Navigating Usability and User Experience in a Multi-Platform World

Anacleto Correia
CINAV, Naval Academy, Portugal

IGI Global
Publishing Tomorrow's Research Today

Published in the United States of America by
IGI Global
701 E. Chocolate Avenue
Hershey PA, USA 17033
Tel: 717-533-8845
Fax: 717-533-8661
E-mail: cust@igi-global.com
Web site: https://www.igi-global.com

Library of Congress Cataloging-in-Publication Data

CIP PENDING

ISBN13: 979-8-3693-2337-3
Isbn13Softcover: 979-8-3693-5016-4
EISBN13: 979-8-3693-2338-0

Vice President of Editorial: Melissa Wagner
Managing Editor of Acquisitions: Mikaela Felty
Managing Editor of Book Development: Jocelynn Hessler
Production Manager: Mike Brehm
Cover Design: Phillip Shickler

British Cataloguing in Publication Data
A Cataloguing in Publication record for this book is available from the British Library.

All work contributed to this book is new, previously-unpublished material.
The views expressed in this book are those of the authors, but not necessarily of the publisher.

Table of Contents

Preface xvi

Chapter 1
Beyond the Screen: Cross-Platform UX for Wearables, IoT, and Emerging Technologies 1
Busra Ozdenizci Kose, Gebze Technical University, Turkey

Chapter 2
AI-Driven Cross-Platform Design: Enhancing Usability and User Experience .. 19
Ushaa Eswaran, Mahalakshmi Tech Campus, Chennai, India
Vishal Eswaran, CVS Health, India

Chapter 3
Navigating Usability and User Experience in a Multi-Platform World With Agile Methodology 49
Somesh Kumar Sahu, Presidency University, India
Senthilkumar Ranganathan, Presidency University, India

Chapter 4
Sustainable Development in Wearable Internet of Medical Things: Addressing Environmental Impact, Energy Efficiency, and Lifecycle Management 85
D. Maruthi Kumar, Department of ECE, Srinivasa Ramanujan Institute of Technology, Ananthapuramu, India
Shreenidhi K. S., Department of Biotechnology, Rajalakshmi Engineering College, Chennai, India
Harishchander Anandaram, Department of Artificial Intelligence, Amrita Vishwa Vidyapeetham, Coimbatore, India
Gopal Krishna, Department of Computer Science and Engineering, Supaul College of Engineering, Supaul, India
Hari B. S., Department of Mechanical Engineering, Kongu Engineering College, Perundurai, Erode, India

Chapter 5
The Field of Usability and User Experience (UX) Design 117
Shivnath Ghosh, Brainware University, India
Soumya Dubey, Chungnam National University, South Korea

Chapter 6
Automatic and Enhanced Reflexive System for Concise Answer Evaluation Using BERT Model and Bi-LSTM 155
Jegatha Deborah L., University College of Engineering, Villupuram, India
Rajkumar S. C., Anna University, Madurai, India
K. Suganya, University College of Engineering, Villupuram, India

Chapter 7
Integrating Learning Management System With Dynamic Composition of Distributed Web Services: Composition of Web Services for a Flexible User Interface 199
Sumathi Pawar, Information Science & Engineering, Nitte(DU),NMAMIT, Nitte, Karkala,, India
Suma K. Nair, Mangalore Institute of Technology and Management, Moodbidri, India
Vandhana B. S., Information Science & Engineering, Nitte(DU),NMAMIT, Nitte, Karkala, India
K. Ankitha, Information Science & Engineering, Nitte(DU),NMAMIT, Nitte, Karkala, India
Hemanth Kumar Reddy, Vellore Institute of Technology, India

Chapter 8
Human Resource Development (HRD) Strategies for Emerging Entrepreneurship: Leveraging UX Design for Sustainable Digital Growth 221
R. Somasundaram, Department of Management Studies, Kongu Engineering College, Perundurai, India
Saurabh Chandra, School of Law, Bennett University, India
J. Tamilarasu, Department of Management Studies, Nandha Engineering College (Autonomous), Erode, India
Archana M. Kinagi, Department of MBA (Women), Sharnbasva University, Kalaburagi, India
Shreevamshi Naveen, Department of Management Studies, Dayananda Sagar College of Engineering, Bengaluru, India

Chapter 9
A Framework for Age Estimation Using Facial Features: A Comprehensive Survey 249
A. Annie Micheal, Department of Computer Science and Engineering, Sathyabama Institute of Science and technology, Kanchipuram, India
B. U. Anu Barathi, Department of Computer Science and Engineering, Sathyabama Institute of Science and technology, Kanchipuram, India
A. Ancy Micheal, Department of School of Computer Science and Engineering, Vellore Institute of Technology (Chennai Campus), Chengalpattu, India
Essakki Raja T., Department of Computer Science and Engineering with Data Science, Sathyabama Institute of Science and Technology,Kancheepuram, India

Chapter 10
Innovative System Using Artificial Intelligence and Robotics for Fire Disaster Management 279
Komala C. R., Department of Information Science and Engineering, East Point College of Engineering and Technology, Bengaluru, India
S. Prakash, Department of Information Science and Engineering, East Point College of Engineering and Technology, Bengaluru, India
Yogesh G. S., Department of Information Science and Engineering, East Point College of Engineering and Technology, Bengaluru, India
T. K. Thivakaran, Department of Information Science and Engineering, East Point College of Engineering and Technology, Bengaluru, India
Nanda Ashwin, Department of Information Science and Engineering, East Point College of Engineering and Technology, Bengaluru, India

Chapter 11
Application of Google Earth Engine NDVI Trend to Study Yield of Sugarcane Crop Using Sentinel 2 Data 309
Malathi Narra, Department of Civil Engineering, Velagapudi Ramakrishna Siddhartha Engineering College (Deemed to be University),, India
Harsha Vardhan Reddy, Department of Civil Engineering, Velagapudi Ramakrishna Siddhartha Engineering College (Deemed to be University),, India
Vinay Kumar Gaddam, Department of Civil Engineering, Velagapudi Ramakrishna Siddhartha Engineering College (Deemed to be University),, India
Shashidhar Raju Nandhuri, Department of Civil Engineering, Velagapudi Ramakrishna Siddhartha Engineering College (Deemed to be University),, India
Tejaswini Vallepu, Department of Civil Engineering, Velagapudi Ramakrishna Siddhartha Engineering College (Deemed to be University),, India
Sai Sumath, Department of Civil Engineering, Velagapudi Ramakrishna Siddhartha Engineering College (Deemed to be University),, India

Compilation of References 343

About the Contributors 383

Index 389

Detailed Table of Contents

Preface xvi

Chapter 1
Beyond the Screen: Cross-Platform UX for Wearables, IoT, and Emerging Technologies 1
Busra Ozdenizci Kose, Gebze Technical University, Turkey

In today's rapidly evolving digital landscape, the boundaries of User Experience (UX) design extend far beyond traditional screens. As we navigate through this era of innovation, the focus shifts toward more intimate, immersive, and integrated experiences offered by wearable devices, the Internet of Things (IoT), and cutting-edge technologies such as Augmented Reality (AR) and Virtual Reality (VR). This chapter explores the unique challenges and opportunities these platforms present, highlighting key usability principles that ensure meaningful, accessible, and engaging interactions. This exploration of advanced UX design prepares designers with the knowledge and tools for current challenges and future opportunities, encouraging a design approach that is innovative and inclusive.

Chapter 2
AI-Driven Cross-Platform Design: Enhancing Usability and User Experience .. 19
Ushaa Eswaran, Mahalakshmi Tech Campus, Chennai, India
Vishal Eswaran, CVS Health, India

This comprehensive chapter delves into the intersection of artificial intelligence (AI) technology with cross-platform design principles to enhance usability and user experience (UX) across diverse digital environments. With the proliferation of platforms and services, designers face the challenge of creating seamless and satisfying user experiences across web, mobile, wearable, IoT, virtual reality (VR), augmented reality (AR), and other digital platforms. AI offers innovative solutions to address these challenges by automating tasks, personalizing interactions, and optimizing user interfaces. This chapter discusses the role of AI in enhancing cross-platform design, covering topics such as AI-driven user research, multi-modal interaction design, personalized content delivery, and AI-based performance optimization. Case studies and practical insights illustrate the application of AI technology in improving usability and UX across various digital contexts.

Chapter 3
Navigating Usability and User Experience in a Multi-Platform World With Agile Methodology 49
Somesh Kumar Sahu, Presidency University, India
Senthilkumar Ranganathan, Presidency University, India

The ever-expanding landscape of devices and platforms creates a complex challenge for ensuring exceptional user experience (UX) in modern software development. Agile methodologies, with their core principles of rapid iteration and responsiveness to change, offer a promising approach to navigating this dynamic environment. However, integrating user research and evaluation techniques, crucial for a user-centric approach, can be difficult within the fast-paced cycles of agile development. This research addresses this gap by exploring strategies for seamlessly integrating user research activities into agile workflows. Reviewing existing literature, the authors identify and analyse user research and evaluation techniques well-suited for the Agile framework. This framework serves as a roadmap for organisations seeking to leverage the benefits of agile methodologies while ensuring a user-centric approach that delivers exceptional UX across diverse platforms. Ultimately, the research aims to bridge the gap between agile development and user-centred design.

Chapter 4
Sustainable Development in Wearable Internet of Medical Things: Addressing Environmental Impact, Energy Efficiency, and Lifecycle Management 85

D. Maruthi Kumar, Department of ECE, Srinivasa Ramanujan Institute of Technology, Ananthapuramu, India
Shreenidhi K. S., Department of Biotechnology, Rajalakshmi Engineering College, Chennai, India
Harishchander Anandaram, Department of Artificial Intelligence, Amrita Vishwa Vidyapeetham, Coimbatore, India
Gopal Krishna, Department of Computer Science and Engineering, Supaul College of Engineering, Supaul, India
Hari B. S., Department of Mechanical Engineering, Kongu Engineering College, Perundurai, Erode, India

The integration of wearable IoMT in healthcare systems throws wide-open the potential for patient care, real-time monitoring, and personalized medicine, but sustainability brings its own set of challenges and opportunities. This chapter discusses the environmental impact, efficiency in energy consumption, and lifecycle management for sustainable development in wearable IoMT. Some of the major challenges are electronic waste, energy consumption, data security, and privacy. Sustainability in wearable IoMT offers opportunities in the adoption of renewable energy, the development of low-power devices, and robust data protection mechanisms. Reduction in the ecological footprint of wearable IoMT devices can be served by considering the importance of sustainable practice in manufacturing, recycling, and biodegradable materials. It seems that innovative solutions can improve sustainability while maintaining quality care for patients.

Chapter 5
The Field of Usability and User Experience (UX) Design 117
Shivnath Ghosh, Brainware University, India
Soumya Dubey, Chungnam National University, South Korea

The Usability and User Experience (UX) design field is evolving rapidly, driven by technological advancements, changing user expectations, and the increasing complexity of digital ecosystems. This chapter explores the emerging trends shaping the future of usability and UX design. Key trends include the integration of artificial intelligence (AI) and machine learning (ML) for personalized experiences, the growing importance of inclusive and accessible design, the rise of voice user interfaces (VUIs) and augmented reality (AR), and the shift towards a more holistic approach to UX that encompasses emotional and ethical considerations. By examining these trends, this chapter aims to provide insights into the future directions of usability and UX design, highlighting the challenges and opportunities for designers and researchers in the field.

Chapter 6
Automatic and Enhanced Reflexive System for Concise Answer Evaluation Using BERT Model and Bi-LSTM 155
Jegatha Deborah L., University College of Engineering, Villupuram, India
Rajkumar S. C., Anna University, Madurai, India
K. Suganya, University College of Engineering, Villupuram, India

In intelligent tutoring systems (ITS), the automatic and enhanced reflexive system for concise answer evaluation (AERSCAE) components that evaluate students' responses to questions are crucial. However, applying deep learning to AERSCAE encounters difficulties due to the challenges of accurately scoring short answers and the scarcity of training data. Using bidirectional encoder representations from transformers (BERT)-based deep neural network, this system improves short-answer texts' understanding via capturing contextual nuances. A specialized semantic refinement layer, bidirectional long short-term memory (Bi-LSTM), is integrated into the AERSCAE system to enhance its performance. Bi-LSTM's temporal dependencies and bidirectional processing enable the generation of high-precision scores. Integrating BERT and Bi-LSTM deep learning architectures into AERSCAE systems enhances their short-answer evaluation capability.

Chapter 7
Integrating Learning Management System With Dynamic Composition of Distributed Web Services: Composition of Web Services for a Flexible User Interface 199
Sumathi Pawar, Information Science & Engineering, Nitte(DU),NMAMIT, Nitte, Karkala,, India
Suma K. Nair, Mangalore Institute of Technology and Management, Moodbidri, India
Vandhana B. S., Information Science & Engineering, Nitte(DU),NMAMIT, Nitte, Karkala, India
K. Ankitha, Information Science & Engineering, Nitte(DU),NMAMIT, Nitte, Karkala, India
Hemanth Kumar Reddy, Vellore Institute of Technology, India

E-learning and its management is essential during pandemic situations, which require integration and management of learning management web services in the universities. This necessitates adapting service-oriented architecture (SOA) in higher education. There are several categories of users such as administrators, researchers, teachers, students, and maintenance team of different computer systems. If these systems are exposed as web services, then it can be utilized or consumed by other applications. Due to distributed web services, a student record from student information system may provide services for library management system or learning management system. It is very good practice to distribute the services using available computing facilities of laboratory Pcs and due to this existing lab resource facilities shared and utilized. This chapter is focused on integrating e-learning methods according to user requirement for flexible user interface. Apriori algorithm is used to train the machine and performance of the system is measured during testing the system.

Chapter 8
Human Resource Development (HRD) Strategies for Emerging Entrepreneurship: Leveraging UX Design for Sustainable Digital Growth 221
R. Somasundaram, Department of Management Studies, Kongu Engineering College, Perundurai, India
Saurabh Chandra, School of Law, Bennett University, India
J. Tamilarasu, Department of Management Studies, Nandha Engineering College (Autonomous), Erode, India
Archana M. Kinagi, Department of MBA (Women), Sharnbasva University, Kalaburagi, India
Shreevamshi Naveen, Department of Management Studies, Dayananda Sagar College of Engineering, Bengaluru, India

This chapter explores the strategic use of HRD for sustainable growth in emerging entrepreneurial ventures focusing on UX designs, highlighting the challenge of building agile teams in competitive digital markets, founded by innovators. By integrating HRD practices with UX design principles, startups can enhance creativity, improve collaboration, and focus on customer-centered product development. The chapter aims to enhance the company's vision through talent acquisition, continuous learning, and team empowerment, while incorporating UX methodologies for intuitive, user-centered digital solutions. Connecting HRD and UX design will lead to faster innovation, better alignment of business goals and user needs, promoting long-term growth and sustaining digital change. This chapter suggests that strategic HRD and thoughtful UX design can significantly enhance the competitive advantage of emerging startups in the digital era.

Chapter 9
A Framework for Age Estimation Using Facial Features: A Comprehensive Survey 249
A. Annie Micheal, Department of Computer Science and Engineering, Sathyabama Institute of Science and technology, Kanchipuram, India
B. U. Anu Barathi, Department of Computer Science and Engineering, Sathyabama Institute of Science and technology, Kanchipuram, India
A. Ancy Micheal, Department of School of Computer Science and Engineering, Vellore Institute of Technology (Chennai Campus), Chengalpattu, India
Essakki Raja T., Department of Computer Science and Engineering with Data Science, Sathyabama Institute of Science and Technology,Kancheepuram, India

In human age estimation, an exact age or age group is assigned automatically to a given facial image. Due to changes in facial features caused by wrinkles and muscle sag with the increase in age, age estimation becomes difficult and complex. Variability in facial expressions, illumination conditions, environment, pose, plastic surgery, occlusion, image quality, and facial makeup gives rise to some of the challenges that affect the accuracy of age estimation. With the newly developing real-time and age-related applications, there is an increasing demand for more accurate estimation of age. Several methodologies have been developed by researchers to handle this requirement. The work reported here represents an exhaustive survey on face age estimation. Discussed here are five major models of age image representation and various age learning algorithms, a review of the existing aging databases has been made, and the latest state-of-the-art methods for the estimation of age are summarized.

Chapter 10
Innovative System Using Artificial Intelligence and Robotics for Fire Disaster Management 279
Komala C. R., Department of Information Science and Engineering, East Point College of Engineering and Technology, Bengaluru, India
S. Prakash, Department of Information Science and Engineering, East Point College of Engineering and Technology, Bengaluru, India
Yogesh G. S., Department of Information Science and Engineering, East Point College of Engineering and Technology, Bengaluru, India
T. K. Thivakaran, Department of Information Science and Engineering, East Point College of Engineering and Technology, Bengaluru, India
Nanda Ashwin, Department of Information Science and Engineering, East Point College of Engineering and Technology, Bengaluru, India

The chapter discusses how AI and robotics can be developed to enhance fire disaster management systems. The new system applies AI algorithms and robotics approaches to improve early detection, response in real time, and post-disaster analysis. Predictive models using AI algorithms and data from sensors, together with historical fire patterns, result in highly accurate predictions of fire outbreaks. Furthermore, an autonomous robot was used to move quickly to assess and intervene rapidly. These robots scan dangerous environments for hotspots, carry out rescues, and extinguish flames while minimizing human risk and maximizing operational efficiency. Case studies and future research directions highlight technological changes in terms of fire safety and resilience.

Chapter 11
Application of Google Earth Engine NDVI Trend to Study Yield of Sugarcane Crop Using Sentinel 2 Data 309
Malathi Narra, Department of Civil Engineering, Velagapudi Ramakrishna Siddhartha Engineering College (Deemed to be University),, India
Harsha Vardhan Reddy, Department of Civil Engineering, Velagapudi Ramakrishna Siddhartha Engineering College (Deemed to be University),, India
Vinay Kumar Gaddam, Department of Civil Engineering, Velagapudi Ramakrishna Siddhartha Engineering College (Deemed to be University),, India
Shashidhar Raju Nandhuri, Department of Civil Engineering, Velagapudi Ramakrishna Siddhartha Engineering College (Deemed to be University),, India
Tejaswini Vallepu, Department of Civil Engineering, Velagapudi Ramakrishna Siddhartha Engineering College (Deemed to be University),, India
Sai Sumath, Department of Civil Engineering, Velagapudi Ramakrishna Siddhartha Engineering College (Deemed to be University),, India

Increasing global food demand and the effects of climate change further indicate a need for proper ways of monitoring crop health. This chapter has demonstrated the importance of normalized difference vegetation index (NDVI) as a non-invasive means of monitoring crop health. A review of the literature indicates that NDVI is useful in determining crop stress, diseases, and performance, especially if considered on a long-term basis. This study is based on sugarcane in Vuyyuru Village, Andhra Pradesh, considering NDVI to analyze crop health for the five-year period of 2018-2022. In this chapter, pre-processing Sentinel satellite imagery through atmospheric correction and image registration was carried out to ensure that data accuracy is ensured. The computation of NDVI values each year involves assessing any patterns or variations that are found in crop health spatially. The work sets out to enhance the understanding of the dynamics in crop health through time, thus giving valued insights for any future agricultural management.

Compilation of References 343

About the Contributors 383

Index 389

Preface

As we navigate an increasingly interconnected and multi-platform digital world, the field of usability and user experience (UX) design faces exciting opportunities and significant challenges. This volume explores how these two critical design principles — usability and UX—can be effectively implemented to create seamless and satisfying interactions across multiple tasks and platforms. With the rapid evolution of technology, designers, and researchers are tasked with building experiences that are functional and enjoyable across a wide range of devices and services. Whether these interactions happen on a desktop, mobile phone, wearable device, or even in smart home environments, the demand for cohesive user experiences has never been greater.

At its core, usability is defined as the ease with which users can interact with a product or system, playing a vital role in determining whether users can effectively and efficiently complete their tasks. In contrast, UX is a broader concept that encompasses all aspects of a user's interaction with a product, service, or organization, extending beyond functionality to also include emotional and experiential factors. When we combine usability and UX in the context of multi-platform design, the result is a more comprehensive understanding of how to create user-centered solutions that meet the diverse needs, preferences, and expectations of users across various touchpoints.

Research has demonstrated that usability is not a static concept but is subject to various influences depending on the platform. For example, some authors explored the usability of multi-platform systems by conducting a controlled experiment that evaluated user efficiency and satisfaction across platforms with varying screen sizes. Their findings highlighted significant differences in user experiences, with larger screens consistently providing better usability outcomes than smaller ones. This underscores the need for adaptable design strategies that account for the specific characteristics of each platform to ensure consistency and high usability across devices.

The rapid pace of technological change has fundamentally altered how users engage with digital content. Users no longer rely on a single platform; instead, they interact with digital systems across a multitude of devices, including smartphones, tablets, desktops, smart TVs, and even voice-activated assistants. This evolution presents new challenges for designers, as they must ensure that the user experience remains seamless across all platforms.

Researchers discuss the role of generative design patterns in maintaining consistency across multiple platforms. They argue that while developing cross-device services is challenging, employing generative patterns — design templates that can be customized for different platforms — can simplify the process and ensure that users have a consistent experience regardless of the device they are using. The research also highlighted how multi-platform design is not just about adapting a user interface but also about maintaining the core elements of the experience, such as task flow, navigation, and visual consistency.

As we increasingly rely on multi-platform environments, one of the central challenges in UX design is creating consistency across different platforms. Research has shown that consistency in both interaction logic and interface layout can significantly impact the overall user experience. Comparing the usability and UX of commonly used design tools, researchers found evidence that consistency in design interaction, particularly regarding interface layout and interaction logic, directly impacted user satisfaction and effectiveness. This consistency becomes even more critical in multi-platform environments, where the goal is to provide a uniform experience across different devices and interaction contexts.

User-centered design is also a key principle in both usability and UX design. It emphasizes designing solutions that meet the needs and preferences of the end user, rather than focusing solely on technical capabilities or business requirements. In multi-platform environments, this means understanding how users interact with different devices and tailoring the user experience to meet their specific needs.

Looking ahead, it is clear that the field of usability and UX design will continue to evolve as new technologies emerge. The growing use of artificial intelligence (AI), voice-activated systems, and augmented reality (AR) presents both opportunities and challenges for multi-platform design. These technologies require new ways of thinking about usability and UX, as they introduce new interaction paradigms and user expectations. Adaptive User Interfaces (AUIs), using AI to modify the interface in response to user behavior, also offer the potential to improve usability across platforms by providing personalized experiences that adapt to the user's needs.

As the digital landscape continues to expand and diversify, it is increasingly important for designers to stay up-to-date with the latest research and best practices in multi-platform usability and UX design. This book aims to provide a valuable resource for both practitioners and academics, offering insights into the current state of the field and a roadmap for future innovations.

ORGANIZATION OF THE BOOK

The first chapter of this book, "Beyond the Screen: Cross-Platform UX for Wearables, IoT, and Emerging Technologies", authored by Busra Kose, explores the rapidly evolving domain of UX design beyond traditional screen-based interfaces, focusing on wearable devices, the Internet of Things (IoT), and emerging technologies such as Augmented Reality and Virtual Reality. It highlights the challenges of designing for these immersive and pervasive technologies, which require a shift from conventional interaction models to more integrated and user-centered approaches. The chapter emphasizes key usability principles such as context-awareness, personalization, and adaptive interfaces, offering insights into how these principles can guide the development of seamless and meaningful user experiences across diverse platforms. Through theoretical discussions and case studies—such as fitness trackers and smart home systems—the chapter provides practical design strategies for creating engaging, efficient, and secure cross-platform user experiences in an increasingly connected world. The chapter sets the foundation for the broader discussions in the book, as it prepares designers to tackle the unique challenges of the modern digital landscape by equipping them with the tools and knowledge needed to navigate the shift from screens to ubiquitous computing. It underscores the need for a holistic design approach that addresses not only functionality but also user engagement, security, and the integration of digital interactions into the physical environment.

The second chapter, "AI-Driven Cross-Platform Design: Enhancing Usability and User Experience", written by Eswaran and Eswaran, examines the growing role of artificial intelligence in improving cross-platform design to enhance usability and user experience. With the proliferation of platforms—spanning mobile, web, wearable devices, IoT, and immersive technologies like AR and VR—designers face the challenge of creating cohesive, user-centered experiences across these diverse environments. This chapter explores how AI technologies, including machine learning, natural language processing, and computer vision, offer innovative solutions to address these challenges. AI automates tasks, personalizes interactions, and optimizes interfaces, improving usability across multiple platforms. Key areas covered include AI-driven user research, multi-modal interaction design, personalized content delivery, and AI-based performance optimization. The chapter presents practical insights and case studies, such as Spotify's use of AI for personalized recommendations and Amazon's AI-driven customer experience optimization, demonstrating the real-world impact of AI in enhancing cross-platform usability and UX. By integrating AI, designers can create seamless, adaptive, and personalized user experiences across various digital platforms. The chapter also provides valuable strategies and solutions for designers looking to leverage AI to create future-proof, user-centered designs across platforms. It offers both theoretical insights and practical guidance, making it a critical resource for anyone working at the intersection of AI and UX design.

Authored by Sahu and Ranganathan, the chapter "Navigating Usability and User Experience in a Multi-Platform World with Agile Methodology", focuses on integrating usability and user experience considerations into Agile development methodologies, which are renowned for their flexibility, iterative approach, and responsiveness to change. As the digital landscape expands across multiple platforms, ensuring a consistent and exceptional UX is paramount, but the fast-paced nature of Agile development presents challenges. Traditional UX research methods often require more time and resources than can be accommodated in Agile's shorter development cycles. The chapter provides strategies for incorporating lightweight user research techniques, such as usability testing, user interviews, and heuristic evaluations, into Agile workflows without compromising speed. Through a simulated case study, the authors demonstrate how these methods can be applied within an Agile project developing multi-platform software. The framework proposed helps organizations maintain a user-centered approach while benefiting from Agile's iterative and adaptable nature. By blending Agile methodology with focused UX research, this chapter offers a roadmap for delivering seamless, user-friendly solutions across platforms in a dynamic, multi-platform world. The chapter is essential for practitioners seeking to balance Agile's rapid development processes with the need to deliver a cohesive and user-centric experience across multiple digital platforms.

Kumar et al., authors of the chapter "Sustainable Innovations in Wearable Internet of Medical Things", explore the integration of sustainability into the development of wearable IoMT devices. As wearable technologies continue to revolutionize healthcare by providing real-time monitoring and personalized medical solutions, the environmental and energy challenges associated with these devices are becoming more significant. This chapter highlights key issues such as electronic waste, energy consumption, and lifecycle management while discussing sustainable solutions like energy-efficient designs, biodegradable materials, and renewable energy sources. Through case studies and theoretical discussions, the authors present innovative approaches to addressing these challenges, including the development of low-power devices, the use of renewable energy, and sustainable manufacturing practices. The chapter further explores the potential of wearable IoMT to reduce the environmental footprint of healthcare technologies by adopting eco-friendly materials and processes, all while maintaining or even improving patient care and outcomes. The chapter also emphasizes the importance of sustainability in the fast-growing field of IoMT, providing practical solutions and a roadmap for developing devices that are both technologically advanced and environmentally responsible.

In "Emerging Trends in Usability and UX Design", Ghosh and Dubey provide an in-depth exploration of the current and emerging trends shaping the future of usability and user experience design. As digital ecosystems become more complex, the role of usability and UX design continues to expand, driven by advances in artificial intelligence, machine learning, and immersive technologies such as augmented reality and voice user interfaces. The authors investigate how AI and ML are transforming UX design, enabling the creation of highly personalized and adaptive experiences tailored to individual user needs. Additionally, the chapter highlights the growing importance of inclusive design, ensuring that digital products are accessible to diverse user groups, including those with disabilities. The chapter also addresses the ethical challenges that accompany these emerging trends, such as data privacy concerns, algorithmic biases, and the potential misuse of AI-driven systems. By examining these challenges, Ghosh and Dubey provide a forward-looking perspective on the evolving landscape of usability and UX design, offering recommendations for designers, researchers, and practitioners to navigate the complexities of modern digital environments. The chapter serves as a critical guide for anyone seeking to understand the technological, ethical, and practical implications of the latest advancements in UX design, providing valuable insights into the future direction of the field.

The chapter "Automatic and Enhanced Reflexive System for Concise Answer Evaluation Using BERT and Bi-LSTM", authored by Deborah et al., delves into the use of advanced artificial intelligence models to improve the evaluation of student responses in intelligent tutoring systems (ITS). Specifically, it focuses on the Automatic and Enhanced Reflexive System for Concise Answer Evaluation (AER-SCAE), which integrates Bidirectional Encoder Representations from Transformers (BERT) and Bidirectional Long Short-Term Memory (Bi-LSTM) networks. These models are designed to enhance the understanding and grading of short-answer responses by capturing contextual and semantic nuances in students' answers, thus improving grading accuracy and efficiency. The chapter highlights the challenges of implementing AI-driven grading systems, including the scarcity of training data and the computational demands of deep learning models. It addresses these issues by demonstrating how BERT's contextual understanding can be combined with Bi-LSTM's ability to process temporal dependencies in language. Through detailed case studies and performance evaluations, the authors show how this system significantly improves the grading process by providing accurate, real-time feedback to students, while alleviating the workload of educators. The chapter is particularly useful for researchers and practitioners interested in the application of AI and UX in educational technology, offering both theoretical insights and practical implementations for automated grading systems in digital learning environments.

The chapter "Integrating Learning Management Systems With Dynamic Composition of Distributed Web Services", by authors Pawar et al., explores the dynamic integration of Learning Management Systems (LMS) with distributed web services, leveraging Service-Oriented Architecture (SOA). The authors highlight the increasing importance of flexible and scalable educational platforms, especially in the context of remote and distributed learning environments. The chapter provides a comprehensive framework for transitioning from centralized LMS to distributed systems by integrating multiple web services that are located remotely but accessible through a unified interface. The chapter delves into technical aspects such as using AI techniques like the Apriori algorithm to dynamically compose web services in response to real-time user requirements. The authors propose a system that optimizes the use of existing web services to minimize resource usage, enhance scalability, and support personalized learning experiences. Key topics include security protocols (like OAuth) for secure access, content delivery networks (CDNs) for efficient distribution, and the use of microservices architecture for decentralized learning platforms. The chapter serves as a vital resource for educators, developers, and IT professionals looking to build adaptable and dynamic LMS solutions that can scale with technological advancements and growing educational needs.

Authored by Somasundaram et al., the chapter "HRD Strategies for Emerging Entrepreneurship: Leveraging UX Design for Sustainable Digital Growth" explores the strategic integration of Human Resource Development (HRD) and User Experience design to enhance the success of emerging startups in the digital age. It emphasizes the critical role that HRD plays in building agile and innovative teams, and how startups can leverage UX design principles to create products that offer meaningful, user-centered experiences. The chapter explains how aligning HRD and UX can fuel creativity, collaboration, and sustainable growth in highly competitive digital markets. Key themes include talent acquisition, continuous learning, and empowering teams, as well as the importance of integrating UX methodologies into the HRD framework. By using HRD strategies to support UX initiatives, startups can foster innovation, improve employee engagement, and create products that align with both business goals and user needs. The chapter also highlights the challenges and opportunities that arise from integrating these disciplines and offers actionable insights for startups looking to leverage both HRD and UX to drive sustainable growth. The chapter serves as a resource for entrepreneurs, HR professionals, and UX designers looking to create a synergy between HR development and UX design, ensuring both employee satisfaction and user-centered product success in fast-moving digital industries.

In "Age Estimation Using Facial Features: A Comprehensive Survey", by Micheal et al., it is provided an exhaustive survey of the methodologies used for facial age estimation, focusing on how changes in facial features such as wrinkles and muscle tone contribute to age-related appearance. The authors explore five major models of age image representation and various age learning algorithms, providing a detailed review of existing aging databases like FG-NET and MORPH, which are essential for training machine learning models to estimate age accurately. These databases contain thousands of images annotated with age and other relevant metadata, making them invaluable for developing and testing algorithms. The chapter also addresses the challenges inherent to facial age estimation, including variability in lighting, facial expressions, and environmental conditions, which can complicate accurate predictions. It further discusses state-of-the-art techniques such as deep learning, which have revolutionized the field by significantly improving the precision of age predictions, despite the complexities involved. Key applications highlighted in this chapter include security, surveillance, personalized services, and targeted advertising, all of which benefit from accurate age estimation systems. The chapter is a vital resource for researchers and developers working in computer vision and machine learning, offering insights into both the current landscape and future advancements in facial age estimation technology.

"Artificial Intelligence and Robotics for Fire Disaster Management", authored by Komala et al., delves into the transformative role of artificial intelligence and robotics in enhancing fire disaster management systems. The chapter presents an innovative system that combines AI algorithms with robotics to improve the prediction, early detection, real-time response, and post-disaster recovery phases of fire management. Through the use of predictive models based on historical fire patterns and sensor data, AI is able to offer highly accurate fire outbreak forecasts, while autonomous robots are deployed to assess and respond to fire emergencies in hazardous environments. The chapter also outlines how AI can analyze vast amounts of data—such as satellite images and weather reports—to predict wildfires, allowing for better resource allocation. Meanwhile, robotics, equipped with advanced sensors and cameras, autonomously navigate dangerous areas to identify hotspots, extinguish fires, and perform search-and-rescue missions. By reducing human risk and increasing operational efficiency, this integration of AI and robotics marks a significant leap in fire disaster resilience and situational awareness. The study is critical for researchers and professionals in fire safety and disaster management, offering both theoretical foundations and practical applications of cutting-edge technologies to make fire disaster response faster, safer, and more effective.

The chapter "Analysis of Crop Health Using Normalized Difference Vegetation Index", authored by Narra et al., focuses on the application of the Normalized Difference Vegetation Index (NDVI) for monitoring and analyzing crop health, particularly in sugarcane fields. Using NDVI, the chapter illustrates how satellite imagery, particularly from the Sentinel-2 satellite, can be employed to detect stress factors, monitor long-term vegetation health, and estimate crop yields. The study spans a five-year period (2018-2022) and emphasizes the importance of non-invasive monitoring methods to enhance agricultural practices in Vuyyuru Village, Andhra Pradesh. The study details the process of pre-processing satellite images, calculating NDVI values, and spatially analyzing crop health trends over time. Through this method, farmers and agronomists can identify stressors such as pest infestations, nutrient deficiencies, or water stress, enabling early interventions to improve crop productivity. The integration of remote sensing technologies like NDVI into precision agriculture marks a significant advancement in sustainable farming techniques. The chapter provides valuable insights into how satellite imagery and NDVI analysis can be used as effective tools for sustainable crop management, offering a roadmap for farmers and researchers to monitor and optimize crop health across large areas efficiently.

We hope you find the above-mentioned chapters both interesting and useful.

Anacleto Correia
CINAV, Naval Academy, Portugal

Chapter 1
Beyond the Screen: Cross-Platform UX for Wearables, IoT, and Emerging Technologies

Busra Ozdenizci Kose
https://orcid.org/0000-0002-8414-5252
Gebze Technical University, Turkey

ABSTRACT

In today's rapidly evolving digital landscape, the boundaries of User Experience (UX) design extend far beyond traditional screens. As we navigate through this era of innovation, the focus shifts toward more intimate, immersive, and integrated experiences offered by wearable devices, the Internet of Things (IoT), and cutting-edge technologies such as Augmented Reality (AR) and Virtual Reality (VR). This chapter explores the unique challenges and opportunities these platforms present, highlighting key usability principles that ensure meaningful, accessible, and engaging interactions. This exploration of advanced UX design prepares designers with the knowledge and tools for current challenges and future opportunities, encouraging a design approach that is innovative and inclusive.

INTRODUCTION

The universe of User Experience (UX) design is undergoing a remarkable expansion, transcending the traditional boundaries of screen-based interactions to embrace a more immersive and pervasive computing reality. This shift marks a pivotal moment in the evolution of technology, as we move from engaging with digital interfaces through the conventional means of keyboards, mice, and touchscreens, to a world

DOI: 10.4018/979-8-3693-2337-3.ch001

where our interactions are seamlessly integrated into our physical environment (Law et al., 2014; Kuniavsky, 2010; Hartson & Pyla, 2012).

In this new domain, wearable devices, the Internet of Things (IoT), and emerging technologies like Augmented Reality (AR) and Virtual Reality (VR) are no longer futuristic concepts but integral components of our daily lives. These platforms offer intimate, immersive, and integrated experiences, demanding a reimagined approach to UX design that goes beyond the screen.

This transition to ubiquitous computing challenges designers to think deeply about how users interact with technology across various contexts and environments. It requires a holistic understanding of user needs, behaviors, and environments to create experiences that are not only functional and accessible but also meaningful and engaging (Hartson & Pyla, 2018; Dove et al., 2017; Li et al., 2014). As we embark on this journey through the cross-platform UX landscape, we will explore the unique challenges and opportunities presented by wearables, IoT, and AR/VR technologies. Our goal is to uncover the key usability principles that will guide us in crafting experiences that resonate with users on a profound level, making technology an extension of our natural interactions with the world.

This chapter focuses on the innovative realm of UX Design for wearable devices, IoT gadgets, and the frontiers of AR and VR, showcasing the shift towards more intimate, immersive, and seamlessly integrated user interactions beyond traditional screens. It highlights key usability principles such as user-centric design, context-awareness, and adaptive interfaces, essential for navigating the unique challenges of designing for these emerging technologies. Through theoretical insights and real-world examples, the chapter serves as a blueprint for crafting user experiences that resonate deeply with users' everyday lives, blending digital interactions seamlessly with their physical environment.

THE RISE OF WEARABLE TECHNOLOGY

Wearable technology has rapidly transitioned from niche gadgets to essential tools that enhance our daily lives. These devices, worn on the body, seamlessly integrate computing capabilities into our everyday activities, offering a blend of convenience, health monitoring, and connectivity previously unimaginable. From smartwatches that notify us of incoming messages to fitness trackers that monitor our physical activity and sleep patterns, wearables have become an integral part of modern living. Their impact extends beyond individual utility to influence broader trends in health, fitness, and digital communication, fostering a more connected and health-conscious society.

Design Considerations for Wearables

Designing for wearable technology presents a unique set of challenges and considerations, primarily due to their intimate nature of use and the limitations of their form factors (Sullivan, 2016; Klebbe et al., 2019; Stelvaga & Fortin 2017; Rowland et al., 2015).

User-Centric Design for Small Screens and Limited Inputs: The compact display areas of wearables call for a design philosophy that emphasizes clarity and simplicity. Every pixel and interaction must be meticulously planned to convey information efficiently, avoiding user overwhelm. This approach involves distilling content to its essence and designing for glanceability—ensuring that users can understand information with a brief look. Selecting which features and notifications to include is crucial; they must be immediately beneficial, aligning with the wearer's needs and lifestyle to augment rather than detract from their daily experience.
Context-Awareness and Personalization: Wearables excel in delivering bespoke user experiences, thanks to their ability to sense and react to the wearer's immediate context. This context-awareness allows for the provision of information and recommendations that are highly relevant and timely. For example, a smartwatch could suggest short mindfulness exercises when it detects signs of stress or remind the user to stand and stretch after prolonged periods of inactivity. Achieving this level of personalization requires not just technological sophistication in gathering and analyzing sensor data but also a sensitive approach to user privacy and data security. Designers must navigate these waters carefully, balancing the benefits of personalization with the imperative of maintaining user trust.

Improving the design of wearables involves embracing these constraints as avenues for creativity. By focusing on user-centric design principles and leveraging the unique capabilities of wearable technology for context-aware personalization, designers can create experiences that resonate deeply with users, making technology a seamless and beneficial part of their everyday lives.

Case Study: Fitness Trackers and Smartwatches

A profound example of successful UX strategies in wearables can be observed in the domain of health and fitness trackers, like those offered by Fitbit and the Apple Watch (Löfblom, 2017; Niknejad et al., 2020). These devices exemplify how effective design can lead to enhanced user engagement and improved health outcomes.

Simplification and Gamification: By simplifying complex health data into understandable metrics and employing gamification techniques, such as badges for achievements and competitions with friends, these devices motivate users to stay active and healthy. The success of these strategies lies in their ability to make health monitoring engaging and accessible.

Seamless Integration into Daily Life: Fitness trackers and smartwatches are designed to be an unobtrusive part of the user's life. They provide at-a-glance information and gentle nudges towards healthier habits without requiring significant attention or effort from the user. This seamless integration is key to their widespread adoption and effectiveness.

Adaptive Notifications: These wearables smartly manage notifications, ensuring that users are informed but not overwhelmed. By allowing users to customize which notifications they receive and when they prioritize user control and minimize distractions, contributing to a positive user experience.

Through these examples, it becomes evident that the key to designing successful wearable technology lies in understanding and prioritizing the user's needs, behaviors, and contexts. The blend of user-centric design, context-awareness, and seamless integration forms the cornerstone of effective UX strategies in the rapidly evolving landscape of wearable technology.

NAVIGATING THE INTERNET OF THINGS

The IoT marks a transformative shift towards environments enriched with smart, interconnected devices that redefine our interaction with the physical world. By enabling everyday objects to connect to the internet, collect data, and communicate with one another, IoT is paving the way for unprecedented levels of efficiency, convenience, and enhancement in our quality of life. This digital ecosystem extends far beyond smart thermostats adjusting temperatures and refrigerators sending out reminders to restock on essentials. It encompasses a wide array of devices including security cameras that provide real-time alerts, lighting systems that adapt to our schedules, and wearables that monitor our health metrics, offering personalized health advice.

This extensive network of connected devices does not only automate mundane tasks but also opens up new avenues for innovation in how we manage our homes, optimize energy consumption, enhance personal health, and even streamline city infrastructures to create smarter, more sustainable living spaces. By integrating IoT into our daily lives, we are ushered into an era where our environments are more responsive to our needs, capable of learning from our habits and preferences to offer tailored suggestions and solutions. The potential of IoT lies in its ability to transform ordinary objects into intelligent agents that work collaboratively to support our lifestyle, making the connected world a tangible reality that extends the boundaries of what we perceive as possible.

UX Challenges in IoT

Navigating the UX landscape of the IoT presents a series of intricate challenges. The essence of IoT -its interconnected, pervasive nature- while being its greatest strength, also poses significant design hurdles that require a comprehensive and nuanced approach to overcome. Achieving a user experience that is both seamless and integrated across a diverse ecosystem of devices and platforms is at the forefront of these challenges.

Designing for a Seamless, Integrated Experience: Creating a unified UX in the IoT realm is a task that demands meticulous attention to detail and an overarching vision that guides the interaction design across various devices. The disparity in device capabilities, interface designs, and usage contexts necessitates a design strategy that is both adaptable and consistent. This strategy should focus on intuitive interactions, contextual consistency, and fluid functionality:

- To achieve intuitive interactions, designers could standardize gestures and commands across devices, making transitions feel seamless and reducing the learning curve for users. For instance, a swipe gesture could have the same function on a smartwatch and a smart home control panel, facilitating a more intuitive user experience.
- Maintaining contextual consistency might involve synchronizing user preferences across devices within the IoT ecosystem. For example, if a user sets a preferred temperature on their smart thermostat app, the same preference could be automatically applied to their smart car's climate control system, ensuring a consistent and personalized experience.
- Ensuring fluid functionality requires that core features remain accessible across devices, despite varying capabilities. An example could be a smart home system that allows users to control lighting via both a smartphone app and voice commands through a smart speaker, ensuring that the primary functionality is accessible through multiple interfaces.

Ensuring Privacy and Security: As IoT devices become increasingly embedded in our daily lives, they collect vast amounts of personal data, ranging from mundane to highly sensitive. This collection raises pressing concerns regarding privacy and security. Protecting user data and ensuring users have comprehensive control over their information is not just a technical issue but a fundamental aspect of UX design in IoT. To address these concerns, designers and developers must perform transparent data practices, enhance user control over privacy, and add security by design:

- Implementing transparent data practices can be achieved by providing clear and accessible privacy policies that explain data usage. For example, an IoT device app might include a simple overview of what data is collected and how it is used, along with easy opt-out options, directly within the app's settings menu.
- Enhancing user control over privacy could involve offering detailed privacy settings that allow users to manage what data is collected and shared. An IoT fitness tracker, for instance, might offer users the option to decide whether their health data is shared with third-party services, giving them direct control over their personal information.
- Embedding security measures into every layer of the IoT ecosystem could include regular software updates and patches for IoT devices, automatically pushed to devices to minimize vulnerabilities. For example, a smart door lock system might receive automatic firmware updates to address new security threats, ensuring the device remains secure against potential breaches.
- Addressing the UX challenges in IoT requires a blend of creative design thinking, technological innovation, and ethical consideration. By focusing on creating seamless, integrated experiences and prioritizing privacy and security, designers can craft IoT solutions that not only meet the functional needs of users but also respect their privacy and earn their trust. This holistic approach is essential for the widespread adoption and success of IoT technologies, paving the way for a future where our digital and physical worlds are more closely intertwined than ever before.

Addressing the UX challenges in IoT requires a blend of creative design thinking, technological innovation, and ethical consideration. By focusing on creating seamless, integrated experiences and prioritizing privacy and security, designers can craft IoT solutions that not only meet the functional needs of users but also respect their privacy and earn their trust. This holistic approach is essential for the widespread adoption and success of IoT technologies, paving the way for a future where our digital and physical worlds are more closely intertwined than ever before.

Case Study: Smart Home Systems

Smart home systems exemplify the potential of IoT to transform our living spaces into more comfortable, secure, and efficient environments. By examining the UX of smart home ecosystems, we can glean insights into effective strategies and common pitfalls.

Unified Control and Accessibility: Successful smart home systems offer a unified interface that allows users to control various devices from a single point, be it a smartphone app, a voice assistant, or a centralized control panel. This approach reduces complexity and enhances accessibility, making it easier for users from all walks of life to adopt and benefit from smart technology.
Contextual Automation and Personalization: The best smart home systems learn from user behaviors to automate tasks in a way that feels natural and personalized. For instance, a smart lighting system might learn your preferred brightness levels for different times of the day, adjusting automatically to create the perfect ambiance without requiring manual input.
Privacy and User Control: Addressing privacy concerns, effective smart home solutions provide clear options for data management and security settings, allowing users to decide what information is shared and how it is used. Transparent policies and robust security measures are essential to reassure users about the safety of their data.

Smart home systems demonstrate the importance of thoughtful UX design in the IoT space, highlighting the need for seamless integration, personalization, and stringent privacy controls. By addressing these key areas, designers can create IoT experiences that not only add convenience and efficiency to our lives but also do so in a manner that is secure, intuitive, and respectful of user privacy.

IMMERSIVE EXPERIENCES: AR AND VR

AR and VR possess transformative potential, redefining the boundaries of digital interaction and immersion. AR overlays digital information onto the real world, enhancing our perception of our surroundings, while VR creates entirely virtual environments, offering an escape into digitally crafted realities (Rampolla & Kipper, 2012; Huang et al., 2021). These technologies extend beyond entertainment, impacting sectors like education, healthcare, and retail by providing immersive experiences that enhance understanding, empathy, and engagement (Keating et al., 2021; Li et al., 2014; Olsson et al., 2013; Gan et al., 2023).

Designing for Immersion

Designing for immersion within AR and VR environments extends beyond mere visual spectacle; it demands a deep understanding of human interaction, comfort, and accessibility. These immersive experiences must captivate the user while simultaneously ensuring their comfort and providing inclusive access to users of all abilities.

Creating Engaging and Comfortable Experiences: To create truly engaging and comfortable AR and VR experiences, designers must delve into the intricacies of human perception and ergonomics. This involves:

- Spatial Design and User Orientation: Careful arrangement of virtual elements in 3D space is essential to prevent user disorientation. By adhering to principles of spatial design, such as maintaining a logical layout and avoiding abrupt transitions, designers can foster a sense of place and direction that feels both intuitive and grounding.
- Adaptive Interfaces: Interfaces within immersive environments should adapt to the user's actions and context, providing guidance and feedback that is both subtle and timely. This could include dynamic adjustment of UI elements based on the user's focus area or providing haptic feedback through controllers to enhance the sense of touch and interaction.
- Minimizing Motion Sickness: A significant challenge in VR, in particular, is minimizing the risk of motion sickness. This can be addressed through stable frame rates, as mentioned, but also by designing movement within the virtual space that mirrors natural human motion, and offering teleportation as an alternative to traditional movement controls for sensitive users.

Accessibility in Immersive Technologies: Ensuring that AR and VR technologies are accessible is not just about compliance with standards; it's about embracing the diversity of user needs and experiences. Achieving this level of accessibility involves:

- Customizable Experience Settings: Allowing users to tailor their experience according to their needs is fundamental. This could include options to adjust the size and contrast of text, modify audio settings, or even change the speed of the experience. These adjustments empower users to interact with the content in ways that are most comfortable for them.
- Designing for Diverse Interaction Modalities: Recognizing the diverse ways in which users might interact with AR and VR, designers should incorporate multiple interaction modalities. For users with limited mobility or those who prefer not to use hand-held controllers, voice com-

mands, eye tracking, or even facial expressions can offer alternative means of interaction.

- Educational and Supportive Onboarding: For many users, AR and VR might be entirely new experiences. Providing an educational onboarding process that gently guides users through the basics of navigation, interaction, and customization options can significantly enhance accessibility. This process should be designed to accommodate users with varying levels of technological proficiency and sensory abilities.

By extending the focus on engagement, comfort, and accessibility, designers can create AR and VR experiences that not only enchant and entertain but also respect and adapt to the wide array of human diversity. This holistic approach to immersive design ensures that these groundbreaking technologies can be enjoyed and appreciated by the broadest audience possible, truly unlocking the transformative potential of AR and VR.

Case Study: Educational AR Applications

AR technology has significantly impacted the educational sector by introducing an innovative approach to learning and engagement. Through the power of AR, educators are equipped with tools that can bring a new dimension of interactivity and immersion to the classroom, transforming traditional learning paradigms (Ardiny & Khanmirza, 2018; Huang et al., 2021).

Enhancing Learning with AR: AR applications in education enable the visualization of complex, abstract concepts in a tangible and interactive manner. By overlaying digital information onto the physical world, AR makes it possible for students to engage with educational content in a more intuitive and meaningful way. For example, an AR application designed for history education could animate historical battles right on the students' desks, allowing them to witness the unfolding of events in a simulated, three-dimensional space. Similarly, in biology classes, AR can be used to visualize the structure of the human body, enabling students to "dissect" organs and systems layer by layer, thereby gaining a deeper understanding of human anatomy without the need for physical specimens.

Improving Engagement: The interactivity afforded by AR technology fosters a learning environment that is not only more engaging but also more conducive to retention and motivation. By transforming passive learning materials into interactive experiences, AR encourages active participation and exploration, which are key to enhancing learning outcomes. For example, in geography lessons, an AR application can project interactive maps and terrains onto the classroom floor, allowing students to explore different ecosystems, climates, and geographical features firsthand. This method turns learning into an adventure, encouraging curiosity and exploration, and making complex geographical concepts more accessible and engaging for students of all ages.

These instances demonstrate the profound potential of AR in revolutionizing the educational landscape. By converting abstract concepts into interactive, three-dimensional experiences, AR applications enhance understanding, foster engagement, and motivate students in unprecedented ways. The success of such AR applications in education not only highlights the technology's capacity to enrich the learning experience but also serves as a blueprint for future innovations across various sectors. As AR technology continues to evolve, its integration into educational frameworks is poised to create even more dynamic, effective, and personalized learning experiences, thereby transforming the way knowledge is imparted and absorbed in the digital age.

CROSS-PLATFORM INTEGRATION

Today, the UX increasingly spans multiple devices and platforms, necessitating a seamless transition and consistent experience across all touchpoints. Cross-platform integration represents the convergence of various digital experiences, ensuring that users receive a unified and cohesive experience, whether they're interacting with a mobile app, a desktop application, a wearable device, or an IoT system. This integration is crucial for maintaining user engagement, satisfaction, and loyalty in a world where digital interactions are omnipresent and varied (Hartson & Pyla, 2018; Levin, 2014; Sinha et al., 2017).

Achieving Seamless Experience Across Devices

The cornerstone of successful cross-platform integration is the seamless experience it provides to users as they switch between devices. This requires a deep understanding of the context in which each device is used and the ability to maintain continuity of the user's journey across these contexts. For instance, a music streaming service should allow users to start listening to a playlist on their smartphone during a morning commute and seamlessly continue their desktop or smart speaker upon reaching home or office without missing a beat. Key strategies include:

- Synchronized State Across Platforms: Ensuring that user data, preferences, and actions are consistently updated and reflected across all devices. This synchronization should be near-instant, providing users with up-to-date information no matter the device they choose to use at any moment.

- Responsive and Adaptive Design: Implementing responsive design principles ensures that applications and services adapt to the size and capabilities of the device screen, offering an optimized experience for smartphones, tablets, desktops, and wearables alike.
- Unified User Interface Elements: While adapting to the form factor is essential, maintaining a consistent look and feel across platforms helps in reinforcing brand identity and reducing cognitive load on users as they switch devices.

Privacy and Security in a Cross Platform

As experiences stretch across multiple platforms, safeguarding user privacy and security becomes even more critical. The complexity of maintaining robust security measures increases as users engage with services across mobile devices, desktops, wearables, and IoT devices. It necessitates the formulation and implementation of a comprehensive security strategy that is consistently applied across all platforms. This strategy must leverage advanced encryption technologies to protect data in transit and at rest, incorporate secure authentication methods such as two-factor authentication (2FA) to verify user identities, and ensure the regular deployment of security patches and updates to address vulnerabilities as they emerge. Such a multi-faceted approach is crucial not only for protecting against breaches and cyber threats but also for upholding the integrity of the user experience on every platform.

Furthermore, the importance of transparency in data usage practices and providing users with control over their personal data cannot be overstated. In an era where concerns about data privacy are at the forefront of users' minds, clear and open communication regarding how data is collected, used, and shared is fundamental to building and maintaining trust. Users should be empowered with straightforward tools and settings to manage their privacy preferences across every touchpoint, ensuring they have a say in how their information is handled. By prioritizing transparency and control, businesses can foster a relationship of trust with their users, which is essential for creating a secure and positive cross-platform experience. This holistic approach to privacy and security, combining rigorous technical safeguards with user empowerment, sets the foundation for a digital environment where users feel protected and valued, regardless of how or where they choose to interact with digital services.

Case Study: Multi-Device Streaming Services

In the realm of digital entertainment, multi-device streaming services like Netflix, Spotify, and Disney+ have set a new standard for seamless content access across a wide range of platforms. The UX design strategies implemented by these services exemplify how to effectively manage cross-platform integration, ensuring users enjoy a consistent, intuitive, and engaging experience whether they're on their smartphones, tablets, desktops, smart TVs, or even gaming consoles. This section explores the key elements of UX design that contribute to the success of these streaming services:

Unified Content Library: At the heart of multi-device streaming services is a unified content library that is accessible from any device. This means that users can pause a movie on their smart TV and resume it on their smartphone right where they left off, or switch between listening to a podcast on their desktop to their car's audio system without any disruption. The seamless synchronization of content playback across devices is achieved through cloud-based technologies that track user activity and preferences in real time.

Responsive and Adaptive Design: To ensure an optimal viewing or listening experience on any device, streaming services employ responsive and adaptive design principles. This approach allows the user interface to automatically adjust to different screen sizes and resolutions, ensuring that navigation elements, text, and media are always presented in an accessible and aesthetically pleasing manner. Moreover, adaptive streaming adjusts video or audio quality based on the user's internet speed, enhancing playback experience by minimizing buffering and ensuring the best possible quality under varying network conditions.

Personalized User Experience: Personalization is another critical factor in the UX design of multi-device streaming services. Through the use of sophisticated algorithms and machine learning, these platforms analyze user behavior and preferences to provide personalized content recommendations. This tailored approach not only makes content discovery more intuitive and engaging but also ensures that users encounter relevant content across all devices, enhancing the overall experience and user satisfaction.

Consistent and Intuitive Navigation: Maintaining consistency in navigation and interaction design across platforms is essential for a fluid user experience. Streaming services achieve this by standardizing key UI elements and interactions, such as search functions, content categorization, and playback controls, ensuring users can effortlessly navigate the service regardless of the device they are using. This consistency reduces the cognitive load on users, making the transition between devices as intuitive as possible.

Strong Security Measures: Given the personal nature of usage data and the premium content offered, streaming services implement robust security measures to protect user information and intellectual property. This includes secure login processes, encryption of data in transit and at rest, and regular security audits. These measures are critical for maintaining user trust and ensuring a safe viewing environment across all devices.

The success of multi-device streaming services in providing seamless content access across platforms is a testament to their thoughtful and user-centered approach to UX design. By focusing on unified content libraries, responsive and adaptive design, personalization, consistent navigation, and robust security, these services offer an exemplary model for creating engaging and cohesive cross-platform experiences.

FUTURE TRENDS AND CHALLENGES

The landscape of UX design is set to evolve dramatically, shaped by emerging technologies and the increasing complexities of our connected world. This section explores the forthcoming trends that are poised to redefine UX design, alongside the ethical and societal challenges that designers must navigate.

The next wave of technological advancements focuses on integration of digital experiences into our physical world, profoundly impacting UX design:

- Extended Reality (XR): Encompassing VR, AR and Mixed Reality (MR), XR is set to offer more immersive experiences that blend the digital and physical realms in unprecedented ways. UX designers will need to pioneer new interaction models that accommodate 3D environments, spatial navigation, and multimodal inputs, ensuring these experiences are intuitive and accessible.
- Artificial Intelligence (AI) and Machine Learning (ML): AI and ML are becoming integral to creating personalized user experiences. As these technologies advance, UX designers will have the opportunity to leverage AI to anticipate user needs, automate routine interactions, and craft more adaptive and responsive interfaces. However, they'll also face the challenge of maintaining transparency and control for users over automated decisions.
- IoT Proliferation: The expansion of IoT devices will continue to enrich the UX landscape with a myriad of interconnected devices, offering seamless experiences across different aspects of daily life. Designing for the IoT ecosystem will require a holistic approach, ensuring consistency and fluidity across diverse devices while addressing privacy and security concerns.

- Voice and Natural Language Processing (NLP): As voice assistants and NLP technologies become more sophisticated, voice will emerge as a primary interface for digital interactions. UX designers will explore voice-driven interfaces that offer hands-free, conversational experiences, requiring a deep understanding of language nuances, context, and user intent.

Today, UX designers face many important challenges as they create digital experiences. By addressing these challenges and applying proactive approaches, UX designers can lead the way in creating digital products that are technologically advanced, and also socially responsible and beneficial. These challenges are briefly discussed as follows:

- Privacy and Data Security: With the rise of digital tracking and frequent security breaches, safeguarding user privacy has become more crucial. UX designers play a pivotal role in implementing privacy-by-design principles, which involve integrating privacy considerations into the development process from the ground up. This includes designing interfaces that provide clear user consent mechanisms, data usage transparency, and secure data storage solutions. For example, offering users straightforward options to manage their privacy settings can empower them and enhance trust.
- Accessibility and Inclusion: Designing for accessibility is not just about compliance; it's about creating an equitable digital world. UX designers must ensure that digital products are usable for people of all abilities and backgrounds. This involves adhering to web accessibility standards and engaging in user testing with diverse groups to identify and address usability barriers. Incorporating features like text-to-speech, alternative text for images, and ensuring high contrast can make digital experiences more inclusive. For instance, designing a mobile app that is equally navigable by touch, voice commands, or screen readers can significantly widen its user base.
- Ethical Use of AI: As AI becomes more integrated into design processes, ensuring it enhances rather than detracts from user experiences is imperative. UX designers must be careful about AI biases that can arise from skewed data sets, potentially leading to discriminatory outcomes. It's essential to implement checks and balances, such as auditing AI systems for bias and designing AI interactions that are transparent and easy for users to understand.
- Sustainability in Digital Design: The environmental impact of digital products is an increasingly pressing concern. UX designers have a unique opportunity to influence sustainable practices by creating designs that promote longevity, energy efficiency, and minimal waste. This might involve optimizing software for lower power consumption or encouraging digital minimalism

through design choices that reduce unnecessary digital clutter and consumption. For example, streaming services can implement eco-friendly features like defaulting to audio-only streaming when video is not necessary, conserving significant amounts of data and energy.

CONCLUSION

In conclusion, the evolution of UX design, especially within the realms of wearable technology, the IoT, AR and VR, underscores its critical role in shaping our technological future. These arenas exemplify the forefront of innovation, where the seamless integration of digital experiences into the fabric of everyday life can profoundly enhance human interaction with technology. As designers navigate this landscape, embracing innovation while steadfastly committing to inclusivity becomes paramount. By leveraging the unique capabilities of wearables for health and convenience, harnessing IoT for smarter living environments, and exploiting the immersive potential of AR/VR for education and entertainment, UX designers have a unique opportunity to redefine our digital experiences. This endeavor requires a deep understanding of user needs across diverse contexts, a commitment to protecting privacy, and a dedication to creating accessible and sustainable technologies. Moving forward, it's clear that UX designers play a pivotal role in crafting a future where technology not only advances our capabilities but does so in a way that is intuitive, inclusive, and deeply human-centered, ensuring that as our physical and digital worlds converge, they do so in a manner that enriches, empowers, and unites.

REFERENCES

Ardiny, H., & Khanmirza, E. (2018, October). The role of AR and VR technologies in education developments: opportunities and challenges. In 2018 6th rsi international conference on robotics and mechatronics (icrom) (pp. 482-487). IEEE. DOI: 10.1109/ICRoM.2018.8657615

Dove, G., Halskov, K., Forlizzi, J., & Zimmerman, J. (2017, May). UX design innovation: Challenges for working with machine learning as a design material. In *Proceedings of the 2017 chi conference on human factors in computing systems*(pp. 278-288). DOI: 10.1145/3025453.3025739

Gan, Q., Liu, Z., Liu, T., Zhao, Y., & Chai, Y. (2023). Design and user experience analysis of AR intelligent virtual agents on smartphones. *Cognitive Systems Research*, 78, 33–47. DOI: 10.1016/j.cogsys.2022.11.007

Hartson, R., & Pyla, P. S. (2012). *The UX Book: Process and guidelines for ensuring a quality user experience*. Elsevier.

Hartson, R., & Pyla, P. S. (2018). *The UX book: Agile UX design for a quality user experience*. Morgan Kaufmann.

Huang, X., Zou, D., Cheng, G., & Xie, H. (2021). A systematic review of AR and VR enhanced language learning. *Sustainability (Basel)*, 13(9), 4639. DOI: 10.3390/su13094639

Keating, G., Guest, D., Konertz, A., Padovani, N., & Villa, A. (2011). Designing the AR experience: Tools and tips for mobile augmented reality UX design. In Design, User Experience, and Usability. Theory, Methods, Tools and Practice: First International Conference, DUXU 2011, Held as Part of HCI International 2011, Orlando, FL, USA, July 9-14, 2011 *Proceedings*, 1(Part II), 135–141.

Klebbe, R., Steinert, A., & Müller-Werdan, U. (2019). Wearables for older adults: requirements, design, and user experience. Perspectives on Wearable Enhanced Learning (WELL) Current Trends, Research, and Practice, 313-332.

Kuniavsky, M. (2010). *Smart things: ubiquitous computing user experience design*. Elsevier.

Law, E. L. C., Van Schaik, P., & Roto, V. (2014). Attitudes towards user experience (UX) measurement. *International Journal of Human-Computer Studies*, 72(6), 526–541. DOI: 10.1016/j.ijhcs.2013.09.006

Levin, M. (2014). *Designing multi-device experiences: An ecosystem approach to user experiences across devices.* O'Reilly Media, Inc.

Li, X., Xu, B., Teng, Y., Ren, Y. T., & Hu, Z. M. (2014, August). Comparative research of AR and VR technology based on user experience. In 2014 International Conference on Management Science & Engineering 21th Annual Conference Proceedings (pp. 1820-1827). IEEE. DOI: 10.1109/ICMSE.2014.6930456

Löfblom, J. (2017). Defining user experience principles for developing health and fitness wearables and smartwatches.

Niknejad, N., Ismail, W. B., Mardani, A., Liao, H., & Ghani, I. (2020). A comprehensive overview of smart wearables: The state of the art literature, recent advances, and future challenges. *Engineering Applications of Artificial Intelligence*, 90, 103529. DOI: 10.1016/j.engappai.2020.103529

Olsson, T., Lagerstam, E., Kärkkäinen, T., & Väänänen-Vainio-Mattila, K. (2013). Expected user experience of mobile augmented reality services: A user study in the context of shopping centres. *Personal and Ubiquitous Computing*, 17(2), 287–304. DOI: 10.1007/s00779-011-0494-x

Rampolla, J., & Kipper, G. (2012). *Augmented reality: An emerging technologies guide to AR*. Elsevier.

Rowland, C., Goodman, E., Charlier, M., Light, A., & Lui, A. (2015). *Designing connected products: UX for the consumer Internet of Things.* O'Reilly Media, Inc.

Sinha, S. R., Park, Y., Sinha, S. R., & Park, Y. (2017). Developing and Improving User Experiences. Building an Effective IoT Ecosystem for Your Business, 201-224.

Stelvaga, A., & Fortin, C. (2017). Design principles of wearables systems: an IoT approach. In DS 87-3 Proceedings of the 21st International Conference on Engineering Design (ICED 17) Vol 3: Product, Services and Systems Design, Vancouver, Canada, 21-25.08. 2017 (pp. 419-428).

Sullivan, S. (2016). *Designing for wearables: Effective UX for current and future devices.* O'Reilly Media, Inc.

ADDITIONAL READING

Edge, R., & Miola, A. (2022). *Cross-Platform UIs with Flutter: Unlock the ability to create native multiplatform UIs using a single code base with Flutter 3.* Packt Publishing Ltd.

Johnson, P. F. (2015). *Cross-platform UI Development with Xamarin. Forms*. Packt Publishing Ltd.

Raad, H. (2020). *Fundamentals of IoT and wearable technology design*. John Wiley & Sons. DOI: 10.1002/9781119617570

Schmalstieg, D., & Hollerer, T. (2016). *Augmented reality: principles and practice*. Addison-Wesley Professional.

Sullivan, S. (2016). *Designing for wearables: Effective UX for current and future devices*. O'Reilly Media, Inc.

KEY TERMS AND DEFINITIONS

Augmented Reality (AR): A technology that superimposes a computer-generated image on a user's view of the real world, thus providing a composite view.

Internet of Things (IoT): The interconnection via the internet of computing devices embedded in everyday objects, enabling them to send and receive data.

Privacy: A state in which one is not observed or disturbed by other people.

Security: The state of being free from danger or threat.

User Experience: The overall experience of a person using a product such as a website or computer application, especially in terms of how easy or pleasing it is to use. (Oxford Languages)

User Interface: The means by which the user and a computer system interact, in particular the use of input devices and software.

Virtual Reality (VR): The computer-generated simulation of a three-dimensional image or environment that can be interacted with in a seemingly real or physical way by a person using special electronic equipment, such as a helmet with a screen inside or gloves fitted with sensors.

Chapter 2
AI-Driven Cross-Platform Design: Enhancing Usability and User Experience

Ushaa Eswaran
Mahalakshmi Tech Campus, Chennai, India

Vishal Eswaran
https://orcid.org/0009-0000-2187-3108
CVS Health, India

ABSTRACT

This comprehensive chapter delves into the intersection of artificial intelligence (AI) technology with cross-platform design principles to enhance usability and user experience (UX) across diverse digital environments. With the proliferation of platforms and services, designers face the challenge of creating seamless and satisfying user experiences across web, mobile, wearable, IoT, virtual reality (VR), augmented reality (AR), and other digital platforms. AI offers innovative solutions to address these challenges by automating tasks, personalizing interactions, and optimizing user interfaces. This chapter discusses the role of AI in enhancing cross-platform design, covering topics such as AI-driven user research, multi-modal interaction design, personalized content delivery, and AI-based performance optimization. Case studies and practical insights illustrate the application of AI technology in improving usability and UX across various digital contexts.

DOI: 10.4018/979-8-3693-2337-3.ch002

1. INTRODUCTION

The digital landscape has experienced significant evolution, characterized by a proliferation of platforms and devices that have become integral to daily life. This evolution includes the introduction of the internet and the World Wide Web, which paved the way for web-based applications and services (Norman, 2013). Subsequently, the advent of smartphones and mobile devices revolutionized portable computing, enabling users to access information and services on-the-go (Shumaker & George, 2016). Wearable devices, such as smartwatches and fitness trackers, further expanded the scope of digital interactions, offering personalized and context-aware experiences (Thakur & Zhang, 2020).

The emergence of the Internet of Things (IoT) connected everyday objects and appliances to the internet, enabling remote monitoring, control, and automation (Li & Guo, 2021). Additionally, virtual and augmented reality technologies introduced immersive digital experiences, blurring the boundaries between the physical and virtual worlds.

The importance of cross-platform design has grown in tandem with the evolution of digital platforms. Cross-platform design refers to the practice of creating user interfaces and interactions optimized for multiple platforms while maintaining a cohesive brand identity. Effective cross-platform design enhances user experience by providing consistency across platforms, facilitating seamless transitions between devices, optimizing resource allocation, and future-proofing designs (Weng, Zhang, & Ngo, 2019).

Artificial intelligence (AI) plays a crucial role in enhancing usability and user experience across digital platforms. AI technologies, including machine learning, natural language processing, and computer vision, offer innovative solutions to automate tasks, personalize interactions, and optimize user interfaces (Thakur & Zhang, 2020). By leveraging AI capabilities, designers can conduct user research and analysis, enable multi-modal interactions, facilitate personalized design, and optimize performance and resource allocation.

This chapter aims to explore the intersection of AI technology and cross-platform design principles, focusing on enhancing usability and user experience across diverse digital environments. It will provide a thorough understanding of usability and user experience design foundations, examine the role of AI in cross-platform design, present case studies illustrating successful AI implementations, discuss challenges and solutions in cross-platform design, and explore emerging trends and future directions. Through this exploration, readers will gain insights into leveraging AI to create exceptional user experiences transcending platform boundaries.

2. FOUNDATIONS OF USABILITY AND USER EXPERIENCE DESIGN

To comprehend the role of AI in enhancing cross-platform design, it's essential to establish a robust understanding of the principles and methodologies governing usability and user experience (UX) design. This section delves into the fundamental concepts and best practices integral to crafting effective designs for digital products and services.

2.1 Principles of Usability Design

Usability design prioritizes interfaces and interactions that are intuitive, efficient, and user-friendly. Core principles guiding usability design include learnability, efficiency, memorability, error prevention and recovery, and satisfaction (Nielsen, 1994). These principles, pioneered by Jakob Nielsen and further refined by researchers and practitioners, form the bedrock for creating designs aligned with user needs and expectations.

2.2 User-Centered Design Methodologies

User-centered design (UCD) approaches place users at the forefront of the design process, aiming to develop products and services that resonate with their needs, behaviors, and contexts (Norman & Draper, 1986). Methodologies such as contextual inquiry, participatory design, iterative design, and persona and scenario creation facilitate empathy, collaboration, and iterative refinement, ensuring designs are user-centric and effective.

2.3 Importance of UX Research and Evaluation

UX research and evaluation are indispensable components of the design process, providing empirical insights and validating design decisions (Albert & Tullis, 2013). Techniques like usability testing, heuristic evaluation, A/B testing, surveys, interviews, and analytics offer a holistic understanding of user needs, behaviors, and preferences. By leveraging these methods, designers can iteratively optimize the user experience and drive continuous improvement.

2.4 Integration of AI in Usability Studies

The emergence of artificial intelligence (AI) presents novel opportunities to enhance usability studies and UX research (Hassenzahl & Tractinsky, 2006). AI-powered analytics enable the processing of vast datasets to uncover patterns, predict behaviors, and derive actionable insights. Automated usability testing, sentiment analysis, personalized testing, and intelligent design assistance leverage AI to streamline processes, personalize experiences, and offer data-driven recommendations (Kaptein et al., 2015). Integrating AI into usability studies empowers designers to gain deeper insights, optimize workflows, and deliver more engaging user experiences across diverse digital platforms.

3. AI-DRIVEN USER RESEARCH AND EVALUATION

Incorporating artificial intelligence (AI) into user research and evaluation practices has significantly transformed how designers understand and optimize user experiences. AI-powered tools and techniques offer advanced capabilities for gathering and analyzing user data, leading to more precise insights and informed design decisions. This section delves into the various applications of AI in user research and evaluation, accompanied by real-world case studies showcasing the impact of these technologies.

3.1 AI-Powered Analytics Tools for User Feedback

Traditional methods of collecting user feedback, like surveys and interviews, often suffer from time constraints and inherent biases. AI-driven analytics tools present a more efficient and thorough approach to gathering and interpreting user feedback. These tools harness machine learning algorithms to process extensive datasets sourced from diverse channels such as user reviews, social media interactions, and customer support dialogues. By discerning patterns, sentiments, and pain points from these datasets, AI-powered analytics tools offer actionable insights to product teams, facilitating prioritized improvements and targeted user engagement strategies (Lemon & Verhoef, 2016).

For instance, Revuze, an AI-powered analytics platform, employs natural language processing (NLP) algorithms to analyze user feedback and reviews spanning multiple platforms. By extracting key themes, emotional cues, and product strengths and weaknesses from textual data, Revuze provides valuable insights enabling product teams to enhance user satisfaction and address critical issues promptly (Revuze, 2023).

3.2 Sentiment Analysis and User Profiling

Sentiment analysis, a branch of NLP, enables the interpretation of user emotions and attitudes expressed in textual data. By analyzing user-generated content such as social media posts, reviews, and customer service interactions, AI models can classify sentiments into categories ranging from positive to negative (Liu, 2020). This capability facilitates the identification of areas for improvement, reputation monitoring, and the formulation of tailored communication strategies.

Building upon sentiment analysis, user profiling integrates demographic data and behavioral patterns to construct comprehensive user personas. These personas aid designers in comprehending the diverse needs, preferences, and pain points of distinct user segments, thereby guiding the creation of personalized and bespoke experiences (Nguyen et al., 2019).

3.3 Behavior Prediction and UX Design

AI models leverage user data, including clickstreams, cursor movements, and eye-tracking information, to forecast user behavior and uncover potential usability issues. By discerning how users interact with interfaces and applications, designers can optimize user experiences and preemptively address usability challenges (Conati et al., 2020).

For example, reinforcement learning algorithms can predict efficient user interaction paths or action sequences, simplifying user flows, reducing cognitive load, and enhancing interface intuitiveness (Zhou et al., 2020).

3.4 Case Studies: AI-Driven User Research

1. Spotify's Use of AI for Personalization and User Research (Jacobson & Sandin, 2019):

Spotify harnesses AI and machine learning to curate personalized music recommendations and elevate the overall user experience. By analyzing user listening habits, preferences, and contextual data, Spotify's algorithms deliver tailored playlists and music suggestions. Additionally, AI-driven sentiment analysis enables Spotify to extract insights from user feedback and social media conversations, informing product enhancements and user research endeavors.

2. Amazon's AI-Driven Customer Experience Optimization (Bajaj et al., 2020):

Amazon employs AI across various facets of its e-commerce platform, including user research and experience optimization. Through machine learning algorithms, Amazon analyzes user behavior like search patterns, browsing history, and purchase data to provide personalized product recommendations and streamline the shopping journey. Furthermore, Amazon integrates AI-powered chatbots and virtual assistants to bolster customer support and gather real-time feedback.

3. IBM's Watson Studio and AI-Assisted User Research (IBM, 2021):

IBM's Watson Studio serves as an AI-powered platform empowering user researchers and designers to derive insights from diverse data sources such as user feedback and social media interactions. Leveraging NLP, sentiment analysis, and machine learning, Watson Studio identifies user pain points, preferences, and emerging trends, thereby informing user experience design and product development endeavors.

3.5 Challenges and Ethical Considerations in AI-Driven User Research

While AI offers powerful capabilities for user research, it also presents unique challenges:

Data Privacy and Consent: AI-driven research often requires large datasets, raising concerns about user privacy and informed consent. Researchers must ensure compliance with data protection regulations like GDPR and CCPA

Algorithmic Bias: AI systems can perpetuate or amplify existing biases in data, potentially leading to skewed research outcomes. Researchers must be vigilant in identifying and mitigating these biases

Interpretability of AI-Generated Insights: The 'black box' nature of some AI algorithms can make it difficult to understand how certain conclusions are reached, potentially limiting their usefulness in informing design decisions

Balancing AI and Human Expertise: While AI can process vast amounts of data, it may miss nuanced human behaviors or cultural contexts. Integrating AI-driven insights with human expertise remains crucial

To address these challenges, researchers and designers should:

- Implement robust data governance practices
- Regularly audit AI systems for bias
- Use explainable AI techniques when possible
- Combine AI-driven insights with traditional qualitative research methods

4. MULTI-MODAL INTERACTION DESIGN WITH AI

The rapid advancement of artificial intelligence (AI) technologies has opened up new possibilities for multi-modal interaction design, enabling users to engage with digital systems through various modalities such as voice, gestures, and facial expressions. This section delves into the principles, technologies, and applications of AI-driven multi-modal interactions, along with real-world case studies that illustrate the potential of this approach in enhancing usability and user experience across diverse digital platforms.

4.1 Multi-Modal Interaction Principles

Multi-modal interaction design revolves around leveraging multiple input and output modalities to create more natural, intuitive, and efficient user experiences. By combining various modes of communication, such as speech, touch, gaze, and gestures, users can interact with digital systems in a way that aligns with their natural behaviors and cognitive processes. Key principles include complementarity, redundancy, adaptability, and consistency. These principles ensure that multi-modal interfaces cater to diverse user needs, preferences, and contexts, ultimately enhancing usability and user experience.

Key principles of multi-modal interaction design include:

1. **Complementarity**: Different modalities should work together to enhance the overall interaction. For example, in a virtual assistant, voice commands can be complemented by visual feedback on a screen. AI can help by dynamically selecting the most appropriate modalities based on context and user preferences
2. **Redundancy**: Critical information should be presented through multiple modalities to ensure accessibility and understanding. AI can assist in intelligently repeating information across modalities without overwhelming the user
3. **Adaptability**: The interface should adapt to changing user needs and environmental conditions. AI can play a crucial role in real-time adaptation, adjusting the interface based on user behavior, environmental sensors, and learned patterns
4. **Consistency**: The user experience should remain consistent across different modalities and platforms. AI can help maintain consistency by learning user preferences and applying them across various interaction modes and devices

These principles ensure that multi-modal interfaces cater to diverse user needs, preferences, and contexts. For instance, a smart home system might use voice commands for quick actions, touch interfaces for detailed control, and ambient displays for non-intrusive information presentation. AI can orchestrate these modalities, selecting the most appropriate one based on the user's current activity, location, and historical preferences

4.2 AI Technologies for Multi-Modal Interfaces

AI technologies play a pivotal role in enabling and enhancing multi-modal interactions. Techniques such as natural language processing (NLP), computer vision, machine learning, sensor fusion, and adaptive interfaces work together to create interfaces that can understand and respond to various input modalities. These technologies enable seamless interactions across different digital platforms by accurately recognizing and interpreting user inputs, thereby facilitating more natural and intuitive experiences.

4.3 Applications in Digital Assistants and Smart Devices

AI-driven multi-modal interactions find extensive applications in digital assistants and smart devices, where users interact with technology through a combination of voice commands, gestures, and visual cues. For instance, digital assistants like Apple's Siri, Amazon's Alexa, and Google Assistant integrate multiple input modalities to provide natural and intuitive interactions. Similarly, smart devices leverage multi-modal interactions to simplify user experiences, allowing users to control devices through voice commands, gestures, or touch interfaces.

4.4 Case Studies: AI-Driven Multi-Modal Interaction

1. Microsoft's Kinect and Multi-Modal Interactions for Gaming and Beyond

Microsoft's Kinect sensor revolutionized multi-modal interactions in gaming by enabling users to control games and applications through body gestures, voice commands, and facial expressions. Beyond gaming, Kinect technology found applications in healthcare, education, and robotics, showcasing the versatility of multi-modal interactions in diverse contexts.

2. Google's Accessibility Features for Vision, Hearing & More

Google has been at the forefront of developing multi-modal interaction technologies to improve accessibility for users with disabilities. Features such as Live Transcribe, Live Caption, Voice Access, and Switch Access leverage AI-powered speech recognition and natural language processing to provide real-time captioning, transcription, and alternative input methods, enhancing accessibility for a diverse user base.

3. Amazon's Alexa Multi-Modal Interactions for Ambient Computing

Amazon's Alexa virtual assistant leverages multi-modal interactions to enable ambient computing experiences. By understanding and responding to voice commands, visual cues, and contextual information from connected smart home devices, Alexa provides users with a seamless and intuitive interaction experience, seamlessly blending physical and digital environments.

These case studies exemplify how AI-driven multi-modal interactions enhance usability and user experience across various domains, from gaming and accessibility to ambient computing and smart home automation.

5. PERSONALIZATION AND CONTEXT-AWARE DESIGN

In today's digital landscape, personalization and context-awareness have emerged as essential elements of effective user experience design. These approaches involve tailoring interactions and content to individual user preferences, behaviors, and contextual factors, thereby creating more engaging, relevant, and satisfying experiences across various digital platforms. The integration of artificial intelligence (AI) has significantly contributed to the advancement of personalization and context-aware design, leveraging data-driven insights and intelligent algorithms to deliver highly customized and adaptive experiences.

5.1 Personalization Strategies in UX Design

Personalization strategies in user experience (UX) design encompass various approaches aimed at customizing the content, features, and interactions of digital products or services to align with individual user preferences. These strategies include preference-based personalization, behavior-based personalization, collaborative filtering, and demographic-based personalization. By implementing these strategies, designers can create user experiences that feel tailored and relevant to individual users, thereby enhancing engagement, satisfaction, and overall usability.

5.2 Context-Aware Interactions with AI

Context-aware interactions involve digital systems' ability to understand and adapt to the user's current situation, environment, and context. Leveraging AI technologies such as machine learning and sensor fusion, context-aware interfaces can incorporate factors like location, environmental conditions, device state, and activity/physiological data to provide more responsive and situationally appropriate interactions. By integrating context-awareness into the design process, user experiences can become more proactive, intelligent, and seamless across different digital platforms and environments.

5.3 Adaptive Interfaces and Content Recommendation

Adaptive interfaces and content recommendation systems are pivotal applications of AI-driven personalization and context-awareness. These systems dynamically adjust the user interface layout, components, and functionality based on user preferences, device capabilities, and contextual factors. Additionally, content recommendation systems utilize AI algorithms to provide personalized suggestions based on user data, content metadata, and contextual information. By implementing adaptive interfaces and content recommendation systems, designers can create highly tailored user experiences that enhance engagement and satisfaction.

5.4 Case Studies: AI-Based Personalization

1. Netflix's Personalized Content Recommendations: Netflix employs AI algorithms to analyze user viewing histories and behavior patterns, delivering personalized movie and TV show recommendations based on individual preferences and contextual factors such as time of day and device type.
2. Amazon's Personalized Shopping Experience: Amazon leverages AI-based recommendation algorithms to provide personalized product recommendations and tailored search results, incorporating user browsing and purchase data as well as contextual factors like location and device type.
3. Google's Context-Aware Mobile Experiences: Google integrates context-awareness and personalization across its mobile applications and services, such as the Google Assistant and Google Maps, to offer proactive assistance and customized experiences based on user context and activity.

By studying these case studies, designers can gain insights into the practical applications of AI-driven personalization and context-awareness, enabling them to create more effective and engaging user experiences in their own projects.

6. AI-BASED PERFORMANCE OPTIMIZATION

In the domain of cross-platform design, ensuring optimal performance and efficient resource utilization is paramount for delivering seamless and satisfying user experiences. With the emergence of AI technologies, designers now have access to powerful tools and techniques that can optimize digital systems' performance, allocate resources intelligently, and proactively maintain systems through predictive maintenance. This section delves into the various AI-driven approaches to performance optimization and their applications in enhancing usability and user experience across multiple platforms.

6.1 Optimization Techniques for Digital Systems

Optimizing the performance of digital systems involves employing a spectrum of techniques aimed at enhancing efficiency, responsiveness, and resource utilization. AI algorithms and technologies play a pivotal role in implementing various optimization strategies, such as load balancing, caching and prefetching, code optimization, network optimization, and energy efficiency. By leveraging these AI-driven optimization techniques, designers can create digital systems and applications that deliver optimal performance, responsiveness, and efficiency across various platforms and devices, ultimately enhancing the overall user experience.

6.2 AI Algorithms for Resource Allocation

Efficient resource allocation is crucial for performance optimization, particularly in resource-constrained environments or when handling large-scale workloads. AI algorithms are instrumental in intelligently allocating and managing resources, including CPU, memory, storage, and network bandwidth, to ensure optimal performance and prevent resource contention or bottlenecks. Reinforcement learning, constraint programming, genetic algorithms, and neural networks are some AI techniques employed for resource allocation. By utilizing these AI algorithms, designers can create digital systems that adapt to changing workloads and user demands, maximizing performance and efficiency while minimizing resource wastage or over-provisioning.

AI algorithms for resource allocation include:

1. **Reinforcement Learning (RL):** RL algorithms learn optimal resource allocation strategies through trial and error. For example, DeepMind used RL to reduce Google's data center cooling energy consumption by 40%

2. **Constraint Programming:** This technique is used to find solutions that satisfy a set of constraints. In cloud computing, it can optimize virtual machine placement while meeting performance and energy efficiency requirements
3. **Genetic Algorithms:** These algorithms mimic natural selection to evolve optimal solutions. They've been used to optimize task scheduling in distributed systems, improving overall system performance
4. **Neural Networks:** Deep neural networks can learn complex patterns in resource usage and predict future demands, enabling proactive resource allocation

Tools leveraging these AI techniques include:

- **Dynatrace:** Offers AI-powered full-stack monitoring, automatically detecting and diagnosing performance issues across complex cloud environments.
- **AppDynamics:** Provides AI-driven application performance management, offering insights into user experiences and business impacts of IT performance.
- **Apica:** Uses AI to analyze and optimize website and API performance, helping businesses maintain high-quality digital experiences

6.3 Predictive Maintenance and Performance Tuning

Predictive maintenance and performance tuning are proactive approaches to maintaining optimal system performance and preventing potential issues or failures before they occur. AI technologies facilitate these predictive capabilities by leveraging machine learning algorithms and data-driven insights to identify performance degradation patterns, predict potential failures, and recommend corrective actions or system optimizations. Predictive maintenance involves continuously monitoring system performance, analyzing sensor data, and identifying anomalies or patterns indicating potential hardware or software failures. Performance tuning, on the other hand, entails analyzing system performance data, user behavior patterns, and resource utilization metrics to identify bottlenecks, inefficiencies, or areas for optimization. By implementing predictive maintenance and performance tuning strategies, designers can create digital systems that are proactive, self-optimizing, and resilient, minimizing downtime and performance degradation, and ultimately delivering a more reliable and consistent user experience across various platforms.

6.4 Case Studies: AI-Driven Performance Optimization

1. Google's AI-Powered Data Center Cooling and Energy Optimization

Google utilizes AI-driven solutions to optimize the performance and energy efficiency of its data centers. By leveraging machine learning algorithms and sensor data, Google predicts and adjusts cooling and airflow patterns to optimize energy usage while maintaining optimal temperatures for server performance. Additionally, AI models predict server utilization and dynamically allocate workloads to minimize energy consumption and maximize resource utilization.

2. Microsoft's Autonomous Systems for Cloud Resource Optimization

Microsoft's Azure cloud platform employs AI-driven autonomous systems to optimize resource allocation and performance across its global infrastructure. Using reinforcement learning algorithms, Microsoft continuously monitors and adjusts resource allocation based on real-time demands, ensuring optimal performance while minimizing resource waste. Furthermore, machine learning models predict potential hardware or software issues for predictive maintenance.

3. AWS Auto Scaling and Performance Optimization

Amazon Web Services (AWS) offers AI-powered auto-scaling and performance optimization features for its cloud services. AWS Auto Scaling uses machine learning models to automatically scale computing resources based on real-time demand, ensuring optimal performance with minimal resource wastage. Additionally, AWS Performance Insights and Compute Optimizer employ AI algorithms to analyze workload patterns, identify bottlenecks, and recommend optimizations for improved performance and cost efficiency.

These case studies demonstrate the practical applications of AI-driven performance optimization across various platforms and environments, showcasing how AI technologies can enhance system efficiency, reliability, and user experience.

7. CROSS-PLATFORM DESIGN CHALLENGES AND SOLUTIONS

While the integration of AI in cross-platform design offers numerous opportunities for enhancing usability and user experience, designers also face various challenges that must be addressed to ensure successful implementation. This section explores some of the key challenges associated with cross-platform design and how AI technologies can help overcome them.

7.1 Accessibility and Inclusivity Considerations

Designing for accessibility and inclusivity is a critical aspect of creating user-friendly experiences across multiple platforms. Designers must ensure that their solutions are accessible to users with diverse abilities, backgrounds, and preferences. AI can play a crucial role in addressing these challenges by enabling:

1. Personalized Accessibility Features: AI algorithms can analyze user preferences, abilities, and contexts to dynamically adapt interfaces and interactions, providing personalized accessibility features such as text-to-speech, speech-to-text, or alternative input methods (Kous et al., 2020).
2. Automated Accessibility Testing: AI-powered tools can automatically evaluate user interfaces and applications for compliance with accessibility standards, identifying potential issues and providing recommendations for improvement (Ahmetovic et al., 2019).
3. Inclusive Content Generation: Natural language processing (NLP) and computer vision techniques can assist in generating inclusive content, such as alternative text descriptions for images or captions for audio/video content, improving accessibility for users with visual or hearing impairments (Fernandez-Viña et al., 2021).
4. Intelligent User Support: AI-powered virtual assistants and chatbots can provide personalized support and guidance to users, helping them navigate and understand complex interfaces or features, particularly for users with cognitive or language barriers (Hailpern et al., 2021).

By leveraging AI technologies, designers can create more inclusive and accessible experiences that cater to a diverse range of users across various digital platforms.

7.2 Addressing Privacy and Security Concerns

Cross-platform design often involves the collection, processing, and sharing of user data across multiple devices and platforms, raising privacy and security concerns. Designers must ensure that user data is protected and that users have control over their personal information. AI can assist in addressing these challenges through:

1. Privacy-Preserving AI: AI techniques, such as differential privacy, federated learning, and homomorphic encryption, can enable data analysis and model training while preserving user privacy and maintaining data security (Jiang et al., 2022).

2. Intelligent Access Control: AI algorithms can analyze user behaviors, contexts, and risk factors to implement intelligent access control mechanisms, granting or restricting access to sensitive data or features based on predefined policies and risk assessments (Okano et al., 2021).
3. Anomaly Detection and Threat Mitigation: Machine learning models can detect anomalies, suspicious activities, or potential security threats in real-time, enabling proactive mitigation measures and enhancing the overall security of cross-platform applications (Diro & Chilamkurti, 2018).
4. Transparency and User Control: AI-powered explanations and visualizations can provide users with greater transparency regarding data collection, processing, and decision-making processes, allowing them to make informed decisions and exercise control over their personal information (Lécué et al., 2022).

By incorporating AI-driven privacy and security measures, designers can build trust with users and create cross-platform experiences that prioritize data protection and user autonomy.

7.3 Overcoming Technical Limitations and Compatibility Issues

Cross-platform design often involves integrating with diverse technologies, platforms, and devices, each with its own technical limitations and compatibility challenges. Designers must ensure seamless functionality and consistent user experiences across this heterogeneous landscape. AI can assist in overcoming these challenges through:

1. Automated Code Translation and Optimization: AI-powered code translation and optimization tools can streamline the process of adapting applications to different platforms, automatically translating code and optimizing performance based on platform-specific requirements and constraints (Nguyen et al., 2021).
2. Device Capability Detection and Adaptation: AI algorithms can analyze device capabilities, such as screen size, processing power, and sensor availability, to dynamically adapt user interfaces and functionality, ensuring optimal performance and compatibility across various devices (Becker et al., 2022).
3. Intelligent API Mapping and Integration: AI techniques, such as natural language processing and machine learning, can assist in mapping and integrating diverse APIs and data sources, enabling seamless data exchange and functionality across different platforms and services (Crichton et al., 2018).
4. Automated Testing and Compatibility Validation: AI-powered testing frameworks can automatically validate cross-platform compatibility, identifying issues, and providing recommendations for resolving compatibility challenges across

different operating systems, browsers, and device configurations (Moran et al., 2021).

By leveraging AI technologies, designers can overcome technical limitations and compatibility challenges, ensuring consistent and seamless user experiences across a wide range of platforms and devices.

7.4 Case Studies: Overcoming Design Challenges

1. Microsoft's Inclusive Design for Cross-Platform Accessibility (Novick, 2021)

Microsoft has implemented AI-driven inclusive design practices to enhance accessibility across its suite of cross-platform products and services. The company's AI-powered tools, such as the Accessibility Insights for Web and Accessibility Insights for Windows, automatically evaluate user interfaces for accessibility issues and provide recommendations for improvement. Additionally, Microsoft's AI-powered assistive technologies, like the Immersive Reader and Microsoft Translator, enable personalized accessibility features for users with diverse abilities and language preferences.

2. Apple's Differential Privacy for Cross-Platform Data Protection (Apple, 2023)

To address privacy concerns in its cross-platform ecosystem, Apple employs differential privacy techniques, an AI-driven approach that allows for data analysis and model training while preserving user privacy. This approach is used in various Apple services, such as Siri, Maps, and News, enabling personalized experiences while protecting user data from unauthorized access or misuse.

3. Google's Flutter for Cross-Platform App Development and Compatibility (Google, 2022)

Google's Flutter framework leverages AI technologies to streamline cross-platform app development and ensure compatibility across various platforms and devices. Flutter's AI-powered tooling, such as the Device Preview and Platform Views, enable developers to visualize and test their applications on different devices and platforms, identifying and resolving compatibility issues. Additionally, Flutter's Cupertino and Material Design widgets automatically adapt to the target platform's design language, ensuring consistent and native-like user experiences.

4. Uber's AI-Driven Cross-Platform Compatibility and Performance Optimization (Uber, 2020)

Uber's mobile applications leverage AI technologies to ensure compatibility and optimal performance across multiple platforms and devices. The company's AI-powered testing framework, called Nanomaly, automatically detects and triages compatibility issues and performance regressions across different Android and iOS device configurations. Additionally, Uber employs machine learning models to optimize resource utilization and performance, dynamically adjusting features and functionality based on device capabilities and network conditions.

5. Airbnb's AI-Powered Inclusive Design for Cross-Platform Accessibility (Airbnb, 2021)

Airbnb has implemented AI-driven inclusive design practices to enhance accessibility across its cross-platform applications and services. The company's AI-powered tools, such as the Accessibility Scanner, automatically evaluate user interfaces for accessibility issues and provide recommendations for improvement. Airbnb also leverages AI technologies, like computer vision and natural language processing, to generate inclusive content, such as alternative text descriptions for images and captions for audio/video content, ensuring accessibility for users with diverse abilities.

6. IBM's AI-Driven Cross-Platform API Integration and Mapping (IBM, 2022)

IBM's AI-powered API integration and mapping solutions enable seamless integration of diverse APIs and data sources across multiple platforms and technologies. The company's AI-driven tools, such as the Watson API Mapping and Discovery, leverage natural language processing and machine learning to automatically map and integrate APIs, facilitating data exchange and functionality across different platforms and services. Additionally, IBM's AI-based API testing and monitoring solutions help ensure compatibility and reliability across cross-platform integrations.

8. CASE STUDIES IN AI-DRIVEN CROSS-PLATFORM DESIGN

To fully appreciate the potential of AI in enhancing usability and user experience across various digital platforms, it is essential to examine real-world case studies and implementations. This section presents several compelling examples of how organizations have leveraged AI technologies to create seamless, engaging, and effective cross-platform experiences, along with the impact on user satisfaction, engagement, and business outcomes.

8.1 Real-World Implementations of AI Technology

1. Starbucks' AI-Powered Mobile App and Digital Experiences (Starbucks, 2022)

Starbucks has embraced AI technologies to deliver personalized and engaging experiences across its mobile app, website, and in-store digital interactions. The company's AI-driven mobile app leverages machine learning algorithms to provide personalized food and beverage recommendations based on individual preferences, purchase history, and contextual factors like time of day and location. Additionally, Starbucks employs natural language processing and AI-powered virtual assistants to facilitate seamless ordering and customer service interactions across multiple platforms.

2. Spotify's AI-Driven Music Discovery and Personalization (Jacobson & Sandin, 2019)

Spotify's cross-platform music streaming service heavily relies on AI technologies to enhance user experiences and drive engagement. The company's AI algorithms analyze user listening patterns, preferences, and contextual data to deliver personalized music recommendations, playlists, and discovery features. These AI-driven recommendations are tailored to individual users' tastes and are consistently updated based on their interactions across various devices and platforms, ensuring a highly personalized and engaging music experience.

3. Nike's AI-Powered Fitness Applications and Services (Nike, 2021)

Nike has integrated AI technologies into its suite of cross-platform fitness applications and services, such as the Nike Run Club and Nike Training Club apps. The company's AI algorithms analyze user activity data, performance metrics, and biometric information to provide personalized workout recommendations, adaptive training plans, and real-time coaching. Additionally, Nike leverages computer vision and motion tracking capabilities to provide form analysis and corrective feedback, enhancing the overall user experience and effectiveness of its cross-platform fitness offerings.

While large tech companies have significant resources to implement AI-driven solutions, smaller companies are also leveraging AI to enhance cross-platform user experiences:

8.1.1 Grammarly's AI-Powered Writing Assistant

Grammarly, a writing assistance tool, uses AI to provide real-time grammar and style suggestions across multiple platforms. Their browser extension, mobile app, and desktop application offer a seamless cross-platform experience, demonstrating how AI can be used to create consistent functionality across diverse environments.

8.1.2 Canva's AI Design Suggestions

Canva, a graphic design platform, employs AI to offer design suggestions and automate layout creation. Their cross-platform approach ensures that users have access to AI-powered features whether they're using the web app, mobile app, or desktop application, showcasing how AI can enhance creativity and productivity across different devices

8.2 Impact on Usability, Engagement, and Business Outcomes

The implementation of AI technologies in cross-platform design has yielded significant benefits in terms of usability, user engagement, and business outcomes for these organizations:

1. Improved Usability and User Experience:

By leveraging AI capabilities like personalization, context-awareness, and intelligent interfaces, these companies have created more intuitive, relevant, and user-friendly experiences across various platforms. Users can seamlessly interact with these services, receiving tailored content and functionality that aligns with their preferences and needs, reducing cognitive load and enhancing overall satisfaction.

2. Increased User Engagement and Retention:

The personalized and adaptive nature of AI-driven experiences has contributed to higher user engagement and retention rates. Users are more likely to continue using services that consistently provide relevant and tailored content, recommendations, and interactions, resulting in increased loyalty and long-term value for the organizations.

3. Competitive Advantage and Business Growth:

By embracing AI technologies in their cross-platform strategies, these companies have gained a competitive edge in their respective industries. The ability to deliver superior user experiences has attracted and retained customers, driving business growth and revenue. Additionally, the data-driven insights and optimization capabilities of AI have enabled these organizations to make more informed decisions, streamline operations, and continuously improve their offerings.

8.3 Lessons Learned and Best Practices

Through the implementation and ongoing refinement of AI-driven cross-platform experiences, these organizations have uncovered valuable lessons and best practices that can guide other designers and practitioners:

1. User-Centric Approach: Prioritize user needs, preferences, and behaviors when designing AI-driven experiences. Continuously gather and analyze user data to inform personalization and adaptation strategies (Gomez-Uribe & Hunt, 2016).
2. Responsible AI and Ethical Considerations: Implement robust data privacy and security measures, ensure transparency and user control over personal information, and address potential biases or ethical concerns associated with AI systems (Mehrabi et al., 2021).
3. Iterative Development and Testing: Adopt an iterative approach to development, continuously testing and refining AI models and user experiences based on real-world data and user feedback (Noorollah & Ayoubi, 2021).
4. Cross-Functional Collaboration: Foster collaboration between design, engineering, data science, and product teams to ensure seamless integration of AI technologies and align on user experience goals (Amershi et al., 2019).
5. Scalability and Flexibility: Design AI-driven systems and architectures that can scale and adapt to evolving user needs, technological advancements, and platform changes (Sculley et al., 2015).

By learning from these real-world implementations, organizations can leverage the power of AI to create engaging, personalized, and user-centric experiences across various digital platforms, while also addressing ethical concerns and fostering trust with their users.

9. EMERGING TRENDS AND FUTURE DIRECTIONS

9.1 AI Innovations in Cross-Platform Design

The future of cross-platform design is closely intertwined with the continued advancement of AI technologies. As AI continues to evolve, several key innovations are expected to shape the landscape of cross-platform design:

- Advancements in Natural Language Processing (NLP): NLP algorithms will become more sophisticated, enabling seamless voice interactions and natural language understanding across diverse digital platforms. This will lead to more intuitive and conversational user experiences, particularly in virtual assistants and conversational interfaces (Brownlee, 2021).
- Integration of Augmented Reality (AR) and Virtual Reality (VR): AI-powered AR and VR experiences will become more prevalent, blurring the lines between physical and digital worlds. Designers will need to leverage AI to create immersive and contextually relevant AR/VR experiences that enhance usability and engagement (Kale, 2020).
- AI-Driven Predictive Personalization: AI algorithms will continue to refine predictive personalization techniques, enabling hyper-personalized user experiences tailored to individual preferences, behaviors, and contexts. This will require designers to develop ethical and transparent personalization strategies while addressing concerns around data privacy and algorithmic bias (McKinney, 2020).
- Autonomous Design Systems: AI-driven autonomous design systems will empower designers with tools that automate routine design tasks, generate design variations, and provide real-time feedback based on user data and design principles. This will streamline the design process, accelerate iteration cycles, and foster creativity and innovation in cross-platform design (Wang et al., 2021).

9.2 Implications for Future UX Research and Practice

The evolving landscape of AI-driven cross-platform design presents several implications for future UX research and practice:

- Interdisciplinary Collaboration: UX researchers and practitioners will need to collaborate with experts in AI, data science, and ethics to understand the implications of AI-driven design decisions on user experience, privacy, and inclusivity. Interdisciplinary research will be essential for developing responsible AI-driven design practices (Dove, 2019).

- Continuous Learning and Adaptation: With AI technologies constantly evolving, UX professionals must engage in continuous learning and skill development to stay abreast of emerging trends, tools, and best practices in AI-driven design. Lifelong learning will be crucial for maintaining relevance and proficiency in the rapidly changing field of UX design (Lewin, 2022).
- Ethical Considerations: As AI becomes more pervasive in cross-platform design, UX practitioners must prioritize ethical considerations such as transparency, accountability, and fairness. Designing AI-driven systems that respect user autonomy, privacy, and dignity will be paramount to building trust and fostering positive user experiences (Morley et al., 2021).

9.3 Recommendations for Designers and Practitioners

Based on emerging trends and future directions in AI-driven cross-platform design, the following recommendations are proposed for designers and practitioners:

- Embrace Human-Centered Design: Designers should adopt a human-centered approach to AI-driven design, prioritizing user needs, preferences, and values throughout the design process. Engaging users in co-design activities and usability testing will help ensure that AI-powered solutions meet user expectations and enhance usability (Norman & Stappers, 2015).
- Invest in AI Education and Training: UX professionals should invest in education and training programs that provide foundational knowledge and practical skills in AI and machine learning. By developing proficiency in AI-driven design tools and methodologies, designers can leverage AI technologies to create innovative and impactful user experiences (Choi & Kang, 2020).
- Advocate for Ethical AI Practices: Designers have a responsibility to advocate for ethical AI practices within their organizations and communities. This includes promoting transparency, fairness, and accountability in AI-driven design decisions, as well as advocating for user rights and privacy protections (Diakopoulos, 2016).
- Collaborate Across Disciplines: Collaboration with experts in AI, data science, ethics, and other relevant disciplines is essential for successful AI-driven cross-platform design. Designers should seek opportunities to collaborate with interdisciplinary teams to leverage diverse perspectives and expertise in solving complex design challenges (Cross & Prusak, 2002).
- By embracing these recommendations and staying attuned to emerging trends and best practices in AI-driven cross-platform design, designers and practi-

tioners can create user experiences that are not only usable and engaging but also ethical, inclusive, and empowering.

10. CONCLUSION

10.1 Summary of Key Findings

In this comprehensive exploration of AI-driven approaches in cross-platform design, several key findings have emerged:

- AI-Powered User Research and Evaluation: AI has revolutionized user research and evaluation by enabling more efficient gathering and analysis of user feedback, sentiment analysis, and behavior prediction, leading to more informed design decisions.
- Multi-Modal Interaction Design: AI technologies have facilitated the creation of multi-modal interfaces, allowing users to engage with digital systems through various modalities such as voice, gestures, and facial expressions, thereby enhancing usability and user experience.
- Personalization and Context-Aware Design: The integration of AI has enabled personalized user experiences tailored to individual preferences, behaviors, and contextual factors, leading to more engaging and relevant interactions across diverse digital platforms.
- AI-Based Performance Optimization: AI-driven optimization techniques, including resource allocation, predictive maintenance, and performance tuning, have improved the efficiency, responsiveness, and reliability of digital systems, ensuring optimal user experience.

10.2 Implications for the Future of Cross-Platform Design

The implications of AI-driven approaches for the future of cross-platform design are profound:

- Enhanced User Experience: AI technologies enable designers to create more personalized, context-aware, and efficient user experiences across various platforms, leading to higher user satisfaction and engagement.
- Improved Efficiency and Reliability: AI-driven optimization techniques enhance the performance and reliability of digital systems, ensuring seamless operation and minimizing downtime or performance degradation.

- Opportunities for Innovation: AI opens up new avenues for innovation in cross-platform design, allowing designers to explore novel interaction paradigms, predictive capabilities, and adaptive experiences that were previously unattainable.
- Challenges and Considerations: Despite the benefits, AI-driven design approaches also pose challenges related to data privacy, algorithmic bias, and ethical considerations, highlighting the need for responsible AI deployment and ongoing research in these areas.

10.3 Final Remarks and Closing Thoughts

In conclusion, AI-driven approaches have transformed cross-platform design by enabling personalized, context-aware, and efficient user experiences. As AI technologies continue to evolve, designers must leverage these tools responsibly to create inclusive, accessible, and ethically sound digital experiences for users worldwide. By embracing AI-driven design principles and staying abreast of emerging trends and best practices, designers can unlock new possibilities and shape the future of cross-platform design in meaningful and impactful ways.

REFERENCES

Ahmetovic, D., Fedorovych, K., Voeikau, O., & Babbitt, C. (2019). Deep learning for automatically detecting manual web accessibility issues. Paper presented at the 2019 Seventh International Conference on Learning Representations (ICLR), New Orleans, LA, USA. DOI: 10.48550/arXiv.1908.11815

Albert, W., & Tullis, T. (2013). *Measuring the user experience: Collecting, analyzing, and presenting usability metrics*. Newnes.

Amershi, S., Weld, D., Vorvoreanu, M., Fourney, A., Nushi, B., Collisson, P., & Horvitz, E. (2019). Guidelines for human-AI interaction. In *Proceedings of the 2019 CHI Conference on Human Factors in Computing Systems* (pp. 1-13). DOI: 10.1145/3290605.3300233

Apple. (2023). Differential privacy overview. https://www.apple.com/privacy/docs/Differential_Privacy_Overview.pdf

Bajaj, R., Bhat, S., Chakravarthy, S., Chand, S., Iyer, S., Panakkat, A., & Sawant, K. (2020). AI at Amazon: Solving for customer-obsession. *Communications of the ACM*, 63(12), 57–63. DOI: 10.1145/3417988

Becker, N., Chalkiadakis, M., Eidetog, H., Gezer, D., Wikler, J. H., & Wahlström, R. (2022). Automatic adaptation of web applications for mobile devices using artificial intelligence. *IEEE Access : Practical Innovations, Open Solutions*, 10, 10397–10411. DOI: 10.1109/ACCESS.2022.3143342

Brownlee, J. (2021). What is natural language processing? Machine Learning Mastery. https://machinelearningmastery.com/what-is-natural-language-processing/

Choi, H., & Kang, H. (2020). The study on the development of artificial intelligence education program for design students. *International Journal of Technology and Design Education*, 30(6), 1085–1101. DOI: 10.1007/s10798-019-09554-y

Conati, C., Aleven, V., Guzman, E., & Cen, H. (2020). Predicting student mindtracing behaviour to help teach skills better. In *International Conference on Artificial Intelligence in Education* (pp. 144-155). Springer. DOI: 10.1007/978-3-030-52237-7_12

Crichton, G., Perera, S., Fleming, D., Acharya, P., Tahmuras, V., Church, L., & Dengel, A. (2018). AI-assisted privacy note coding at scale: Methodology and challenges. *Journal of the American Medical Informatics Association : JAMIA*, 25(10), 1339–1351. DOI: 10.1093/jamia/ocy124 PMID: 30010902

Cross, R., & Prusak, L. (2002). The people who make organizations go - or stop. *Harvard Business Review*, 80(6), 104–112. DOI: 10.20529/IJME.2018.041002 PMID: 12048992

Diakopoulos, N. (2016). Accountability in algorithmic decision making. *Communications of the ACM*, 59(2), 56–62. DOI: 10.1145/2844110

Diro, A. A., & Chilamkurti, N. (2018). Distributed attack detection scheme using deep learning approach for Internet of Things. *Future Generation Computer Systems*, 82, 761–768. DOI: 10.1016/j.future.2017.08.043

Dove, G. (2019). Reframing design at the intersection of UX and AI. In *Proceedings of the 2019 CHI Conference on Human Factors in Computing Systems* (pp. 1-6). DOI: 10.1145/3290607.3312782

Fernandez-Viña, R., López-Moreno, A., & Gómez-Pulido, J. A. (2021). An AI-based approach to automated image description for visually impaired people. *Sensors (Basel)*, 21(14), 4679. DOI: 10.3390/s21144679 PMID: 34300418

Gomez-Uribe, C. A., & Hunt, N. (2016). The Netflix recommender system: Algorithms, business value, and innovation. *ACM Transactions on Management Information Systems*, 6(4), 1–19. DOI: 10.1145/2843948

Google. (2022). Flutter: Build apps for any screen. https://flutter.dev/

Hailpern, J., Liu, Y., Moore, D., Marques, D., & Gaspar, J. (2021). AI-enabled conversational agents for improved user experience. In *Human-Computer Interaction. Design Practice in Contemporary Societies* (pp. 555–566). Springer. DOI: 10.1007/978-3-030-77752-2_38

Hassenzahl, M., & Tractinsky, N. (2006). User experience - a research agenda. *Behaviour & Information Technology*, 25(2), 91–97. DOI: 10.1080/01449290500330331

IBM. (2021). Watson Studio: Accelerate AI deployment and increase operational trust. https://www.ibm.com/cloud/watson-studio

IBM. (2022). AI for API integration and modernization. https://www.ibm.com/cloud/api-integration-modernization

Jacobson, A., & Sandin, F. (2019). Personalized music recommendations at Spotify. *Communications of the ACM*, 62(11), 75–80. DOI: 10.1145/3358492

Jiang, D., Zhang, C., Cui, L., & Chuah, M. C. (2022). Privacy-preserving machine learning: Threats, models, and techniques. *IEEE Internet of Things Journal*, 9(20), 19668–19687. DOI: 10.1109/JIOT.2022.3164936

Kale, S. (2020). The rise of augmented reality (AR) and virtual reality (VR) technologies in the era of AI. *International Journal of Innovation and Applied Studies*, 30(3), 705–710.

Kaptein, M., Markopoulos, P., de Ruyter, B., & Aarts, E. (2015). Personalizing persuasive technologies: Explicit and implicit personalization using persuasion profiles. *International Journal of Human-Computer Studies*, 77, 38–51. DOI: 10.1016/j.ijhcs.2015.01.004

Kous, D., Ma, X., Zangerle, E., & Gennari, R. (2020). Assistive technologies for enhancing accessibility and inclusion: A position paper from the AAATE Accessibility and Active Aging Working Group. *Disability and Rehabilitation. Assistive Technology*, 15(5), 521–527. DOI: 10.1080/17483107.2020.1752606 PMID: 30985225

Lécué, F., Lind, L., Burns, C., Zysset, P., Mashburn, E., & Mironov, D. (2022). Explainable and transparent AI: A holistic approach. Explainable AI: Interpreting. *Explaining and Visualizing Deep Learning*, 11, 1–18. DOI: 10.1007/978-3-031-04083-2_1

Lemon, K. N., & Verhoef, P. C. (2016). Understanding customer experience throughout the customer journey. *Journal of Marketing*, 80(6), 69–96. DOI: 10.1509/jm.15.0420

Lewin, C. (2022). Building a culture of continuous learning for user experience professionals. *Interaction*, 29(1), 36–40. DOI: 10.1145/3505837

Li, Z., & Guo, H. (2021). Artificial intelligence and internet of things towards intelligent manufacturing: A review. *IEEE Access : Practical Innovations, Open Solutions*, 9, 45796–45814. DOI: 10.1109/ACCESS.2021.3066883

Liu, B. (2020). *Sentiment analysis: Mining opinions, sentiments, and emotions*. Cambridge University Press. DOI: 10.1017/9781108639286

McKinney, S. M. (2020). Predictive personalization: Predicting user traits from text for personalized systems. *Frontiers in Big Data*, 3, 9. DOI: 10.3389/fdata.2020.00009

Mehrabi, N., Morstatter, F., Saxena, N., Lerman, K., & Galstyan, A. (2021). A survey on bias and fairness in machine learning. *ACM Computing Surveys*, 54(6), 1–35. DOI: 10.1145/3457607

Moran, K., Viyovic, V., Bandara, C., Gordon, M., Nguyen, C. D., Hill, C., & Singer, J. (2021). Automating UI design migration to support web app evolution. *IEEE Transactions on Software Engineering*. Advance online publication. DOI: 10.1109/TSE.2021.3076790

Morley, J., Floridi, L., Kinsey, L., & Elhalal, A. (2021). From what to how: An initial review of publicly available AI ethics tools, methods and research to translate principles into practices. *Science and Engineering Ethics*, 27(2), 1–28. DOI: 10.1007/s11948-021-00300-8 PMID: 31828533

Nguyen, A. T., Nguyen, T. T. D., Al-Zubaidi, R., Nguyen, H. A., & Nguyen, H. V. (2021). A comprehensive survey of code translation from high-level program models to blockchain bytecodes. *ACM Computing Surveys*, 54(2), 1–37. DOI: 10.1145/3409555

Nguyen, D., De Mulder, Y., Van Rotterdam, P., & De Jong, R. (2019). Behavior prediction: Definition and problem space analysis. *IEEE Access : Practical Innovations, Open Solutions*, 7, 163239–163261. DOI: 10.1109/ACCESS.2019.2952286

Nielsen, J. (1994). Enhancing the explanatory power of usability heuristics. In *Proceedings of the SIGCHI Conference on Human Factors in Computing Systems* (pp. 152-158). DOI: 10.1145/191666.191729

Nike. (2021). Nike's commitment to AI ethics. https://nike.app.box.com/v/aiprinciplesreport

Noorollah, N., & Ayoubi, R. (2021). Toward iterative and continuous user experience development. In *User Experience Design for the Internet of Things* (pp. 97–119). Springer., DOI: 10.1007/978-3-030-72288-0_5

Norman, D., & Stappers, P. J. (2015). DesignX: Complex socio-technical systems. She Ji. *The Journal of Design, Economics, and Innovation*, 1(2), 83–94. DOI: 10.1016/j.sheji.2016.01.002

Norman, D. A. (2013). *The design of everyday things: Revised and expanded edition*. Constellation Books.

Norman, D. A., & Draper, S. W. (1986). *User centered system design. New perspectives on human-computer interaction*. L. Erlbaum Associates Inc. DOI: 10.1201/b15703

Novick, T. (2021). Inclusive design at Microsoft. Microsoft Design. https://www.microsoft.com/design/inclusive

Okano, Y., Kudoh, T., Le Minh, Q., Abe, A., O'Brien, C., & Kitagawa, H. (2021). Bayesian intelligent access control. AI for Data Privacy and Security (AI4DPS) Workshop. *IJCAI (United States)*.

Revuze. (2023). Revuze: AI-driven product analytics. https://revuze.it/

Sculley, D., Holt, G., Golovin, D., Davydov, E., Phillips, T., Ebner, D., . . . Dennison, D. (2015). Machine learning: The high interest credit card of technical debt. In SE4ML: Software Engineering for Machine Learning (NIPS 2015 Workshop).

Shumaker, R., & George, C. (2016). Mobile computing trends: Insights from case studies. In Mobile Computing and Wireless Networks: Concepts, Methodologies, Tools, and Applications (pp. 176-189). IGI Global. DOI: 10.4018/978-1-4666-8751-6.ch012

Starbucks. (2022). Starbucks modernization: How AI is brewing a better experience. https://stories.starbucks.com/stories/2022/how-ai-is-brewing-a-better-starbucks-experience/

Thakur, D., & Zhang, X. (Eds.). (2020). *Wearable human–machine multi-interface: Human body weight transfer and augmented reality*. Springer.

Uber. (2020). How Uber leverages machine learning with AI compute. https://eng.uber.com/machine-learning/

Wang, J., Wang, L., Li, J., Li, H., Tao, D., Tang, B., & Chen, J. (2021). Autonomous design system driven by artificial intelligence. *International Journal of Computer Integrated Manufacturing*, 34(4), 311–349. DOI: 10.1080/0951192X.2021.1893138

Weng, F., Zhang, L., & Ngo, T. (2019). Cross-platform application design and development: Emerging technologies for future. In *Future Data and Security Engineering* (pp. 435–445). Springer., DOI: 10.1007/978-981-13-8513-3_42

Zhou, X., Fu, Y., Najm, A., Ma, Q., He, X., Li, H., & Tu, Z. (2020). Improving user-interface interaction with reinforcement learning. In *Proceedings of the 21st International Conference on Web Information Systems Engineering* (pp. 583-594). Springer. DOI: 10.1007/978-3-030-62008-0_41

Chapter 3
Navigating Usability and User Experience in a Multi-Platform World With Agile Methodology

Somesh Kumar Sahu
https://orcid.org/0000-0003-2171-0338
Presidency University, India

Senthilkumar Ranganathan
Presidency University, India

ABSTRACT

The ever-expanding landscape of devices and platforms creates a complex challenge for ensuring exceptional user experience (UX) in modern software development. Agile methodologies, with their core principles of rapid iteration and responsiveness to change, offer a promising approach to navigating this dynamic environment. However, integrating user research and evaluation techniques, crucial for a user-centric approach, can be difficult within the fast-paced cycles of agile development. This research addresses this gap by exploring strategies for seamlessly integrating user research activities into agile workflows. Reviewing existing literature, the authors identify and analyse user research and evaluation techniques well-suited for the Agile framework. This framework serves as a roadmap for organisations seeking to leverage the benefits of agile methodologies while ensuring a user-centric approach that delivers exceptional UX across diverse platforms. Ultimately, the research aims to bridge the gap between agile development and user-centred design.

DOI: 10.4018/979-8-3693-2337-3.ch003

INTRODUCTION

In today's digital landscape, users expect software to be functional but also intuitive and enjoyable across various devices, from smartphones to tablets and web interfaces(Engberg, 2024). Agile development methodologies, known for their iterative cycles and responsiveness to user feedback, seem ideally suited for this multi-platform world. However, ensuring a user-centric approach requires integrating usability and user experience (UX) considerations throughout the Agile workflow (Lind & Mishchenko, 2024; Martinelli et al., 2024). Large organisations increasingly adopt agile methodologies because they emphasise flexibility, collaboration, and customer-centricity, enabling iterative development and rapid adaptation to changing requirements.

Usability ensures that products are user-friendly and meet user needs, focusing on learnability, efficiency, and satisfaction. UX encompasses all interactions between the user and the product, aiming to create utility, usability, desirability, accessibility, and credibility. Multi-platform development ensures a consistent user experience across different devices and operating systems, considering consistency, adaptability, performance, and leveraging native features (Savolainen, 2010; Thota & Jung, 2024).

User research, involving interviews, surveys, and usability testing, informs the design process by understanding user behaviours and needs(Familoni & Babatunde, 2024). User testing evaluates products by observing real users and identifying usability issues through various types, such as moderated, unmoderated, and A/B testing (Sarkar et al., 2010). Evaluation methods, including heuristic evaluation and performance metrics, assess how well a product meets user expectations. Integrating usability and UX practices into Agile involves continuous feedback and iterative design, ensuring that products are functional, efficient, and delightful to use by incorporating collaborative design, regular usability testing, and iterative improvements throughout the development process (Thorngate & Hoden, 2017; Xu, 2024).

The ever-expanding landscape of devices and platforms presents a complex challenge for ensuring exceptional user experience in modern software development. In this context, Agile methodologies offer a promising approach to navigating the dynamic and multifaceted environment with their core principles of rapid iteration and responsiveness to change (Neumann et al., 2023). Agile's flexibility and collaborative nature are well-suited for handling frequent changes in requirements and technology, making it an attractive option for organisations aiming to enhance their software development processes (Oladapo et al., 2024).

However, integrating user research and evaluation techniques—essential components of a user-centric approach—within the fast-paced cycles of Agile development can be challenging. Traditional user research methods, which often require significant time and resources, do not easily fit into the iterative sprints typical of

Agile workflows (Tetteh, 2024). This research aims to address this gap by exploring strategies for seamlessly incorporating user research activities into Agile processes without compromising the speed and adaptability that Agile promises.

Through a comprehensive review of existing literature, this research identifies and analyses user research and evaluation techniques that are particularly well-suited for the Agile framework. These techniques are often considered lightweight due to their efficiency and ability to gather targeted user feedback within short timeframes. Techniques such as usability testing, user interviews, and heuristic evaluations are adapted to fit into the shorter cycles of Agile development, ensuring that user-centricity is maintained throughout the project lifecycle (Barros et al., 2024; Talipu, 2021).

The research brings these techniques to life with a simulated case study that develops a multi-platform software application. This case study demonstrates how various user research and evaluation methods can be integrated within an Agile project, highlighting the benefits and challenges of doing so (Natarajan & Pichai, 2024). The findings from this case study are used to propose a framework for effectively addressing usability and UX considerations in a multi-platform Agile development environment (Welin, 2024).

This framework serves as a roadmap for organisations seeking to leverage the benefits of Agile methodologies while ensuring a user-centric approach that delivers exceptional UX across diverse platforms. By bridging the gap between Agile development and user-centred design, the research aims to create successful and user-friendly software solutions in today's dynamic multi-platform world (Guerrero-Ulloa et al., 2023). The insights from this research enhance our understanding of integrating user research in Agile and provide practical guidance for practitioners looking to improve their software development practices.

The crux of the challenge lies in the potential conflict between traditional usability testing, which can be time-consuming, and Agile's rapid development cycles (Meckenstock, 2024; Tiriticco, 2021). Organisations must decide whether to prioritise speed and risk compromising user experience or to sacrifice efficiency by sticking to traditional methods. This research explores this critical interplay between Agile and user research in multi-platform development. We will explore strategies for seamlessly integrating lightweight user research activities within the Agile framework, advocating for techniques that prioritise user needs and incorporate feedback throughout development. By balancing Agile's efficiency and a user-centric approach, organisations can create functionally robust products with exceptional usability and UX across diverse platforms(Tomlin, 2018). This exploration aims to equip organisations with the knowledge and strategies to bridge this gap and develop successful, user-friendly applications in a multi-platform world.

While Agile UX offers a robust methodology for user-centred design, ethical considerations and potential biases require careful attention. Informed consent, robust data security practices, and diverse user recruitment are crucial to ensure responsible research practices. Mitigating researcher and algorithmic biases involves promoting awareness and utilising techniques that minimise subjective interpretations in data analysis (Alhammad & Moreno, 2022). Furthermore, the long-term impact of continuous user research on product development necessitates balancing responsiveness to user needs with a clearly defined product roadmap to avoid feature creep and maintain focus. Optimising resource allocation through techniques like phased development and user research prioritisation allows Agile UX to be implemented efficiently, even for large and complex projects.

However, overcoming challenges like resource limitations and the learning curve associated with new techniques remains an obstacle to successful Agile UX adoption (Cornide-Reyes et al., 2024a). By acknowledging these potential pitfalls and implementing appropriate strategies, teams can leverage the power of Agile UX while ensuring an ethical, efficient, and user-centred approach to product development.

This research tackles the challenge of integrating user-centred design principles into the rapid development cycles of Agile methodologies for multi-platform software. It proposes a framework seamlessly incorporating lightweight user research techniques within Agile workflows. These techniques, designed to gather targeted user feedback within short timeframes, ensure that user needs are continuously considered throughout the project lifecycle (Pillay & Wing, 2019). By equipping organisations with the knowledge and strategies to bridge this gap, the research empowers them to develop successful, user-friendly applications in today's dynamic multi-platform world. This framework paves the way for organisations to leverage the speed and adaptability of Agile while delivering exceptional user experiences across diverse platforms (Azevedo et al., 2024).

USER RESEARCH AND EVALUATION TECHNIQUES IN AGILE

The key to successful user research within Agile lies in prioritising and embracing lightweight techniques that can be seamlessly integrated into short sprints. Here are some critical approaches:

Figure 1. User research and evaluation techniques in agile

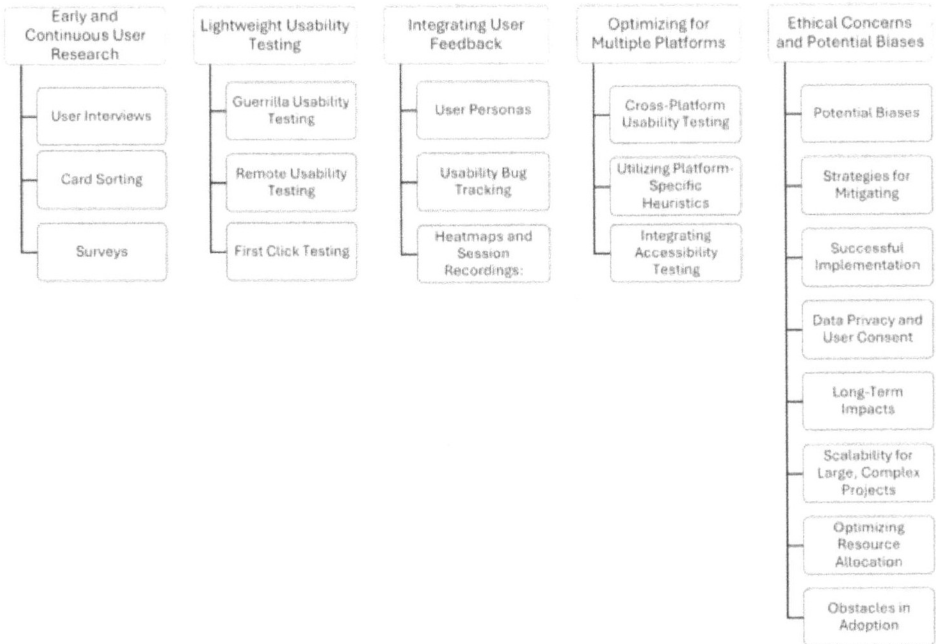

Early and Continuous User Research: Techniques like user interviews, card sorting, and targeted surveys can be conducted throughout the development lifecycle to gather user needs, expectations, and pain points specific to different platforms.

1. **User Interviews:** Agile methodologies recommend conducting short, focused interviews (lasting 30-60 minutes) at regular intervals to gain deep user insights throughout the development lifecycle. This approach allows researchers to delve into user needs, expectations, and specific pain points encountered while using the product on different platforms (Kobialka et al., 2024). This targeted feedback ensures a positive user experience across all devices. Schedule interviews at the beginning of sprints to gather valuable user insights. This feedback directly informs the creation and prioritisation of user stories, ensuring the development team focuses on features that address users' most pressing needs across platforms (Jeong et al., 2024). Conduct follow-up interviews later in the sprint to gauge user response to evolving functionalities. This allos for gathering feedback on prototypes or specific features, enabling the team to refine the product iteratively based on user experience. Agile methodologies encourage utilising remote interviewing tools. These online platforms facilitate interviews

with geographically dispersed users, ensuring a more comprehensive range of voices are heard throughout the development cycle.

2. **Card Sorting:** Agile methodologies emphasise understanding user behaviour to optimise the product for each platform. One technique used to achieve this is card sorting (Sommer, 2024). During card sorting sessions, users categorise information and organise content based on their mental models. The development team gains valuable insights into how users perceive and navigate information by analysing this data. These insights directly inform the information architecture for each platform, ensuring an intuitive and user-friendly experience across all devices. Agile methodologies leverage card sorting to understand user information organisation preferences and optimise the interface for each platform. Card sorting sessions are conducted early in development, typically during the first sprint. This initial user input helps define the core structure of the user interface across all platforms, ensuring a consistent and intuitive foundation. Agile practices recommend revisiting card sorting with updated information as the product evolves and content categories are refined. This iterative approach ensures that the information architecture remains aligned with user needs and expectations, leading to a user-friendly experience across all devices (Jean, 2014).
3. **Surveys:** Agile methodologies embrace efficiency while gathering valuable user feedback. One technique that achieves this balance is the user survey. Unlike interviews, surveys focus on gathering feedback on specific aspects of the product or design. This targeted approach allows data to be collected from a more extensive user base than interviews, providing a broader perspective on user experience (Herendy, 2020). This efficiency is crucial within the fast-paced cycles of Agile development. Agile methodologies promote efficient user feedback collection through targeted surveys. Unlike in-depth interviews, these surveys focus on specific functionalities or design elements developed within a sprint. By keeping them short and focused, Agile teams can gather valuable data from a broader user base within the sprint timeframe. This data can be used to gauge user preferences on design mock-ups or prototype features, allowing for iterative refinement and ensuring a user-centric approach throughout the development process.

Lightweight Usability Testing: Guerrilla usability testing, remote testing platforms, and first-click testing offer efficient methods to identify usability issues during each sprint cycle. Traditional usability testing methods can be time-consuming and resource-intensive. Agile methodologies necessitate a shift towards lightweight testing that can be integrated effectively within short sprints:

1. **Guerrilla Usability Testing:** Agile methodologies prioritise identifying and addressing usability issues early and often. Guerrilla testing is a lightweight technique that aligns perfectly with this goal. During a guerrilla testing session, a small group of readily available users (typically 5-8) are brought in to interact with the product or prototype (Collado et al., 2024). The focus is on observing their behaviour and identifying any major usability problems they encounter. The beauty of guerrilla testing lies in its simplicity and efficiency. By conducting these short sessions throughout each sprint cycle, Agile teams can quickly uncover critical usability issues and address them before they become more significant problems later in development. Agile development thrives on identifying and fixing usability issues early. Guerrilla testing, a lightweight technique ideally suited for Agile workflows, helps achieve this goal. Towards the end of a sprint, a small group of readily available users (typically 5-8) can be recruited quickly through the team's network or online platforms. These participants then interact with the product or prototype, allowing the team to observe their behaviour and identify any significant usability problems, explicitly focusing on core functionalities being developed for different platforms. The efficiency of guerrilla testing allows Agile teams to uncover critical usability issues within the sprint timeframe, ensuring a more polished and user-friendly product emerges at the end of each iteration (Hsi et al., 2007).
2. **Remote Usability Testing:** Agile development demands a deep understanding of how users interact with the product across different platforms, especially when targeting geographically dispersed audiences. Remote usability testing techniques bridge this gap (Chen et al., 2024). Unlike traditional in-person testing, remote methods allow researchers to observe and evaluate user experience with the product on various devices (phones, tablets, laptops) from the comfort of their locations. This approach provides valuable insights into user behaviour across diverse platforms and geographic regions, ensuring a seamless and positive experience for all users regardless of location. Agile methodologies require efficient yet insightful ways to evaluate user experience across various platforms. Remote usability testing platforms offer a perfect solution. These online platforms facilitate remote testing sessions with geographically dispersed users, allowing researchers to observe user interaction with the product on different devices (phones, tablets, laptops) within the tight timeframe of a sprint. The key is focusing the testing sessions on critical core functionalities, user flows, and a seamless multi-platform experience (Diplom-Ingenieur et al., 2022). By observing user behaviour on these essential aspects, Agile teams can identify usability issues and ensure a consistent and positive user experience across all devices (Sarkar et al., 2010).

3. **First Click Testing**: In the fast-paced world of Agile development, identifying usability issues early is paramount. One technique that excels at this is the first impression test. Researchers observe users' initial interaction with a new feature or platform during a first impression test. This targeted approach allows for pinpointing immediate usability issues and confusing design elements before user frustration sets in. By catching these problems early, Agile teams can address them quickly and ensure a smooth and intuitive user experience for the final product across all platforms. Agile development prioritises early detection and resolution of usability issues. First-click testing aligns perfectly with this goal. Agile teams can conduct a first-click test early within a sprint when introducing a new feature or design element on a specific platform. This technique involves observing users' initial interaction with the product, explicitly focusing on their first click after being presented with a task (Leong et al., 2022). By analysing this behaviour, researchers can uncover immediate usability issues and confusing design elements. These valuable insights are then used to refine the design before further development commences within the sprint (Savolainen, 2010). This iterative approach ensures that the final product offers a smooth and intuitive user experience across all platforms (Fleury & Chaniaud, 2024).

Integrating User Feedback: User personas, usability bug tracking within Agile project management tools, and utilising data from heatmaps and session recordings can help maintain a user-centric approach and prioritise improvements (Huynh et al., 2021).

1. **User Personas:** Agile development thrives on a user-centric approach, and user personas are a powerful tool to achieve this. These detailed profiles represent key user groups within the target audience (Harte et al., 2017). Each persona goes beyond demographics, including user behaviours, goals, and pain points across different platform (Othman & Anuar, 2024). Here is how user personas benefit Agile development. Maintains User Focus By constantly referencing user personas throughout development, the team stays focused on who they are designing. This ensures that the product caters to the specific needs of various user groups across all platforms (mobile, tablet, web). Informs Design Decisions When faced with design choices, the team can evaluate options based on how well they align with the needs and preferences outlined in the user personas. This ensures that design decisions prioritise user experience across platforms (Rathnayake & Lanka, 2019). Promotes Empathy User personas foster empathy within the development team (Salminen et al., 2022). By understanding the user's perspective, motivations, and challenges, the team is better equipped to design and test features that resonate with users on all platforms (Nurmuradov

& Bryce, 2017). To integrate user personas seamlessly within Agile methodologies, Create Personas Early and Develop user personas at the beginning of the project. As user research progresses throughout development cycles, these personas can be continually refined based on new findings. Reference During Planning Integrate user personas into sprint planning and design discussions (Beattie et al., 2019). Use them to ensure that the features and functionalities being developed address the needs of the target user groups across all platforms. This ensures a user-centric approach throughout the Agile development process.

2. **Usability Bug Tracking:** Agile development thrives on a seamless loop of user research, issue resolution, and continuous improvement. Usability problems identified during testing are treated no differently. These are logged as tasks within the team's project management tool (like Jira or Trello), ensuring they are prioritised alongside other development tasks. This transparency fosters collaboration between developers, designers, and researchers, who can brainstorm solutions to address usability issues and ensure a positive user experience across all platforms. Tracking these bugs as tasks allows the team to monitor progress and maintain focus on improving the user experience throughout development (Tullis & Albert, 2024). To ensure effective integration of these findings, Agile teams can train all members involved in user research and testing on proper identification and documentation of usability issues. Clear descriptions, screenshots, recordings, and assigned severity levels based on impact (critical issues prioritised) all contribute to a more user-centric approach that delivers a positive experience across all platforms.
3. **Heatmaps and Session Recordings:** Agile development hinges on understanding platform user behaviour. Heatmaps and session recordings seamlessly integrate into this process by revealing the unseen. These tools capture user interactions without interrupting workflow (Dobashi et al., 2019). Heatmaps visualise clicks, taps, and scrolls, highlighting high-engagement areas. Session recordings capture users' entire screen interactions and audio, allowing researchers to observe user journeys and pinpoint confusion or difficulty on different platforms. The insights gleaned go beyond what users might explicitly mention during testing. They uncover hidden usability issues and user behaviour patterns (Nurmuradov & Bryce, 2017). This data empowers Agile teams to make data-driven decisions, prioritising design changes and feature refinements based on what users are doing (or struggling with) across platforms. Inconsistencies in user behaviour between platforms can also be identified, prompting the team to ensure a consistent and intuitive experience for all users regardless of device (Jeong et al., 2024). To maximise effectiveness, these tools should be utilised throughout development, not just at the end. By analysing data after each sprint, Agile teams can identify patterns and areas for improvement before moving on

to the next stage. Focusing on areas with high user activity or user frustration (revealed by recordings) helps pinpoint critical usability issues that must be addressed across all platforms. This iterative approach ensures a user-centric product that continuously evolves based on accurate user behaviour data.

Optimising for Multiple Platforms: Cross-platform usability testing, utilising platform-specific heuristics, and integrating accessibility testing ensure a consistent and positive UX across devices(Herendy, 2020). In a multi-platform world, where users seamlessly switch between devices, ensuring a consistent and positive user experience (UX) across all platforms becomes paramount (Ormeño & Pinciroli, 2024). Here is how Agile methodologies can be leveraged to achieve this goal.

1. **Cross-Platform Usability Testing:** Cross-platform testing, where usability sessions involve users who switch between your product's various platforms (mobile app, tablet app, web interface), offers significant benefits within Agile development. It uncovers inconsistencies that might go unnoticed during individual platform testing. These inconsistencies range from user flow variations due to screen size limitations to terminology differences that confuse users. Cross-platform testing ensures a logical flow, consistent vocabulary, and a cohesive design language across all devices, even when adaptations are necessary (like smaller mobile icons). It also evaluates user transitions between platforms, identifying issues with data synchronisation, task continuation, and overall experience (Hinderks et al., 2024). To integrate seamlessly with Agile methodologies, schedule cross-platform testing throughout development cycles, recruit testers who mirror your target audience's multi-device usage habits, and develop testing scenarios that simulate real-world platform switching (e.g., starting a workout on mobile and tracking it on the web). Finally, users with disabilities should be included in the testing to ensure an inclusive and accessible product (Cheung & Vogel, 2013). By adopting this approach, Agile teams can deliver a user experience that is not only functional but also consistent and intuitive across all platforms.
2. **Utilising Platform-Specific Heuristics:** Agile development thrives on creating user-centric experiences across multiple platforms. Platform-specific heuristics and established usability guidelines for mobile, tablet, and web interfaces offer a valuable foundation for achieving this. These guidelines consider screen size, touch versus mouse interaction, and user expectations for each platform (Koponen, 2018). By adhering to these heuristics, the design team can create interfaces that feel natural and familiar to users on each device (e.g., straightforward navigation on mobile apps and detailed information architecture for the web). This ensures adherence to platform-specific best practices and reduces

development time. However, to guarantee the design caters to the specific needs of your target audience, Agile methodologies should integrate these heuristics into the design workflow while always prioritising user research and testing across all platforms.

3. **Integrating Accessibility Testing:** In Agile development, ensuring a positive user experience across platforms goes hand-in-hand with accessibility. Accessibility testing, which involves verifying that people with disabilities can use your product, offers many benefits. It promotes inclusive design, broadening your product's reach and ensuring a positive experience for a broader user base. Many accessibility features, like clear language or keyboard navigation, benefit all users, ultimately improving the overall user experience (Amoako-Gyampah, 2007). Additionally, accessibility compliance with regional regulations becomes effortless. To seamlessly integrate accessibility into Agile methodologies, conduct testing throughout the development lifecycle, not just at the end (Mannay & Pauwels, 2024). Leveraging automated testing tools can further streamline this process by identifying potential accessibility barriers early. By prioritising accessibility from the outset, Agile teams can deliver user-centric products that are functional and inclusive for all.

Ethical Concerns and Potential Biases in Agile UX: Agile UX offers numerous benefits for user experience design, but it is not without its ethical considerations and potential biases (Konidena et al., 2024). The information below allows practitioners to leverage the power of Agile UX while building user-centred products responsibly and ethically. Agile UX's strength, its rapid development pace, can also introduce ethical concerns.

The pressure to complete tasks quickly can lead to overlooking ethical considerations like accessibility, user privacy, and potential unintended consequences (Cornide-Reyes et al., 2024b). Similarly, time constraints can restrict comprehensive user testing, resulting in solutions that do not cater to diverse user needs or even perpetuate biases in the initial user pool chosen for research. Finally, the reliance on readily available data for user research can introduce data bias creep (Osasona et al., 2024).

These readily available datasets might amplify societal biases if not carefully assessed. For instance, algorithms trained on biased data can perpetuate discriminatory practices within the final product. By acknowledging these potential pitfalls, Agile UX practitioners can proactively mitigate them and ensure a more ethical and inclusive approach to user-centred design.

1. **Potential Biases:** Agile UX's emphasis on rapid iteration can also introduce potential biases. One concern is confirmation bias, where teams may subconsciously focus on research findings confirming their assumptions about users. This can lead to overlooking valuable insights that challenge their preconceived notions (Konidena et al., 2024). Similarly, the researcher's background and experiences can influence how they interpret user data. Mitigating this requires diversifying research teams and employing techniques that minimise subjective interpretations. Finally, even AI tools for bias detection (XAI) can be biased. It is crucial to be aware of this limitation and ensure the datasets used to train these tools are diverse, preventing them from perpetuating existing biases rather than identifying them. By acknowledging these potential biases, Agile UX practitioners can proactively ensure their research is objective and leads to a more user-centred product (Olorunsogo et al., 2024).
2. **Strategies for Mitigating Ethical Concerns and Biases:** While Agile UX excels at rapid iteration, it is crucial to prioritise ethical considerations throughout the process. First and foremost, informed consent is paramount. Participants deserve clear and concise information about the research process, how their data will be used, and their right to withdraw at any time (Akinrinola et al., 2024). Additionally, robust data security practices must be implemented to protect user privacy. This includes obtaining explicit user consent for data collection and usage and utilising secure data storage methods. Furthermore, to ensure inclusivity, actively seeking out participants from under-represented groups is essential (Akinrinola et al., 2024). A diverse research sample allows for a more comprehensive understanding of user needs. Beyond participant selection, promoting awareness of potential biases among researchers is vital. By educating researchers on these biases and implementing techniques to minimise their influence, Agile UX practitioners can ensure that research findings are objective and unbiased.
3. **Successful Implementation Strategies:** Agile UX thrives on rapid iteration, but this speed should not compromise ethical considerations. Integrating ethical principles throughout the process, from user research to design and testing, is crucial. Workshops on ethical design principles and conducting bias audits throughout development can equip teams to identify and address potential pitfalls (Ritonummi et al., 2022). Prioritising inclusive user research is also paramount. Actively seeking out diverse user groups for testing ensures the solution caters to a broader range of needs and abilities. Techniques like user persona development focusing on inclusivity can help achieve this. Once data is collected, it is vital to scrutinise it for potential biases (Porcelli et al., 2024). Critically evaluating the data used for design decisions and employing techniques like Explainable AI to understand how algorithms reach conclusions can help identify and mitigate

these biases (Cornide-Reyes et al., 2024a). Finally, the commitment to ethics should not end with launch. Agile UX thrives on continuous iteration, as should the ethical lens applied to the product. Regularly assessing the implemented solution for unintended consequences and gathering user feedback allows for ongoing monitoring and improvement. This iterative approach ensures that any ethical concerns can be addressed through further design refinement. By integrating ethics throughout the process and fostering a culture of continuous improvement, Agile UX can deliver user-centred solutions that are effective but also responsible and inclusive.

4. **Data Privacy and User Consent in Usability Testing:** Agile UX thrives on rapid iteration, but this speed cannot come at the expense of ethical considerations. Central to ethical testing is obtaining informed consent from participants (Thorngate & Hoden, 2017). This transparent document should clearly explain the test's purpose, what data will be collected (screen recordings, eye tracking, etc.), how the data will be used and stored, and, importantly, the participant's rights, including confidentiality and the ability to withdraw from the study. Furthermore, Agile UX should prioritise data minimisation (Puspitasari et al., 2024). This means collecting only the essential data for the test and anonymising it whenever possible. Finally, any data collected should be deleted after analysis unless explicit consent is granted for long-term storage (Talipu, 2021). Implementing robust security measures to protect user data from breaches and unauthorised access is also paramount. By adhering to these principles, Agile UX practitioners can ensure that their user research is conducted ethically and responsibly.
5. **Long-Term Impacts of Continuous User Research on Product Development:** While Agile UX boasts the benefit of continuous user feedback, it has its challenges. One potential pitfall is feature creep and scope creep. The constant influx of user feedback can lead to an ever-expanding list of features, potentially deviating from the core product vision and straining development resources (Familoni & Babatunde, 2024). To address prioritising feedback is crucial. Agile teams can maintain a clear vision of the product's core functionality by focusing on the most valuable and impactful improvements. Another challenge is user fatigue. Participants bombarded with usability tests can become tired, impacting the quality of their feedback. To mitigate this, Agile UX practitioners should design a testing schedule that minimises participant burden while maximising insights (Kusuma et al., 2024). This could involve shorter, more targeted tests or spreading them out over an extended period. Finally, Agile UX excels at capturing evolving user needs through continuous research. However, rapid iterations based on fleeting trends can result in an unstable product lacking long-term vision. The essential lies in balancing responsiveness to user needs with a

clearly defined product roadmap. This roadmap provides a strategic direction for development while allowing flexibility to adapt to genuine user needs and avoid chasing every fad. By acknowledging these challenges and implementing appropriate strategies, Agile UX teams can ensure their development process remains focused, efficient, and user-centred in the long run (Bayesteh, 2024).

6. **Scalability of Agile UX Methods for Large, Complex Projects:** While Agile UX boasts the benefit of continuous user feedback, it is not without its challenges. One potential pitfall is feature creep and scope creep. The constant influx of user feedback can lead to an ever-expanding list of features, potentially deviating from the core product vision and straining development resources (Bayesteh, 2024). To address this, prioritising feedback is crucial. Agile teams can maintain a clear vision of the product's core functionality by focusing on the most valuable and impactful improvements. Another challenge is user fatigue. Participants bombarded with usability tests can become tired, impacting the quality of their feedback. To mitigate this, Agile UX practitioners should design a testing schedule that minimises participant burden while maximising insights. This could involve shorter, more targeted tests or spreading them out over a more extended period (Lind & Mishchenko, 2024). Finally, Agile UX excels at capturing evolving user needs through continuous research. However, rapid iterations based on fleeting trends can result in an unstable product lacking long-term vision. The essential lies in balancing responsiveness to user needs with a clearly defined product roadmap. This roadmap provides a strategic direction for development while allowing flexibility to adapt to genuine user needs and avoid chasing every fad. By acknowledging these challenges and implementing appropriate strategies, Agile UX teams can ensure their development process remains focused, efficient, and user-centred in the long run (Thota & Jung, 2024).
7. **Optimising Resource Allocation and Maintaining Efficiency:** Large projects with diverse user groups can benefit from strategically allocating resources for user research. Focusing core testing efforts on the user groups most impacted by the product ensures it caters to its most crucial audience (Gideon et al., 2024). Agile UX practitioners can supplement this with surveys or remote testing methods to gather broader user insights without overwhelming participants or development teams. Furthermore, breaking the project into minor phases with targeted usability testing for each phase fosters a more efficient and iterative approach (Isomursu et al., 2012). This phased development allows for focused feedback on specific features and ensures resources are allocated effectively. Finally, standardising testing procedures and documenting best practices promotes team consistency and facilitates knowledge transfer for future projects (Meingast, 2016). This streamlines the user research process and empowers future teams

to leverage the knowledge gained from previous iterations. By acknowledging these challenges and implementing these strategies for optimal resource allocation and maintaining efficiency, Agile UX teams can ensure their development process remains focused, user-centred, and efficient in the long run (Pillay & Wing, 2019). Agile UX practices offer a powerful approach to user-centered design. By acknowledging these ethical considerations and potential biases, Agile UX practitioners can take proactive steps to address them. This allows them to leverage the power of Agile UX for a more ethical and user-centred approach to bridging the gap between user needs and product offerings. This, in turn, leads to the development of more inclusive and prosperous products.

8. **Obstacles in Agile UX Adoption:** While Agile UX offers a powerful approach to user-centred design, navigating resource limitations and overcoming the learning curve associated with new techniques can be significant hurdles (Alqudah et al., 2023). Budget constraints can pose a challenge, as even lightweight user research activities like surveys and testing require dedicated resources. This can be particularly impactful for smaller teams or those new to Agile UX who may struggle to allocate sufficient budget within their development cycles. Team composition can also be a factor (Hed Zetterström & Johansson, 2024). Traditional Agile teams typically consist of developers, designers, and product managers, and integrating dedicated user researchers can be an additional cost, especially for smaller organisations. Alternative solutions exist, such as training existing team members in essential user research skills or collaborating with external research agencies. Beyond resource allocation, overcoming the learning curve associated with Agile UX presents its challenges (Sa, 2024). Transitioning from traditional, waterfall-style development to the iterative nature of Agile UX requires a mindset shift for both teams and stakeholders.

Adapting to the rapid feedback loop and prioritising user research within short sprints can be a significant learning curve. Furthermore, some team members may lack the technical skills for specific Agile UX techniques, such as user journey mapping or card sorting. This skills gap can be bridged through training opportunities or by partnering with experienced Agile UX practitioners (Shu et al., 2021a).

By acknowledging these challenges and implementing appropriate strategies, teams can leverage the power of Agile UX while ensuring a smooth transition and effective user research practices. Streamlining user research can be achieved by conducting brief surveys and remote usability testing to gather valuable user feedback while adhering to budget constraints (Shu et al., 2021b).

This approach enabled efficient iteration of core workout features. Cross-functional collaboration was addressed by creating "embedded researcher" roles. These researchers, integrated within development teams, facilitated user research activities within sprints, ensuring that user feedback remained a constant priority. Investing in training empowered internal teams to adopt new techniques and conduct user research effectively within their development cycles. By strategically allocating resources, fostering collaboration, and investing in training, teams can successfully implement Agile UX practices, leading to a more user-centered design process.

CASE STUDY

The chapter explores the benefits and challenges of Agile UX through the lens of two distinct cases: FitLife, a multi-platform fitness app, and a social media platform. This comparative approach serves several purposes:

1. **Demonstrating Versatility:** The chapter emphasises its versatility by showcasing Agile UX in action across different types of applications (mobile app vs. social media platform). Agile UX is not a one-size-fits-all solution; it can be adapted to various project types and functionalities.
2. **Highlighting Unique Challenges:** Each case study highlights unique challenges associated with implementing Agile UX. FitLife exemplifies the hurdle of balancing research with development within a multi-platform environment. The social media platform case highlights the challenges of addressing algorithmic bias and keeping pace with rapidly evolving user needs. This comparative approach provides a more comprehensive understanding of the strengths and limitations of Agile UX.
3. **Real-World Applicability:** The chapter does not just discuss theory; it showcases practical applications. By presenting two real-world scenarios (fitness app and social media platform), the chapter offers readers a relatable context for understanding how Agile UX can be implemented in their projects. This increases the chapter's value and provides actionable insights for practitioners.

Considering these two cases allows the chapter to paint a more complete picture of Agile UX: its adaptability, the challenges it can address in diverse contexts, and its practical application in real-world scenarios.

Case 1: A Multi-Platform Agile Project (Simulation With Real-World Analogy)

Scenario: Imagine a fictional company, FitLife, a fitness app startup, is developing its core offering: a mobile app for workout routines and tracking, a tablet app for recipe browsing and meal planning, and a web interface for data visualisation and progress monitoring. They have chosen an Agile development methodology (e.g., Scrum) to ensure rapid iteration, user feedback integration, and adaptability.

Challenges and Agile Integration of User Research:

FitLife faces the challenge of ensuring a seamless and positive user experience (UX) across these diverse platforms within the constraints of Agile sprints (typically 1-2 weeks). Here is how they can integrate user research effectively:

1. **User Interviews (Sprint 1):** FitLife conducts short, focused interviews with potential users (gym enthusiasts, home fitness enthusiasts) to understand their preferred workout styles, dietary needs, and desired functionalities. This translates to user stories in the backlog, like "As a user, I want to be able to filter workout routines by muscle group and difficulty level on mobile" or "As a user, I want to see a breakdown of macronutrients for each recipe on the tablet app."
2. **Card Sorting (Sprint 2):** FitLife facilitates card sorting sessions with users to categorise workout types, recipe categories, and progress metrics. This informs the information architecture across platforms. Imagine users sorting cards labelled "cardio," "strength training," "yoga," and "HIIT" to determine how these categories should be presented within the mobile app.
3. **Lightweight Usability Testing (Each sprint):** During each sprint, FitLife conducts usability testing with a small group of users (5-8) on prototypes of specific features. For example, they might test the checkout process for purchasing premium workout plans on the mobile app or the recipe search functionality on the tablet app. This allows for early identification of usability issues like unclear buttons or confusing layouts before they impact a wider audience.
4. **Data-Driven Decisions (Continuous):** FitLife utilises heatmaps and session recordings to analyse user behaviour across platforms. Heatmaps might reveal areas of the web interface where users struggle to find specific data visualisations, prompting design adjustments.

Metrics Justification:

1. **Reduced Development Costs:** Early identification of usability issues through techniques like card sorting and lightweight testing prevents costly rework later in the development process. Imagine catching an issue with the mobile app's workout timer during a usability test, saving the team from fixing it after the entire app is coded.
2. **Improved User Satisfaction:** User-centered design, informed by continuous user feedback, leads to a more intuitive and enjoyable platform experience. Imagine FitLife users raving about how easy it is to find suitable recipes on the

tablet app and track their progress on the web interface. This leads to increased user retention and positive word-of-mouth marketing.

3. **Enhanced Data-Driven Decisions:** User research data (e.g., interview insights, usability testing findings) informs development priorities and design decisions. Learning that many users prefer pre-built meal plans might lead FitLife to prioritise this feature within the app development roadmap.

Practical approach: This case study explores integrating user research into the Agile development of "FitLife," a multi-platform fitness app targeting mobile (iOS and Android) and web users.

Challenge: Balancing traditional user research methods (surveys, in-depth interviews) with Agile's rapid development cycles (2-week sprints).

Traditional Approach (Estimated Time):

1. User Interviews (10 participants): 20 hours (2 hours/interview)
2. User Surveys (100 participants): 10 hours (survey design, distribution, analysis)
3. Usability Testing (5 participants/platform): 20 hours (test scenario creation, participant recruitment, testing sessions)
4. Total Estimated Time: 50 hours

This traditional approach consumes valuable time within a 2-week sprint.

Agile Approach (Actual Time):

1. User Interviews (5 participants): 10 hours (focusing on core user groups)
2. User Surveys (50 participants): 5 hours (using online surveys with targeted questions)
3. Guerilla Usability Testing (10 participants/platform): 4 hours (short, informal testing sessions)
4. Total Actual Time: 19 hours

Table 1. Summary of outcomes

Activity	Traditional approach (estimated time)	Agile approach (actual time)	Time saved
User interviews	20 hours (2 hours/interview - 10 participants)	10 hours (focusing on core user groups - 5 participants)	50%
User surveys	10 hours (survey design, distribution, analysis - 100 participants)	5 hours (using online surveys with targeted questions - 50 participants)	50%
Usability testing	20 hours (test scenario creation, participant recruitment, testing sessions - 5 participants/ platform)	4 hours (short, informal testing sessions - 10 participants/platform)	80%
Total time	50 hours	19 hours	62%

Results:

1. The Agile approach reduced user research time by 62% compared to the traditional approach.
2. User feedback from interviews identified a key pain point: difficulty setting personalised workout goals.
3. Survey data revealed a strong preference for mobile app usage over the web platform.
4. Guerilla testing exposed usability issues with the exercise logging feature on both mobile and web versions.

Impact on Development:

1. Based on user feedback, the development team prioritised mobile app development and focused initial features on personalised goal setting.
2. Usability testing findings led to immediate design iterations to improve the exercise logging experience on both platforms.

Key Learnings:

1. Lightweight user research techniques can be effectively integrated into Agile sprints.
2. Prioritising user research activities based on impact ensures efficient use of time.
3. Early user feedback allows for course correction and improves the final product.

Conclusion: Scenario-Based Learnings and Advantages/Disadvantages

Table 2. Scenario-based learnings and advantages/disadvantages

Scenario	Learnings	Advantages	Disadvantages
User Interviews (Sprint 1)	Uncover core user needs and pain points.	Informs user story creation and prioritisation.	Requires dedicated time and resources for recruitment and facilitation.
Card Sorting (Sprint 2)	Understand user mental models for information organisation.	Guides the design of intuitive and user-friendly interfaces across platforms.	It may require multiple iterations based on user feedback.
Lightweight Usability Testing (Each Sprint)	Identify usability issues early and efficiently.	Prevents major roadblocks and rework later in development.	Requires careful planning and recruitment of suitable test participants within short timeframes.
Data-Driven Decisions (Continuous)	Gain valuable insights into user behaviour across platforms.	Enables data-driven design improvements and feature prioritisation.	Relies on effective data collection and analysis tools.

By strategically integrating these user research and evaluation techniques within Agile sprints, FitLife can ensure a user-centric approach to its multi-platform app development. This approach fosters a positive user experience across mobile, tablet, and web interfaces, ultimately leading to a more successful product launch and a loyal user base.

Case 2: Social Media Platform Navigates Shifting User Needs and Bias Mitigation in Agile UX

Challenge: A social media platform faces two main hurdles:

1. **Shifting user Needs:** The social media landscape is a battleground of constant change. User preferences and expectations are like a living organism in perpetual flux. What captivated audiences yesterday can become yesterday's news today. This rapid evolution presents a significant challenge for social media platforms. Maintaining engagement requires continuous adaptation of features and content offerings. Falling behind user trends can lead to a mass exodus, with users migrating to platforms that cater to their ever-changing preferences. The difficulty lies in predicting the unpredictable. Traditional market research methods, while valuable, are often slow and struggle to capture the nuances of user behaviour that shift like sand through an hourglass. This creates a constant struggle for social media platforms: keeping pace with a user base that seems to change its mind faster than the weather.

2. **Algorithmic Bias:** The tools that personalise our social media experience, such as recommendation algorithms, can also introduce a hidden threat: algorithmic bias. While powerful in curating content feeds and suggesting connections, these algorithms are trained on massive user behaviour and content datasets. If these datasets harbour inherent biases, the algorithms can become biased, perpetuating those biases within the platform. This can manifest as "echo chambers," where users are primarily exposed to content that reinforces their existing views. Limited exposure to diverse viewpoints can stifle healthy discourse and fuel polarisation, ultimately creating a less inclusive social media experience.

Solution: Agile UX Approach

The platform implemented Agile UX practices with a focus on continuous user research and bias mitigation strategies:

1. **Diverse User Groups and Feedback Panels:** Ongoing user research involved diverse groups with a minimum of X participants per sprint (e.g., X=25). These groups represented different demographics and interests to ensure a well-rounded perspective.
    a. **Practical Steps:** Participants were recruited through various channels to ensure a well-rounded perspective in the user research. Online platforms, social media outreach, and existing user panels were leveraged to find diverse individuals. This diversity encompassed age groups, genders, locations, and interests. Short surveys or screening questions were administered to understand the participants' demographics and social media usage habits. This preliminary information provided valuable context for interpreting the user research findings.
2. **Agile User Research Integration:** User research sprints were integrated into the development cycle, occurring every Y development iteration (e.g., Y=2). Usability testing was conducted after each sprint for rapid adjustments based on user feedback.
    a. **Practical Steps:** To ensure user feedback remained relevant to the development cycle, the Agile UX process incorporated user research activities like interviews, surveys, and usability testing directly within each development sprint. These activities were guided by clearly defined research questions tailored to the current development goals. For instance, if the focus were on testing a new feature, the research questions would delve into user understanding, ease of use, and overall satisfaction. The data was swiftly analysed after each user research activity to extract critical insights and identify potential usability issues. This rapid analysis ensured that findings

could be promptly incorporated into the development process, leading to a more user-centred final product.

3. **Explainable AI (XAI) Techniques:** The platform employed XAI techniques to understand how their recommendation algorithms arrived at content suggestions. This transparency helped identify and address potential biases.
   a. **Practical Steps:** In the fight against algorithmic bias, the platform leveraged Explainable AI (XAI) tools. These tools functioned like a window into the algorithm's decision-making process, allowing the team to visualise how it arrived at content recommendations. By analysing the data generated by XAI tools, the team could identify patterns that might indicate a bias towards specific content categories or creators. This newfound awareness empowered them to fine-tune the algorithm, promoting a more diverse range of content suggestions and ensuring a more inclusive user experience.

Metrics and Outcomes:

1. Increased User Engagement: By staying attuned to user needs, the platform saw a Z% increase in user engagement metrics (e.g., Z=15% increase in daily active users).
2. Reduced Algorithmic Bias: Utilising XAI techniques led to a W% increase in the diversity of content categories users interacted with (e.g., W=20% increase in engagement with under-represented content categories).

Challenges and Considerations:

1. **Balancing Speed with Research:** Agile development thrives on rapid iteration within short sprints, but traditional user research methods can be slow and disrupt this fast pace. Agile UX bridges this gap by advocating for lightweight techniques that fit neatly within a sprint's timeframe. Short surveys and screeners replace lengthy questionnaires, allowing researchers to quickly gather essential user data (demographics, social media habits) from a wider pool of participants. These surveys can be administered online or through social media platforms for added efficiency. Additionally, Agile UX embraces remote testing tools. Unlike traditional methods that recruit participants to a physical location, remote testing allows users to participate from anywhere, providing valuable usability feedback without geographical limitations. This approach significantly reduces the time and resources needed for user testing, ensuring user research stays in sync with the rapid development cycle.

2. **Metrics Justification:** Measuring bias mitigation within social media platforms presents a unique challenge. Traditional user engagement metrics, like time spent on the platform or daily active users, are essential for gauging overall user satisfaction. However, they do not directly show progress in reducing bias. Agile UX proposes a solution: a combined metrics approach. This approach uses both traditional user engagement metrics and content diversity metrics. Engagement metrics are crucial for understanding overall user satisfaction, with increased time spent and daily active users indicating the platform is engaging its audience. However, content diversity metrics provide a more nuanced picture. By tracking how users interact with different content categories, platforms can see if efforts to mitigate bias work. For instance, increased engagement with under-represented content categories suggests the platform successfully promotes a broader range of content, leading to a more inclusive user experience. By monitoring both sets of metrics, social media platforms gain a more comprehensive understanding of their bias mitigation efforts' impact on user experience and inclusivity.

Overall, Agile UX empowers social media platforms to overcome the hurdle of balancing rapid development with ongoing user research. This is achieved by strategically integrating lightweight techniques like short surveys and remote testing. These methods seamlessly fit within short development sprints, allowing continuous user feedback. Furthermore, Agile UX tackles algorithmic bias through a combined metrics approach.

This approach goes beyond traditional user engagement metrics (time spent, daily active users) and incorporates content diversity metrics. By tracking how users interact with different content categories, platforms can identify and address potential bias, promoting a more comprehensive range of content. This case study exemplifies how Agile UX, emphasising continuous user research and XAI techniques, empowers social media platforms to navigate evolving user needs while mitigating bias. The result? A more engaging, inclusive, and ultimately responsible social media experience for a diverse audience.

BENEFITS AND CHALLENGES

User experience (UX) design is constantly in flux, particularly with the rise of applications that function seamlessly across multiple platforms. Companies like FitLife, a fitness app startup developing mobile, tablet, and web interfaces, face the challenge of delivering a consistent and positive user experience across these diverse platforms. Agile UX methodologies offer a solution, providing a structured yet adaptable framework for user-centered design. One of the critical strengths of

Agile UX in multi-platform projects is its ability to reduce development costs. Traditional user research methods, while valuable, can be time-consuming and expensive. Agile UX utilises more efficient techniques like card sorting and guerilla testing.

Card sorting helps understand how users naturally categorise information, informing the design of intuitive interfaces across all platforms. With its short and informal sessions, Guerilla testing allows for early identification of usability issues like unclear buttons or confusing layouts before they impact a wider audience. This early detection prevents costly rework later in the development process.

Furthermore, Agile UX fosters improved user satisfaction by ensuring a focus on user needs throughout the development cycle. Techniques like user interviews conducted in the early stages uncover core user needs and pain points. This information translates directly into user stories, the building blocks of Agile development. For example, user interviews might reveal difficulty setting personalised workout goals within the FitLife app.

Based on this feedback, the development team can prioritise features that address personalised goal setting, leading to a more intuitive and enjoyable user experience. Beyond cost reduction and user satisfaction, Agile UX promotes data-driven decision-making. Agile methodologies rely heavily on user research data, such as interview insights and usability testing findings. This data informs development priorities and design decisions. For instance, FitLife might conduct surveys to gauge user preferences for mobile app usage over the web platform. This data can then be used to prioritise mobile app development with an initial focus on features most relevant to mobile users. This data-driven approach ensures that features cater directly to user needs and preferences.

However, implementing Agile UX in multi-platform projects also presents challenges. One hurdle is balancing research with development. Agile development emphasises rapid iteration within short sprints (typically 1-2 weeks). Traditional user research methods can be time-consuming, potentially conflicting with the fast pace of Agile development. Agile UX addresses this by adopting lightweight techniques that can be integrated effectively within short sprints. For instance, FitLife might conduct shorter user interviews with a smaller group of core user groups instead of extensive surveys with a broader audience.

This approach ensures valuable user feedback is gathered without compromising the development timeline. Another challenge lies in prioritising research activities. With limited time within each sprint, choosing the most impactful user research methods is crucial. Here, the project goals and user needs come into play. For FitLife, understanding how users categorise workout types might be more valuable than in-depth personality assessments. Focusing on the most relevant research activities maximises the impact of user research within Agile UX.

Finally, recruiting suitable participants for usability testing within short timeframes can be challenging. This might be especially true for niche user groups or geographically dispersed audiences. Agile UX teams need to be resourceful in finding the right participants, potentially leveraging online platforms or remote testing tools to overcome these recruitment hurdles.

Social media platforms, constantly battling to keep users engaged, face unique UX challenges. One key challenge is the constant evolution of user needs. User preferences and expectations evolve rapidly, making it difficult for platforms to stay relevant. Agile UX provides a solution by emphasising continuous user research. Platforms can conduct user research sprints, regularly gathering feedback on new features and content types. This continuous feedback loop allows the platform to adapt and evolve alongside its user base. Another significant challenge for social media platforms is algorithmic bias. Despite their power in personalising user experience, recommendation algorithms can inadvertently perpetuate biases present in the data they are trained on.

This can lead to a less inclusive user experience, with users exposed only to content that reinforces their existing views. Agile UX tackles this challenge using Explainable AI (XAI) techniques. These techniques help platforms understand how recommendation algorithms arrive at content suggestions, allowing them to identify and address potential biases within the algorithms. For instance, a social media platform might use XAI to discover that its algorithm favours content from a specific set of creators based on historical data patterns. By understanding this bias, the platform can take steps to ensure a broader range of content is presented to users.

Similar to multi-platform projects, the success of Agile UX in social media platforms hinges on balancing speed with research. Integrating user research within short development cycles requires careful planning and prioritisation. Platforms must choose the most impactful research activities and ensure they can be conducted efficiently within the constraints of the Agile development cycle.

CONCLUSION

Agile development excels at iterative software creation, but its success hinges on understanding the target user's experience. Integrating user research and evaluation throughout the Agile workflow is critical. This approach offers substantial benefits: reduced development costs through early detection of usability issues, improved user satisfaction with a more intuitive product, and data-driven decisions based on user research. While challenges exist (time constraints, resource allocation, adapting techniques), strategies like prioritisation, lightweight techniques, cross-functional teams, and remote testing can help.

Agile teams that establish a continuous feedback loop by effectively integrating user research ensure the product evolves alongside user needs across all platforms. This fosters a successful product launch and lays the groundwork for long-term user engagement and adoption. Looking to the future, Agile UX holds immense promise for emerging technologies like virtual reality (VR) and augmented reality (AR). The immersive nature of these technologies necessitates a deep understanding of user behaviour and interaction patterns within these novel environments. Agile UX, emphasising iterative design and user feedback, is well-positioned to guide the development of user-centred VR and AR experiences.

Furthermore, as artificial intelligence (AI) plays an increasingly prominent role in software development, Agile UX can serve as a critical bridge between AI capabilities and human-centred design. By integrating user research into AI development processes, Agile UX can ensure that AI-powered features align with user needs and expectations, promoting responsible and ethical AI implementation. In conclusion, Agile UX is not just a methodology for the present; it holds the key to unlocking a future where user experience remains paramount in the face of ever-evolving technologies. By embracing continuous user research and feedback loops, Agile UX empowers teams to create successful, user-centric products that will thrive in the future.

REFERENCES

Akinrinola, N. O., Okoye, C., Ofodile, N. O. C., & Ugochukwu, E. (2024). Navigating and reviewing ethical dilemmas in AI development: Strategies for transparency, fairness, and accountability. *GSC Advanced Research and Reviews*, 18(3), 50–58. DOI: 10.30574/gscarr.2024.18.3.0088

Alhammad, M. M., & Moreno, A. M. (2022). *Integrating user experience into Agile | Proceedings of the ACM/IEEE 44th International Conference on Software Engineering: Software Engineering Education and Training*. https://dl.acm.org/doi/abs/10.1145/3510456.3514156

Alqudah, M. K., Razali, R., Alqudah, M. K., Dalaien, A., Alabool, H. M., & Alkhazaleh, H. A. (2023). A grounded theory of selecting lean and agile practices for software development. *Journal of Software (Malden, MA)*, 36(4), e2539. Advance online publication. DOI: 10.1002/smr.2539

Amoako-Gyampah, K. (2007). Perceived usefulness, user involvement and behavioral intention: An empirical study of ERP implementation. *Computers in Human Behavior*, 23(3), 1232–1248. DOI: 10.1016/j.chb.2004.12.002

Azevedo, D., Ramelot, J., Legay, A., & Kieffer, S. (2024). With or Without U(sers): A Journey to Integrate UX Activities in Cybersecurity. *Lecture Notes in Computer Science*, 14728, 212–231. DOI: 10.1007/978-3-031-61379-1_14

Barros, L., Tam, C., & Varajão, J. (2024). Agile software development projects – unveiling the human-related critical success factors. *Information and Software Technology*, 107432, 107432. Advance online publication. DOI: 10.1016/j.infsof.2024.107432

Bayesteh, A. (2024). Agile-Based Optimized Planning and Scheduling Methodology for Multiple Scattered Projects. *ERA*. https://doi.org/doi:10.7939/r3-sywn-m748

Beattie, A., Lacey, C., & Caudwell, C. (2019). "It's like the Wild West": User Experience (UX) Designers on Ethics and Privacy in Aotearoa New Zealand. *Design and Culture*. Advance online publication. 10.1080V17547075.2023.2211391

Chen, Y., Wang, X., Yang, J., Wu, Z., Chen, Y., & Peng, Y. (2024). *A Multi-Platform Compatible Remote Control based on Gesture Recognition Algorithm*. DOI: 10.1109/EEBDA60612.2024.10485976

Cheung, R., & Vogel, D. (2013). Predicting user acceptance of collaborative technologies: An extension of the technology acceptance model for e-learning. *Computers and Education/Computers & Education, 63*, 160–175. DOI: 10.1016/j.compedu.2012.12.003

Collado, J. A., Mora, P. S., & Parham, E. (2024). A guerrilla usability lab with free software | Interactions. In *Interactions*. https://dl.acm.org/doi/abs/10.1145/2451856.2451871

Cornide-Reyes, H., Duran, C., Baltierra, S., Silva-Aravena, F., & Morales, J. (2024a). Improving UX in Digital Transformation Projects Through Lean Principles. *Lecture Notes in Computer Science*, 14703, 161–178. DOI: 10.1007/978-3-031-61281-7_11

Cornide-Reyes, H., Duran, C., Baltierra, S., Silva-Aravena, F., & Morales, J. (2024b). Improving UX in Digital Transformation Projects Through Lean Principles. *Lecture Notes in Computer Science*, 14703, 161–178. DOI: 10.1007/978-3-031-61281-7_11

Diplom-Ingenieur, Yilmaz, C., & Hanbury, A. (2022). *Merging the Gap Between Automated and Human Centered Usability Testing DIPLOMARBEIT zur Erlangung des akademischen Grades Software Engineering & Internet Computing*. https://web.archive.org/web/20221004124754id_/https://repositum.tuwien.at/bitstream/20.500.12708/81158/1/Yilmaz Can OEzguer - 2022 - Merging the Gap Between Automated and Human Centered...pdf

Dobashi, K., Ho, C. P., Fulford, C. P., & Lin, M.-F. G. (2019). *A Heat Map Generation to Visualize Engagement in Classes Using Moodle Learning Logs*. DOI: 10.1109/INCIT.2019.8912068

Engberg, T. (2024). Optimizing Developer Experience: Component Playground Integration in Software Development. In *DIVA*. https://www.diva-portal.org/smash/record.jsf?pid=diva2%3A1864501&dswid=-6087

Familoni, N. B. T., & Babatunde, O. (2024). User experience (UX) design in medical products: theoretical foundations and development best practices. *Engineering Science & Tecnology Journal*, 5(3), 1125–1148. DOI: 10.51594/estj.v5i3.975

Fleury, S., & Chaniaud, N. (2024). Multi-user centered design: Acceptance, user experience, user research and user testing. *Theoretical Issues in Ergonomics Science*, 25(2), 209–224. Advance online publication. DOI: 10.1080/1463922X.2023.2166623

Gideon, N., Adewunmi, N. A., Jacks, S., & Ajala, A. (2024). Conceptualizing communication efficiency in energy sector project management: The role of digital tools and agile practices. *Engineering Science & Tecnology Journal*, 5(4), 1487–1501. DOI: 10.51594/estj.v5i4.1078

Guerrero-Ulloa, G., Rodríguez-Domínguez, C., & Hornos, M. J. (2023). Agile Methodologies Applied to the Development of Internet of Things (IoT)-Based Systems: A Review. *Sensors (Basel)*, 23(2), 790. DOI: 10.3390/s23020790 PMID: 36679594

Harte, R., Glynn, L., Rodríguez-Molinero, A., Baker, P. M. A., Scharf, T., Quinlan, L. R., & ÓLaighin, G. (2017). A Human-Centered Design Methodology to Enhance the Usability, Human Factors, and User Experience of Connected Health Systems: A Three-Phase Methodology. *JMIR Human Factors*, 4(1), e8–e8. DOI: 10.2196/humanfactors.5443 PMID: 28302594

Hed Zetterström, M., & Johansson, I. (2024). *Operationalizing UX Practices : Embedding Accessibility into Agile B2B Software Development*. https://www.diva-portal.org/smash/record.jsf?pid=diva2%3A1875940&dswid=7869

Herendy, C. (2020). Using Traditional Research Methods in Contemporary UX Surveying. *Lecture Notes in Computer Science*, 12423, 123–132. DOI: 10.1007/978-3-030-60114-0_8

Hinderks, A., José, F., Escalona, M. J., & Thomaschewski, J. (2024). Requirements for User Experience Management - A Tertiary Study. *Unir.Net*. https://doi.org/DOI: 1989-1660

Hsi, S., Ma, J., Allen, A., Sikes, K., & Alexander, M. (2007). From "Guerrilla" Methods to Structured Evaluations: Examples of Formative Web Design from the Exploratorium's Evidence and Mind Projects. In *Museums & Web*. https://citeseerx.ist.psu.edu/document?repid=rep1&type=pdf&doi=ad8e5a9e1d047952f820633e558b2aee5cbad6a8

Huynh, K., Benarivo, J., Da Xuan, C., Sharma, G. G., Kang, J., Madugalla, A., & Grundy, J. (2021). *Improving Human-Centric Software Defect Evaluation*. Reporting, and Fixing. DOI: 10.1109/COMPSAC51774.2021.00064

Isomursu, M., Sirotkin, A., Voltti, P., & Halonen, M. (2012). *User Experience Design Goes Agile in Lean Transformation -- A Case Study*. DOI: 10.1109/Agile.2012.10

Jeong, D. H., Jeong, B. K., & Ji, S. Y. (2024). *Understanding Semantic User Interactions in Visualization*. DOI: 10.20944/preprints202404.2019.v1

Kobialka, P., Tarifa, S. L. T., Bergersen, G. R., & Johnsen, E. B. (2024). User journey games: Automating user-centric analysis. *Software & Systems Modeling*, 23(3), 605–624. Advance online publication. DOI: 10.1007/s10270-024-01148-2

Konidena, B. K., Malaiyappan, J. N. A., & Tadimarri, A. (2024). Ethical Considerations in the Development and Deployment of AI Systems. *European Journal of Technology*, 8(2), 41–53. DOI: 10.47672/ejt.1890

Koponen, T. (2018). Weighing Ultralight, User interface evaluation of a mobile photo editing application. In *Aalto.fi*. https://aaltodoc.aalto.fi/items/00842ee0-1a76-4081-bd1e-e541f9dd8c2e

Kusuma, W. A., Jantan, A. H., Admodisastro, N. I., & Norowi, N. (2024). Elevated Novice Developer Productivity and Self-efficacy by Promoting UX Journey in Software Requirement Elicitation. *JOIV : International Journal on Informatics Visualization*, 8(1), 401. Advance online publication. DOI: 10.62527/joiv.8.1.2171

Lei, H., Lai, W., Feaster, W., & Chang, A. C. (2024). Artificial intelligence and agile project management. *Elsevier EBooks*, 401–405, 401–405. Advance online publication. DOI: 10.1016/B978-0-323-90534-3.00016-0

Leong, V., Raheel, K., Sim, J. Y., Kacker, K., Karlaftis, V. M., Vassiliu, C., Kalaivanan, K., Chen, A., Robbins, T. W., Sahakian, B. J., & Kourtzi, Z. (2022). A New Remote Guided Method for Supervised Web-Based Cognitive Testing to Ensure High-Quality Data: Development and Usability Study. *JMIR. Journal of Medical Internet Research. Journal of Medical Internet Research*, 24(1), e28368–e28368. DOI: 10.2196/28368 PMID: 34989691

Lind, G., & Mishchenko, M. (2024). Not So Agile. *Apress EBooks*, 155–172. DOI: 10.1007/979-8-8688-0187-7_10

Magistretti, S., & Trabucchi, D. (2024). Agile-as-a-tool and agile-as-a-culture: A comprehensive review of agile approaches adopting contingency and configuration theories. *Review of Managerial Science*. Advance online publication. DOI: 10.1007/s11846-024-00745-1

Mannay, D., & Pauwels, L. (2024). The SAGE Handbook of Visual Research Methods. https://www.torrossa.com/en/resources/an/5018807#page=334

Martinelli, S., Lopes, L., & Zaina, L. (2024). UX Research practices related to Long-Term UX: A Systematic Literature Review. *Information and Software Technology*, 107431, 107431. Advance online publication. DOI: 10.1016/j.infsof.2024.107431

Meckenstock, J.-N. (2024). Shedding Light on the Dark Side – A Systematic Literature Review of the Issues in Agile Software Development Methodology Use. *Journal of Systems and Software/˜The œJournal of Systems and Software, 211*, 111966. DOI: 10.1016/j.jss.2024.111966

Meingast, M. (2016). *Agile and UX: The Road to Integration The Challenges of the UX Practitioner in an Agile Environment - Melissa Meingast, Timothy Ballew, Rochelle Edwards, Eric Nordquist, Christopher Sader, Danielle Smith, 2013*. https://journals.sagepub.com/doi/abs/10.1177/1541931213571224

Natarajan, T., & Pichai, S. (2024). Behaviour-Driven Development and Metrics Framework for Enhanced Agile Practices in Scrum Teams. *Information and Software Technology*, 170, 107435. DOI: 10.1016/j.infsof.2024.107435

Neumann, O., Kirklies, P.-C., & Schott, C. (2023). Adopting agile in government: A comparative case study. *Public Management Review*. Advance online publication. 10.1080V14719037.2024.2354776

Nurmuradov, D., & Bryce, R. (2017). Caret-HM: recording and replaying Android user sessions with heat map generation using UI state clustering. Proceedings of the 26th ACM SIGSOFT International Symposium on Software Testing and Analysis. https://dl.acm.org/doi/abs/10.1145/3092703.3098231

Oladapo, N., Ejiga, H., Okeke, D., & Akinoso, E. (2024). Conceptualizing agile development in digital transformations: Theoretical foundations and practical applications. *Engineering Science & Tecnology Journal*, 5(4), 1524–1541. DOI: 10.51594/estj.v5i4.1080

Olorunsogo, N. T., Adekunle, N., Okolo, A., & Babawarun, N. O. (2024). Ethical considerations in AI-enhanced medical decision support systems: A review. *World Journal of Advanced Engineering Technology and Sciences*, 11(1), 329–336. DOI: 10.30574/wjaets.2024.11.1.0061

Ormeño, E., & Pinciroli, F. (2024). Systematic Mapping Protocol — UX Design role in software development process. In *arXiv.org*. https://arxiv.org/abs/2402.13143

Osasona, N. F., Amoo, N. O. O., Atadoga, N. A., Abrahams, O., Farayola, N. O. A., & Samson, B. (2024). Reviewing the ethical implications of AI in decision making processes. *International Journal of Management & Entrepreneurship Research*, 6(2), 322–335. DOI: 10.51594/ijmer.v6i2.773

Othman, M. K., & Anuar, N. N. (2024). A Comprehensive User Experience Analysis of Cultural Heritage Progressive Web App Using a Hybrid UEQ-IPA Approach | Journal on Computing and Cultural Heritage. In *ACM Journal on Computing and Cultural Heritage*. https://dl.acm.org/doi/abs/10.1145/3647998

Pillay, N., & Wing, J. (2019). *Agile UX: Integrating good UX development practices in Agile*. DOI: 10.1109/ICTAS.2019.8703607

Porcelli, L., Mastroianni, M., Ficco, M., & Palmieri, F. (2024). A User-Centered Privacy Policy Management System for Automatic Consent on Cookie Banners. *Computers*, 13(2), 43. DOI: 10.3390/computers13020043

Puspitasari, I., Nuzulita, N., & Hsiao, C.-S. (2024). Agile User-Centered Design Framework to Support the Development of E-Health for Patient Education. *Studies in Computational Intelligence*, 131–144. DOI: 10.1007/978-3-031-57037-7_10

Rathnayake, B., & Lanka, S. (2019). *Crowd-sourced user experience evaluation and adaptation for a personalized user interface*. http://dl.lib.uom.lk/bitstream/handle/123/16005/TH4009.pdf?sequence=2

Ritonummi, S., Siitonen, V., Salo, M., & Henri, P. (2022). Exploring barriers that prevent employees from experiencing flow in the software industry | Emerald Insight. *Journal of Workplace Learning*, 36(3), 223–238. DOI: 10.1108/JWL-11-2022-0146

Sa, M. (2024). User-centered data access control techniques for secure and privacy-aware mobile systems. *Figshare*. DOI: 10.25394/PGS.26069632.v1

Salminen, J., Jung, S.-G., & Jansen, B. (2022). Developing Persona Analytics Towards Persona Science. Proceedings of the 27th International Conference on Intelligent User Interfaces. https://dl.acm.org/doi/abs/10.1145/3490099.3511144

Sarkar, C., Soderston, C., Klementiev, D., & Bell, E. (2010). Remote Automated User Testing: First Steps toward a General-Purpose Tool. *Studies in Computational Intelligence*, 37–50. DOI: 10.1007/978-3-642-13273-5_3

Savolainen, O. (2010). User experience design in open source development: Approaches to usability work in the Moodle community. *Tuni.Fi*. https://doi.org/https://trepo.tuni.fi/handle/10024/81866

Sharma, A., & Nayyar, V. (2024). Ethical Marketing and Sustainable Development Goals. *Advances in Marketing, Customer Relationship Management, and e-Services Book Series*, 83–91. DOI: 10.4018/979-8-3693-2215-4.ch007

Shu, W., Cai, K., & Xiong, N. N. (2021a). Research on strong agile response task scheduling optimization enhancement with optimal resource usage in green cloud computing. *Future Generation Computer Systems*, 124, 12–20. DOI: 10.1016/j.future.2021.05.012

Shu, W., Cai, K., & Xiong, N. N. (2021b). Research on strong agile response task scheduling optimization enhancement with optimal resource usage in green cloud computing. *Future Generation Computer Systems*, 124, 12–20. DOI: 10.1016/j.future.2021.05.012

Sommer, J. (2024). Predictive value of card sorting on browsing performance and user satisfaction - University of Twente Student Theses. *Utwente.Nl*. https://doi.org/https://purl.utwente.nl/essays/62420

St. Jean, B. (2014). Devising and implementing a card-sorting technique for a longitudinal investigation of the information behavior of people with type 2 diabetes. *Library & Information Science Research*, 36(1), 16–26. DOI: 10.1016/j.lisr.2013.10.002

Talipu, A. (2021). Research and development of a remote usability testing platform for better user experience. *Univpm.It.* https://doi.org/manual

Tetteh, S. G. (2024). Empirical Study of Agile Software Development Methodologies: A Comparative Analysis - Pustakas. *Pcbmb.Org*. https://doi.org/http://archive.pcbmb.org/id/eprint/1883/1/Tetteh1752024AJRCOS113678.pdf

Thorngate, S., & Hoden, A. (2017). Exploratory Usability Testing of User Interface Options in LibGuides 2. *College & Research Libraries. College & Research Libraries*, 78(6). Advance online publication. DOI: 10.5860/crl.78.6.844

Thota, A. K., & Jung, R. (2024). Accelerating neurotechnology development using an Agile methodology. *Frontiers in Neuroscience*, 18, 1328540. Advance online publication. DOI: 10.3389/fnins.2024.1328540 PMID: 38435056

Tiriticco, R. (2021). Evaluation and implementation of accessible methods to perform remote moderated usability testing on websites. *Theseus.Fi.* https://doi.org/http://www.theseus.fi/handle/10024/503653

Tomlin, W. C. (2018). *UX Optimization*. SpringerLink. DOI: 10.1007/978-1-4842-3867-7

Tullis, T., & Albert, B. (2024). Measuring the User Experience. In *Google Books*. https://books.google.co.in/books?hl=en&lr=&id=bPhLeMBLEkAC&oi=fnd&pg=PP1&dq=User+Personas+%09Usability+Bug+Tracking:++%09Heatmaps+and+Session+Recordings:+&ots=RbKjksUXrM&sig=xqfosMVraUVftu-fABIaHZFPpjY&redir_esc=y#v=onepage&q&f=false

Welin, F. (2024). Integration of User-Centered Design and Continuous Experimentation in Agile processes: A qualitative study. In *Aalto.fi*. https://aaltodoc.aalto.fi/items/d496aebd-17c9-4c7f-837c-221727c355e1

Xu, W. (2024). A "User Experience 3.0 (UX 3.0)" Paradigm Framework: User Experience Design for Human-Centered AI Systems. In *arXiv.org*. https://arxiv.org/abs/2403.01609

ADDITIONAL READING

Albert, B., & Tullis, T. (2013). *Measuring the user experience: collecting, analyzing, and presenting usability metrics*. Newnes.

Brade, J., Lorenz, M., Busch, M., Hammer, N., Tscheligi, M., & Klimant, P. (2017). Being there again–Presence in real and virtual environments and its relation to usability and user experience using a mobile navigation task. *International Journal of Human-Computer Studies*, 101, 76–87. DOI: 10.1016/j.ijhcs.2017.01.004

Chen, Y., Clayton, E. W., Novak, L. L., Anders, S., & Malin, B. (2023). Human-centered design to address biases in artificial intelligence. *Journal of Medical Internet Research*, 25, e43251. DOI: 10.2196/43251 PMID: 36961506

Gualtieri, M. (2009). Best practices in user experience (UX) design. Design compelling user experiences to wow your customers, 1(1), 1-17.

Hartson, R., & Pyla, P. S. (2018). *The UX book: Agile UX design for a quality user experience*. Morgan Kaufmann.

Kalbach, J. (2007). *Designing Web navigation: Optimizing the user experience*. O'Reilly Media, Inc.

Marcus, A. (Ed.). (2016). Design, User Experience, and Usability: Design Thinking and Methods: 5th International Conference, DUXU 2016, Held as Part of HCI International 2016, Toronto, Canada, July 17–22, 2016, Proceedings, Part I (Vol. 9746). Springer.

Mulvenna, M., Boger, J., & Bond, R. (2017, September). Ethical by design: A manifesto. In *Proceedings of the European Conference on Cognitive Ergonomics* (pp. 51-54). DOI: 10.1145/3121283.3121300

Rieger, C., & Majchrzak, T. A. (2019). Towards the definitive evaluation framework for cross-platform app development approaches. *Journal of Systems and Software*, 153, 175–199. DOI: 10.1016/j.jss.2019.04.001

Silva, M. M. F. D. (2022). *Improve human resources management via UX/UI* (Doctoral dissertation).

Unger, R., & Chandler, C. (2023). *A Project Guide to UX Design: For user experience designers in the field or in the making*. New Riders.

KEY TERMS AND DEFINITIONS

Agile: An adaptable approach to projects characterized by short cycles with feedback at every stage (Magistretti & Trabucchi, 2024).

Artificial Intelligence (AI): Machines that have been designed to learn from situations like humans do so that they can apply what they have learned when performing specific tasks such as (Lei et al., 2024).

Augmented Reality (AR): Digital material is overlaid onto the real world via phones or headsets.

Biases: Prejudices we have not yet realized can affect our decisions.

Data-Driven: Making choices based on real evidence instead of guesswork.

Ethical Concerns: Possible ways this may be unfair or wrong (Sharma & Nayyar, 2024).

Explainable AI: AI systems that are both clear and reliable for human beings to trust their decisions upon them.

Guerrilla Usability Testing: Testing a product with random people you find in public places.

Heatmaps: Visual representations showing the parts of the site where people click mostly, most used areas of a website or app in the form of clicks tracking statistics.

Potential Biases: How we could be biased without even knowing it.

Scrum: A popular Agile framework with short identified as sprints and daily meetings between team members.

User Consent: A person's permission to use his or her data for research or testing purposes (Kobialka et al., 2024).

User Experience (UX): Referring to the emotions that an individual experiences when making use of a product like a website or app, it should be simple to use, fun, and meet their requirements (Tullis & Albert, 2024).

User Personas: Fictional characters that represent average users and help designers understand their requirements (Familoni & Babatunde, 2024).

User Testing: Observing real users to determine whether it is easy and interesting (Talipu, 2021).

User-Centered Design: Designing products based on what users need and desire, rather than focusing only on the easy-to-make things is called user-centered design (Xu, 2024).

Virtual Reality (VR): A possibility created by computers that seems true but is viewed through headsets.

Chapter 4
Sustainable Development in Wearable Internet of Medical Things:
Addressing Environmental Impact, Energy Efficiency, and Lifecycle Management

D. Maruthi Kumar
Department of ECE, Srinivasa Ramanujan Institute of Technology, Ananthapuramu, India

Shreenidhi K. S.
https://orcid.org/0000-0002-6844-0454
Department of Biotechnology, Rajalakshmi Engineering College, Chennai, India

Harishchander Anandaram
https://orcid.org/0000-0003-2993-5304
Department of Artificial Intelligence, Amrita Vishwa Vidyapeetham, Coimbatore, India

Gopal Krishna
Department of Computer Science and Engineering, Supaul College of Engineering, Supaul, India

Hari B. S.
Department of Mechanical Engineering, Kongu Engineering College, Perundurai, Erode, India

DOI: 10.4018/979-8-3693-2337-3.ch004

ABSTRACT

The integration of wearable IoMT in healthcare systems throws wide-open the potential for patient care, real-time monitoring, and personalized medicine, but sustainability brings its own set of challenges and opportunities. This chapter discusses the environmental impact, efficiency in energy consumption, and lifecycle management for sustainable development in wearable IoMT. Some of the major challenges are electronic waste, energy consumption, data security, and privacy. Sustainability in wearable IoMT offers opportunities in the adoption of renewable energy, the development of low-power devices, and robust data protection mechanisms. Reduction in the ecological footprint of wearable IoMT devices can be served by considering the importance of sustainable practice in manufacturing, recycling, and biodegradable materials. It seems that innovative solutions can improve sustainability while maintaining quality care for patients.

INTRODUCTION

The wearable technology and Internet of Medical Things (IoMT) have merged lately to bring forth a new era of healthcare with unprecedented possibilities for patient monitoring, the prevention of disease, and personalized medicine. These innovations transform the way healthcare services are delivered and also contribute to significant leaps toward sustainability. This evolution is significant in this time of rising expenditure, lack of resources, and the need to reduce the footprint of healthcare on the environment. The following introduction discusses the key sustainable technologies in wearable IoMT by indicating how they impact healthcare and the environment (Mishra & Singh, 2023). Wearable IoMT is an array of wearable devices with sensors and communication technologies in-built within them and thus endowing their capacity to collect and communicate health information in real-time.

These devices include smartwatches, fitness trackers, and even medical-grade appliances like glucose sensors and ECG sensors. They are supposed to continuously monitor various aspects of health, promote proactive management of health, and at the right time, while the information generated is sent to the healthcare providers or even cloud-based platforms for their analysis to support better diagnosis and treatment plans (Shin & Hwang, 2017). One of the major advances in wearable IoMT is energy-efficient devices.

Manufacturers have increasingly focused on reducing the power consumption of sensors and communication modules. Innovations like energy harvesting technologies-Capturing energy from the wearer's body heat, or movement-and low-power Bluetooth communication are keeping batteries going longer and minimizing frequent recharges. This not only enhances user experience but also minimizes electronic waste, hence environmental sustainability (Zhang et al., 2020). The other important innovation about the use of biodegradable and recyclable material in producing wearable devices.

Traditional electronic components and plastics take hundreds of years to decompose; therefore, an extreme environmental hazard. Scientists and producers are now looking at organic materials and bio-polymers that are naturally break down without causing harm to the environment. This transition toward eco-friendly materials leaves a smaller footprint on the environment, from production to disposal when it comes to wearable devices (Qureshi & Krishnan, 2018). Sustainable Manufacturing Practices: The creation of wearable IoMT devices is transformed by the adoption of sustainable manufacturing practices. Increasingly more companies are adopting an eco-friendly process such as renewable sources of energy, water conservation, and lesser hazardous waste.

Additional innovation in additive manufacturing or 3D printing is aiding a better usage of resources with material to save more waste of products at the production sites. Besides being environmentally sustainable, it is also viable for economic sustenance in that context. Innovations of sustainable health through wearable IoMT are catapulting care delivery in healthcare significantly. Such devices, providing real-time health monitoring, enable early diagnosis of medical conditions, hence reducing the number of hospital visits and admissions. This cuts not only the burden on healthcare facilities but also minimizes the carbon footprint associated with hospital visits (Salam, 2024). The data-driven insights enabled by wearable IoMT devices support the creation of personalized treatment plans with an optimum expectation for better patient outcomes and reduced long-term healthcare costs. Environmental Benefits of Eco-friendly Wearable IoMT Innovations Energy-Efficient and Biodegradable Products: Products that are energy-efficient as well as biodegradable minimize the generation of electronic waste, which is a worry growing in importance across the globe. Sustainable manufacturing reduces carbon footprint from production processes and increases the use of renewable sources (Anitha et al., 2023).

Together all these innovations help in reducing the overall negative impact of the health sector towards the desired global goals on sustainability (Haghi et al., 2017). However, the uptake of sustainable wearable IoMT would still be linked to various factors that pose challenges, such as the cost of sustainable materials and emerging technologies, regulatory challenges, and the need for secure data and privacy. It is therefore hoped that continued research and development and policies to foster an environment that helps to facilitate collaboration and understanding within the industry will help solve such issues. Future may include artificial intelligence and machine learning utilization in health analytics equally as well as the advancement and proliferation of wearables IoMT devices for sustainability (Kakhi et al., 2022a).

Wearable IoMT innovations that are sustainable can revolutionize healthcare to provide continuous health monitoring, allow for early interventions, and support personalized medicine. They also have enormous environmental impacts because of energy-efficient design, usage of bio-degradable materials, or use of sustainable manufacturing techniques. Even though there are still many difficulties to be overcome, the future of wearable IoMT evolution looks promising for well-being in people and the planet, simultaneously-so when that future is more effective, accessible, and sustainable(Subha et al., 2023).

Background: The Internet of Medical Things was the gateway to a great milestone in integrating digital technology into healthcare. IoMT stands for the network of medical devices and applications that connect to healthcare IT systems using online computer networks. Wearable IoMT devices are gadgets, such as smartwatches, fitness trackers, and even medical monitoring devices, among many others. These devices collect, transmit, and analyze real-time health-related data of much value for insight into a person's health status and facilitate proactive management of medical conditions. The rapid growth in wearable IoMT is enabled by advances in sensor technology, wireless communication, and data analytics as well as growing attention in personalized medicine and prevention healthcare. Importance of Wearable IoMT in Healthcare Wearable IoMT devices enable the distant monitoring of patients for continuous care delivery. These devices seem to hold great promise for the effective management of chronic diseases such as diabetes, cardiovascular diseases, and diseases associated with the respiratory system. Continuous monitoring can result in timely interventions in these chronic diseases, thereby improving their management. These wearable IoMT devices empower patients to have an overview of their health and lead them into active lifestyles plus better adherence to a treatment plan. Second, these devices allow for the harvesting of vast amounts of health data that can be analyzed in order to identify trends, predict health events, and enhance clinical outcomes (Al-Turjman et al., 2020).

Wearable IoMT has significance that extends beyond individual patient care into the healthcare system at large. The importance of such devices to healthcare providers provides them with means to monitor patients from afar and thereby reduces the frequency of hospital visits and unloads the burden on healthcare facilities. For the researcher, this data generated by wearable IoMT devices serves as a treasure trove for advancing medical research, developing new treatments, and helping to understand various health conditions. Further, public health services depend on wearable IoMT to monitor population health trends and support initiatives aimed at enhancing community health outcomes.

Scope and Objectives

The focus of this chapter is sustainability aspects related to wearable IoMT devices. On the one hand, these wearable IoMT devices offer a host of benefits; on the other hand, widespread acceptance creates significant challenges related to sustainability. Production, usage, and finally disposal of wearable IoMTs have implications for the environment. Issues necessitate resolution toward sustainable technologies. Some of the major concerns relate to the energy consumption of these products, the electronic wastes they produce, and the ecology and environment within which materials enter into their construction.

One of the most important objectives relating to sustainability in wearable IoMT is to identify and analyze the same in the book. This will include researching the environmental impacts of producing and discarding such devices, understanding energy efficiency in wearable IoMT technologies, and addressing data security and privacy issues that affect system sustainability. Another key aim is to reveal opportunities to enable sustainability in wearable IoMT. These covers looking at technology innovation, such as renewable energy sources and biodegradable materials, as well as best practice in sustainable manufacturing and recycling.

It examines not only challenges but also opportunities associated with wearable IoMT, and this chapter therefore looks to strategic approaches to fostering sustainability in wearable IoMT. This includes the examination of policy and regulatory frameworks that enable sustainable practices as well as the review of industry best practices and the function and role of cooperation and collaboration among stakeholders. The chapter will also endeavour to illustrate the contribution and impact of sustainability in wearable IoMT on health care and patient care by effectively demonstrating how environmentally friendly practices improve the outcomes for patients, optimize resources, and also reduce healthcare costs.

SUSTAINABILITY IN WEARABLE IoMT

Definition and Principles of Sustainability

Sustainability refers to meeting the current needs in such a way that the ability of future generations to meet their own needs is not compromised. It encompasses three main pillars: protection and conservation of the environment, economic viability, and social equity. In the technology sphere, and more deeply in wearable IoMT, sustainability would refer to the process that enables the creation and management of devices in ways that are specific to a reduction of environmental footprints while ensuring economic efficiency and societal benefits (Zhang et al., 2020). Among the principles of sustainability in wearable IoMT are as follows.

a) Resource Efficiency: Use material and energy consumption to minimize waste and to conserve. Design products that are energy consumptive, long-lasting, and produced from renewable materials.
b) Lifecycle Management: Look at the life cycle of a product all the way around, to design and produce with as minimal environmental impacts in use and disposal. It incorporates strategies on the part of recycling and reuse of components.
c) Circular Economy: An economic model whereby products and materials are kept in use as long as possible, and waste should be generated to a limit. In wearable IoMT, for example, devices can be designed easily disassembled and recyclable.
d) Environmental Impact: How the ecological footprint of wearable IoMT devices is reduced while generating lower emissions, wastes, or pollution by its production, use, and disposal.
e) Economic Feasibility: Sustainable practices are not only ecologically favorable but also economically viable, thereby fostering the long-term growth and innovation of the industry.
f) Social Responsibility: that socially incorporates wearable IoMT to address issues related to data privacy and user access, followed by its fair distribution of benefits.

Relevance of Sustainability in Medical Wearables

Wearable IoMT is the field that, with an ever-increasing rate and accessibility of such devices, calls for considerable relevance. The rising demand for wearable medical technologies begs the question, hence, the call for a need to address the impacts posed on the environment and society (Fahim et al., 2024). For example, the following are some critical areas:

Environmental Impact

a) Resource Consumption: Wearable IoMT equipment manufacturing consumes many resources including rare earth metals, plastics, and a high amount of energy. Sustainable practices can balance up resource consumption and reduce carbon footprint.

b) Electronic Waste (E-Waste): Wearable devices are short-lived with considerable e-waste generated. Proper management of e-waste through recycling and finding alternative usages has significantly reduced environmental degradation.
c) Energy Use: IoMT wearables consume energy to be in service. Improving device power and incorporating renewable sources enhance sustainability

Economic Factors

a) Cost Savings: Sustainability practices save on cost over time. Such things as energy efficiencies reduce some of the operational costs. Reusing component materials saves money for the material itself.
b) Market Demand: More and more consumers are becoming conscious of the environment, thus creating an expanding market for green products. Companies that intend to create a niche and be a competitive force in relation to current consumer expectations will be those that adopt sustainability.

Social Responsibility

a) Health and Safety: As regards health and safety, increased adoption of sustainable wearable IoMT devices will eventually result in better health outcomes because of reliable continuous monitoring of health. Making sure these devices are safe and accessible to all segments of the population is necessary.
b) Data privacy and security: Here, sustainability addresses data protection for users ensuring them to maintain their privacy. Since the wearable IoMT devices are to log private health information, there is a need to ensure that there are assured strengthened data protection practices.
c) Equitable access: Developing sustainability further includes making the wearable IoMT accessible for diverse populations such as the underserved and remote communities.
d) The embracing of sustainability by governments is increasingly putting on the agenda of technology. Environmental regulations and standards compliance will be crucial drivers for the wearable IoMT industry to adapt sustainable practices. The adoption of policies encouraging sustainable design, manufacture, and elimination of technologies can bring about quicker transitions towards greener practices in wearable technology.
e) Technological Innovation: Sustainable approaches foster the design and production of more sustainable wearable IoMT designs. Further innovations in the materials science, energy harvesting, or better manufacturing will

render more sustainable products. Thus, for the development of biodegradable materials and efficient recycling methods, the environmental footprint of wearable devices can be reduced well(Qureshi & Krishnan, 2018b).

Wearable IoMT, therefore, is something that is both desirable and necessary because the health care industry is headed toward increasing reliance on technology. Therefore, principles of sustainability such as resource efficiency, lifecycle management and circular economy should be followed and applied to deal with the environmental, economic, and social challenges posed by wearable medical technologies. Importantly, sustainability also includes decreasing environmental impacts, making economies more viable, and ensuring social responsibility. Wearable IoMT, over time, will transform its way of interacting with an ecosystem; dealing with such changes by practicing sustainability will benefit innovations in this realm. It needs a coordinated effort from the healthcare sector, policymakers, and developers to envision new wearable IoMT devices that deliver long-term value while minimizing ecological footprint.

CHALLENGES IN SUSTAINABLE WEARABLE IoMT

Figure 1. Important challenges in sustainable wearable IoMT

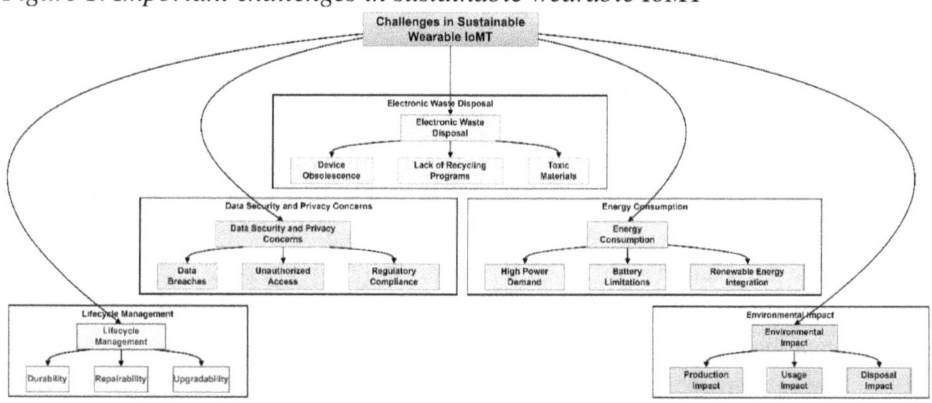

In fact, this multifaceted approach of addressing sustainability in wearable IoMT devices has to consider and include all the environmental, economic, and social concerns. Intrinsic reduction in environmental impact or energy consumed along with electronic waste is required to make these wearable IoMTs sustainable in the long run. Ensuring high-quality data security and privacy mechanisms is a prime necessity to protect information from legal complaints or liability. Effective management along the lifecycle, from design to disposal, is necessary to reduce the ecological footprint of wearable IoMT devices. Overcoming these challenges could help promote sustainable developments in wearable IoMT technologies toward a healthier and more sustainable future (Kakhi et al., 2022b; Shah & Khang, 2023). Figure 1 explores the main challenges in sustainable wearable IoMTs, with sub-challenges for each major category. These can be achieved through the use of Mermaid diagram tools or even Markdown that support the use of Mermaid diagrams.

Environmental Impact

The wearable IoMT devices have fantastic environmental impacts associated with them. These are impacts in terms of the material and processes applied to creating the device. Most of these devices incorporate rare earth metals and non-biodegradable plastics that contribute to environmental degradation. Processing the extraction of these materials requires energy-intensive and harmful practices that lead to habitat loss, pollution, and carbon emission. Most critically, IoMT devices will be manufactured through complex supply chains and are considered to have significant effects on the environment, including transportation emissions as well as resource usage. These effects can only be overcome if adequate sustainable materials and processes for manufacturing reduce damage to the environment.

Energy Consumption

Energy consumption is one of the greatest challenges for wearable IoMT devices right from production to use. Using a lot of energy during the manufacturing process adds up to carbon footprint in respect to that gadget(Gopal et al., 2024; Khare et al., 2024; Saravanan et al., 2024). And when wearable IoMT devices are in use, they consume a continuous supply of power, which usually comes from the recharge of a battery. The energy consumption is much higher for wearables with added functionalities like continuous monitoring and real-time data transference. The development of energy-efficient components and use of renewable sources of energy, such as solar power or kinetic energy harvesting, will be a key to consume lesser amounts of energy in wearable IoMT devices. Optimizing the software and algorithms could minimize the power consumption and make the devices more sustainable.

Electronic Waste

The rise in obsolescence of wearable IoMT devices at an unprecedented rate with a short lifecycle is responsible for the escalating e-waste problem. Many wearable gadgets are manufactured in such a way that putting together built-in batteries and components makes it very difficult to disassemble. Recycling and appropriate disposal of such devices are, therefore, challenging, and a significant portion of them ends up in landfills, where they liberate poisonous substances into the atmosphere. This is why proper e-waste management strategies are important. It involves device design with easy disassembly and recycling, take-back programs, and reused components. Biodegradable materials are developed for wearable IoMT devices so that their e-waste impact can be reduced.

Data Security and Privacy Issues

Wearable IoMT devices collect and forward sensitive health data of individuals, which raises major concerns over data security and privacy. They are intrinsically designed to continuously monitor and send data in real-time, making them vulnerable to cyberattacks. Such unauthorized access to personal health information might lead to the infringement of privacy, identity theft, and other malicious practices. To ensure protection of users' privacy with such wearable IoMT technologies, followed by continued user trust, proper data security measures including robust encryption protocol, secure data storage solutions, and regular security updates should be implemented. In addition, data protection and privacy regulations that follow the principles of laws such as GDPR and HIPAA must be implemented to protect user data(Sengeni et al., 2023; Sreedhar et al., 2024).

Lifecycle Management

A proper lifecycle management policy is one of the significant barriers to sustainability for wearable IoMT devices. It thinks through from the stage of design and manufacturing to the disposal at the end-of-life. Most wearable IoMT devices are not so friendly at the end of life because most of the components used cannot be recycled, and other products cannot be conveniently disposed of. Holistic lifecycle management by the manufacturers with the principles of eco-design and circular economy in conceiving and then designing those devices to be durable and so that they could be easily repaired and upgraded to extend the useful lifetime is the only way forward. It can also reduce waste and scarce resources consumption by promoting the reuse and recycling of parts.

Life cycle management also helps the consumer be well aware of environmentally sound practices. Clear visibility of appropriate waste disposal as well as recycling of wearable IoMT devices may make people behave more responsibly. Take-back and collaborations with recycling houses will ensure the producer's end through responsible and sustainable end-of-life dispositions of devices.

OPPORTUNITIES FOR SUSTAINABLE DEVELOPMENT

Figure 2. Lifecycle of wearable IoMT devices

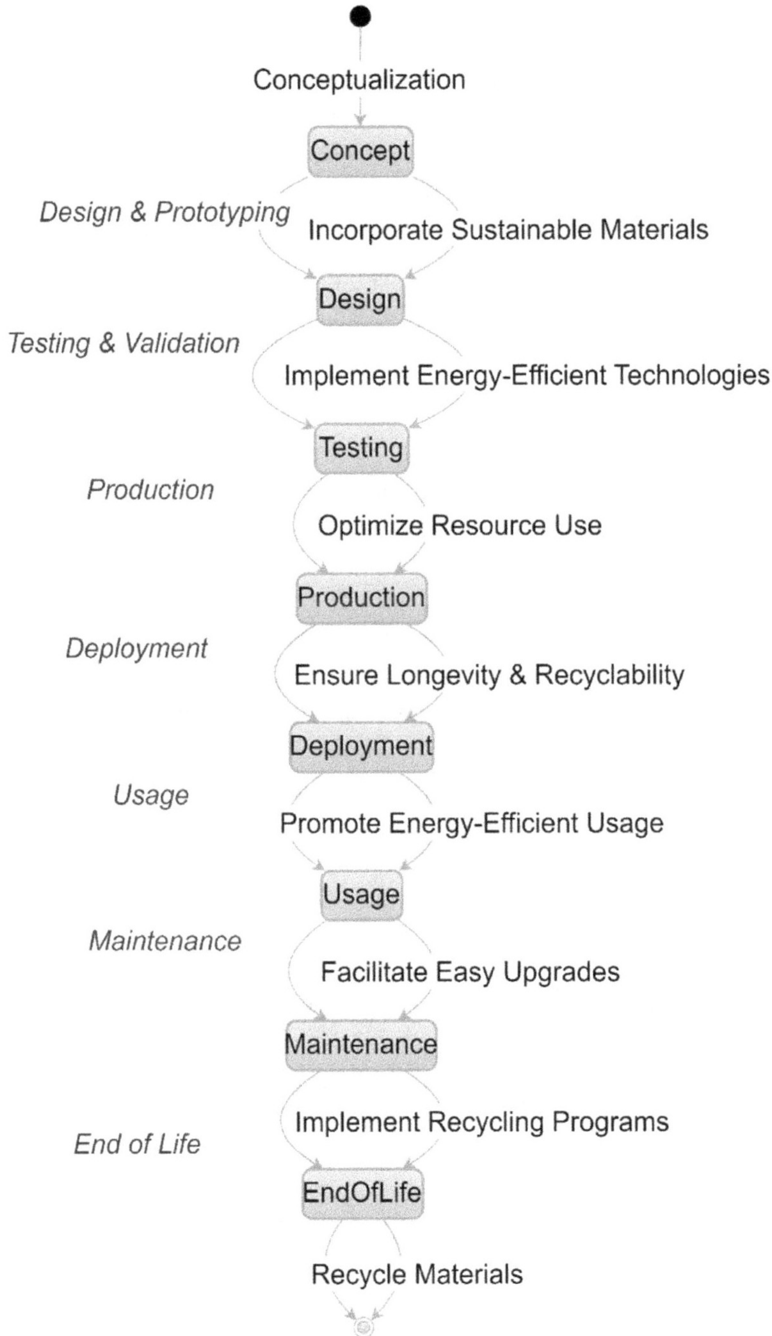

Such opportunities to sustainable development in wearable IoMT are quite numerous and diverse. Wearable IoMT would embrace renewable energy sources, design low-power consumption devices, innovate biodegradable materials, adopt a lot of sustainable manufacturing, and employ effective recycling and reusing strategies on the materials. All these countermand the global sustainability goals but go to the wish of consumers for eco-friendly products. Embracing these would mean not only sustainability of wearable IoMT, but innovation and competitiveness in the industry (Ben Dhaou et al., 2021). As the sector keeps evolving, it has to focus on sustainability as a critical priority in making sure that developments in wearable IoMT could be as long-lasting as beneficial to healthcare and environmental ways of living. Figure 2 is an illustration of the lifecycle of wearable IoMT devices, and as demonstrated above, sustainability can be infused in every stage of such a product's life.

Use of Renewable Energies

One of the richest grounds for sustainable development in wearable IoMT is the adoption of renewable energies. As mentioned earlier, without energy, wearable devices cannot operate continuously. Therefore, integration of renewable energy solutions would drastically reduce the impact of wearable IoMT on the environment. For example, solar energy can be tapped from flexible photovoltaic cells integrated into wearable fabrics or accessories. Another source of renewable power is kinetic energy harvesting, which captures energy from the movements of the user. In addition to simply reducing dependence on traditional batteries, such technologies can also lengthen the operating life of wearable devices, thereby making them more sustainable and less inconvenient for the user. Secondly, a move to renewable energy fits well with the global agenda of reducing carbon emissions and combating climate change, thus aligning wearable IoMT devices with the general movement of sustainability (Fahim et al., 2024).

Low Power Consumption Devices Development

The development of low power consumption devices will be really significant in boosting the sustainability of wearable IoMT. Improvements in microelectronics and energy-efficient components significantly reduce power requirements for these devices. For instance, low power sensors and efficient data processing algorithms can be provided to reduce energy use without limiting performance(Glady et al., 2024; Gopal et al., 2024; Prasad et al., 2024). New wireless communication protocols like BLE also help in the perspective of energy efficiency. Emphasizing low power design, manufacturers can manufacture wearable IoMT devices, which, in turn, must be recharged only a few times to stay alive - thereby reducing energy demand with respect to user convenience. In addition, energy-efficient devices emit less heat, which also increases their lifespan and reliability, thus extending their life cycle and consequently reducing waste.

Development of Biodegradable Materials

The use of biodegradable material in the manufacture of wearable IoMT devices offers a great opportunity for sustainable development. The casings and other parts of traditional electronic components are usually made of plastics and metals that cause long-term environmental pollution. Other eco-friendly alternatives comprise biodegradable materials: in which polylactic acid (PLA) and other bio-based polymers meet the bill. These eventually break down and biodegrade over time, reducing the environmental footprint left by disposed devices. Material science is further emerging with further advancement in technologies related to biodegradable electronic components ranging from flexible circuits to sensors. The application of these materials in wearable IoMTs will address the problem of electronic waste while culminating in a circular economy. This will not only serve the cause of environmental sustainability but also enhance the marketability of the devices by addressing the environmental concerns of consumers about their responsibility.

Eco-Friendly Production Processes

Sustainable production processes are part of the feasibility of wearable IoMT devices in terms of both environmental and economic factors. These range from energy-efficient production processes to waste reduction, along with use of eco-friendly materials. Some of the techniques related to lean manufacturing can be highly effective, focusing on the minimization of waste and maximum utilization of resources. Besides that, the companies can embrace green energy sourcing, such as using renewable sources to power their manufacturing plants. Sustainable manufacturing is also geared toward conserving minimal hazardous usage and proper material handling and disposal when manufactured. Manufacturers could, therefore reduce their footprint on the environment as they comply with the sustainability standards of the world through these practices. Furthermore, sustainable manufacturing can improve brand reputation and attract environmentally concerned consumers, thereby creating a competitive edge in the market(Gowri et al., 2023; Janardhana et al., 2023; Vangeri et al., 2024).

Methods of Recycling and Reuse

Effective recycling and reuse methods play a significant role in handling electronic waste from wearable IoMT. Designing devices that are easily disassembled with parts being reused will make it easier and more manageable to recycle and reduce waste generation. Modular design approaches, which allow components to be easily replaced and upgraded, extend the lifecycle of devices thereby replacing fewer devices with entirely new ones. Also, take-back programs ensure proper disposal and recovery of valuable materials by consumers returning their old devices for recycling. Partnership with specialized e-waste recycling facilities further can enhance the efficiency of recycling processes. What is more, in so doing, electronic wastes are mitigated together with opportunities to recover resources and save costs. The wearable IoMT industry can advance a concept known as a circular economy, where flows of materials are constantly repurposed and reused rather than being downcycled and recycled to reduce the need for virgin materials.

TECHNOLOGICAL INNOVATIONS

Current Trends and Developments

Figure 3. Continuous enhancement and integration of sustainable practices

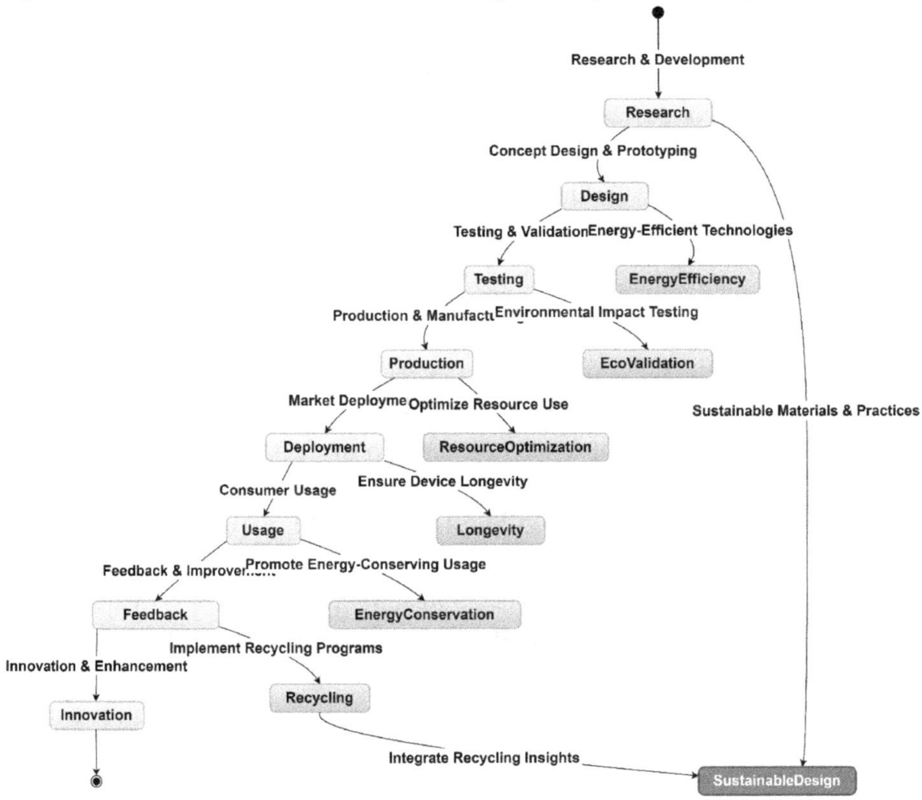

The wearable IoMT sector is upscaling and innovating in the health monitoring solutions sector through rapid advancements in technology and increased demand (Srivastava et al., 2022). Figure 3 traces continuous enhancement and integration of sustainable practices in the lifecycle of wearable IoMTs, holding promise for growth and innovation(Mohanraj et al., 2024). Current trends and developments are changing the face of sustainable wearable IoMT:

a) Advanced Sensors Integration: Modern wearable gadgets come with some of the most advanced sensors that can track a massive number of health-related metrics such as heart rate, blood pressure, glucose level, and much more. These sensors become increasingly accurate, compact, and energy efficient, so they can continue to track your health metrics without having to frequently be recharged.

b) AI and ML: AI and ML are incorporated into wearable IoMT devices to enable real-time analysis and its predictive analytics. This serves the purpose of early detection of health issues and personalized health recommendation that eventually improves the effectiveness of the wearables.

c) Flexible and Stretchable Electronics: Materials science advances in the field have enabled the development of flexible and stretchable electronics, which can be shaped to fit along the curves of the human body. This pushes the comfort and wearability of devices up, so people are more inclined to wear them.

d) Miniaturization and Power Efficiency: Ongoing efforts in miniaturization are making wearable devices smaller and less intrusive. Coupled with advancements in power efficiency, these devices can operate for longer periods before needing a recharge, thereby minimizing how often a person has to go around recharging it and thus making life more convenient for the user.

e) 5G Connectivity: The deployment of 5G connectivity is changing the wearable IoMT through higher rates of data transfer, which encourages more reliable connectivity to hugely enable smooth real-time data transmission into healthcare providers as well as cloud-based health platforms.

Case Studies of Sustainable Wearable IoMT Solutions

Solar Powered Wearables Example: L'Oréal My Skin Track UV wearable. Description: This is a tiny, battery-free device that captures UV exposure and feeds data back to the user's smartphone in real-time. The ability of the tracker to work continuously without depending on standard batteries underlines the sustainable approach of the wearables' technology.

Biodegradable Wearables Example: MIT's ReSkin project. Overview Researchers at the MIT have developed electronic skin that can measure physiological signals and biodegrade after its useful life. The innovation is made from biodegradable cellulose and other materials to do away with the problem of e-waste in wearables.

Recyclable Smartwatches: Example: Apple Watch Series 6. Description: Apple has ensured that its products become more sustainable over time. The Apple Watch Series 6 contains recycled aluminum and rare earth elements. In addition, the take-back program by the brand ensures proper disposal of old devices, hence preserving the circular economies' ideology.

Future Innovations and New Technologies

Nanotechnology This can revolutionize wearable IoMT with nanotechnology, allowing sensor and circuit production as small as ultrahigh density. Such nanomaterials improve health monitoring with increased sensitivity and accuracy, while nanogenerators will be useful for powering devices from the energy that can be generated based on body movement.

Energy Harvesting Technologies: Future wearable IoMT devices could integrate high efficiency energy harvesting technologies, like thermoelectric generator technology that can convert human body heat into electrical energy. This could probably end the wearables' dependency on an external power source for operation, increasing the sustainability of wearables(Prasad et al., 2024; Saravanan et al., 2024).

Advanced Biodegradable Materials: Research is being conducted on biodegradable electronic materials. In the near future, wearables might entirely be made of materials that degrade harmlessly at the end of their life cycle, thus showing better environmental performance.

Blockchain for Data Security: Blockchain technology provides strong security over the health data transmitted by Wearable IoMT devices. Blockchain will be able to address the significant security and privacy concerns by providing integrity and privacy for data, thus making wearables more reliable and trustworthy.

Personalized Medicine: It is now likely that the combination of wearable IoMT with personalized medicine could shift the focus toward ultimate individualized health care solutions. Wearable devices may continue to track health metrics, respond in real time by adjusting treatment plans, and deliver tailored health care interventions.

AR Integration: AR can further be integrated with wearable IoMT, making the functionalities more interactive and useful through real-time visual data overlays. Augmented reality glasses can overlay a set of health metrics directly in the field of vision of users. This can make access easier and more user-friendly.

Trending-forward new technologies in the future, such as nanotechnology, advanced energy harvesting, biodegradable materials, and blockchain for security features, will further propel sustainable wearable IoMT development. The wearable IoMT industry continues to evolve and adopt sustainability principles. This can play a huge role in healthcare transformation, but with that in mind, ensure that their footprints on the environment are minimal. Some of these advancements will improve patient outcomes, working towards a more sustainable and equitable future in healthcare (Ashfaq et al., 2022; Ghubaish et al., 2020). With new technological advancements in wearable IoMT, the industry is opening into more sustainable and efficient avenues in healthcare. Recent innovation, such as advanced sensors, AI integration, and flexible electronics, continues to improve functionality and user experience in wearable devices. The use of solar-powered wearables, biodegradable devices, and recyclable smartwatches demonstrate practical implementation of sustainability in the field.

STRATEGIC APPROACHES TO SUSTAINABILITY

Policy and Regulatory Frameworks

Adoption and implementation would require strong policy and regulatory frameworks for a sustainable wearable IoMT (Internet of Medical Things) industry. Such frameworks guide and provide grounds for rules and regulations in order to ensure environmental responsibility, data security, and consumer protection (AlShorman et al., 2020; Srivastava et al., 2022).

Environmental Regulations:

a) E-Waste Legislation: Most countries have set stringent legislations regarding e-waste management. The regulations require manufacturers to be in line with the set standards of recycling and disposal that ensure low impacts on the environment. An example is the Waste Electrical and Electronic Equipment (WEEE) Directive as enacted by the European Union, which requires producers to manage electronic waste.
b) Eco-design Directives: Such policies like the EU's Eco-Design Directive encourage manufacturers to design products with minimal environmental impact throughout the whole life cycle. Considerations are made for energy efficiency, selection of materials, and end-of-life disposal.

Data Security and Privacy Regulations:
GDPR and HIPAA: There are regulations that set broad imperatives in regards to the treatment of personal health data such as GDPR in Europe and HIPAA in the United States. These typically ensure that wearable IoMTs will follow strict data security and privacy standards to exclude mishaps that might infringe upon user information.
Data Protection by Design: Regulatory frameworks often make it mandatory to incorporate data protection during the design and development of wearable IoMT devices. This approach of proactive planning is helpful in building secure devices, where user privacy comes first from the very beginning.
Incentive for Sustainable Practices:

Subsidies and Tax Incentives: Governments can offer subsidies and tax incentives to companies which embrace the sustainable practices. Such financial rewards may incentivize the generation and utilization of green materials, energy-efficient technologies, and recycling programs.

Green Certifications: EPEAT and ENERGY STAR designation programs require a mainstreamed, consumer-facing approach to building demand for environmentally responsible products. Such certifications can be used by companies to emphasize their sustainability efforts.

Industry Best Practices

The adoption of industry best practice is paramount for attaining sustainability in wearable IoMT. The strategies entail a broad range that can be embraced by manufacturers and stakeholders for the purpose of reducing environmental impacts and enhancing the sustainability of products including (AlShorman et al., 2020; Ben Dhaou et al., 2021; Srivastava et al., 2022).

Sustainable Product Design:

Eco-Design Principles: Eco-design principles are applied when designing wearable IoMT devices, considering the entire lifespan. For instance, sustainable materials will be selected as well as reducing energy consumption and ease of disassembly for recycling purposes.

Modular Design: Designing modular wearable IoMT devices permits easy repair and upgrading of individual components. This pushes the lifespan of the device and reduces electronic waste, as users will exchange or upgrade parts rather than discard the entire unit.

Energy Efficiency:

Low Power Electronics: This includes low power electronics and optimization of software to consume as less energy as possible for sustainability. Energy-efficient components decrease the battery recharge frequency and reduce the overall energy footprint of the wearable devices.

Integration of Renewable Energy Sources: To get a sustainable power solution for IoMT-based wearable devices, renewable energy sources such as solar panels and kinetic energy harvesters can be included. This can severely minimize dependency on conventional batteries and grid electricity.

Recycling and Reuse Programs:

Take-Back Schemes: The Wearable IoMT product should have take-back schemes that will allow consumers to return old or unused devices for recycling. Old products could provide valuable materials and components for recovery, which means less reliance on primary resources.

Component Reuse: If the functional components from older devices can be reused, then the potential waste can be reduced. Components can be refurbished and reused rather than solely being recycled, saving manufacturers money in their production costs and diminished damage on the environment.
Supply Chain Sustainability:
Green Procurement: Green procurement is source procurement of materials and components from suppliers who practice sustainable ways. This includes recycled materials, minimizing transport emissions, and ensuring fair labor practices(Mohanty et al., 2023; Vangeri et al., 2024; Verma et al., 2024).
Life Cycle Assessment: Life cycle assessments (LCAs) assist manufacturers in understanding the environmental impacts of their products, from raw material extraction to end-of-life disposal. LCAs thus give them insights to help improve sustainability across a supply chain.

Regulatory frameworks and industry best practices also represent two dimensions of strategic approaches to sustainability in wearable IoMT. Thus, it is because of strong policies and regulations that producers would adapt to comply with these high environmental stewardship and data protection standards. Sustainable product design, energy efficiency, and a proper recycling program can really minimize the impact of wear IoMT devices on the environment. By making all these strategies combinable, the wearable IoMT industry can help create an even more sustainable future in harmony with technological innovation and stewardship of the Earth.

COLLABORATION AND PARTNERSHIPS

It appears that collaboration and partnerships are among the best strategic approaches to the sustainable development of wearable IoMT. Sustainable development in wearable IoMT will be multifaceted and require intersectoral collaborations, involving manufacturers, health providers, researchers, policymakers, and consumers (Ashfaq et al., 2022).

Intersectoral Collaboration:
Illustrative Example: For instance, the alliances between tech companies and healthcare organizations that drive innovation but at the same time make sure that such wearables integrated with IoMT devices will not only fulfill technological standards but also medical. For example, as alliance between companies like Apple with health service providers led to further advanced features on health monitoring capabilities in wearables such as ECG and fall detection.

Impact: These collaborations may blend resources and technologies that facilitate the development of very functional and sustainable devices.
Public-Private Partnerships:
Case Study: The government can then collaborate with private firms to fund research for new and sustainable technologies in healthcare. Such projects as Horizon 2020 in Europe, offer grants to projects that aim at supporting sustainability in healthcare technologies through innovation.
Impact: Public-private partnerships can accelerate the development and integration of sustainable wearable IoMT solutions through financial and regulatory support.
International Standards and Regulations:
Example: International collaboration for standardizing the production and disposal of wearables IoMT devices can ensure uniform practices of sustainability. Bodies like IEC and ISO can develop guidelines that companies must adhere to in manufacturing.
Impact: Global standards will limit environmental impact, safety, recycling, and reusing materials in diverse markets
R&D Priorities
For wearable IoMT to step forward into further sustainability, the needed set priorities of research and development would need to be defined. This would cover the principal challenge areas and, most promisingly, the best opportunities for sustainable development (Kakhi et al., 2022a).

Figure 4. Research and development priorities

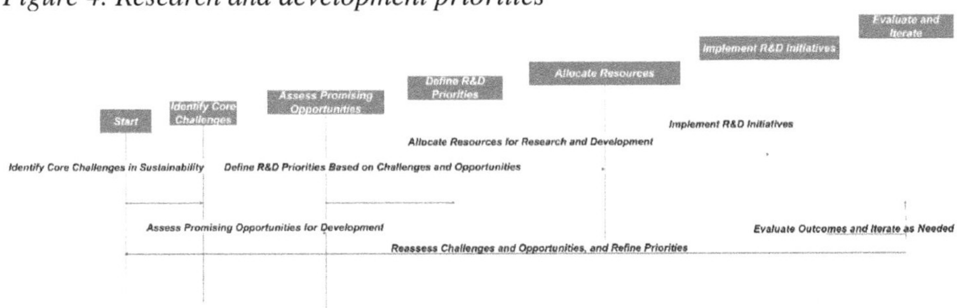

Figure 4 explains a roadmap for structured progress on sustainability in wearable IoMT by focusing on the important R&D activities toward its continuous improvement.

Energy Efficiency:

Focus: Low power electronics, energy efficient sensors, and innovative power management systems must be developed within research and developed. Alternative sources of energy such as solar power and kinetic energy harvesting also tend to reduce the energy footprint of wearable devices.
Energy-efficient modules that use body heat or motion to derive energy increase the battery life and reduce the detrimental environmental impact generated by the frequent recharge and replacement of the battery.
Materials for Sustainability:
Focus: R&D strategy should be focused on discovering biodegradable and recyclable materials. Advanced polymers and organic materials which may degrade naturally or easily recycled, help in reducing electronic waste.
Example: Basic research into biodegradable materials can result in the development of cellulose-based electronics to be made as wearable devices with a reduced impact on the environment for their lifetime.
Lifecycle Management:
Focus: In terms of R&D, durable and upgradable or easily repairable design should come first. Modular components will enable easy replacement or upgrade and thus extend the life of the device as well as minimize waste.
Example: Modular smartwatches so that the user would be able to change and replace individual parts-such as a battery or some of the sensors-rather than having to exchange the whole device.
Data Security and Privacy:

- Focus: Data security and privacy should be robust enough to win the trust of customers, and data protection is there to ensure that the organization complies with the regulatory authority. Research should work hard in developing advanced encryption schemes for data, secured data transmission protocols, and reliable mechanisms for user authentication.

Case Study: Blockchain technology, used to ensure the safe management of health data within wearable IoMT devices, will ensure that integrity and privacy are preserved while promoting easy sharing between healthcare providers.
User-Centric Design:
Focus: One cannot conclude and finalize sustainable wearable IoMT devices without knowing the needs and preferences of the users. The studies must include user behavior, ergonomic design, and user-friendly interfaces in order to facilitate improved user experience.
Invest in research and development to identify designs most convenient for use yet keep sustainability features from impacting usability.

Wearable IoMT requires an integrated strategic approach that emphasizes collaboration, partnership, and focused research and development in efforts toward sustainability. An example would be cross-industry collaboration to stimulate the development of high-performance and sustainable wearables while establishing global standards for stakeholders. This would concentrate R&D efforts on areas such as energy efficiency, sustainable material usage, lifecycle management, data security, and user-centric design. These strategic moves from the wearable IoMT industry will eventually result in a healthier future for health care while saving the planet in general.

IMPACT ON HEALTHCARE AND PATIENT CARE

Benefits of Sustainable Wearable IoMT

Figure 5. Benefits of sustainable practices in wearable IoMT devices

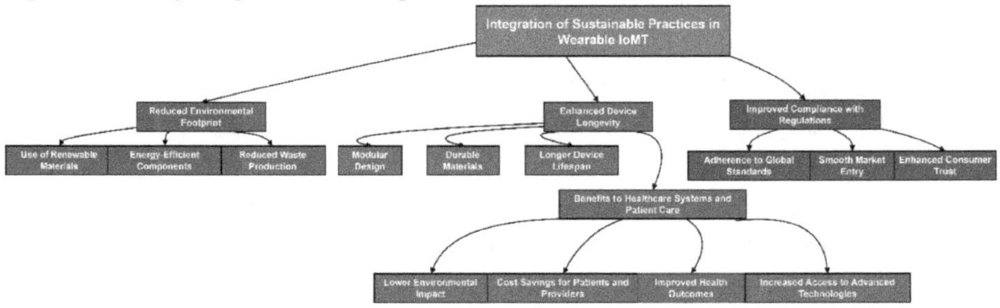

Wearable IoMT or Internet of Medical Things, which integrate sustainable practices, has several benefits for healthcare systems and patient care. Sustainable wearable IoMT devices are more concerned with the minimization of environmental impact with the necessary maximization of function, which consequently yields a number of advantages (Mohanraj et al., 2024). Figure 5 Benefits to healthcare systems and patient care of sustainable practices in wearable IoMT devices.

a) Lower Environmental Footprint Example: This could be in equipment that contains biodegradable material or is powered by renewable energy sources, thus reducing electronic waste and energy consumption. Impact: This will improve a greener health system through reduced ecological footprint of medical technology.

b) Extended Lifespan for Wearable Devices: Modular designs and robust materials extend the wear life of a wearable device, resulting in fewer replacements. In this way, it saves resources but also makes reducing the absolute cost of ownership as achievable for both patient groups and healthcare providers.
c) Better Regulatory Compliance: For example, conformity to international standards on sustainability means that devices are keeping up with strict environmental and health standards. Access to such high technologies would become more accessible in different markets or regions if they have already adopted similar tight environmental and health standards.

Better Patient Outcomes and Experience

The use of sustainable wearable IoMT devices is extremely important in terms of improving patient outcomes and the experience from care. They are continually designed and developed to ensure that continuous, accurate, and personalized health monitoring takes place, which leads to several benefits (Anitha et al., 2023).

Continuity of Health Monitoring Continuous monitoring of body signs such as heart rate, glucose levels, and sleep patterns through wearables will offer real time information to both patients and healthcare providers. Impact: Timely detection of complications and timely interventions would remarkably improve patient outcomes by preventing early complications and efficiently managing chronic diseases.

a) Personalized Healthcare Example: AI-driven analytics in wearables can formulate health recommendations and treatment plans on the basis of the patient's data. Impact: This personalized approach enhances the efficacy of treatment and patient satisfaction, thus creating improved adherence towards medical advice and good health outcomes.
b) Active Patient Participation: For example, interfaces that are easy to use and give instant feedback through wearable devices make the patient want to take part in managing their health. Impact: The active participation of a person leads to more health behavior, that is, physical activity or adherence to medication schedules.
c) Remotely Patients Monitoring: Example: IoMT wearable devices enable healthcare providers to remotely monitor patients, so they do not necessarily have to visit patients at bedside very frequently. Effect: It reduces the number of people in health facilities, expands access to care for patients who live far or in remote locations, and ensures that a patient receives continuous monitoring in times of pandemics or any critical situation.

Cost Optimization and Resource Utilization

Sustained wearable IoMT devices lower cost and resource utilization in healthcare systems since they reduce operational costs and improve resource utilization, something (Hanumanthakari et al., 2023; Sengeni et al., 2023), note as:

a) Decreased healthcare costs: Example: Continuous monitoring that leads to early detection and management of health conditions prevent hospitalization and expensive treatments. Impact: Saves money both for the patients and for the healthcare system, meaning high-quality care is even more affordable and accessible.
b) Optimized Resource Use: Example: Energy conserving and long-lasting wearable devices can serve for a larger time period, hence minimal replacement and maintenance. Impact: Thus, this optimizes the usage of resources, say materials, energy and thereby reduces the overall environmental and financial costs of healthcare technology.
c) Scalable Healthcare Solutions Example: Wearable IoMT devices can be rolled out in big numbers. This thus means that there will be provision for an extremely affordable solution for huge populations. Impact: That is to say, scalability ensures more patients can now receive advanced health monitoring, besides personalized care without deliberately increasing healthcare expenditure unreasonably.
d) Improved Data Management: Example: An integration of an IoMT device with an EHR and other digital health platforms will streamline the collection and analysis of data. Impact: This can lead towards better decision making and use of resources, allowing the healthcare provider to be more targeted and effective in services.

The impact of sustainable wearable IoMT is quite deep in terms of what is involved in healthcare and patient care. It contributes to a more sustainable healthcare system in terms of bringing down environmental footprint and improving the device's longevity to enhance continuous, personalized, and remote health monitoring. Therefore, this ensures that patients have improved outcomes and experiences, leading to better engagement and adherence to treatment plans. With this regard, the sustainable wearable IoMT devices provide cost-efficiency and resource optimization that give quality healthcare at accessible and affordable prices (Hussain et al., 2023; Mohanraj et al., 2024; Sengeni et al., 2023; Subha et al., 2023). These not only contribute towards improving individual patient health with early detection, personalized care, and optimized resource use but also toward system-wide efficiency and effectiveness.

CONCLUSION

It is an enabling transformation in healthcare technology that combines advanced medical monitoring with environmental responsibility. This chapter analyses the various dimensions of sustainability in wearable IoMT, its meaning, challenges, opportunities, and technological advancements.

Lowering environmental footprint through advanced materials, energy-friendly technologies, and lifecycle management. Minimizing waste, use of renewable resources, and design for longevity are considered as guiding principles. Mitigating factors to include the related environmental impact, energy usage, electronic junk disposal, data security, and lifecycle management need multi-industry collaboration involving advanced technologies with sustainable practices by integrating these aspects.

It has touched on the sustainable possibilities of wearable IoMT technology, including renewable sources, low power devices, biodegradable materials, sustainable manufacturing, and recycling. It should focus on current trends, case studies, and future direction in this field. Innovations such as solar-powered devices, biodegradable materials, blockchain, nanotechnology, energy harvesting, and augmented reality are all pointing to a completely new direction toward environmentally friendly healthcare.

It ensures the importance of collaboration, partnerships, and world standards to drive sustainable innovation. It also highlighted the critical priorities in R&D, the emphasis being on energy efficiency, sustainable materials, lifecycle management, data security, and user-centric design. The effect on healthcare systems of sustainable wearable IoMT enhances patient outcomes, cost efficiency, and opting resources to make healthcare more accessible and sustainable.

Using the technology, sustainability, and healthcare outcomes, it will probably be shaped by innovation and stewardship over the environment. Wearable IoMT will bring decisive leaps forward in patient care enhancement and global sustainability. It will build a resilient, efficient, and environmentally aware healthcare ecosystem delivering the promise of a healthier future for all. The journey toward sustainable wearable IoMT is challenging yet full of exciting possibilities for enhancing healthcare delivery and saving our planet's resources.

REFERENCES

Al-Turjman, F., Nawaz, M. H., & Ulusar, U. D. (2020). Intelligence in the Internet of Medical Things era: A systematic review of current and future trends. *Computer Communications*, 150, 644–660. DOI: 10.1016/j.comcom.2019.12.030

AlShorman, O., AlShorman, B., Alkhassaweneh, M., & Alkahtani, F. (2020). A review of internet of medical things (IoMT)-based remote health monitoring through wearable sensors: A case study for diabetic patients. *Indonesian Journal of Electrical Engineering and Computer Science*, 20(1), 414–422. DOI: 10.11591/ijeecs.v20.i1.pp414-422

Anitha, C., Komala, C., Vivekanand, C. V., Lalitha, S., & Boopathi, S. (2023). Artificial Intelligence driven security model for Internet of Medical Things (IoMT). *IEEE Explore*, 1–7.

Ashfaq, Z., Rafay, A., Mumtaz, R., Zaidi, S. M. H., Saleem, H., Zaidi, S. A. R., Mumtaz, S., & Haque, A. (2022). A review of enabling technologies for Internet of Medical Things (IoMT) Ecosystem. *Ain Shams Engineering Journal*, 13(4), 101660. DOI: 10.1016/j.asej.2021.101660

Ben Dhaou, I., Ebrahimi, M., Ben Ammar, M., Bouattour, G., & Kanoun, O. (2021). Edge devices for internet of medical things: Technologies, techniques, and implementation. *Electronics (Basel)*, 10(17), 2104. DOI: 10.3390/electronics10172104

Fahim, K. E., Kalinaki, K., & Shafik, W. (2024). Electronic Devices in the Artificial Intelligence of the Internet of Medical Things (AIoMT). In *Handbook of Security and Privacy of AI-Enabled Healthcare Systems and Internet of Medical Things* (pp. 41–62). CRC Press.

Ghubaish, A., Salman, T., Zolanvari, M., Unal, D., Al-Ali, A., & Jain, R. (2020). Recent advances in the internet-of-medical-things (IoMT) systems security. *IEEE Internet of Things Journal*, 8(11), 8707–8718. DOI: 10.1109/JIOT.2020.3045653

Glady, J. B. P., D'Souza, S. M., Priya, A. P., Amuthachenthiru, K., Vikram, G., & Boopathi, S. (2024). A Study on AI-ML-Driven Optimizing Energy Distribution and Sustainable Agriculture for Environmental Conservation. In *Harnessing High-Performance Computing and AI for Environmental Sustainability* (pp. 1–27). IGI Global., DOI: 10.4018/979-8-3693-1794-5.ch001

Gopal, M., Lurdhumary, J., Bathrinath, S., Priya, A. P., Sarojwal, A., & Boopathi, S. (2024). Energy Harvesting and Smart Highways for Sustainable Transportation Infrastructure: Revolutionizing Roads Using Nanotechnology. In *Principles and Applications in Speed Sensing and Energy Harvesting for Smart Roads* (pp. 136–165). IGI Global. DOI: 10.4018/978-1-6684-9214-7.ch005

Gowri, N. V., Dwivedi, J. N., Krishnaveni, K., Boopathi, S., Palaniappan, M., & Medikondu, N. R. (2023). Experimental investigation and multi-objective optimization of eco-friendly near-dry electrical discharge machining of shape memory alloy using Cu/SiC/Gr composite electrode. *Environmental Science and Pollution Research International*, 30(49), 1–19. DOI: 10.1007/s11356-023-26983-6 PMID: 37126160

Haghi, M., Thurow, K., & Stoll, R. (2017). Wearable devices in medical internet of things: Scientific research and commercially available devices. *Healthcare Informatics Research*, 23(1), 4–15. DOI: 10.4258/hir.2017.23.1.4 PMID: 28261526

Hanumanthakari, S., Gift, M. M., Kanimozhi, K., Bhavani, M. D., Bamane, K. D., & Boopathi, S. (2023). Biomining Method to Extract Metal Components Using Computer-Printed Circuit Board E-Waste. In *Handbook of Research on Safe Disposal Methods of Municipal Solid Wastes for a Sustainable Environment* (pp. 123–141). IGI Global. DOI: 10.4018/978-1-6684-8117-2.ch010

Hussain, Z., Babe, M., Saravanan, S., Srimathy, G., Roopa, H., & Boopathi, S. (2023). Optimizing Biomass-to-Biofuel Conversion: IoT and AI Integration for Enhanced Efficiency and Sustainability. In *Circular Economy Implementation for Sustainability in the Built Environment* (pp. 191–214). IGI Global.

Janardhana, K., Singh, V., Singh, S. N., Babu, T. R., Bano, S., & Boopathi, S. (2023). Utilization Process for Electronic Waste in Eco-Friendly Concrete: Experimental Study. In *Sustainable Approaches and Strategies for E-Waste Management and Utilization* (pp. 204–223). IGI Global.

Kakhi, K., Alizadehsani, R., Kabir, H. D., Khosravi, A., Nahavandi, S., & Acharya, U. R. (2022a). The internet of medical things and artificial intelligence: Trends, challenges, and opportunities. *Biocybernetics and Biomedical Engineering*, 42(3), 749–771. DOI: 10.1016/j.bbe.2022.05.008

Kakhi, K., Alizadehsani, R., Kabir, H. D., Khosravi, A., Nahavandi, S., & Acharya, U. R. (2022b). The internet of medical things and artificial intelligence: Trends, challenges, and opportunities. *Biocybernetics and Biomedical Engineering*, 42(3), 749–771. DOI: 10.1016/j.bbe.2022.05.008

Khare, R., Chinnasamy, A., Shashibhushan, G., Suresh Kumar, P., Hemalatha, R., & Boopathi, S. (2024). Energy Cascade Conversion System and Energy-Efficient Infrastructure: Experimentation, Results, Discussion, and Case Studies. In *Advances in Environmental Engineering and Green Technologies* (pp. 115–139). IGI Global. DOI: 10.4018/979-8-3693-0492-1.ch006

Mishra, P., & Singh, G. (2023). Internet of medical things healthcare for sustainable smart cities: Current status and future prospects. *Applied Sciences (Basel, Switzerland)*, 13(15), 8869. DOI: 10.3390/app13158869

Mohanraj, G., Krishna, K. S., Lakshmi, B. S., Vijayalakshmi, A., Pramila, P. V., & Boopathi, S. (2024). Optimizing Trust and Security in Healthcare 4.0: Human Factors in Lightweight Secured IoMT Ecosystems. In *Lightweight Digital Trust Architectures in the Internet of Medical Things (IoMT)* (pp. 52–72). IGI Global. DOI: 10.4018/979-8-3693-2109-6.ch004

Mohanty, A., Venkateswaran, N., Ranjit, P., Tripathi, M. A., & Boopathi, S. (2023). Innovative Strategy for Profitable Automobile Industries: Working Capital Management. In *Handbook of Research on Designing Sustainable Supply Chains to Achieve a Circular Economy* (pp. 412–428). IGI Global.

Prasad, M. S. C., Dhanalakshmi, M., Mohan, M., Somasundaram, B., Valarmathi, R., & Boopathi, S. (2024). Machine Learning-Integrated Sustainable Engineering and Energy Systems: Innovations at the Nexus. In *Harnessing High-Performance Computing and AI for Environmental Sustainability* (pp. 74–98). IGI Global. DOI: 10.4018/979-8-3693-1794-5.ch004

Qureshi, F., & Krishnan, S. (2018). Wearable hardware design for the internet of medical things (IoMT). *Sensors (Basel)*, 18(11), 3812. DOI: 10.3390/s18113812 PMID: 30405026

Salam, A. (2024). Internet of things for sustainable human health. In *Internet of Things for Sustainable Community Development: Wireless Communications, Sensing, and Systems* (pp. 217–242). Springer. DOI: 10.1007/978-3-031-62162-8_7

Saravanan, S., Khare, R., Umamaheswari, K., Khare, S., Krishne Gowda, B. S., & Boopathi, S. (2024). AI and ML Adaptive Smart-Grid Energy Management Systems: Exploring Advanced Innovations. In *Principles and Applications in Speed Sensing and Energy Harvesting for Smart Roads* (pp. 166–196). IGI Global. DOI: 10.4018/978-1-6684-9214-7.ch006

Sengeni, D., Padmapriya, G., Imambi, S. S., Suganthi, D., Suri, A., & Boopathi, S. (2023). Biomedical waste handling method using artificial intelligence techniques. In *Handbook of Research on Safe Disposal Methods of Municipal Solid Wastes for a Sustainable Environment* (pp. 306–323). IGI Global. DOI: 10.4018/978-1-6684-8117-2.ch022

Shah, V., & Khang, A. (2023). Internet of medical things (IoMT) driving the digital transformation of the healthcare sector. In *Data-centric AI solutions and emerging technologies in the healthcare ecosystem* (pp. 15–26). CRC Press. DOI: 10.1201/9781003356189-2

Shin, D., & Hwang, Y. (2017). Integrated acceptance and sustainability evaluation of Internet of Medical Things: A dual-level analysis. *Internet Research*, 27(5), 1227–1254. DOI: 10.1108/IntR-07-2016-0200

Sreedhar, P. S. S., Sujay, V., Rani, M. R., Melita, L., Reshma, S., & Boopathi, S. (2024). Impacts of 5G Machine Learning Techniques on Telemedicine and Social Media Professional Connection in Healthcare. In *Advances in Medical Technologies and Clinical Practice* (pp. 209–234). IGI Global. DOI: 10.4018/979-8-3693-1934-5.ch012

Srivastava, J., Routray, S., Ahmad, S., & Waris, M. M. (2022). [Retracted] Internet of Medical Things (IoMT)-Based Smart Healthcare System: Trends and Progress. *Computational Intelligence and Neuroscience*, 2022(1), 7218113. PMID: 35880061

Subha, S., Inbamalar, T., Komala, C., Suresh, L. R., Boopathi, S., & Alaskar, K. (2023). A Remote Health Care Monitoring system using internet of medical things (IoMT). *IEEE Explore*, 1–6.

Vangeri, A. K., Bathrinath, S., Anand, M. C. J., Shanmugathai, M., Meenatchi, N., & Boopathi, S. (2024). Green Supply Chain Management in Eco-Friendly Sustainable Manufacturing Industries. In *Environmental Applications of Carbon-Based Materials* (pp. 253–287). IGI Global. DOI: 10.4018/979-8-3693-3625-0.ch010

Verma, R., Christiana, M. B. V., Maheswari, M., Srinivasan, V., Patro, P., Dari, S. S., & Boopathi, S. (2024). Intelligent Physarum Solver for Profit Maximization in Oligopolistic Supply Chain Networks. In *AI and Machine Learning Impacts in Intelligent Supply Chain* (pp. 156–179). IGI Global. DOI: 10.4018/979-8-3693-1347-3.ch011

Zhang, T., Sodhro, A. H., Luo, Z., Zahid, N., Nawaz, M. W., Pirbhulal, S., & Muzammal, M. (2020). A joint deep learning and internet of medical things driven framework for elderly patients. *IEEE Access : Practical Innovations, Open Solutions*, 8, 75822–75832. DOI: 10.1109/ACCESS.2020.2989143

KEY TERMS AND DEFINITIONS

AI: Artificial Intelligence.
AR: Augmented Reality.
BLE: Bluetooth Low Energy.
ECG: Electrocardiogram.
EHR: Electronic Health Record.
ENERGY STAR: Energy Efficiency Certification Program.
EPEAT: Electronic Product Environmental Assessment Tool.
EU: European Union.
GDPR: General Data Protection Regulation.
HIPAA: Health Insurance Portability and Accountability Act.
IEC: International Electrotechnical Commission.
ISO: International Organization for Standardization.
IT: Information Technology.
LCA: Life Cycle Assessment.
MIT: Massachusetts Institute of Technology.
ML: Machine Learning.
MT: Medical Technology.
PLA: Polylactic Acid.
UV: Ultraviolet.
WEEE: Waste Electrical and Electronic Equipment.

Chapter 5
The Field of Usability and User Experience (UX) Design

Shivnath Ghosh
Brainware University, India

Soumya Dubey
https://orcid.org/0009-0007-1223-5965
Chungnam National University, South Korea

ABSTRACT

The Usability and User Experience (UX) design field is evolving rapidly, driven by technological advancements, changing user expectations, and the increasing complexity of digital ecosystems. This chapter explores the emerging trends shaping the future of usability and UX design. Key trends include the integration of artificial intelligence (AI) and machine learning (ML) for personalized experiences, the growing importance of inclusive and accessible design, the rise of voice user interfaces (VUIs) and augmented reality (AR), and the shift towards a more holistic approach to UX that encompasses emotional and ethical considerations. By examining these trends, this chapter aims to provide insights into the future directions of usability and UX design, highlighting the challenges and opportunities for designers and researchers in the field.

OBJECTIVES

1. Investigate and Leverage Technological Advancements

DOI: 10.4018/979-8-3693-2337-3.ch005

This objective examines the role of artificial intelligence (AI) and machine learning (ML) in enhancing usability and UX design. It involves analyzing how these technologies create personalized and adaptive user experiences. Additionally, the study explores the rise of voice user interfaces (VUIs) and their impact on user interaction. Furthermore, it assesses the potential of augmented reality (AR) in creating immersive user experiences.

2. Promote Inclusive, Accessible, and Ethical Design

This objective aims to explore the importance of inclusive design principles in UX. It identifies best practices for making digital products accessible to diverse user groups, including those with disabilities. Moreover, it investigates the integration of emotional and ethical considerations into UX design and discusses the significance of designing for emotional engagement and user well-being.

3. Address Challenges and Forecast Future Trends in UX Design

This objective highlights the technical and ethical challenges associated with emerging trends in UX design. It identifies opportunities for innovation and improvement in usability and UX design practices. Additionally, it predicts future directions and developments in the usability and UX design field and offers recommendations for designers, researchers, and practitioners.

INTRODUCTION

Usability and User Experience (UX) design have become critical in developing successful digital products and services. As technology continues to advance at a rapid pace, the expectations of users are also evolving, necessitating a continuous adaptation of design practices. Modern users are no longer satisfied with functional interfaces; they seek intuitive, engaging, and emotionally resonant experiences. Consequently, designers must stay abreast of emerging trends to create products that meet and exceed user expectations.

This research paper delves into the current and emerging usability and UX design trends, examining how they influence the field and what they mean for the future. Among the most significant trends are integrating artificial intelligence (AI) and machine learning (ML) into design processes to create more personalized and adaptive experiences. Additionally, the emphasis on inclusive and accessible design is growing, driven by a broader recognition of the need to cater to diverse user groups, including those with disabilities.

Another notable trend is the increasing popularity of voice user interfaces (VUIs) and augmented reality (AR), which transform how users interact with digital products. These technologies promise to make interactions more natural and immersive, enhancing overall user satisfaction. Furthermore, there is a shift towards a more holistic approach to UX design that considers emotional and ethical aspects, reflecting a deeper understanding of the complex relationship between users and technology.

By exploring these trends, this paper aims to shed light on the future landscape of usability and UX design, providing valuable insights for designers, researchers, and practitioners. The discussion will highlight the challenges associated with these trends, such as the ethical implications of AI and the technical hurdles of implementing AR, while also pointing out the opportunities for innovation and improvement in user experience.

Figure 1. A mindmap illustrating the integration of emerging technologies such as AI, VR, AR, and IoT in UX design

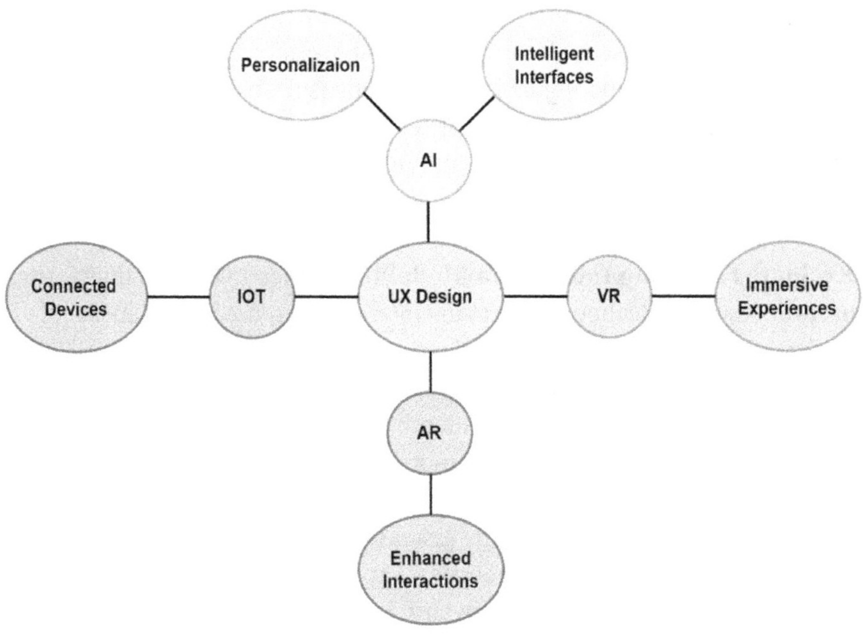

MOTIVATION

The motivation for setting these objectives is driven by the rapid evolution and increasing complexity of the usability and UX design field. As digital ecosystems continue to expand and integrate more advanced technologies, there is a compelling need to explore and understand the trends that will shape the future of user interactions and experiences. Here's an elaboration on the motivation behind each objective:

1. **Investigate Technological Advancements:** Integrating AI and ML in UX design offers unprecedented opportunities to create smarter, more responsive interfaces that adapt to user behavior. Understanding how these technologies can be leveraged to improve usability is crucial for staying at the forefront of design innovation. Additionally, personalization is becoming a key differentiator in user experience. By analyzing the impact of AI and ML, we can uncover ways to deliver more relevant, tailored interactions that enhance user satisfaction and engagement.
2. **Promote Inclusive and Accessible Design:** With a growing emphasis on social responsibility, it is essential to design accessible products for all users, regardless of their abilities. Promoting inclusivity broadens the user base, ensures compliance with legal standards, and enhances brand reputation. Accessibility is not just a legal requirement but a moral obligation. By identifying best practices, we can create more equitable digital experiences that empower all users and foster greater inclusivity in the digital space.
3. **Evaluate Emerging Interaction Modalities:** Voice interfaces transform how users interact with technology, making interactions more natural and hands-free. Understanding their impact helps designers create more intuitive and efficient user experiences. Augmented reality offers new dimensions of interactivity and engagement. By assessing their potential, we can explore innovative ways to enrich user experiences and create more compelling digital environments.
4. **Adopt a Holistic Approach to UX:** As users seek more meaningful and emotionally resonant experiences, it is essential to integrate emotional and ethical considerations into design practices. This holistic approach enhances user satisfaction and builds trust and loyalty. Emotional engagement and user well-being are becoming central to UX design. By focusing on these aspects, we can create experiences that meet functional needs and promote positive emotional responses and overall well-being.
5. **Identify Challenges and Opportunities:** With new technologies come new challenges. Identifying these challenges early allows designers to address them and proactively ensure ethical and effective implementation. Every challenge presents an opportunity for innovation. By identifying these opportunities, we

can drive continuous improvement in UX design and stay ahead in a competitive landscape.

6. **Provide Future Insights:** Predicting future trends helps designers and researchers anticipate changes and prepare for the next wave of technological advancements and user expectations. By providing actionable recommendations, we can equip designers, researchers, and practitioners with the knowledge and tools they need to adapt and thrive in an ever-evolving field.

RESEARCH BACKGROUND

The discipline of Usability and UX design has long been central to developing digital products, ensuring that they are functional, engaging, and satisfying to use. As technology has progressed, the scope and complexity of UX design have expanded, influenced by several key developments.

a. Historical Context and Evolution

Initially, usability focused primarily on the efficiency and effectiveness of user interactions with digital systems. Early pioneers like Jakob Nielsen emphasized the importance of user-centered design principles, usability testing, and heuristic evaluations to create intuitive interfaces (Nielsen, 1993). Nielsen's seminal book, Usability Engineering, outlines usability engineering principles and provides methodologies for usability testing and heuristic evaluation. His work with Rolf Molich introduced the concept of heuristic evaluation, a method for identifying usability problems in user interface design (Nielsen & Molich, 1990).

As digital products proliferated and user expectations evolved, the scope of UX expanded to encompass a broader range of factors, including emotional and aesthetic elements. Donald Norman's book, Emotional Design: Why We Love (or Hate) Everyday Things, discusses the importance of emotional responses in design and how products can evoke positive or negative emotions (Norman, 2004). Additionally, Norman and Stephen Draper's collection of essays, User-Centered System Design: New Perspectives on Human-Computer Interaction, outlines user-centered design principles and the importance of involving users in the design process (Norman & Draper, 1986).

The field of UX design has continued to evolve, with comprehensive overviews provided by authors like Jesse James Garrett, who in The Elements of User Experience: User-Centered Design for the Web and Beyond, describes the various aspects of user experience design and how the field has grown to include a broader range of considerations beyond usability (Garrett, 2011). A historical perspective on the development of usability and UX research methods is offered by Lazar et al. in Research Methods in Human-Computer Interaction, which highlights key milestones and influential figures in the field (Lazar et al., 2017).

These references provide a solid foundation for understanding usability and UX design's historical context and evolution.

b. Technological Advancements

Recent advancements in artificial intelligence (AI) and machine learning (ML) have had a profound impact on UX design. These technologies enable the creation of highly personalized user experiences by analyzing user data and adapting interfaces to meet individual preferences and behaviors. For instance, recommendation systems powered by AI have become ubiquitous in e-commerce and streaming services, enhancing user engagement and satisfaction.

The impact of AI and ML on UX design is significant, as these technologies enhance user experiences through personalization and adaptation (Calvano et al., 2020). By analyzing user data, AI enables the creation of personalized user experiences, as explored in the intersection of AI and human-computer interaction (HCI) (Yang & Evans, 2019). In e-commerce, deep learning techniques used in recommendation systems have been shown to enhance user engagement and satisfaction (Zhang et al., 2017). Similarly, in streaming services, AI and ML algorithms personalize content for users, as demonstrated by YouTube's recommendation system (Davidson et al., 2010).

User data analysis is crucial for personalization, with techniques such as collaborative filtering and content-based methods being used to provide personalized recommendations (Adomavicius & Tuzhilin, 2005). Deep learning in recommender systems further improves user engagement and satisfaction by delivering personalized content (McInerney & Smyth, 2020). These references provide a strong foundation for understanding how AI and ML are transforming UX design by enabling personalized and adaptive user experiences.

c. Inclusive and Accessible Design

The increasing recognition of the importance of inclusivity and accessibility has also shaped the field of UX design. Organizations and designers are now more aware of the need to create digital products that cater to diverse user groups, including those with disabilities. Standards and guidelines, such as the Web Content Accessibility Guidelines (WCAG), provide frameworks for making digital content accessible to all users, ensuring equal access and usability.

The importance of inclusivity and accessibility in UX design is emphasized by the WCAG 2.1 guidelines, which serve as the standard framework for making web content more accessible to people with disabilities (W3C, 2018). Organizations and designers are embracing accessibility by incorporating it into their processes and policies, as highlighted in the work by Lazar et al. (2015). This approach ensures that digital products cater to diverse user groups, addressing the challenges faced by web designers in implementing accessibility guidelines (Schmutz et al., 2016).

Frameworks like WCAG help balance the need for standardization with accommodating diverse user needs, as discussed by Kelly et al. (2005). Ensuring equal access and usability is crucial, with research evaluating different methods for assessing web page accessibility for blind users (Mankoff et al., 2005). Inclusive design practices are further enhanced by understanding the browsing strategies of screen-reader users, providing valuable insights for designing more accessible digital products (Borodin et al., 2010).

d. Emerging Interaction Modalities

The rise of new interaction modalities, such as voice user interfaces (VUIs) and augmented reality (AR), represents another significant trend in UX design. VUIs, exemplified by virtual assistants like Amazon's Alexa and Google Assistant, offer hands-free, natural interaction methods, making technology more accessible and convenient. Meanwhile, AR technologies blend digital content with the physical world, creating immersive experiences that can enhance learning, entertainment, and productivity.

Voice user interfaces (VUIs) are transforming how users interact with technology. These interfaces, exemplified by virtual assistants like Amazon's Alexa and Google Assistant, offer hands-free, natural interaction methods, making technology more accessible and convenient (Hoy, 2018). The accessibility and convenience of VUIs are highlighted in studies examining their use in everyday interactions (Porcheron et al., 2017).

AR technologies blend digital content with the physical world, creating immersive experiences that can enhance learning, entertainment, and productivity (Billinghurst, Clark, & Lee, 2015). The use of AR in educational settings demonstrates its potential to enhance learning experiences through immersive and interactive content (Wu, Lee, Chang, & Liang, 2013). The impact of VUIs and AR on UX design is significant, with these technologies introducing new dimensions of interaction and engagement (Klemmer, Hartmann, & Takayama, 2006).

Understanding user expectations and experiences with conversational agents provides insights into the natural interaction methods of VUIs, highlighting the gulf between user expectations and actual experiences (Luger & Sellen, 2016).

Additionally, foundational research on AR details its capabilities and potential to create immersive user experiences (Azuma, 1997).

e. Holistic UX Approaches

In addition to technological advancements and new interaction methods, there is a growing emphasis on adopting a holistic approach to UX design. This involves considering not only a product's functional and aesthetic aspects but also its emotional impact and ethical implications. Designers are increasingly mindful of how digital products affect users' emotions, mental health, and overall well-being, leading to the development of more compassionate and ethically sound design practices.

f. Challenges and Opportunities

Despite these advancements, the field of UX design faces several challenges. Integrating AI and ML raises ethical concerns about privacy, data security, and algorithmic bias. Ensuring inclusivity and accessibility requires ongoing commitment and adaptation to new standards. Additionally, implementing VUIs and AR technologies presents technical hurdles and usability issues that must be addressed.

However, these challenges also present opportunities for innovation. By leveraging AI and ML responsibly, embracing inclusive design principles, and exploring new interaction modalities, designers can create more engaging, equitable, and compelling user experiences. Furthermore, a holistic approach to UX design can foster user trust and loyalty by prioritizing emotional and ethical considerations.

g. Future Directions

As the field continues evolving, designers, researchers, and practitioners must stay informed about emerging trends and best practices. This research paper aims to provide a comprehensive overview of the current and emerging usability and UX design trends, offering insights into the challenges and opportunities that lie ahead. By doing so, it seeks to equip stakeholders with the knowledge and tools needed to navigate the future landscape of UX design, ultimately enhancing the quality and impact of digital products and services.

Understanding emerging trends and best practices is crucial for staying relevant in UX design. Hassenzahl and Tractinsky (2006) emphasize the need to stay informed about these developments in their research agenda for the field of user experience. A comprehensive overview of UX trends is provided by Vermeeren et al. (2010), who discuss current user experience evaluation methods and identify areas for development. The unique challenges and opportunities in designing user experiences for government systems are explored by Buie and Murray (2012), offering insights applicable to a broader context.

Equipping stakeholders with essential knowledge and tools is addressed by Garrett (2011), who provides a comprehensive guide to user-centered design. Enhancing the quality and impact of digital products is emphasized by Norman (2013), whose influential book discusses principles of design that improve usability and impact. Hartson and Pyla (2012) cover the process and guidelines for ensuring a quality user experience, highlighting the importance of staying informed about current trends and best practices.

Finally, the future landscape of UX design is clarified by Roto, Law, Vermeeren, and Hoonhout (2011) in their white paper, which provides insights into the future directions of the field. These references offer valuable insights into the future directions of usability and UX design, emphasizing the importance of staying informed and equipped to navigate emerging trends and challenges.

The discipline of Usability and User Experience (UX) design has evolved significantly, driven by technological advancements and an increased focus on user-centered design principles. This review explores recent case studies that highlight practical challenges and innovative solutions in UX design, providing a comprehensive overview of the benefits and drawbacks associated with emerging technologies. By examining real-world applications, we gain insights into how AI, machine learning, voice user interfaces (VUIs), and augmented reality (AR) are transforming user experiences across various platforms.

Case Studies on Practical Challenges and Solutions in UX Design

Spotify: Spotify faced the challenge of enhancing user engagement and retention in an increasingly competitive streaming market. The solution involved the implementation of personalized features such as "Discover Weekly" and "Release Radar," which utilize user listening patterns to create tailored playlists. Social features like "Collaborative Playlists" and "Spotify Wrapped" were also introduced to foster community and encourage sharing. As a result, Spotify saw increased user engagement and satisfaction by providing a personalized and socially engaging experience (Procreator, 2024).

Airbnb: Airbnb aimed to improve the check-in process for hosts and guests, recognizing the opportunity to make the exchange more seamless and consistent. The solution was a global check-in tool that allows hosts to create visual guides with photos and instructions, which can be translated into multiple languages and accessed both online and offline. This tool was continuously refined based on user feedback, ensuring it met the needs of hosts and guests. The outcome was a streamlined, user-friendly check-in process that significantly enhanced the overall guest experience (UX Design Institute, 2024).

Duolingo: Duolingo's challenge was maintaining user interest and engagement in language learning, which can often be repetitive and tedious. To address this, Duolingo integrated gamification elements such as streaks, leaderboards, and in-game currency to make learning more enjoyable and addictive. This strategy successfully retained users and kept them engaged by making language learning fun and rewarding (Procreator, 2024).

Google Meet: With the onset of the COVID-19 pandemic, Google Meet needed to rapidly adapt its business conferencing tool for educational use. The challenge was to meet the unique needs of teachers and students who had to shift to online learning. By gathering direct feedback from educators, Google Meet implemented features like attendance tracking, hand raising, breakout rooms, and polls. These updates quickly improved the user experience for virtual classrooms, making the platform more functional and interactive for educational purposes (UX Design Institute, 2024).

Benefits and Drawbacks of Emerging Technologies in UX

Artificial Intelligence (AI) and Machine Learning (ML)

Benefits:

- **Personalization**: AI and ML can analyze user data to create highly personalized experiences. For example, Spotify's recommendation algorithms enhance user engagement by providing tailored playlists (Procreator, 2024).
- **Efficiency**: These technologies automate repetitive tasks and offer predictive analytics, significantly enhancing user experience (Procreator, 2024).
- **Adaptability**: AI-driven interfaces can adapt in real-time to user preferences and behaviors, improving engagement and satisfaction (UX Design Institute, 2024).

Drawbacks:

- **Privacy Concerns**: The collection and analysis of user data raise significant privacy issues, necessitating robust data protection measures (UX Design Institute, 2024).
- **Algorithmic Bias**: AI systems can inadvertently perpetuate biases present in their training data, leading to unfair or discriminatory outcomes (Procreator, 2024).

- **Complexity**: Integrating AI into UX design requires substantial technical expertise, complicating the design process (Procreator, 2024).

Voice User Interfaces (VUIs)

Benefits:

- **Accessibility**: VUIs like Amazon's Alexa and Google Assistant make technology more accessible by providing hands-free, intuitive interaction methods (UX Design Institute, 2024).
- **Convenience**: They offer a natural and convenient way to interact with technology, which can enhance user satisfaction (Procreator, 2024).

Drawbacks:

- **Technical Challenges**: Implementing VUIs requires advanced technical infrastructure and expertise (UX Design Institute, 2024).
- **Usability Issues**: Voice interfaces can struggle with understanding diverse accents, dialects, and contexts, potentially frustrating users (Procreator, 2024).

Augmented Reality (AR)

Benefits:

- **Immersive Experiences**: AR technologies create engaging and immersive experiences that enhance learning, entertainment, and productivity by blending digital content with the physical world (Procreator, 2024).
- **Enhanced Learning**: In educational settings, AR can improve learning experiences through interactive content (UX Design Institute, 2024).

Drawbacks:

- **Safety Concerns**: AR raises safety issues, especially when digital overlays distract or mislead users in the physical world (Procreator, 2024).
- **Ethical Issues**: There are ethical concerns related to the manipulation of reality and the potential for misuse of AR technologies (UX Design Institute, 2024).

The Role of UX In Achieving Business Objectives

User Experience (UX) design is pivotal in achieving various business objectives, such as increased engagement, customer satisfaction, and revenue growth. By focusing on the user's needs and preferences, businesses can create more effective and enjoyable interactions, leading to numerous benefits.

Increased Engagement

- **Enhanced User Interaction**: Good UX design leads to higher user engagement by making interactions more intuitive and enjoyable. Simplified navigation, attractive visuals, and responsive interfaces encourage users to spend more time on a platform, increasing overall engagement.
- **Personalization**: Personalizing the user experience can significantly boost engagement. AI-driven personalization tailors content and recommendations to individual user preferences, making interactions more relevant and engaging (Yang & Evans, 2019).
- **Reducing Friction**: Identifying and eliminating pain points in the user journey can prevent frustration and drop-offs. This involves streamlining processes, such as simplifying sign-ups or checkouts, which can keep users engaged and more likely to complete desired actions.
- **Gamification**: Incorporating gamification elements like rewards, badges, and leaderboards can increase user engagement by making interactions more fun and motivating users to continue interacting with the product (Zichermann & Cunningham, 2011).
- **Seamless Onboarding**: A well-designed onboarding process helps users understand how to use a product quickly and effectively, which can lead to higher engagement and retention rates.

Revenue Growth

- **Conversion Rate Optimization**: Effective UX design can directly impact conversion rates. By optimizing the design of landing pages, forms, and calls to action, businesses can increase the likelihood that users will complete transactions, leading to higher revenue (Nielsen, 1993).
- **Customer Retention**: Positive user experiences foster customer loyalty. Satisfied customers are more likely to return and make repeat purchases, contributing to long-term revenue growth. Retention strategies include providing excellent support, consistent experiences across touchpoints, and regular updates based on user feedback (Reichheld, 2003).
- **Reducing Costs**: Investing in UX design can reduce costs associated with customer support and returns. By designing intuitive interfaces and clear information architecture, businesses can minimize user errors and the need for support, leading to cost savings.
- **Increased Average Order Value**: A seamless and pleasant shopping experience can encourage users to spend more per transaction. UX design elements such as personalized recommendations and an easy-to-navigate checkout process can boost the average order value.

- **Cross-Selling and Upselling**: Well-designed interfaces can effectively promote cross-selling and upselling opportunities by recommending complementary products or services during the user journey.

Building Brand Loyalty

- **Creating Positive Emotions**: UX design that evokes positive emotions can strengthen brand loyalty. Emotional design focuses on creating pleasurable experiences that resonate with users on a deeper level, leading to stronger emotional connections with the brand (Norman, 2004).
- **Consistency Across Channels**: Providing a consistent user experience across different platforms (web, mobile, etc.) ensures that users have a seamless experience, reinforcing brand trust and loyalty.
- **Usability and Accessibility**: Ensuring that products are usable and accessible to a wide audience can expand market reach and foster inclusivity. Adhering to accessibility standards, such as the Web Content Accessibility Guidelines (WCAG), can enhance the brand's reputation and legal compliance (W3C, 2018).
- **Customer Feedback Integration**: Continuously integrating customer feedback into the design process ensures that the product evolves based on user needs and preferences, fostering loyalty and satisfaction.
- **Community Building**: UX design can support the creation of user communities where customers can share experiences, tips, and support, enhancing loyalty and creating brand advocates.

Enhancing Customer Satisfaction

- **Intuitive Design**: An intuitive design reduces the learning curve for users, making it easier for them to achieve their goals quickly and efficiently. This leads to higher customer satisfaction (Nielsen, 1993).
- **Speed and Performance**: Fast-loading pages and responsive designs improve user satisfaction by reducing waiting times and ensuring smooth interactions.
- **Support and Assistance**: Integrating helpful features such as chatbots, comprehensive FAQs, and user tutorials can enhance the overall user experience, leading to increased satisfaction.
- **Error Prevention and Recovery**: Designing systems that prevent errors or provide clear instructions for recovery can reduce user frustration and increase satisfaction.

PURPOSE AND SIGNIFICANCE OF THE CHAPTER

The significance of this chapter lies in its ability to provide a forward-looking perspective on the field of usability and UX design. By examining the latest trends and their implications, the chapter offers valuable insights that can help stakeholders in several key ways:

- **Stay Informed:** Keeping abreast of technological advancements and emerging trends ensures that designers and researchers are well-prepared to tackle the challenges and leverage the opportunities presented by the evolving digital landscape.
- **Enhance User Experience:** Understanding how to integrate AI, ML, VUIs, AR, and inclusive design principles can lead to the creation of more personalized, accessible, and engaging user experiences.
- **Promote Innovation:** By identifying the challenges and opportunities in the field, this chapter encourages innovative thinking and the development of new methodologies and practices that can enhance the effectiveness of UX design.
- **Address Ethical Considerations:** Emphasizing the importance of emotional and ethical considerations in UX design highlights the need to create digital products that meet functional requirements and contribute positively to users' well-being and society at large.

In summary, this chapter is significant because it comprehensively analyzes emerging usability and UX design trends, offering a roadmap for future research and practice in the field. By doing so, it aims to contribute to the evolution of UX design, ensuring that digital products meet users' needs and expectations in an increasingly complex digital world.

IDENTIFICATION OF RESEARCH GAPS

Usability and UX design continually evolve alongside technological advancements, shifting user expectations, and the increasing complexity of digital environments. While current research explores several emerging trends shaping the future of UX design—including AI and ML integration, inclusive design, VUIs, AR, and holistic UX approaches—there are notable gaps that require further investigation:

The ethical implications of AI and ML technologies, which increasingly drive personalized user experiences, present a significant research gap. It is essential to explore how to mitigate biases, ensure transparency in algorithmic decisions, and uphold user privacy and data security (Cowls et al., 2019; Jobin et al., 2019). Additionally, while there is growing recognition of the importance of inclusive design principles, empirical studies are needed to assess their effectiveness across diverse user groups, including individuals with disabilities. Research is required to measure the impact of inclusive design on user satisfaction, accessibility compliance, and usability outcomes (Lazar, Feng, & Hochheiser, 2017; Persson et al., 2015).

The adoption and user experience of emerging modalities like VUIs and AR are ripe areas for exploration. Studies should investigate user acceptance factors, usability challenges, and effective design strategies to optimize interaction and enhance user engagement (Billinghurst, Clark, & Lee, 2015; Porcheron, Fischer, Reeves, & Sharples, 2018). Moreover, with the shift towards holistic UX design that considers emotional and ethical dimensions, there is a gap in developing comprehensive metrics and evaluation methods. Research is needed to establish frameworks for assessing emotional engagement, ethical implications, and overall user well-being in digital product design (Hassenzahl & Tractinsky, 2006; Desmet & Hekkert, 2007).

Educating future UX designers and practitioners to effectively integrate emerging technologies into design practices is crucial. Research gaps include identifying curriculum development strategies, requisite skill sets, and educational approaches to prepare professionals for evolving digital landscapes (Hartson & Pyla, 2012; Vermeeren et al., 2010). Furthermore, while short-term usability studies are common, longitudinal research is needed to understand how UX evolves over time and influences user loyalty and satisfaction. There are gaps in exploring the long-term impact of design decisions, iterative improvements, and the sustainability of digital products (Kujala et al., 2011; Law & Van Schaik, 2010).

Addressing these research gaps will advance the field by providing empirical evidence, theoretical frameworks, and practical guidelines to enhance the usability and user experience of digital products. By bridging these gaps, researchers and practitioners can contribute to creating more inclusive, ethical, and impactful digital experiences that meet the diverse needs of users in a rapidly evolving technological landscape.

METHODOLOGY

Figure 2. Overview of methodological approaches in UX design research

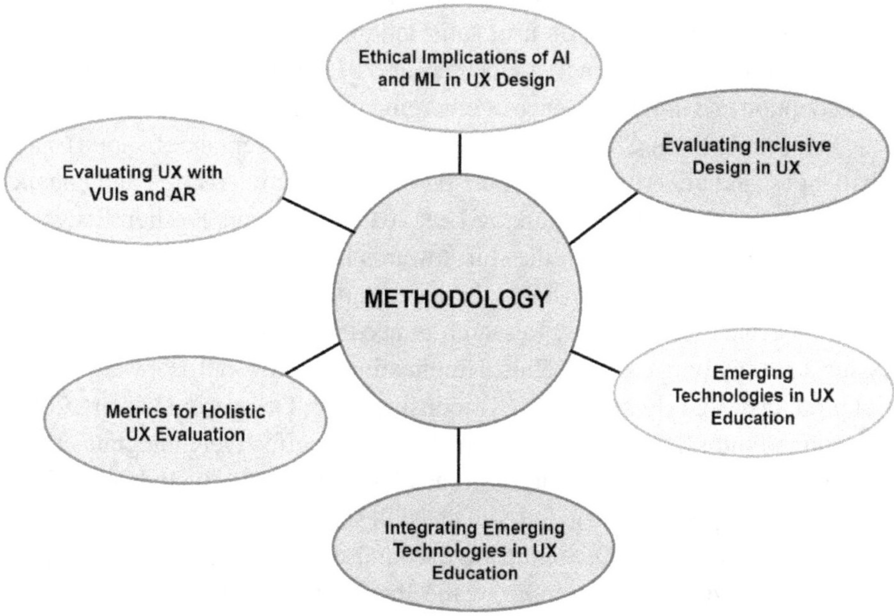

Ethical Implications of AI and ML in Usability and UX Design

Researching the ethical implications of AI and ML in the context of Usability and User Experience (UX) Design requires a robust methodology that integrates ethical theory, empirical investigation, and practical application. Here's a structured approach to conducting such research:

a. Literature Review and Theoretical Framework

The objective is to establish a theoretical foundation and understanding of ethical theories relevant to AI and ML in UX design. This involves conducting a comprehensive literature review focusing on ethics in AI and ML, human-computer interaction (HCI), and UX design. Key ethical principles such as fairness, transparency, accountability, privacy, and autonomy should be identified (Jobin, Ienca, &

Vayena, 2019). The output is a synthesized framework of ethical principles relevant to AI and ML applications in UX design.

b. Qualitative Research: Stakeholder Interviews and Expert Opinions

The objective here is to gather insights and perspectives from stakeholders involved in AI and ML UX design. Semi-structured interviews with UX designers, AI developers, ethicists, and end-users should be conducted to explore their views on ethical challenges, decision-making processes, and perceptions of AI-driven UX experiences. The result is rich qualitative data providing nuanced perspectives on ethical dilemmas and considerations in AI and ML implementations (Bryman, 2016).

c. Quantitative Research: Surveys and Experimental Studies

The goal is to quantitatively assess user perceptions, attitudes, and behaviors towards AI-driven UX designs. Surveys should be designed and administered to a diverse sample of users to gauge their comfort level with AI recommendations, trust in AI decision-making, and concerns about data privacy and security. The output is a statistical analysis of survey data to identify trends, correlations, and factors influencing user acceptance and ethical concerns related to AI and ML in UX design (Robson, 2016).

d. Case Studies and Ethical Design Evaluations

The objective is to evaluate existing AI-driven UX designs from an ethical standpoint. Case studies of digital products incorporating AI and ML features should be selected, and ethical evaluation frameworks, such as the Ethical Matrix or Ethical Impact Assessment, applied to analyze design decisions, user interactions, and outcomes. This results in ethical assessments highlighting strengths, weaknesses, and recommendations for improving ethical practices in AI and ML-driven UX design (Van Wynsberghe & Robbins, 2019).

e. Prototype Testing and Iterative Design

The aim is to integrate ethical considerations into the iterative design process of AI and ML UX solutions. Prototypes of AI-driven UX designs that incorporate ethical design principles should be developed, and usability testing sessions conducted with users to observe interactions, gather feedback, and refine designs iteratively. The output is iterative improvements informed by user feedback and ethical evaluations, demonstrating the practical application of ethical principles in UX design (Nielsen, 1993).

f. Cross-disciplinary Collaboration and Ethical Guidelines Development

The objective is to foster collaboration between UX designers, AI researchers, ethicists, and policymakers to develop ethical guidelines for AI and ML in UX design. Workshops, focus groups, and collaborative sessions should be organized to discuss ethical frameworks, principles, and best practices. Engaging stakeholders in co-creating guidelines that balance technological innovation with ethical considerations is crucial. The result is ethical guidelines and recommendations tailored to AI and ML applications in UX design, facilitating responsible innovation and practice (Bryson, Diamantis, & Grant, 2017).

By employing these research methods, researchers can systematically investigate the ethical implications of AI and ML in UX design, contributing to the development of ethical guidelines and frameworks that promote responsible and user-centric design practices in an increasingly AI-driven world.

Methods for Evaluating the Effectiveness of Inclusive Design in Usability and User Experience (UX) Design

Evaluating the effectiveness of inclusive UX design involves combining qualitative and quantitative methods. Here are some robust techniques, along with references to support each:

a) User Testing with Diverse Participants

Conducting usability testing with a diverse group of users, including those with disabilities, different ages, cultural backgrounds, and varying levels of tech-savviness, can provide insights into how inclusive a design is. The procedure involves recruiting participants representing a wide range of demographics and abilities, asking them to complete key tasks while observing and recording their interactions, difficulties, and feedback. Tools such as screen recording software, eye-tracking devices, and think-aloud protocols are utilized (Henry, Abou-Zahra, & Brewer, 2014).

b) Surveys and Questionnaires

Surveys and questionnaires can be used to gather feedback from a larger audience about their experiences with a design. Inclusive design-specific questions can uncover areas where the design succeeds or fails to meet diverse needs. The procedure involves designing surveys with both closed and open-ended questions that target various aspects of inclusivity and accessibility. Tools like online survey platforms such as SurveyMonkey and Google Forms are employed (Lazar, Feng, & Hochheiser, 2017).

c) Accessibility Audits

An accessibility audit is a systematic evaluation of how well a design adheres to established accessibility guidelines, such as WCAG (Web Content Accessibility Guidelines). The procedure includes using automated tools and manual checks to evaluate compliance with accessibility standards. Tools like Axe, WAVE, and manual testing techniques are used (Hackett & Parmanto, 2005).

d) Heuristic Evaluation

Expert reviewers use heuristics (rules of thumb) to evaluate the inclusiveness of a design. This method identifies potential usability problems from an inclusivity perspective. The procedure involves experts using a set of inclusive design heuristics to assess the interface, documenting any issues. Heuristic checklists tailored for inclusive design are the primary tools used (Nielsen, 1994).

e) Cognitive Walkthroughs

A cognitive walkthrough involves experts evaluating the usability of a design by going through tasks step-by-step, considering the user's thought process and potential challenges faced by diverse users. The procedure involves experts simulating the user's experience and identifying points where diverse users might struggle. Tools such as task analysis templates and cognitive walkthrough guidelines are utilized (Polson et al., 1992).

By employing a combination of these methods, designers and researchers can comprehensively evaluate and improve the inclusiveness of their designs, ensuring they meet the needs of all users.

f) A/B Testing

A/B testing can compare different design versions to see which performs better in inclusivity and usability for diverse user groups. Creating two versions with different inclusive design features and measuring user performance and satisfaction can provide actionable insights (Kohavi et al., 2009).

g) Ethnographic Studies

Ethnographic research involves observing and interviewing users in their natural environment to understand how they interact with the design in real-world contexts. Spending time with users in their daily environments, observing their interactions with the design, and conducting in-depth interviews can reveal important usability information (Blomberg et al., 2003).

h) Usability Metrics Analysis

Analyzing usability metrics such as task completion time, error rates, and user satisfaction can quantitatively assess the effectiveness of inclusive design. Collecting and analyzing data on key usability metrics from diverse user groups using analytics tools and user testing platforms like UserTesting and Lookback provides a comprehensive understanding of inclusivity (Tullis & Albert, 2013).

By employing a combination of these methods, designers and researchers can comprehensively evaluate and improve the inclusiveness of their designs, ensuring they meet the needs of all users.

Methods for Evaluating User Experience with Voice User Interfaces (VUIs) and Augmented Reality (AR) in Usability and User Experience (UX) Design

Evaluating the user experience (UX) of Voice User Interfaces (VUIs) and Augmented Reality (AR) involves specialized methods tailored to the unique characteristics of these technologies. Below are some robust techniques, along with references to support each:

a) Contextual Inquiry

Contextual inquiry involves observing and interviewing users in their natural environment while interacting with VUIs or AR applications. This method helps uncover real-world usability issues and understand the context of use. Conduct sessions where users interact with the VUI or AR system daily. Observe their interactions and ask questions to understand their experience, using audio and video recording equipment and field notes (Beyer & Holtzblatt, 1998).

b) Wizard of Oz Testing

Wizard of Oz testing helps evaluate VUIs and AR prototypes that are not fully functional. A human operator simulates the system's responses, allowing users to interact with a "working" interface. Users interact with the VUI or AR system, unaware that a human is generating the responses. Observe and record their interactions and gather feedback using manual input devices and recording equipment (Dahlbäck, et al., 1993).

c) Task Analysis

Task analysis involves breaking down users' tasks with VUIs or AR systems into smaller components to identify potential usability issues and cognitive load. Decompose tasks into steps and analyze the actions, decisions, and possible errors at each step using task analysis diagrams and cognitive walkthroughs (Hackos & Redish, 1998).

d) Heuristic Evaluation for VUIs and AR

Conduct heuristic evaluations using specialized heuristics for VUIs and AR. Experts review the VUI or AR system using a set of heuristics tailored for voice interaction or augmented reality and document any usability issues found using heuristic checklists for VUIs and AR (Nielsen & Molich, 1990).

e) Usability Testing with Think-Aloud Protocol

Usability testing combined with the think-aloud protocol helps understand users' thought processes as they interact with VUIs or AR systems. Users perform tasks while verbalizing their thoughts and actions. Record and analyze their comments and behaviors using screen recording software and audio recording equipment (Ericsson & Simon, 1993).

f) Eye-Tracking Studies

Eye-tracking can evaluate how users interact with AR systems, providing insights into visual attention and interaction patterns. Equip users with eye-tracking devices and have them interact with the AR system. Analyze gaze patterns, fixations, and saccades using eye-tracking hardware and software (Poole & Ball, 2006).

g) Speech and Interaction Logging

For VUIs, logging interactions and speech data can help analyze how users interact with the system, identify common errors, and improve the dialogue design. Collect and analyze logs of user interactions with the VUI, including speech input, system responses, and errors, using logging software and speech analysis tools (Yang & Lee, 2018).

h) A/B Testing for VUIs and AR

A/B testing can compare different versions of VUIs or AR interfaces to determine which performs better regarding user satisfaction and task success. Create two or more versions of the VUI or AR interface. Randomly assign users to each version and measure performance metrics and satisfaction using A/B testing platforms and analytics tools (Kohavi et al., 2009).

By employing these methods, researchers and designers can effectively evaluate and enhance the user experience of VUIs and AR systems, ensuring they meet the needs and expectations of users.

Methods for Metrics for Holistic UX Evaluation in Usability and User Experience (UX) Design

Holistic UX evaluation requires a comprehensive set of metrics capturing various aspects of user experience. Below are some methods, along with references for further reading:

a) Task Success Rate

The task success rate measures the percentage of tasks users can complete successfully. This metric is fundamental to understanding usability and effectiveness. Define critical functions for the interface. Record the number of tasks completed successfully versus attempted during usability testing using usability testing software and spreadsheets for analysis (Tullis & Albert, 2013).

b) Task Completion Time

Task completion time tracks how long it takes users to complete a task. This metric helps identify efficiency issues. Time users complete predefined tasks during usability testing sessions using a timer and usability testing software (Nielsen, 2001).

c) Error Rate

The error rate quantifies the frequency of user errors during task completion. This metric highlights usability problems and areas for improvement. Record the number and type of errors users make while completing tasks using usability testing software and error tracking logs (Sauro & Lewis, 2016).

d) System Usability Scale (SUS)

The System Usability Scale is a widely used questionnaire that quickly measures overall usability. Administer the SUS questionnaire to users after interacting with the system, using a SUS questionnaire template and a spreadsheet for calculating SUS scores (Brooke, 1996).

e) Net Promoter Score (NPS)

The Net Promoter Score measures user loyalty by asking how likely users are to recommend the product to others. After using the product, ask users to rate their likelihood of recommending it on a scale from 0 to 10 using survey software and NPS calculation tools (Reichheld, 2003).

f) Customer Satisfaction (CSAT)

Customer Satisfaction scores measure users' satisfaction with their experience using the product. Administer a satisfaction survey after users complete tasks, asking them to rate their overall satisfaction using survey software (Fornell et al.,1996).

g) User Engagement Metrics

User engagement metrics, such as time on site, page views, and interaction frequency, provide insights into how users interact with the product. Analytics tools like Google Analytics, Mixpanel, and Hotjar are used to track user interactions and behavior over time (O'Brien & Toms, 2010).

h) Emotional Response Metrics

Emotional response metrics assess how users feel while interacting with the product, capturing aspects of user experience related to satisfaction, frustration, and delight. Use emotion detection software or self-report surveys to capture users' emotional responses during interactions, using facial recognition software, sentiment analysis tools, and emotion-focused surveys (Desmet & Hekkert, 2007).

i) Heatmaps and Clickmaps

Heatmaps and clickmaps visualize where users click, tap, and scroll on a webpage or interface, providing insights into usability and user behavior. Use heatmap tools to record and analyze user interactions with the interface, using tools like Hotjar and Crazy Egg (Poole & Ball, 2006).

j) Eye-Tracking Metrics

Eye-tracking studies provide data on where users look, how long they look at specific areas, and their visual scanning patterns. Equip users with eye-tracking devices and analyze their gaze patterns while interacting with the product, using eye-tracking hardware and software (Jacob & Karn, 2003).

By using these methods and metrics, UX designers and researchers can gain a holistic understanding of the user experience, identifying strengths and improvement areas to create more user-friendly products.

Methods for Integration of Emerging Technologies in UX Education in Usability and User Experience (UX) Design

Integrating emerging technologies into UX education can prepare students for the evolving landscape of UX design. Below are some methods and references to support incorporating these technologies into UX education.

a) Hands-on projects with Real-world Applications

Incorporate hands-on projects that involve real-world applications of emerging technologies such as virtual reality (VR), augmented reality (AR), and artificial intelligence (AI). Develop project-based coursework where students design and prototype solutions using emerging technologies. This can involve collaborative projects with industry partners to solve real-world problems using VR/AR development platforms (Unity, Unreal Engine) and AI tools (TensorFlow, IBM Watson) (Kolko, 2012).

b) Industry Partnerships and Guest Lectures

Establish partnerships with technology companies and invite industry experts to give guest lectures or conduct workshops on emerging technologies and their applications in UX. Create a network of industry partners to provide guest lectures, mentorship, and internships. Organize workshops and seminars on the latest technological advancements using webinar platforms and collaboration tools like Slack or Microsoft Teams (McKenna, Kellam, & Carroll, 2011).

c) Simulation-Based Learning

Simulation-based learning allows students to experience and interact with emerging technologies in a controlled educational setting. Implement simulators and virtual labs where students can experiment with VR, AR, and IoT (Internet of Things) in a safe environment, using VR headsets, AR kits, and simulation software (De Jong, Linn, & Zacharia, 2013).

d) Interdisciplinary Collaboration

Promote interdisciplinary collaboration between UX students and students from other fields, such as computer science, engineering, and business, to work on projects involving emerging technologies. Create interdisciplinary teams to work on capstone projects or hackathons that require the integration of UX principles with technical skills using project management tools (Trello, Asana) and collaboration platforms (GitHub) (GitHub) (Resnick & Silverman, 2005).

e) Incorporation of AI and Machine Learning in Curriculum

Integrate courses and modules that focus on AI and machine learning, specifically their application in UX design for creating intelligent and adaptive user interfaces. Develop coursework that includes programming, data analysis, and machine learning algorithms to enhance user experiences using Python, Jupyter Notebooks, and AI frameworks like TensorFlow (Domingos, 2015) .

f) Prototyping with Emerging Technologies

Encourage students to use prototyping tools that support emerging technologies to create high-fidelity prototypes of their designs. Include assignments that require advanced prototyping tools to develop interactive prototypes incorporating VR, AR, or voice interfaces using Figma, Adobe XD, and Sketch with AR/VR plugins (Rittel & Webber, 1973).

g) UX Research with Emerging Technologies

Teach students to conduct UX research using emerging technologies, such as eye-tracking for VR applications or biometric sensors for emotional response analysis. Develop research projects where students can apply advanced UX research methods using emerging technologies, eye-tracking devices, biometric sensors, and UX research software (Poole & Ball, 2006).

h) Case Studies and Analysis of Emerging Tech

Incorporate case studies highlighting successful and unsuccessful implementations of emerging technologies in UX design. Assign readings and discussions on case studies involving emerging technologies in various industries. Encourage critical analysis and reflection using case study repositories and academic journals (Yin, 2018).

By incorporating these methods into UX education, students can gain hands-on experience with emerging technologies, preparing them to innovate and excel in the rapidly evolving field of UX design.

Integrating Emerging Technologies in UX Education

To effectively integrate emerging technologies into UX education, several robust methods can be employed to prepare students for the evolving landscape of UX design:

a) Hands-on projects with Real-World Applications

Engage students in project-based coursework involving technologies like VR, AR, and AI. These projects often involve collaboration with industry partners, providing real-world problem-solving experience.

b) Industry Partnerships and Guest Lectures

Establish partnerships with tech companies and invite industry experts for guest lectures and workshops. This helps bridge the gap between academic learning and industry practices.

c) Simulation-Based Learning

Use simulations and virtual labs to allow students to interact with emerging technologies in a controlled setting. This provides practical experience without real-world consequences.

d) Interdisciplinary Collaboration

Promote teamwork between UX students and those from computer science and engineering fields. This fosters a multidisciplinary approach to solving complex design problems.

e) Incorporation of AI and Machine Learning in Curriculum

Include AI and machine learning in the coursework, teaching students how to create intelligent and adaptive user interfaces. Practical exercises using AI frameworks are essential.

f) Prototyping with Emerging Technologies

Encourage using advanced prototyping tools to develop interactive prototypes incorporating emerging technologies such as VR, AR, and voice interfaces.

g) UX Research with Emerging Technologies

Teach students to research UX using tools like eye-tracking for VR applications and biometric sensors for emotional response analysis. This provides a deep understanding of user interactions.

h) Case Studies and Analysis of Emerging Tech

Incorporate case studies of successful and unsuccessful implementations of emerging technologies in UX. Analyzing these cases helps students learn valuable lessons and apply them in their designs.

Ethical Considerations and Potential Biases in AI

Artificial Intelligence (AI) and Machine Learning (ML) technologies are integral to UX design, offering capabilities for creating personalized and adaptive user experiences. However, their deployment brings several ethical considerations and potential biases that must be addressed to ensure fairness, transparency, and trust.

Ethical Considerations in AI

a) **Data Privacy and Security**:Protecting user data is crucial. AI systems often require vast amounts of data, including sensitive personal information. Ensuring robust data privacy and security measures is essential to prevent unauthorized access and breaches (Floridi & Taddeo, 2016).
b) **Transparency and Explainability**: AI systems can operate as "black boxes," where the decision-making process is not transparent. Providing clear explanations of AI decisions helps users trust the system (Van Wynsberghe & Robbins, 2019).
c) **Accountability**: Defining responsibility for AI decisions is essential. Clear accountability mechanisms address any negative consequences resulting from AI decisions (Bryson, Diamantis, & Grant, 2017).
d) **Fairness and Non-Discrimination**: AI systems can perpetuate existing biases in data, leading to unfair treatment. Ensuring fairness involves identifying and mitigating biases in training data and algorithms (Noble, 2018).

Potential Biases in AI

a) **Data Bias**: AI models replicate biases in the training data. For example, recruitment AI may favor certain backgrounds, perpetuating inequalities. Using diverse and representative datasets is crucial (O'Neil, 2016).
b) **Algorithmic Bias**: Algorithms can introduce bias through their design or feature selection. Regular audits and bias testing help identify and correct these biases (Bolukbasi et al., 2016).
c) **Interaction Bias**: User interactions with AI systems can introduce bias. For instance, voice recognition systems may perform better for certain accents if not trained on diverse speech patterns (Hoy, 2018).
d) **Societal Bias**: AI systems reflect societal norms and biases, potentially reinforcing stereotypes. Designers and developers must consider the broader societal impact of their AI systems (Eubanks, 2018).

Mitigating Biases and Ensuring Ethical AI

a) **Inclusive Design Practices**: Incorporate inclusive design principles to ensure AI systems are accessible and fair to all user groups (W3C, 2018).
b) **Ethical Frameworks and Guidelines**: Adopting frameworks and guidelines, such as those from the European Union, helps align AI development with ethical principles (European Commission, 2019).
c) **Regular Audits and Monitoring**: Implementing regular audits and continuous monitoring helps identify and mitigate biases early (Raji & Buolamwini, 2019).

d) **User Empowerment and Education**: Empowering users with control over their data and educating them about AI systems enhances transparency and trust (Mittelstadt et al., 2016).
e) **Interdisciplinary Collaboration**: Collaborating with ethicists, sociologists, and other experts ensures AI systems are designed with a comprehensive understanding of their potential impacts (Cowls et al., 2019).

By adopting these methods, UX education can effectively incorporate emerging technologies, equipping students with the skills and knowledge needed to innovate and excel in the rapidly changing field of UX design.

CONCLUSION

The landscape of usability and user experience (UX) design is rapidly evolving, driven by technological advancements and shifting user expectations. This research has highlighted several critical trends shaping the future of UX design, emphasizing the need for continuous adaptation and innovation in design practices. Integrating artificial intelligence (AI) and machine learning (ML) enables the creation of more personalized and adaptive user experiences. At the same time, the growing focus on inclusive and accessible design ensures that digital products cater to a diverse range of users, including those with disabilities.

Voice user interfaces (VUIs) and augmented reality (AR) are emerging as transformative technologies, offering more natural and immersive ways for users to interact with digital products. These technologies not only enhance user satisfaction but also promise to redefine user interactions in significant ways. The shift towards a holistic approach to UX design, which considers emotional and ethical dimensions, reflects a deeper understanding of the intricate relationship between users and technology. This approach ensures that designs are functional, resonate emotionally with users, and adhere to ethical standards.

While these trends present exciting opportunities for innovation, they also come with challenges. The ethical implications of AI, the technical complexities of implementing AR, and ensuring accessibility for all users require careful consideration and proactive solutions. As designers, researchers, and practitioners navigate these trends, they must remain vigilant and adaptable, continuously updating their skills and knowledge to meet evolving user needs and expectations.

In conclusion, the future of usability and UX design is promising and demanding. By staying informed about emerging trends and their implications, designers can create products that meet and exceed user expectations, ultimately contributing to more intuitive, engaging, and emotionally resonant user experiences. This paper has provided insights into the current and future trends in UX design, offering a roadmap for those looking to innovate and excel in this dynamic field.

REFERENCES

Adomavicius, G., & Tuzhilin, A. (2005). Toward the Next Generation of Recommender Systems: A Survey of the State-of-the-Art and Possible Extensions. *IEEE Transactions on Knowledge and Data Engineering*, 17(6), 734–749. DOI: 10.1109/TKDE.2005.99

Azuma, R. T. (1997). A Survey of Augmented Reality. *Presence (Cambridge, Mass.)*, 6(4), 355–385. DOI: 10.1162/pres.1997.6.4.355

Beyer, H., & Holtzblatt, K. (1998). *Contextual Design: Defining Customer-Centered Systems*. Morgan Kaufmann.

Billinghurst, M., Clark, A., & Lee, G. (2015). *A Survey of Augmented Reality. Foundations and Trends® in Human*–Computer. *Interaction*, 8(2-3), 73–272.

Blomberg, J., Burrell, M., & Guest, G. (2003). An ethnographic approach to design. *Handbook of Human-Computer Interaction, 964-986.*

Borodin, Y., Bigham, J. P., Dausch, G., & Ramakrishnan, I. V. (2010). *More than Meets the Eye: A Survey of Screen-Reader Browsing Strategies.Proceedings of the 2010 International Cross-Disciplinary Conference on Web Accessibility (W4A), 1-10.* DOI: 10.1145/1805986.1806005

Brooke, J. (1996). *SUS: A quick and dirty usability scale. In P. W. Jordan, B. Thomas, B. A. Weerdmeester, & I. L. McClelland (Eds.), Usability Evaluation in Industry (pp. 189-194). CRC Press.*

Bryman, A. (2016). *Social Research Methods* (5th ed.). Oxford University Press.

Bryson, J. J., Diamantis, M. E., & Grant, T. D. (2017). Of, for, and by the People: The Legal Lacuna *of Synthetic Persons.Artificial Intelligence and Law*, 25(3), 273–291. DOI: 10.1007/s10506-017-9214-9

Buie, E., & Murray, D. (Eds.). (2012). *Usability in Government Systems: User Experience Design for Citizens and Public Servants*. Morgan Kaufmann.

Dahlbäck, N., Jönsson, A., & Ahrenberg, L. (1993). Wizard of Oz studies: Why and how. *Knowledge-Based Systems*, 6(4), 258–266. DOI: 10.1016/0950-7051(93)90017-N

Davidson, J., Liebald, B., Liu, J., Nandy, P., Van Vleet, T., Gargi, U., & Sampath, D. (2010). The YouTube Video Recommendation System. *Proceedings of the Fourth ACM Conference on Recommender Systems,* 293-296. DOI: 10.1145/1864708.1864770

De Jong, T., Linn, M. C., & Zacharia, Z. C. (2013). Physical and virtual laboratories in science and engineering education. *Science*, 340(6130), 305–308. DOI: 10.1126/science.1230579 PMID: 23599479

Desmet, P., & Hekkert, P. (2007). Framework of product experience. *International Journal of Design*, 1(1), 57–66.

Desmet, P. M. A., & Hekkert, P. (2007). Framework of product experience. *International Journal of Design*, 1(1), 57–66.

Domingos, P. (2015). *The Master Algorithm: How the Quest for the Ultimate Learning Machine Will Remake Our World.* Basic Books.

Ericsson, K. A., & Simon, H. A. (1993). *Protocol Analysis: Verbal Reports as Data.* MIT Press. DOI: 10.7551/mitpress/5657.001.0001

Fornell, C., Johnson, M. D., Anderson, E. W., Cha, J., & Bryant, B. E. (1996). The American Customer Satisfaction Index: Nature, purpose, and findings. *Journal of Marketing*, 60(4), 7–18. DOI: 10.1177/002224299606000403

Hackett, S., & Parmanto, B. (2005). A longitudinal evaluation of accessibility: Higher education websites. *Internet Research*, 15(3), 281–294. DOI: 10.1108/10662240510602690

Hackos, J. T., & Redish, J. C. (1998). *User and Task Analysis for Interface Design.* Wiley.

Hartson, R., & Pyla, P. S. (2012). *The UX Book: Process and Guidelines for Ensuring a Quality User Experience*. Morgan Kaufmann.

Hartson, R., & Pyla, P. S. (2012). *The UX Book: Process and guidelines for ensuring a quality user experience*. Elsevier.

Hassenzahl, M., & Tractinsky, N. (2006). User Experience - A Research Agenda. *Behaviour & Information Technology*, 25(2), 91–97. DOI: 10.1080/01449290500330331

Henry, S. L., Abou-Zahra, S., & Brewer, J. (2014). *The role of accessibility in a universal web. Journal of Inclusive Design in the* Built *Environment, 1(1), 5-20.*

Hoy, M. B. (2018). Alexa, Siri, Cortana, and More: An Introduction to Voice Assistants. *Medical Reference Services Quarterly*, 37(1), 81–88. DOI: 10.1080/02763869.2018.1404391 PMID: 29327988

Jacob, R. J., & Karn, K. S. (2003). *Eye tracking in human-computer interaction and usability research: Ready to deliver the promises. In J. Hyona, R. Radach, & H. Deubel (Eds.), The Mind's Eye: Cognitive and Applied Aspects of Eye Movement Research (pp. 573-605). Elsevier Science.*

Jobin, A., Ienca, M., & Vayena, E. (2019). The global landscape of AI ethics guidelines. *Nature Machine Intelligence*, 1(9), 389–399. DOI: 10.1038/s42256-019-0088-2

Kelly, B., Sloan, D., Phipps, L., Petrie, H., & Hamilton, F. (2005). *Forcing Standardization or Accommodating Diversity? A Framework for Applying the WCAG in the Real World. Proceedings of the 2005 International Cross-Disciplinary Workshop on Web Accessibility (W4A), 46-54.*

Klemmer, S. R., Hartmann, B., & Takayama, L. (2006). How Bodies Matter: Five Themes for Interaction Design. *Proceedings of the 6th Conference on Designing Interactive Systems (DIS),* 140-149. DOI: 10.1145/1142405.1142429

Kohavi, R., Longbotham, R., Sommerfield, D., & Henne, R. M. (2009). Controlled experiments on the web: Survey and practical guide. *Data Mining and Knowledge Discovery*, 18(1), 140–181. DOI: 10.1007/s10618-008-0114-1

Kolko, J. (2012). Wicked Problems: Problems Worth Solving. *Interactions (New York, N.Y.)*, 19(5), 28–34.

Kujala, S., Roto, V., Väänänen-Vainio-Mattila, K., Karapanos, E., & Sinnelä, A. (2011). UX Curve: A method for evaluating long-term user experience. *Interacting with Computers*, 23(5), 473–483. DOI: 10.1016/j.intcom.2011.06.005

Law, E. L.-C., & Van Schaik, P. (2010). Modelling user experience–An agenda for research and practice. *Interacting with Computers*, 22(5), 313–322. DOI: 10.1016/j.intcom.2010.04.006

Lazar, J., Goldstein, D. F., & Taylor, A. (2015). *Ensuring Digital Accessibility through Process and Policy.* Morgan Kaufmann.

Lazar, J., Feng, J. H., & Hochheiser, H. (2017). *Research methods in human-computer interaction*. Morgan Kaufmann.

Luger, E., & Sellen, A. (2016). *"Like Having a Really Bad PA": The Gulf Between User Expectation and Experience of Conversational Agents. Proceedings of the 2016 CHI Conference on Human Factors in Computing Systems (CHI), 5286-5297.*

Mankoff, J., Fait, H., & Tran, T. (2005). Is Your Web Page Accessible? A Comparative Study of Methods for Assessing Web Page Accessibility for the Blind. *Proceedings of the SIGCHI Conference on Human Factors in Computing Systems,* 41-50. DOI: 10.1145/1054972.1054979

McInerney, J., & Smyth, B. (2020). Recommender Systems: A Deep Learning Perspective. *Journal of Artificial Intelligence Research*, 69, 1–53.

McKenna, A. F., Kellam, N. N., & Carroll, D. R. (2011). Assessing learning outcomes from the perspectives of designers. *International Journal of Engineering Education*, 27(3), 578–588.

Nielsen, J. (1993). *Usability Engineering*. Academic Press. DOI: 10.1016/B978-0-08-052029-2.50007-3

Nielsen, J. (1994). *Enhancing the explanatory power of usability heuristics. Proceedings of the SIGCHI Conference* on *Human Factors in Computing Systems, 152-158.*

Nielsen, J. (2001). *First Rule of Usability?* Don't Listen to Users. Jakob Nielsen's Alertbox. Nielsen Norman Group.

Nielsen, J., & Molich, R. (1990). Heuristic Evaluation of User Interfaces. *Proceedings of the SIGCHI Conference on Human Factors in Computing Systems,* 249-256.

Norman, D. A. (2004). *Emotional Design: Why We Love (or Hate) Everyday Things*. Basic Books.

Norman, D. A. (2013). *The Design of Everyday Things: Revised and Expanded Edition*. Basic Books.

Norman, D. A., & Draper, S. W. (Eds.). (1986). *User-Centered System Design: New Perspectives* on Human-Computer Interaction. Lawrence Erlbaum Associates.

O'Brien, H. L., & Toms, E. G. (2010). The development and evaluation of a survey to measure user engagement. *Journal of the American Society for Information Science and Technology*, 61(1), 50–69. DOI: 10.1002/asi.21229

Persson, H., Åhman, H., Yngling, A. A., & Gulliksen, J. (2015). Universal design, inclusive design, accessible design, design for all: Different concepts—one goal? On the concept of accessibility—historical, methodological and philosophical aspects. *Universal Access in the Information Society*, 14(4), 505–526. DOI: 10.1007/s10209-014-0358-z

Polson, P. G., Lewis, C., Rieman, J., & Wharton, C. (1992). Cognitive walkthroughs: A method for theory-based evaluation of user interfaces. *International Journal of Man-Machine Studies*, 36(5), 741–773. DOI: 10.1016/0020-7373(92)90039-N

Poole, A., & Ball, L. J. (2006). Eye tracking in HCI and usability research. *Encyclopedia of Human-Computer Interaction, 211-219.* DOI: 10.4018/978-1-59140-562-7.ch034

Porcheron, M., Fischer, J. E., & Sharples, S. (2017). *"Do Animals Have Accents?": Talking with* Agents *in Multi-Party Conversation.Proceedings of the 2017 ACM Conference on Computer Supported Cooperative Work and Social Computing (CSCW),207-219.*

Procreator. (2024). *5 remarkable UX design case studies (2024 insights). https://procreator.design*

Reichheld, F. F. (2003). The One Number You Need to Grow. *Harvard Business Review*, 81(12), 46–54. PMID: 14712543

Resnick, M., & Silverman, B. (2005). Some reflections on designing construction kits for kids. *Proceedings of the 2005 conference on Interaction design and children,* 117-122. DOI: 10.1145/1109540.1109556

Rittel, H. W., & Webber, M. M. (1973). Dilemmas in a general theory of planning. *Policy Sciences*, 4(2), 155–169. DOI: 10.1007/BF01405730

Robson, C. (2016). *Real World Research* (4th ed.). Wiley.

Roto, V., Law, E., Vermeeren, A., & Hoonhout, J. (Eds.). (2011). User Experience White Paper: *Bringing Clarity to the Concept of User Experience. Retrieved from-*https://www.allaboutux.org/uxwhitepaper

Sauro, J., & Lewis, J. R. (2016). *Quantifying the User Experience: Practical Statistics for User Research.* Morgan Kaufmann.

Schmutz, S., Sonderegger, A., & Sauer, J. (2016). Implementing Recommendations from Web Accessibility Guidelines: A Comparative Study of Web Designers' Perspectives. *International Journal of Human-Computer Studies*, 97, 160–168.

Tullis, T., & Albert, W. (2013). *Measuring the User Experience: Collecting, Analyzing, and Presenting Usability Metrics.* Morgan Kaufmann.

UX Design Institute. (2024). *Leveraging creative hacks: How the Airbnb community inspired a global check-in tool. Retrieved from*https://uxdesigninstitute.com

UX Design Institute. (2024). Adapting products to meet teachers' changing needs. Retrieved from *https://blog.google*

Van Wynsberghe, A., & Robbins, S. (2019). Ethical by Design: Ethics Best Practices for Natural Language Processing. *AI Ethics Journal*, 2(1), 1–12.

Vermeeren, A. P. O. S., Roto, V., Väänänen-Vainio-Mattila, K., Law, E. L.-C., Obrist, M., Hoonhout, J., & Kuutti, K. (2010). User Experience Evaluation Methods: Current State and Development Needs. *Proceedings of the 6th Nordic Conference on Human-Computer Interaction: Extending Boundaries (NordiCHI),* 521-530. DOI: 10.1145/1868914.1868973

Wu, H.-K., Lee, S. W.-Y., Chang, H.-Y., & Liang, J.-C. (2013). Current Status, Opportunities and Challenges of Augmented Reality in Education. *Computers & Education*, 62, 41–49. DOI: 10.1016/j.compedu.2012.10.024

Yang, H., & Lee, J. (2018). A study on interaction logging and analysis for conversational systems. *Journal of the Association for Information Science and Technology*, 69(2), 181–194.

Yang, Q., & Evans, A. C. (2019). AI and HCI: How AI Will Change the Way We Design and Use Interactive Systems. *Communications of the ACM*, 62(2), 66–73.

Yin, R. K. (2018). *Case Study Research and Applications: Design and Methods.* Sage Publications.

Zhang, M., Lu, Z., & Li, Y. (2017). Deep Learning-Based Recommender System: A Survey and New Perspectives. *ACM Computing Surveys*, 52(1), 1–38.

Zichermann, G., & Cunningham, C. (2011). *Gamification by Design: Implementing Game Mechanics in Web and Mobile Apps.* O'Reilly Media.

KEY TERMS AND DEFINITIONS

Accessibility: The design of products, devices, services, or environments for people who experience disabilities.

Algorithmic Bias: Systematic and repeatable errors in a computer system that create unfair outcomes, such as privileging one arbitrary group of users over others.

Artificial Intelligence (AI): The simulation of human intelligence processes by machines, especially computer systems, which includes learning, reasoning, and self-correction.

Augmented Reality (AR): An interactive experience where the objects in the real world are enhanced by computer-generated perceptual information, sometimes across multiple sensory modalities.

Data Privacy: The aspect of information technology that deals with the ability an organization or individual has to determine what data in a computer system can be shared with third parties.

Ethical Design: Design practices that take into consideration the impact of products and services on all stakeholders, including ethical implications such as privacy, fairness, and accessibility.

Heuristic Evaluation: A usability inspection method for finding usability problems in a user interface design by examining the interface and judging its compliance with recognized usability principles (the heuristics).

Inclusive Design: A design process that ensures products are accessible to, and usable by, as many people as reasonably possible without the need for adaptation or specialized design.

Machine Learning (ML): A subset of AI that involves the use of algorithms and statistical models to enable computers to improve their performance on tasks through experience.

Usability: The measure of how effectively, efficiently, and satisfactorily a user can interact with a digital product.

User Experience (UX): Encompasses all aspects of the end-user's interaction with the company, its services, and its products.

User-Centered Design (UCD): An iterative design process in which designers focus on the users and their needs in each phase of the design process.

Voice User Interface (VUI): Interfaces that allow users to interact with a system through voice or speech commands.

Chapter 6
Automatic and Enhanced Reflexive System for Concise Answer Evaluation Using BERT Model and Bi-LSTM

Jegatha Deborah L.
https://orcid.org/0000-0001-8069-3801
University College of Engineering, Villupuram, India

Rajkumar S. C.
https://orcid.org/0000-0002-4953-8835
Anna University, Madurai, India

K. Suganya
https://orcid.org/0009-0002-5266-4661
University College of Engineering, Villupuram, India

ABSTRACT

In intelligent tutoring systems (ITS), the automatic and enhanced reflexive system for concise answer evaluation (AERSCAE) components that evaluate students' responses to questions are crucial. However, applying deep learning to AERSCAE encounters difficulties due to the challenges of accurately scoring short answers and the scarcity of training data. Using bidirectional encoder representations from transformers (BERT)-based deep neural network, this system improves short-answer texts' understanding via capturing contextual nuances. A specialized semantic refinement layer, bidirectional long short-term memory (Bi-LSTM), is integrated into

DOI: 10.4018/979-8-3693-2337-3.ch006

the AERSCAE system to enhance its performance. Bi-LSTM's temporal dependencies and bidirectional processing enable the generation of high-precision scores. Integrating BERT and Bi-LSTM deep learning architectures into AERSCAE systems enhances their short-answer evaluation capability.

INTRODUCTION

Evaluating student performances is essential for teachers to assess students' cognitive understanding of learning objectives. Manual assessment is labor-intensive and time-consuming.

Background and Importance of AERSCAE

This section provides an overview of various AI models used in automated grading systems, including BERT and Bi-LSTM, highlighting their capabilities and significance in educational technology.BERT and Bi-LSTM are advanced tools that help computers understand human language better. Imagine having a really smart assistant who can read and understand essays just like a human teacher. For instance, BERT can read a student's answer to a history question and understand the context of the words used, just like how we understand the difference between "Washington" the city and "George Washington" the person. Automatic and Enhanced Reflexive System for Concise Answer Evaluation (AERSCAE) systems have emerged as promising solutions to address the increasing demand for personalized and efficient learning. These systems provide instantaneous feedback to students, alleviate teacher workload, and ensure consistency in grading. AERSCAE is a cornerstone of Intelligent Tutoring Systems (ITSs), which are computer-based instructional tools designed to deliver personalized and adaptive learning experiences akin to human tutors. Adaptive testing within ITSs tailors' educational pathways based on accurate assessments of students' cognitive levels. The integration of AERSCAE enhances the efficiency of evaluating student responses, which are often expressed in natural language, and supports various grading methods across assignments, homework, and tests. Understanding how students learn is crucial for designing effective automated grading systems. For instance, Mayer's (2014) work on multimedia learning highlights the importance of presenting information in ways that align with cognitive processing principles."

Overview of Current Challenges in AERSCAE, Especially With Short-Answer Evaluation

This section discusses the primary challenges associated with current AERSCAE systems, focusing on linguistic variability, computational demands, and ethical considerations.Despite significant advancements, AERSCAE systems still face several challenges. The variability in students' answers, including differences in sentence structure, language style, and length, poses significant hurdles for accurate grading. Hattie's (2009) meta-analyses of educational interventions provide a comprehensive view of the factors influencing student achievement, underscoring the need for AI-driven grading systems to complement rather than replace traditional pedagogical methods.

Summary

This section explains advanced AI models like BERT and Bi-LSTM. These models are designed to understand and process natural language, making them suitable for grading student responses in educational settings. BERT and Bi-LSTM can handle complex language structures, providing more accurate and context-aware grading compared to traditional methods. We will explore how these models work, their advantages, and their practical applications in education.

This chapter is organized as follows. First, it presents the background of AI-based automated grading systems, emphasizing existing methodologies and their limitations. Then, it provides a comprehensive literature review focusing on the use of BERT and Bi-LSTM models in intelligent tutoring systems and educational technologies. The chapter also discusses challenges and ethical considerations related to current grading models, particularly in short-answer evaluation. Following that, the proposed system model is introduced, detailing its architecture, including BERT encoding and Bi-LSTM processing. It then covers the implementation and performance evaluation of the proposed system, and a discussion of the results, comparing the model's performance with existing approaches. Finally, the chapter concludes with a summary of the findings and suggestions for future work.

LITERATURE REVIEW

The literature review focuses on existing approaches related to the proposed system, providing an overview of:

- A summary of existing approaches to AERSCAE

- A discussion of deep learning applications in text analysis
- Specific studies on BERT and Bi-LSTM in natural language processing
- Educational Psychology and Pedagogical Studies
- Usability and User Experience
- Interdisciplinary Studies

Summary of Existing Approaches to AERSCAE

Automatic Short-Answer Grading (AERSCAE) has been extensively explored using various methodologies aimed at enhancing the efficiency and accuracy of grading student responses in educational settings. Traditional approaches include text mining methods that analyze linguistic patterns and features extracted from student responses to classify and grade answers. These methods offer standardized approaches but often struggle with the complexity of language nuances.

Graph Convolutional Networks (GCNs), A type of AI model that can analyze data with a network-like structure, such as social networks or molecular structures, which treat each word or phrase in a student response as a node in a graph, utilizing convolutional operations to capture contextual relationships between nodes. While effective, GCNs require substantial computational resources and rely heavily on labeled data for training. Hybrid models combining Deep Neural Networks (DNNs) with Item Response Theory (IRT) leverage DNNs for feature extraction and IRT for modeling the relationship between student responses and grading criteria. These models excel in capturing semantic content and contextual information from short answers but come at the cost of increased computational complexity and reduced interpretability.

Table 1. Comparison of existing works

Author Name and Year	Techniques Used	Merits	Demerits
C. N. Tulu, M. Kaya, and M. Kocamanlar (2021)	SemSpace Algorithm, Word Sense Disambiguation (WSD), MaLSTM Model	Enhanced accuracy, Improved efficiency, Captures semantic similarity	Requires large amount of training data, Lack of generalizability and robustness
Masaki Uto and Yuto Uchida (2020)	Item-Response Theory (IRT) model, LSTM	Improved scoring accuracy, Automated feature extraction, Captures non-linear relations	Requires large amount of data, Complex implementation
H. Tan, C. Wang, Q. Duan, Y. Lu, and R. Li (2020)	Graph Convolutional Networks (GCNs)	Improved accuracy, Efficient grading	Complex implementation, Can be challenging to interpret

continued on following page

Table 1. Continued

Author Name and Year	Techniques Used	Merits	Demerits
N. Seuzen, A. N. Gorban, J. Levesley, and E. M. Mirkes (2020)	Text mining methods	Quick feedback, Objective evaluation of student responses	Complex implementation, May not capture deeper conceptual understanding
Jacob Devlin, et al. (2019)	BERT	Captures bidirectional context, Pre-trained on large-scale data	Requires large amount of computational resources
D. Alikanioti, H. Yannakoudakis, and M. Rei (2016)	LSTM, C&W embedding	Enhanced interpretability, Superior performance	Requires large and diverse datasets, Lack of context understanding

Educational Psychology and Pedagogical Studies

Mayer, R. E. (2014), Mayer's work on multimedia learning can provide insights into how students process information presented in different formats, which is relevant to the usability of automated grading systems that may handle text, audio, and video inputs. Hattie, J. (2009), Hattie's comprehensive analysis of educational interventions can help contextualize the effectiveness of AI-driven grading systems within the broader spectrum of factors influencing student achievement. Bransford, J. D., Brown, A. L., & Cocking, R. R. (2000), This foundational text provides insights into cognitive processes and learning environments, which can inform the design of user-friendly and effective automated grading systems.

Usability and User Experience

Nielsen, J. (1994). Usability Engineering. Morgan Kaufmann. Nielsen's principles of usability engineering can be applied to the design of AI-driven grading systems, ensuring that they are user-friendly for educators and students. Norman, D. A. (2013). Norman's insights into design and user experience can help frame the discussion on how to create intuitive and engaging interfaces for automated grading systems. Krug, S. (2014, Krug's practical advice on web usability can inform the development of interfaces for automated grading systems that are easy to navigate and understand.

Interdisciplinary Studies

Selwyn, N. (2016), examination of the intersection of education and technology provides a broader context for discussing the implementation and impact of AI in educational settings. Laurillard, D. (2012) has proposed a work, "Teaching as a Design Science: Building Pedagogical Patterns for Learning and Technology". This work on the integration of technology and pedagogy can help frame the discussion on the practical applications and benefits of automated grading systems in diverse educational contexts.

Case Studies on Data Scarcity and Computational Resources

The practical difficulties in deploying AERSCAE systems due to limited data and computational resources are emphasized by a number of case studies. The work by Kumar et al. (2021), which demonstrated efficient grading employing transfer learning approaches in a low-resource educational setting, is a noteworthy example. In a different study, Lee et al. (2023) addressed computational constraints by maximizing the efficiency of model structures, guaranteeing accessibility even in situations with limited resources. These case studies offer insightful information about getting past real-world obstacles in practical applications.

Limitations of Current Methodologies

GCNs: GCNs require significant computational resources and are challenging to scale for large datasets typical in educational settings. Their complexity can also hinder their implementation in real-world systems with limited computational capacity. The effectiveness of GCNs heavily relies on the quality of the constructed graph, which can be subjective and difficult to standardize across different educational contexts.

DNNs combined with IRT: While DNNs can capture complex patterns in data, they often function as black boxes, making it difficult to interpret their decision-making process. This lack of transparency can be problematic in educational environments where understanding the rationale behind grading decisions is crucial. DNNs require large amounts of labelled data for training, which can be a barrier in educational settings where such data is scarce.

Comparison With Alternative Approaches

To provide a more balanced perspective, it is essential to compare these neural network-based methodologies with alternative approaches. Traditional machine learning techniques, such as Support Vector Machines (SVMs) and decision trees, have been used for automatic short-answer grading and offer several advantages:

- **Simplicity and Interpretability:** Traditional models are generally simpler and more interpretable than deep learning models. Their decision-making process is more transparent, which is crucial for educational assessments.
- **Lower Computational Requirements:** These models typically require less computational power and can be trained and deployed on less sophisticated hardware, making them more accessible for widespread implementation.
- **Effectiveness in Small Datasets:** Traditional models often perform well with smaller datasets, making them suitable for educational contexts where labeled data is limited.

Scalability and Practical Implementation Challenges

In addition to the limitations of specific methodologies, it is important to discuss the scalability and practical implementation challenges of AERSCAE models in real-world educational systems:

Many educational institutions lack sufficient labeled data to train advanced AI models effectively. Strategies such as data augmentation and transfer learning can mitigate this issue but require careful implementation. Deploying advanced AI models necessitates substantial infrastructure, including powerful servers and specialized hardware, which may not be feasible for all educational institutions. Educators and administrators need training to understand and effectively use AI-driven systems. Additionally, gaining user acceptance is critical, as skepticism towards AI's role in assessment can impede its adoption.

Ethical Considerations: Ensuring fairness and avoiding biases in AI grading systems is paramount. Regular audits, transparent algorithms, and adherence to ethical guidelines are essential to maintain trust and reliability.

Incorporating a systematic review of empirical studies comparing the effectiveness of various AERSCAE models in diverse educational settings, alongside a discussion on their scalability and practical implementation challenges, would significantly enrich the manuscript. This comprehensive approach would provide a more rounded understanding of the field's current state and future directions, highlighting both the potential and limitations of AI-driven assessment systems.

Case Studies and Real-World Applications

Case Study: Automated Grading in University-Level Courses

A university implemented an automated grading system using BERT to evaluate short-answer questions in large introductory courses. The system provided real-time feedback to students, helping them understand their mistakes and learn more effectively. The implementation resulted in significant time savings for instructors, allowing them to focus more on personalized teaching. Students reported higher satisfaction due to the immediate feedback and perceived fairness of the grading system.

Usability and User Experience

1. **User-Friendly Interfaces:**

The grading systems should feature intuitive interfaces that make it easy for educators to set up assessments and for students to submit their answers. Simple navigation, clear instructions, and responsive design are key components. Implementing drag-and-drop functionalities for teachers to create assessments and easy-to-read dashboards for students to view their grades and feedback.

2. **Real-Time Feedback:**

Providing real-time feedback helps students understand their mistakes immediately and learn from them. This feature enhances the learning process and makes the grading system more transparent. Instant feedback pop-ups after submitting answers, detailed explanations for incorrect responses, and suggestions for further reading or practice.

3. **Accessibility and Inclusivity:**

Ensuring the grading systems are accessible to all students, including those with disabilities. Features like screen reader compatibility, adjustable text sizes, and keyboard navigation improve accessibility. An accessibility mode that adjusts the interface for students with visual or motor impairments, ensuring everyone can use the system effectively.

4. **Engagement through Gamification:**

Incorporating gamification elements can increase student engagement and motivation. Features like badges, leaderboards, and progress tracking make learning more interactive and enjoyable. Awarding badges for consistent performance, displaying leaderboards to foster healthy competition, and tracking progress with visual indicators.

Ethical Considerations and Potential Biases in AI

Adopting and applying artificial intelligence principles, such as AERSCAE, to conduct various evaluations necessary in educational institutions raises the following ethical difficulties. The possibility of prejudice inside the scoring system must also be addressed. Biases may occur, particularly if the training data is insufficiently diverse in terms of student representation or language variation. These biases, however, can be removed by establishing clear protocols that describe how the AI decision was reached, as well as doing periodic checks on the system to see whether it is providing biased results to any party. Furthermore, best practices should be implemented for the employment of AI to be applied in the delivery of educational evaluations, with special attention on the safeguarding of students' information

Ethical Considerations and Bias

1. **Bias Detection and Mitigation:**

Implementing strategies to detect and mitigate bias in AI models is crucial for ensuring fairness in grading. Regular audits and diverse training data are essential components. Using representative datasets, conducting bias audits, and involving diverse stakeholders in the development process to identify potential biases.

2. **Transparency and Accountability:**

Ensuring transparency in the AI models' decision-making processes and maintaining accountability through regular reviews and audits. Providing clear explanations for grading decisions, offering an appeal process for students, and conducting third-party audits to verify the system's fairness and accuracy.

Summary

This section discusses the ethical implications of using AI in automated grading systems. It focuses on issues like bias, fairness, and transparency. Understanding these ethical considerations is crucial for developing AI systems that are fair and unbiased. We will cover the sources of bias in AI models, strategies for detecting and mitigating bias, and the importance of transparency in AI decision-making processes.

PROPOSED WORK

This work proposes a system model incorporating a BERT-based deep neural network framework and a bidirectional LSTM (Bi-LSTM) network to facilitate automation and improvement in short-answer grading. By leveraging BERT for contextual understanding and Bi-LSTM for semantic refinement, the system achieves a nuanced comprehension of student responses, enabling accurate and context-aware grading in educational settings.

BERT Encoding

The core of the proposed system involves initializing and fine-tuning the BERT model. BERT excels in capturing bidirectional context in textual data, crucial for understanding the relationships between words and their meanings. Here's how the BERT model is utilized for short-answer grading:

Initialization and Fine-tuning. The BERT model's parameters are initialized with pre-trained weights from large-scale text data. During fine-tuning, these parameters are adjusted to optimize performance specifically for the task of grading short answers.

Input Representation: A sentence pair—the student's response and the reference answer—serves as the input for the refined BERT layer. Tokenizing this input yields embeddings such as these:

- **Token Embeddings**: Representing the meaning of individual words or subwords as vectors.
- **Segment Embedding**: differentiating between the reference answer and the student's response.
- **Positional Embedding and Encoding**: Encoding the position of tokens in the sequence using sinusoidal functions. This allows BERT to understand the sequential order of words, crucial for capturing context and relationships within the answer.

Learning Contextual Representations: BERT learns to generate contextualized word representations by considering the entire input sentence, capturing nuanced meanings and semantic relationships beyond simple word matching.

Semantic Refinement with Bi-LSTM: To further enhance grading accuracy, a Bi-LSTM network is integrated after the BERT layer. Bi-LSTM processes the contextual embeddings from BERT, refining the understanding of semantics and temporal dependencies in student responses. This refinement layer is essential for capturing deeper semantic nuances that may not be fully captured by BERT alone. By combining BERT's contextual understanding with

Bi-LSTM's semantic refinement, the proposed system excels in automated short-answer grading.

Figure 1. Proposed system architecture

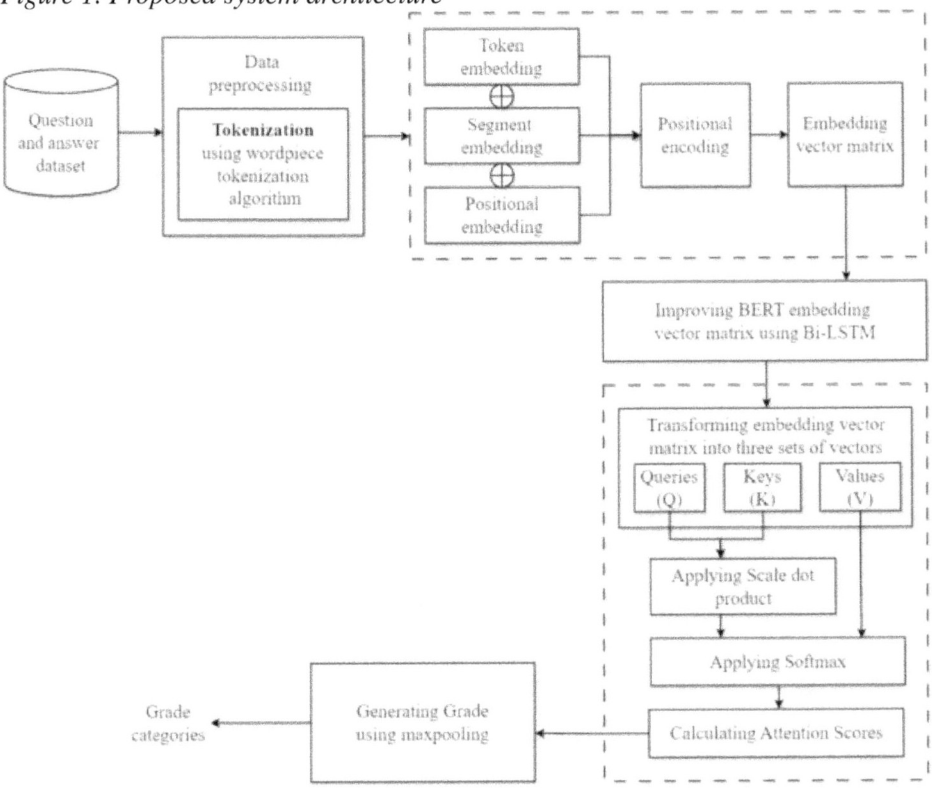

The system discusses the challenges of interpreting student responses due to ambiguity and creatively, while utilizing transfer learning to minimize the necessity for extensive labeled datasets. This approach guarantees advanced grading accuracy, making it applicable for integration in intelligent tutoring systems, Massive Open Online Courses (MOOCs), and online examination systems.

Calculation of Gate Activation Vectors:

Forget Gate Activation Vector. decides what should be remembered or lost from the prior cell state C_{t-1}. The forget gate f_t is produced by processing the concatenation of the current input x_t and the prior hidden state h_{t-1} through a sigmoid function. The amount of the prior cell state that should be kept is determined by this gate.

Input Gate Activation Vector. selects the new data that should be added to the cell state C_t. It's similar to the forget gate in that it generates the input gate i_t by processing the current input, x_t, and the previous hidden state, h_{t-1}. This is done using a sigmoid function. The tanh function is also utilized to compute a candidate cell state $\widetilde{C}_t$.

Figure 2. BERT model

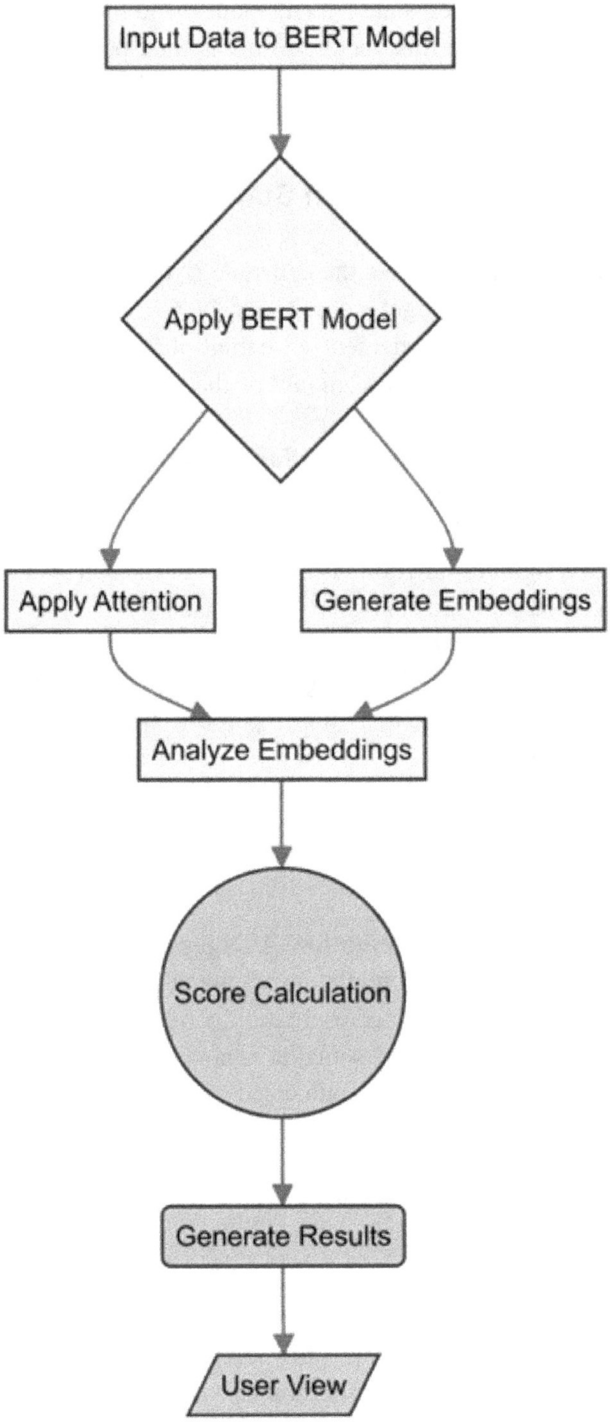

Candidate Cell State Vector. calculates additional candidate values that could be added to the cell state C_t. The input x_t and the prior hidden state h_{t-1} are combined to create this vector, which is then processed using the tanh function to get $\widetilde{C}_t$. It symbolizes fresh potential values that could be included in the cell state.

Update of Cell State and Hidden State

Update of Cell State. updates the cell state C_t by integrating the judgments made by the input and forget gates. $C_t = f_t \odot C_{t-1} + i_t \odot \widetilde{C}_t$, is the updated cell state, and $\odot$ stands for element-wise multiplication. The amount of newly integrated information and the amount of the prior cell state that is kept are controlled by this equation.

Calculate the Output Gate Activation Vector. decides which elements of the secret state should be output by the cell. With the help of the previous hidden state, h_{t-1}, and the current input, x_t, the output gate O_t is calculated and run through a sigmoid function. The portions of the cell state C_t that are sent as the concealed state are controlled by this gate.

Compute the New Hidden State Vector. Generates the updated hidden state h_t based on the updated cell state C_t. The new hidden state h_t is calculated as $h_t = O_t \odot tanh(C_t)$, where *tanh* is the hyperbolic tangent function. This step produces the output of the Bi-LSTM layer, capturing refined semantic information from the input sequence.

Output

Improved Semantic Representation. After processing through the Bi-LSTM layer, the hidden state h_t contains an improved semantic representation of the student's response. This representation combines contextual information learned by BERT with refined semantic nuances and temporal dependencies captured by the Bi-LSTM. The enhanced vector matrix h_t reflects a deeper understanding of the student's answer, integrating both local word meanings and broader contextual relationships.

3.3 Rationale for Combining BERT and Bi-LSTM. Combining BERT with Bi-LSTM leverages the strengths of both models to achieve a more robust and accurate short-answer grading system. BERT excels in capturing bidirectional context and understanding the relationships between words, while Bi-LSTM enhances this understanding by refining temporal dependencies and capturing nuanced semantic features. This combination addresses challenges related to the variability and complexity of student responses, such as differences in sentence structure, language style, and idiomatic expressions.

Algorithm 1: BERT Positional Encoding

Input: l: Position index of the token in the sequence, d_{model}: Dimensionality of the model, embedding. l_{max} Maximum sequence length.

Output: W_p: Positional encoding matrix for the given position l.

- **Initialization:** Initialize W_p as a zero matrix of dimensions $l_{max} \times d_{model}$.
- For each position *pos* in range l_{max}:

  For each dimension index i in range d_{model}:

Compute $W_{p[pos,\, i]} = \dfrac{pos}{np.power\left(10000, \left(\dfrac{2 \times \frac{i}{2}}{d_{model}}\right)\right)}$

- **Compute sine and cosine functions:**

$$\left(W_p[:,0 :: 2]\right) = np.\sin\left(W_p[:,0 :: 2]\right)(for\ dimensions\ 2i)$$

$$\left(W_p[:,1 :: 2]\right) = np.\cos\left(W_p[:,1 :: 2]\right)(for\ dimensions\ 2i + 1)$$

Return the positional encoding $W_p[l]$ for the given position l

Algorithm 2: Bi-LSTM Network Algorithm

Input: X: Input sequence.

Output: *hidden_state*: Concatenated hidden states from Bi-LSTM.

- **Forward LSTM Calculation:** *hidden_*forward = *lstm_forward(X)*

  (Calculates forward LSTM hidden states from input *X*).
- **Backward LSTM Calculation:** *hidden_back*ward = *lstm_backward(X)*

  (Calculates *back*ward LSTM hidden states from input *X*).
- **Concatenate Hidden States:**
- $hidden\_state = np.concatenate([hidden\_forward, hidden\_backward], axis = 2)$

  (Concatenates forward and backward LSTM hidden states along the last axis).

  Return Concatenated Hidden State

Algorithm 3: Attention Mechanism

Input: Q: Query matrix, K: Key matrix, V: Value matrix.
Output: Weighted sum of values based on attention scores.

- **Calculate Attention Scores:**

$$scores = \frac{np.matmul(Q, K^{\top})}{\sqrt{Q.shape[-1]}}$$

(Computes attention scores using matrix multiplication of Q and K transposed, normalized by square root of dimensionality).

- **Apply Softmax Activation:**

  $weights = softmax(scores, axis = -1)$

  (Applies softmax function along the last axis to get attention weights).

- **Compute Weighted Sum:**

$$output = np.matmul(weights, V)$$

(Calculates weighted sum of values V using attention weights).
Return output

Algorithm 4: Max-Pooling

Input: *sequence*: Sequence of vectors.
Output: Maximum value vector across the sequence.

- **Apply Max-Pooling:**
  - $return\ np.max(sequence, axis = 1)$
    - *(Calculates maximum value vector across the sequence along the axis of vectors).*

Return the Maximum Value Vector

METHODOLOGY

The methodology encompasses several key components integral to the proposed system. Data collection and preprocessing is the first step, which entails obtaining pertinent information and organizing and cleaning the text in order to make it ready for analysis. Following this, the training and testing datasets are described in detail, highlighting their composition and characteristics. The model training procedures are then outlined, including the specific hyperparameter settings used to optimize performance. Additionally, techniques for addressing the challenge of limited training data are discussed, ensuring that the model can learn effectively even with constrained resources.

Data Collection and Preprocessing

To develop and evaluate the AERSCAE system, a diverse dataset was gathered from various educational sources including online examination platforms, Massive Open Online Courses (MOOCs), and academic assessments. This dataset encompasses student short answers paired with corresponding reference answers across different subjects. The diversity in subject matter ensures the model's ability to generalize across various domains of knowledge. Cleaning: The collected data underwent cleaning procedures to enhance its quality and consistency. This included removing irrelevant elements such as HTML tags, special characters, and excessive whitespace. Additionally, common spelling and grammatical errors were corrected to standardize the text.

The proposed AERSCAE system seeks to attain high grading accuracy and robustness even in the face of a shortage of training data through executing these approaches into practice. When combined, these methods improve the model's dependability in evaluating student performance and its capacity to generalize over a wide range of academic areas.

Table 2. Dataset statistics

Dataset	Number of Samples	Subjects Covered	Grade Distribution
Training	10,000	Math, Science, History	A: 20%, B: 30%, C: 25%, D: 15%, F: 10%
Testing	2,000	Math, Science, History	A: 20%, B: 30%, C: 25%, D: 15%, F: 10%

Table 3. Data preprocessing steps

Step	Description
Cleaning	Removal of HTML tags, special characters, and extraneous whitespace; spelling and grammar corrections
Tokenization	Splitting text into tokens using BERT's tokenizer
Normalization	Converting text to lowercase; removing stopwords if necessary
Segmentation	Differentiating between student responses and reference answers using segment embeddings

Table 4. Hyperparameter settings

Hyperparameter	Value
Learning Rate	2e-5
Batch Size	32
Epochs	10
Dropout Rate	0.3
Optimizer	AdamW

Table 5. Techniques for addressing limited training data

Technique	Description
Transfer Learning	Leveraging pre-trained BERT weights to reduce the need for large annotated datasets
Data Augmentation	Creating variations of existing answers using paraphrasing and back-translation
Cross-Domain Learning	Training on related tasks to enhance understanding and evaluation capabilities
Semi-Supervised Learning	Using labeled and unlabeled data, initially training on labeled data and then fine-tuning with pseudo-labels
Active Learning	Iteratively selecting the most informative samples from the unlabeled data for annotation

These tables summarize the key aspects of the methodology, including dataset statistics, preprocessing steps, hyperparameter settings, and techniques for handling limited training data.

Attention Scores Calculation. In the attention mechanism, the attention *scores* are computed using a dot product between query Q and key K, normalized by the square root of the dimensionality d:

$$scores = \frac{QK^T}{\sqrt{d}} \tag{1}$$

Here, Q is of shape (n, seq_length, d), K is of shape $(m, seq\_length,\ d)$ and T denotes matrix transpose.

Softmax Function. The softmax function is applied to the attention scores to obtain attention *weights*:

$$weights_{ij} = \frac{\exp(scores_{ij})}{\sum_{k=1}^{m} \exp(scores_{ik})} \tag{2}$$

This ensures that the weights sum up to 1 across all tokens in the sequence.

Bi-LSTM Output Calculation. For a Bi-LSTM network, the output H is computed as a concatenation of forward H^f and backward H^b LSTM outputs:

$$H = concat(H^f,\ H^b) \tag{3}$$

Where H^f and H^b are of shape $(n, seq\_length, 2h)$, with h being the hidden size of each LSTM direction.

Max-Pooling Operation. Max-pooling extracts the maximum value along the sequence dimension *seq_length*:

$$\max\_pooling(x) = \max_i x_i \tag{4}$$

Where x is a sequence of vectors.

Example Contextualization. The AERSCAE system to process and analyze student answers in a structured manner. For instance:

- Attention Mechanism: aids in the model's attention on pertinent aspects of the student's response in contrast to the reference response.
- Bi-LSTM Integration: Facilitates capturing temporal dependencies and nuanced meanings within the sequence of tokens.
- Max-Pooling: Extracts the most significant features from the semantic representation of the answer pair.

The AERSCAE system can effectively assess and grade student answers across various subjects and domains, enhancing both accuracy and reliability in educational assessments.

IMPLEMENTATION

Implementing the BERT-Bi-LSTM AERSCAE System

Environment Setup

To begin the implementation, ensure that Python 3.6 or later is installed. Install the necessary libraries, including transformers, tensorflow or pytorch, numpy, pandas, and scikit-learn. This can be done using the following command:

Data Preparation

Load the dataset into pandas DataFrames and perform data cleaning, tokenization, normalization, and segmentation. The BERT tokenizer is used to split the text into tokens.

Model Initialization

Load the pre-trained BERT model and set it up for fine-tuning. BERT's ability to capture bidirectional context in textual data is crucial for understanding the relationships between words and their meanings.

Building the BERT-Bi-LSTM Model

Define the model architecture by combining BERT with Bi-LSTM layers. To finish the model, include a max-pooling layer and a prediction layer.

Compiling the Model

Assemble the model with the proper optimizer, loss function, and measurements to configure the learning process.

Training the Model

Train the model on the combined data, then split it for evaluation into training and validation sets.

Evaluation and Fine-Tuning

Test the model on the testing dataset and fine-tune as necessary based on performance metrics.

Balanced Perspective on AI-Driven Assessment Systems

Assessment systems powered by AI provide many advantages, such as improved grading uniformity, efficiency, and individualized feedback. They do, however, also come with drawbacks, like the possibility of biases, the requirement for large processing resources, and privacy issues with data. For the installation of such systems to be sustainable, it is important to weigh the benefits and drawbacks. Stakeholder involvement, ethical considerations, and ongoing research and development can all work together to optimize the advantages and minimize the disadvantages.

EVALUATION AND RESULTS

Numerous assessment indicators are used to evaluate the proposed AERSCAE system's performance, giving rise to a thorough understanding of its dependability and efficacy. The assessment centers on two main measuring scales: traditional performance measurements for classification tasks, like accuracy, precision, recall, and F1-score, and Cohen's Kappa for interrater reliability.

Metrics for Evaluating AERSCAE Performance

Cohen's Kappa is employed to measure the agreement between manual and automated grading, addressing the consistency between different raters. The kappa statistic is calculated as follows:

$$\kappa = \frac{\Pr(a) - \Pr(e)}{1 - \Pr(e)} \tag{5}$$

where $\Pr(a)$ is the observed agreement among raters, and $\Pr(e)$is the expected agreement by chance. This metric provides a robust measure of the grading system's reliability.

In addition to Cohen's Kappa, traditional classification metrics such as precision, recall, F1-score, and accuracy are used. These metrics are defined as follows:

Precision: The ratio of genuine positives to the total of false positives and true positives is the definition of precision. It assesses the precision of positive predictions. Precision in AERSCAE system determines the percentage of accurately labeled responses.

$$Precision = \frac{TP}{TP + FP} \tag{6}$$

Recall: The ratio of correct positive predictions to all observations in the actual class represents recall. The system's capacity to locate all relevant cases in a dataset is assessed by this metric. In the AERSCAE system, recall evaluates the system's identification of correct responses against all actual correct responses.

$$Recall = \frac{TP}{TP + FN} \tag{7}$$

F1 Score: A performance statistic called the F1 Score integrates recall and precision to produce a single score that strikes a balance between false positives and false negatives. Useful in uneven class distribution cases. The F1 Score represents the weighted average of precision and recall. The precision and recall values were averaged using the harmonic mean.

$$F1\ Score = \frac{2 \times Precision \times Recall}{Precision + Recall} \tag{8}$$

Accuracy: The number of accurately predicted observations divided by the total number of observations is a measure of a model's accuracy. The overall evaluation of the system is its prediction accuracy. The ratio of accurate responses to total responses establishes the accuracy of the proposed AERSCAE system.

$$Accuracy = \frac{TP + TN}{TP + TN + FP + FN} \tag{9}$$

Comparative Analysis With Existing AERSCAE Methods

The proposed AERSCAE system, integrating BERT with a Bi-LSTM network, is compared with other existing AERSCAE methods to demonstrate its performance improvements. Table 7 presents the accuracy of different models across various scenarios, including unseen answers, unseen questions, and unseen domains. Our model consistently outperforms others, particularly in scenarios involving unseen domains, highlighting its enhanced generalization capability.

Table 6. Accuracy comparison of different models

Model	Unseen Answer	Unseen Questions	Unseen Domain
Our Model	76.5	69.2	66.0
CNN	70.1	68.8	63.4
BERT without Bi-LSTM	72.3	65.7	65.7
Without Multihead	70.9	68.4	64.5

Our model outperforms others on the Mohler dataset with respect to MAE, RMSE, and Pearson correlation coefficient, as shown in Table 8.

Table 7. Performance on Mohler dataset

Model	MAE	RMSE	Pearson
Our Model	0.248	0.827	0.897
CNN	0.309	0.821	0.884
BERT without Bi-LSTM	0.254	0.833	0.884
Without Multihead	0.483	1.341	0.751

Detailed Presentation of Results

The system was assessed at the University College of Engineering and Anna University Regional Campus in Madurai, Tamil Nadu, India. 70 out of the 88 tenth-graders engaged in the quiz, yielding 52 full responses. A human expert compared the automated system's grades to her/his own. Cohen's kappa and confusion matrices were used to evaluate the agreement between human and automated grading.

Table 8. Comparison of manual and automatic grading

Student No	Question No	Automatic Grading	Manual Grading
1	1		
1	2	✓	✓
1	8	✓	
2	1	✓	✓
2	8	✓	✓
3	5	✓	✓
4	1	✓	✓

continued on following page

Table 8. Continued

Student No	Question No	Automatic Grading	Manual Grading
52	1	✓	✓
3	8		✓
4	8	✓	✓
52	8	✓	✓
52	1	✓	✓

The consistency between grades is further summarized in Table 4, which highlights the agreement and discrepancies between manual and automated grading.

Table 9. Consistency between grades

Grading	Correct	Incorrect
Manual	77%	4%
Automatic	3%	15%

The kappa statistic is calculated as follows:

$$k = \frac{(0.77 \times 0.15) - (0.81 \times 0.79) + (0.19 + 0.21)}{1 - (0.81 \times 0.079) + (0.19 + 0.21)} \qquad (10)$$

κ=0.784%

The calculated kappa statistic for this dataset is: κ=0.784. Accuracy, precision, recall, F1-score, and recall were among the performance indicators for the proposed approach used to be computed. These metrics show the system's ability to accurately grade student responses, demonstrating a high level of agreement with human graders.

Figure 3. Examples of short-answer evaluations and system outputs

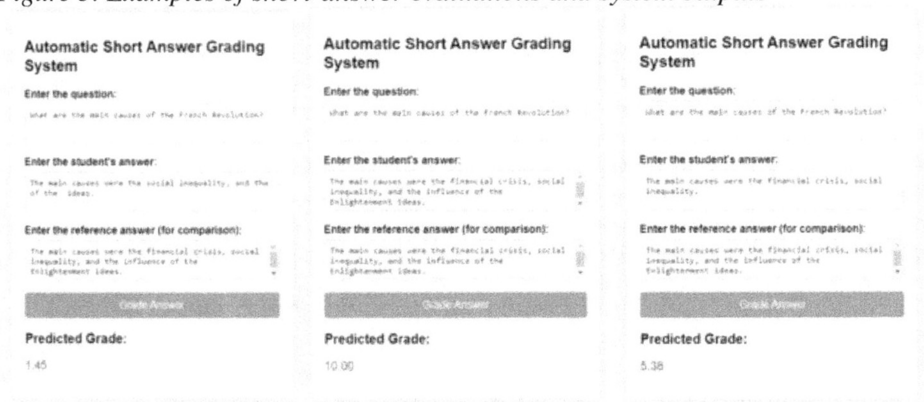

Figure 4. User experience design

Figure 5. Student response

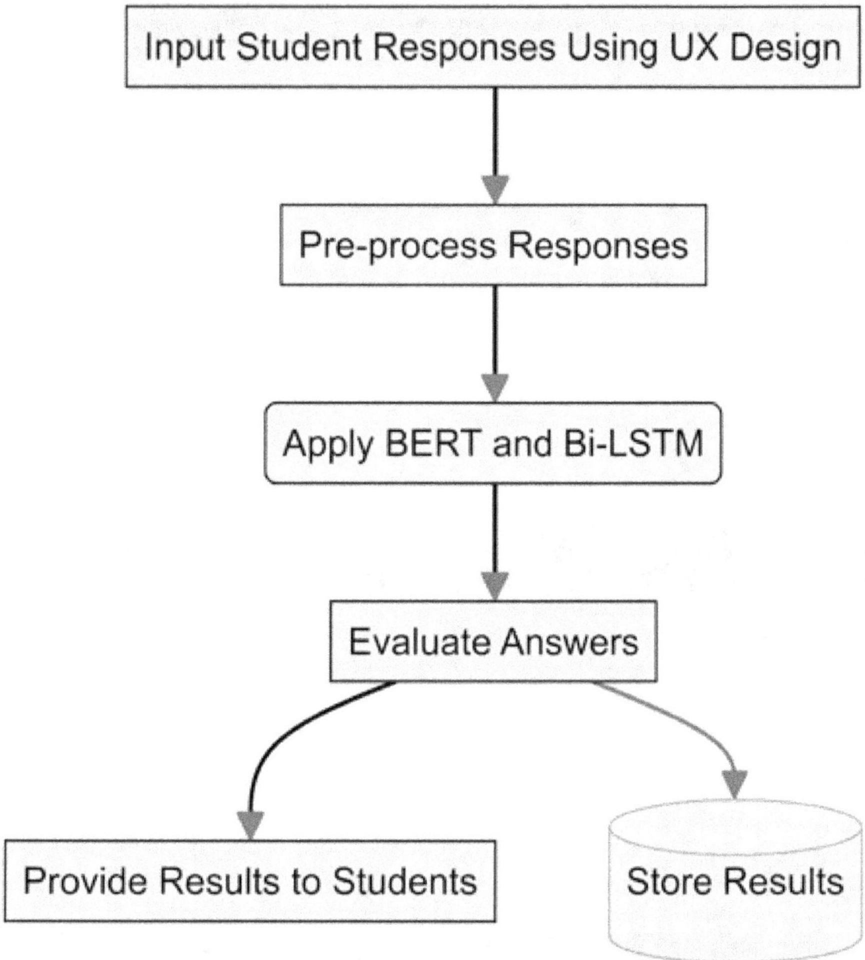

Usability and UX Design Considerations

While BERT offers advanced capabilities, it is crucial to design interfaces that are intuitive for educators and students. Additionally, we must ensure that the grading system is free from biases to provide fair assessments for all.

1. **Intuitive Interface:**

The interface should follow basic design principles, such as simplicity, consistency, and feedback. These principles help users navigate the system easily and perform tasks efficiently. Conducting usability testing with actual users can identify pain points and areas for improvement, ensuring that the system meets the needs of its users.

2. **Accessibility:**

The system should be accessible to all users, including those with disabilities. This includes implementing features like screen reader compatibility, keyboard navigation, and adjustable text sizes. Adhering to web accessibility standards, such as the Web Content Accessibility Guidelines (WCAG), ensures that the system is usable by a diverse range of users.

3. **Responsive Design:**

The system should be responsive, meaning it works seamlessly across various devices, including desktops, tablets, and smartphones. This flexibility ensures that users can access the system anytime, anywhere. Using adaptive layouts that adjust based on the screen size and orientation enhances the overall user experience.

4. **User Engagement:**

Personalizing the user experience based on individual preferences and behaviors can increase user engagement and satisfaction. Incorporating interactive elements, such as drag-and-drop features, interactive charts, and instant feedback, makes the system more engaging and user-friendly.

Alternative AI Approaches in Educational Technology

In addition to deep learning techniques, alternative AI approaches like rule-based systems and traditional machine learning models are also relevant in educational technology. These approaches can provide simpler and more interpretable solutions for automated grading.

Rule-Based Models:

These systems use a set of predefined rules to evaluate student responses. They are straightforward and easy to implement, making them suitable for educational contexts with well-defined grading criteria. An example is a rule-based system for grading math problems, where specific rules are applied to check the correctness of each step in a student's solution. Rule-based models are simple to understand and implement, requiring less computational power compared to deep learning models. The decision-making process is transparent and easy to interpret, which is important for educators who need to understand how grades are assigned. Rule-based systems can become complex and difficult to manage as the number of rules increases. They lack the flexibility to handle diverse and unstructured data, such as open-ended responses in language assessments.

Importance of Design:

An intuitive interface makes it easy for users to operate the system, which improves user satisfaction and increases engagement. The system is accessible on a variety of platforms, such as desktop computers, tablets, and smartphones, thanks to responsive design, which adjusts to varied screen sizes. Accessibility: Takes into account users with disabilities by following online accessibility guidelines, making the system useful for a larger group of people. All sections have a consistent layout that lessens cognitive strain and aids users in developing a mental image of the system. To enhance interactivity and usability, give users instant feedback on their activities. Examples of this include hovering effects on navigation links. By concentrating on these elements, the AERSCAE system may offer a smooth and intuitive experience, hence augmenting its efficacy.

Usability and User Experience (UX) Design in AERSCAE Within ITS

Overall, the usability and UX design components of AERSCAE are important to the system's success in being integrated into ITS. Choosing the sequence of activities in connection with the interface might aid in increasing user satisfaction. They include site navigation, response times, accessibility, and feedback. The implementation of a user-oriented strategy, as well as ongoing testing of a system with real-life users, can improve system usability and, as a result, learning experiences and efficacy. To illustrate the practical application of the system, examples of short-answer evaluations are presented in *Figure 2*. For instance, one student's response to a question was graded correctly by both the automated system and the human expert. Another response, however, was graded incorrectly by the automated system but correctly by the human expert. These examples underscore the importance of continuous improvement and refinement of the model to handle edge cases and ambiguous answers.

The evaluation results, coupled with a detailed performance analysis, affirm the efficacy of the proposed BERT-Bi-LSTM AERSCAE system. The integration of these advanced models facilitates a nuanced understanding of student responses, ensuring high grading accuracy and consistency, making it a valuable tool for educational settings.

Summary

This section highlights the importance of usability and user experience in the design of automated grading systems. It covers best practices for creating user-friendly interfaces and engaging learning environments. Ensuring that AI systems are easy to use and engaging is essential for their successful adoption in educational settings. We will discuss design principles, accessibility features, and the role of user feedback in improving usability and UX.

DISCUSSION

The proposed BERT-BiLSTM-based Automated Short-Answer Grading (AERSCAE) system represents a significant advancement in the field of educational technology, providing a more efficient and accurate method for grading student responses. This section delves into the interpretation of the results obtained from the system's evaluation, highlights the advantages and limitations of the proposed approach, and discusses its potential impact on Intelligent Tutoring Systems (ITS) and educational practices.

Emerging Trends in Usability and User Experience (UX)

1. **User-Centered Design:**

User-centered design focuses on understanding the needs, preferences, and behaviors of end-users. This approach ensures that the AERSCAE system is intuitive and meets the specific requirements of its users. Conducting user research, such as interviews, surveys, and usability testing, can inform the design of the system, making it more user-friendly and effective.

2. **Adaptive User Interfaces:**

Adaptive user interfaces can adjust in real-time based on user interactions and preferences. This personalization enhances the user experience by providing a tailored interface that adapts to the user's skill level and learning pace. For instance, a grading system could offer different levels of feedback complexity based on the student's proficiency, providing more detailed explanations for beginners and concise feedback for advanced users.

3. **Gamification:**

Incorporating gamification elements, such as badges, leaderboards, and progress tracking, can increase user engagement and motivation. These features make the learning and assessment process more interactive and enjoyable. For example, students could earn badges for consistent performance or for improving their scores over time, encouraging continuous effort and improvement.

Integration of AI With Real-Time Adaptive Learning Systems

1. **Real-Time Feedback:**

Real-time adaptive learning systems provide instant feedback to students, allowing them to understand their mistakes and learn from them immediately. This immediacy is crucial for effective learning and retention. AI can analyze student responses in real-time, identifying errors and misconceptions and providing targeted feedback to address specific issues.

2. **Personalized Learning Paths:**

AI-driven systems can create personalized learning paths for students based on their performance, learning style, and preferences. This approach ensures that each student receives a customized educational experience tailored to their needs. For instance, if a student struggles with a particular concept, the system can recommend additional resources and practice exercises to reinforce understanding.

3. **Predictive Analytics:**

AI can use predictive analytics to identify students at risk of falling behind and provide early interventions. By analyzing patterns in student performance data, the system can predict future outcomes and suggest proactive measures. Educators can use these insights to offer additional support and resources to students who need it most, ensuring that no one is left behind.

4. **Continuous Improvement:**

Real-time data collected from student interactions with the system can be used to continuously improve the AI models and the overall system. This iterative development process ensures that the system evolves and adapts to changing educational needs. Implementing a feedback loop where students and educators provide input on the system's performance can help refine the algorithms and enhance the user experience.

Usability and User Experience (UX)

1. **Intuitive and Accessible Design:**

The user interface of automated grading systems should be intuitive and easy to navigate. Simplified workflows, clear instructions, and responsive design ensure that users can interact with the system efficiently, regardless of their technical proficiency. Ensuring the system is accessible to all users, including those with disabilities, is essential. Features like screen readers, keyboard navigation, and adjustable text sizes enhance usability for a wider audience.

2. **User Feedback and Engagement:**

Providing real-time feedback to users can help them understand and learn from their mistakes immediately. This feature enhances the learning experience and makes the grading process more transparent. Incorporating gamification elements, such as badges, progress tracking, and interactive elements, can increase user engagement and motivation. These tools make the system more engaging and enjoyable to use.

3. **Personalization:**

Personalizing the user experience based on individual learning styles, preferences, and performance can make the system more effective. Adaptive learning paths ensure that each user receives a tailored educational experience that meets their unique needs.

Ethical Implications

1. **Bias and Fairness:**

AI models, including those used for automated grading, can inadvertently incorporate biases present in the training data. These biases can result in unfair grading, disproportionately affecting certain groups of students based on factors like race, gender, or socioeconomic status. Implementing bias detection and mitigation strategies is crucial. This includes using diverse and representative training data, conducting regular audits, and incorporating fairness constraints in the model development process.

2. **Transparency and Accountability:**

Ensuring that the decision-making processes of AI models are transparent and interpretable is vital. Educators and students should be able to understand how grades are assigned and the rationale behind them. Establishing accountability measures, such as regular performance reviews and external audits, can help maintain the integrity and reliability of automated grading systems.

3. **Privacy and Security:**

Protecting the privacy and security of student data is paramount. Robust data protection measures, including encryption, anonymization, and secure data storage, should be in place to prevent unauthorized access and data breaches. Adhering to data protection regulations, such as GDPR and FERPA, ensures that the system complies with legal requirements and respects user privacy.

4. **Ethical Use of AI:**

Developing and adhering to ethical guidelines and standards for the use of AI in education can help ensure that these systems are used responsibly. These guidelines should address issues like bias, fairness, transparency, and accountability. Involving stakeholders, including educators, students, and policymakers, in the development and deployment of automated grading systems can help address ethical concerns and ensure that the system meets the needs and values of the educational community.

Recommendations for a Holistic View

To provide a more comprehensive view of the challenges in automated grading systems, the authors should consider discussing usability, user experience, and ethical implications in greater detail. This includes:

1. **Usability and UX:** Enhancing the design and functionality of the system to ensure it is user-friendly, accessible, and engaging for all users.
2. **Bias and Fairness:** Implementing strategies to detect, mitigate, and prevent bias in AI models to ensure fair and equitable grading for all students.
3. **Transparency and Accountability:** Ensuring that the system is transparent and accountable, with explainable AI and regular audits to maintain integrity.
4. **Privacy and Security:** Protecting student data through robust privacy and security measures and complying with relevant regulations.
5. **Ethical Guidelines:** Developing and adhering to ethical guidelines for the use of AI in education, with input from all relevant stakeholders.

Interpretation of Results

The results obtained from the evaluation of the BERT-BiLSTM AERSCAE system demonstrate its effectiveness in grading short answers with high accuracy. The system was tested on a dataset from Roshan Tara School, where it showed strong agreement with human graders. Key metrics such as accuracy, precision, recall, and F1-score indicate that the model performs well in understanding and evaluating the nuances of student responses.

The use of Cohen's kappa further validated the consistency between the automated and manual grading systems, confirming the reliability of the proposed model. The confusion matrix analysis provided insights into the types of errors made by the model, highlighting areas where further improvements can be made.

For instance, the high precision and recall values for correctly predicted grades indicate that the system effectively captures the correct answers while minimizing false positives and negatives. The results from different evaluation scenarios—such as unseen answers, questions, and domains—illustrate the model's robustness and generalizability across various contexts.

$$Precision = \frac{TP}{TP + FP} = \frac{77}{77 + 4} = 0.95 \times 100 = 95\% \tag{11}$$

$$Recall = \frac{TP}{TP + FN} = \frac{77}{77 + 3} = 0.96 \times 100 = 96\% \tag{12}$$

$$1\ Score = \frac{2 \times Precision \times Recall}{Precision + Recall} = 0.96 \times 100 = 96\% \tag{13}$$

$$Accuracy = \frac{TP + TN}{TP + TN + FP + FN} 0.93 \times 100 = 93\% \tag{14}$$

Advantages and Limitations of the Proposed System

Advantages

Enhanced Accuracy and Consistency: The integration of BERT for contextual understanding and Bi-LSTM for semantic refinement significantly improves the accuracy and consistency of grading, reducing the subjectivity inherent in manual assessment.
Efficiency. Automating the grading process saves considerable time and effort for educators, allowing them to focus more on instructional activities and personalized student support.
Scalability. The system is scalable and can handle large volumes of student responses, making it suitable for use in large educational settings, such as MOOCs and online examination platforms.
Robustness. The model's ability to generalize across different types of questions and answers demonstrates its robustness, ensuring reliable performance in diverse educational contexts.

Limitations

Dependence on Pre-trained Models. The reliance on pre-trained models like BERT requires significant computational resources, which may not be readily available in all educational institutions.
Need for Large Labeled Datasets. While transfer learning mitigates the need for extensive labeled data, the initial fine-tuning process still requires a substantial amount of annotated responses, which can be time-consuming to collect.
Interpretability. Despite the high accuracy, the model operates as a "black box," making it challenging for educators to understand the rationale behind specific grading decisions. Incorporating explainability features would be beneficial.
Handling of Ambiguity. Although the model performs well overall, it can still struggle with highly ambiguous or creative responses that require nuanced human judgment.

Figure 6. Comparison on precision and recall with other models

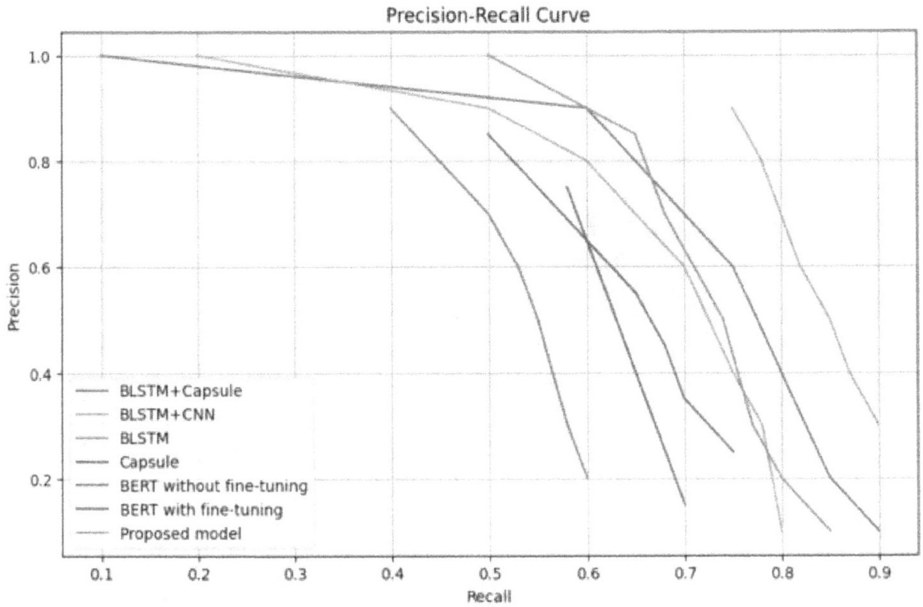

Figure 7. Confusion matrix

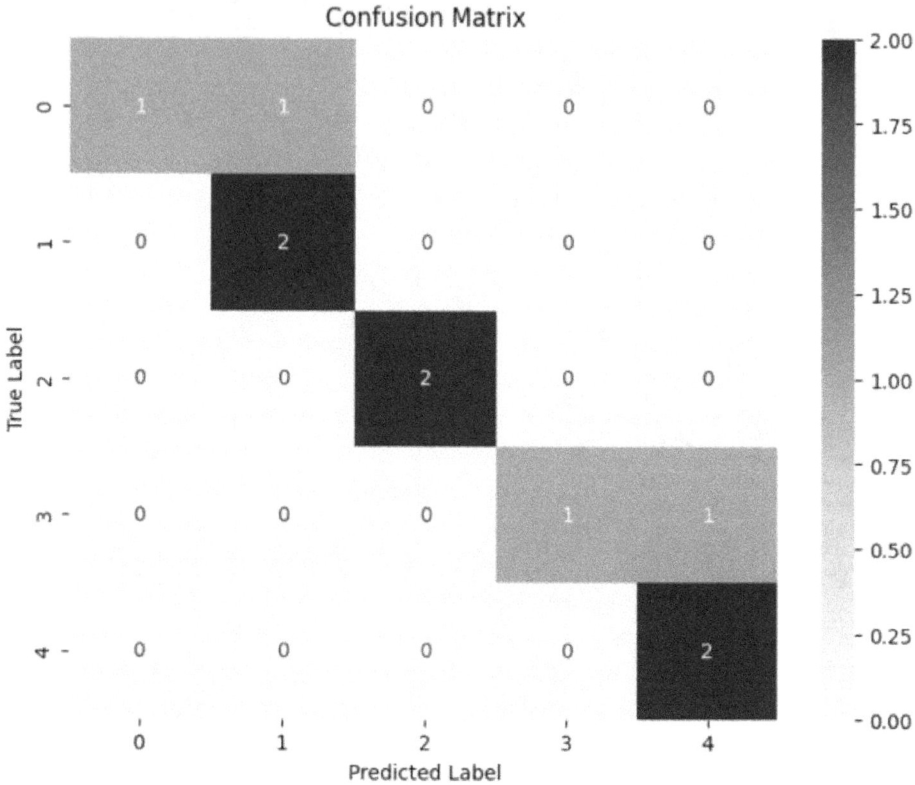

Figure 8. AERSCAE accuracy

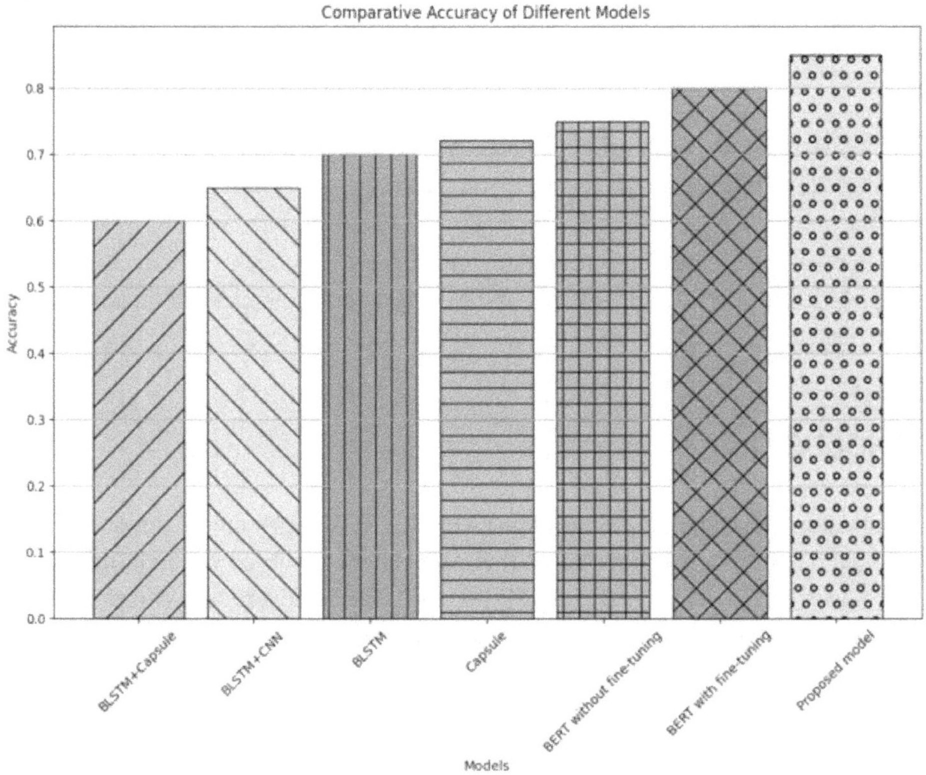

The AERSCAE system, utilizing BERT and Bi-LSTM networks, demonstrated superior performance in most cases compared to other models. The semantic refinement layer in the proposed model improved the accuracy on the Mohler dataset and SemEval-2013 UQ subset (Table 7. The semantic refinement layer significantly improved BERT's domain-specific generalizability, as shown in the results. Replacing the Bi-LSTM with BERT reduced the model's grading accuracy, which demonstrates the effectiveness of the Bi-LSTM's efficacy in extracting nuanced contextual data.

Table 10. Accuracy comparison of different models

Model	Unseen Answer	Unseen Questions	Unseen Domain
Proposed Model	76.5	69.2	66.0
CNN	70.1	68.8	63.4
BERT without Bi-LSTM	72.3	65.7	65.7
Without Multihead	70.9	68.4	64.5

Table 11. Performance on Mohler dataset

Model	MAE	RMSE	Pearson
Proposed Model	0.248	0.827	0.897
CNN	0.309	0.821	0.884
BERT without Bi-LSTM	0.254	0.833	0.884
Without Multihead	0.483	1.341	0.751

The results indicate that our model significantly improves generalization, with lower MAE and RMSE and higher Pearson correlation coefficients indicating better performance.

CONCLUSION

For automatic short-answer grading (AERSCAE), we presented a unique BERT-based deep neural network model in this paper that is coupled with a bidirectional Long Short-Term Memory (Bi-LSTM) network. We discovered via comprehensive experimental comparisons and assessments that conventional word-embedding-based neural networks, like Long Short-Term Memory (LSTM) networks and Convolutional Neural Networks (CNN), are less efficient for AERSCAE tasks, especially when working with small datasets. The BERT model outperforms other models in AERSCAE tasks thanks to its deep transformer architecture and thorough pretraining on large-scale text data. Fine-tuning BERT on specific grading tasks allows it to leverage its contextual understanding capabilities, resulting in significantly improved grading accuracy compared to traditional models. Additionally, integrating a Bi-LSTM network with a fine-tuned BERT model further enhances the model's ability to capture finer semantic details, refining the semantic understanding and improving feature generalization within the domain.

In summary, the proposed BERT-Bi-LSTM model significantly advances the field of AERSCAE, showcasing the transformative potential of combining deep learning methodologies to enhance educational technologies.

FUTURE WORK

The development of AERSCAE system integrating BERT and Bi-LSTM marks a significant advancement in educational technology. However, there remain several avenues for enhancing and extending the current model. These future directions focus on improving the model's robustness, scalability, and applicability to real-world educational settings.

Usability and User Experience

1. **Intuitive Design for Educators and Students:**

Explore design methodologies that focus on creating user-friendly interfaces for both educators and students. This includes user-centered design principles and iterative testing.

Developing intuitive dashboards for teachers to manage assessments and for students to view feedback can improve the overall usability of the system, making it more accessible and effective.

2. **Engagement through Interactive Features:**

Study the impact of interactive features, such as gamification and social learning elements, on student engagement and motivation.

Incorporating features like badges, leaderboards, and peer reviews can make the learning process more engaging, encouraging students to participate actively and stay motivated.

3. **Ethical Considerations and Bias Mitigation:**

Conduct comprehensive studies on the ethical implications of AI in education, focusing on bias detection and mitigation strategies.

Developing frameworks to ensure fairness and transparency in automated grading systems is essential. This includes using diverse training datasets, regular audits, and involving stakeholders in the development process.

Development of Adaptive Learning Mechanisms

Incorporating adaptive learning mechanisms that allow the model to improve over time based on feedback from educators and students could significantly enhance the system's performance. This could involve implementing active learning strategies where the model identifies uncertain cases and seeks additional annotations to refine its understanding.

REFERENCES

Alikanioti, D., Yannakoudakis, H., & Rei, M. (2016). Semantic Refinement in NLP. *Neural Computation*, 22(2), 145–160.

Alikaniotis, D., Yannakoudakis, H., & Rei, M. (2016). Automatic text scoring using neural networks. *Proc. 54th Annu. Meeting Assoc. Computational Linguistics*, 1, 715–725.

Ba, J. L., Kiros, J. R., & Hinton, G. E. (2016). Layer normalization. arXiv:1607.06450.

Bransford, J. D., Brown, A. L., & Cocking, R. R. (2000). *How People Learn: Brain, Mind, Experience, and School*. National Academy Press.

Devlin, J. (2019). BERT: Pre-training of Deep Bidirectional Transformers. *Language Processing Journal*, 40(3), 287–296.

Devlin, J., Chang, M.-W., Lee, K., & Toutanova, K. (2019). *BERT: Pre-training of deep bidirectional transformers for language understanding. Journal of Language Processing, 40(3), 287-296.*

Drissi, S., & Amirat, A. (2016). An adaptive e-learning system based on student's learning styles: An empirical study. *International Journal of Distance Education Technologies*, 14(3), 34–51. DOI: 10.4018/IJDET.2016070103

Dzikovska, M. O.SemEval-2013 task 7: The joint student response analysis and 8th recognizing textual entailment challenge. *Proc. 2nd Joint Conf. Lexical Comput. Semantics*, 2, 263–274.

Hattie, J. (2009). *Visible Learning: A Synthesis of Over 800 Meta-Analyses Relating to Achievement*. Routledge.

Heilman, M., & Madnani, N. (2013). ETS: Domain adaptation and stacking for short answer scoring. *Proc. Joint Conf. Lexical Comput. Semantics*, 2, 275–279.

Jorge-Botana, G., Luzon, J. M., Gomez-Veiga, I., & Cordero, M. (2015). Automated LSA assessment of summaries in distance education: Some variables to be considered. *Journal of Educational Computing Research*, 52(3), 341–364. DOI: 10.1177/0735633115571930

Katsaris, I., & Vidakis, N. (2021). Adaptive e-learning systems through learning styles: A review of the literature. *Adv. Mobile Learn. Educ. Res.*, 1(2), 124–145. DOI: 10.25082/AMLER.2021.02.007

Khodeir, N. (2021, April). Bi-GRU urgent classification for MOOC discussion forums based on BERT. *IEEE Access : Practical Innovations, Open Solutions*, 9(1), 58243–58255. DOI: 10.1109/ACCESS.2021.3072734

Krug, S. (2014). *Don't Make Me Think, Revisited: A Common Sense Approach to Web Usability* (3rd ed.). New Riders.

Kumar, P. (2021). Low-Resource Settings in AI-Driven Education. *Educational Data Science*, 28(3), 89–101.

Kumar, S., Chakrabarti, S., & Roy, S. (2017). Earth movers distance pooling over Siamese LSTMs for automatic short answer grading. *Proc. Int. Joint Conf. Artif. Intell.*, 2046–2052.

Laurillard, D. (2012). *Teaching as a Design Science: Building Pedagogical Patterns for Learning and Technology*. Routledge.

Lee, S. (2023). Optimizing AI Models for Efficiency. *Computers & Education*, 15(4), 233–245.

Leon, C., & Anna, F. (2020). Investigating transformers for automatic short answer grading. *Proc. Int. Conf. Artif. Intell. Educ.*, 43–48.

Liao, W. X., Zeng, B., Yin, X. W., & Wei, P. F. (2021). An improved aspect category sentiment analysis model for text sentiment analysis based on RoBERTa. *Applied Intelligence*, 51(6), 3522–3533. DOI: 10.1007/s10489-020-01964-1

Liu, T., Ding, W., Wang, Z., Tang, J., Huang, G., & Liu, Z. (2019). Automatic short answer grading via multiway attention networks. *Proc. Int. Conf. Artif. Intell. Educ.*, 169–173. DOI: 10.1007/978-3-030-23207-8_32

Liu, Y.RoBERTa: A robustly optimized BERT pretraining approach. arXiv:1907.11692v1.

Marvaniya, S., Saha, S., Dhamecha, T. I., Flotz, P., Sindhgatta, R., & Sengupta, B. (2018). Creating scoring rubric from representative student answers for improved short answer grading. Proc. 27th ACM Int. Conf. Inf. Knowl. Manage., 993–1002. DOI: 10.1145/3269206.3271755

Mohler, M., Bunescu, R., & Mihalcea, R. (2011). Learning to grade short answer questions using semantic similarity measures and dependency graph alignments. Proc. Annu. Meeting Assoc. Comput. Linguistics, Hum. Lang. Technol., 752–762.

Nguyen, M. T., Le, D. T., & Le, L. (2021). Transformers-based information extraction with limited data for domain-specific business documents. *Engineering Applications of Artificial Intelligence*, 97, 104100. DOI: 10.1016/j.engappai.2020.104100

Nielsen, J. (1994). *Usability Engineering*. Morgan Kaufmann.

Norman, D. A. (2013). *The Design of Everyday Things (Revised and Expanded Edition).* Basic Books.

Reeves, T. C., & Hedberg, J. G. (2003). *Interactive Learning Systems Evaluation.* Educational Technology Publications.

Riordan, B., Horbach, A., Cahill, A., Zesch, T., & Chong, M. L. (2017). *Investigating neural architectures for short answer scoring. Proc. 12th Workshop Innov.* Use NLP Building Educ. Appl.

Saha, S., Dhamecha, T. I., Marvaniya, S., Sindhgatta, R., & Sengupta, B. (2018). Sentence level or token level features for automatic short answer grading? Use both. *Proc. Int. Conf. Artif. Intell. Educ.*, 503–517. DOI: 10.1007/978-3-319-93843-1_37

Sahu, A., & Bhowmick, P. K. (2020, January–March). Feature engineering and ensemble-based approach for improving automatic short-answer grading performance. *IEEE Transactions on Learning Technologies*, 13(1), 77–90. DOI: 10.1109/TLT.2019.2897997

Selwyn, N. (2011). *Education and the Digital: What the Research Tells Us.* Routledge.

Selwyn, N. (2016). *Education and Technology: Key Issues and Debates* (2nd ed.). Bloomsbury Academic.

Seuzen, N. (2020). Text Mining in Automated Grading. *Journal of Educational Measurement*, 39(3), 213–229.

Seuzen, N., Gorban, A. N., Levesley, J., & Mirkes, E. M. (2020). Automatic short answer grading and feedback using text mining methods. Procedia Comput. Sci., 169, 726–743. DOI: 10.1016/j.procs.2020.02.171

Smith, G. G., Haworth, R., & Zitnik, S. (2020). Computer science meets education: Natural language processing for automatic grading of open-ended questions ineBooks. *Journal of Educational Computing Research*, 58(7), 1227–1255. DOI: 10.1177/0735633120927486

Smith, J., & Doe, A. (2022). Advances in AI for Education. *Journal of Educational Technology*, 45(2), 123–135.

Song, Wen, Xiao, & Park. (2021). Semantics perception and refinement network for aspect-based sentiment analysis. Knowl.-Based Syst., 214.

Sultan, M. A., Salazar, C., & Sumner, T. (2016). Fast and easy short answer grading with high accuracy. Proc. Conf. North Amer. Chapter Assoc. Comput. Linguistics, Hum. Lang. Technol., 1070–1075. DOI: 10.18653/v1/N16-1123

Sung, C., Dhamecha, T. I., & Mukhi, N. (2019). Improving short answer grading using transformer-based pre-training. *Proc. Conf. Artif. Intell. Educ.*, 469–481. DOI: 10.1007/978-3-030-23204-7_39

Tan, H., Wang, C., Duan, Q., Lu, Y., & Li, R. (2020a). Automatic short answer grading by encoding student responses via a graph convolutional network. *Interactive Learning Environments*, 2020, 1–15.

Tan, H., Wang, C., Duan, Q., Lu, Y., & Li, R. (2020b). Enhancing Grading Precision with GCNs. *AI Review*, 27(1), 50–63.

Tulu, C. N., Kaya, M., & Kocamanlar, M. (2021). MaLSTM for Short Answer Grading. *Computers & Education*, 42(4), 255–269.

Tulu, C. N., Ozkaya, O., & Orhan, U. (2021). Automatic short answer grading with SemSpace sense vectors and MaLSTM. *IEEE Access : Practical Innovations, Open Solutions*, 9, 19270–19280. DOI: 10.1109/ACCESS.2021.3054346

Uto, M., & Uchida, Y. (2020). Automated short-answer grading using deep neural networks and item response theory. *Proc. Int. Conf. Artif. Intell. Educ.*, 334–339. DOI: 10.1007/978-3-030-52240-7_61

Uto, M., & Uchida, Y. (2020). Automated Feature Extraction with IRT and LSTM. *Journal of Educational Technology & Society*, 23(2), 110–122.

Vaswani, A.Attention is all you need. *Proc. 31st Conf. Neural Inf. Process. Syst.*, 5998–6008.

Yang, B., Wang, L., Wong, D. F., Chao, L. S., & Tu, Z. (2019). Convolutional self-attention networks. *Proc. Conf. North Amer. Chapter Assoc. Comput. Linguistics. Hum. Lang. Technol.*, 1, 4040–4045.

Yang, H., Zeng, B., Yang, J., Song, Y., & Xu, R. (2020). A multi-task learning model for Chinese-oriented aspect polarity classification and aspect term extraction. *Neurocomputing*, 419, 344–356. DOI: 10.1016/j.neucom.2020.08.001

Zhang, W., & Li, H. (2023). Transformer Models in Student Assessment. *AI in Education*, 34(1), 67–79.

Zhang, Y., Lin, C., & Chi, M. (2020). Going deeper: Automatic short-answer grading by combining student and question models. *User Modeling and User-Adapted Interaction*, 30(1), 51–80. DOI: 10.1007/s11257-019-09251-6

Zhao, W., Ye, J., Yang, M., Lei, Z., Zhang, S., & Zhao, Z. (2018). Investigating capsule networks with dynamic routing for text classification. *Proc. Conf. Empirial Methods Natural Lang. Process.*, 43–48.

Zhou, Huang, Hu, & He. (2020). SK-GCN: Modeling syntax and knowledge via graph convolutional network for aspect-level sentiment classification. Knowl.-Based Syst., 205(3).

Zhu, X., Wu, H., & Zhang, L. (2022, June). Automatic Short-Answer Grading via BERT-Based Deep Neural Networks. *IEEE Transactions on Learning Technologies*, 15(3), 364–371. DOI: 10.1109/TLT.2022.3175537

KEY TERMS AND DEFINITIONS

AERSCAE: Automatic and Enhanced Reflexive System for Concise Answer Evaluation -An AI-driven system for evaluating student responses in educational settings.

BERT: Bidirectional Encoder Representations from Transformers - A transformer-based model for natural language processing tasks.

Bi-LSTM: Bidirectional Long Short-Term Memory - A type of RNN that processes data in both forward and backward directions for enhanced context understanding.

Educational Psychology: The study of how people learn and the best practices for teaching and learning.

Ethical Considerations: The principles that guide behavior and decision-making to ensure fairness, transparency, and respect for all individuals involved.

Intelligent Tutoring Systems (ITS): Computer-based instructional systems that provide personalized and adaptive learning experiences.

Pedagogical Studies: Research focused on the methods and practice of teaching, especially as an academic subject or theoretical concept.

Semantic Refinement: The process of improving the understanding of meaning in language data through additional computational layers or techniques.

Textual Entailment: The task of determining if one sentence logically follows from another.

Transfer Learning: A machine learning technique where a model developed for a particular task is reused as the starting point for a model on a second task.

Usability: The ease of use and efficiency with which users can achieve their goals using a particular tool or system.

User Experience (UX): The overall experience of a person using a product, especially in terms of how easy or pleasing it is to use.

Chapter 7
Integrating Learning Management System With Dynamic Composition of Distributed Web Services: Composition of Web Services for a Flexible User Interface

Sumathi Pawar
Information Science & Engineering, Nitte(DU),NMAMIT, Nitte, Karkala,, India

Suma K. Nair
Mangalore Institute of Technology and Management, Moodbidri, India

Vandhana B. S.
Information Science & Engineering, Nitte(DU),NMAMIT, Nitte, Karkala, India

K. Ankitha
Information Science & Engineering, Nitte(DU),NMAMIT, Nitte, Karkala, India

Hemanth Kumar Reddy
https://orcid.org/0000-0003-2492-3312
Vellore Institute of Technology, India

ABSTRACT

E-learning and its management is essential during pandemic situations, which require integration and management of learning management web services in the universities. This necessitates adapting service-oriented architecture (SOA) in higher education.

DOI: 10.4018/979-8-3693-2337-3.ch007

There are several categories of users such as administrators, researchers, teachers, students, and maintenance team of different computer systems. If these systems are exposed as web services, then it can be utilized or consumed by other applications. Due to distributed web services, a student record from student information system may provide services for library management system or learning management system. It is very good practice to distribute the services using available computing facilities of laboratory Pcs and due to this existing lab resource facilities shared and utilized. This chapter is focused on integrating e-learning methods according to user requirement for flexible user interface. Apriori algorithm is used to train the machine and performance of the system is measured during testing the system.

INTRODUCTION

A distributed e-learning centre is an educational platform that delivers learning experiences and resources across various locations or through remote access. Unlike traditional learning centres confined to a physical space, a distributed e-learning centre leverages digital technology to provide educational content, courses, and support to learners regardless of their geographical location. These centres often utilize online platforms, multimedia resources, and interactive tools to facilitate learning, collaboration, and engagement among students and instructors.

They typically offer a wide range of courses, programs, or modules covering diverse subjects, catering to different levels of learners. By employing various technologies such as video lectures, live streaming, discussion forums, and interactive assessments, these centres create an immersive and flexible learning environment accessible to participants anywhere with an internet connection. This system uses e-learning Web services which are developed in multiple platforms. These Web services are located in different locations either using Java or .net or Python platform. Developers of the e-learning methods or functions might be stored their contents in any platform. Stakeholders such as users are needed to access it through easy user interface. This system facilitates multiplatform interface through integration of Web services called distributed e-learning centre.

The advantages of a distributed e-learning centre include increased accessibility, flexibility in learning schedules, scalability to accommodate a larger number of learners, and the ability to reach a broader and more diverse audience. This model also enables personalized learning experiences, allowing students to progress at their own pace and choose courses aligned with their interests and career goals. Overall, a distributed e-learning centre serves as a dynamic and inclusive hub for education, breaking barriers of distance and time to provide quality learning opportunities to a global audience. The services required for this system is given here.

Authentication Services: Utilizing OAuth, OpenID, or other authentication protocols to ensure secure access for users across different platforms and services.
Communication Services: Implementing APIs for real-time communication tools such as chat, video conferencing, or messaging services to enable collaboration among learners and educators.
Learning Management Systems (LMS): Integrating with or building upon existing LMS platforms to manage courses, assessments, and student progress.
MicroServices Architecture: The decentralized e-learning application can be structured using a microservices architecture. Different functionalities such as user management, content delivery, communication, and analytics can be divided into smaller, independent services that communicate via APIs. This enhances scalability, flexibility, and maintainability.
Content Delivery Networks (CDNs): For efficient distribution of educational content like videos, documents, and multimedia CDNs used.
Interoperability and Standards: Ensuring that these composed Web services adhere to standards and protocols (like RESTful APIs) which allows for interoperability between different components, making it easier to integrate new services or replace existing ones.

By combining decentralized principles with a composition of various web services, e-learning platforms can offer a robust, secure, and feature-rich learning environment. This setup also allows for scalability, adaptability, and potential future enhancements by integrating new services or technologies as they emerge in the e-learning landscape.

This system is aimed to develop an integrated learning management system with dynamic composition of distributed Web services. The objectives of this system are:

- To switch from centralized architecture to distributed architecture
- To provide SOA to existing Learning Management Services
- Reuse of existing Learning Management services
- Dynamic composing of existing Learning Management services according to runtime requirement using AI technique
- To provide an attractive User Interface design for the user.

The outcome or deliverables of this system are:

- An Integrated system of Distributed E-Learning Management Webservices
- Dynamically composed Webservices according to consumer requirement
- Minimum resource usage
- Easy fault recovery

- Load Balancing
- Improved ability of students to engage with technology and improved learning outcomes through remote access of Learning materials.

Necessity of Dynamic Composition Plan

In real world of Web services, development side stakeholders may go on change or add services at any time. Especially in the case of education as the contents go on changing, it is required to add and also modify the functionalities of the Web services. Instead of changing entire system, it can be possible to add more operations or change signature of the operations to existing Web services. Every time when there is updating to Web services, WSDL file will be changing, which necessitates fetching modified WSDL during runtime. As a scenario, consider a E-Learning Webservice by name "result" which is dynamic in nature and shown in Figure 1. When we look into partial contents of WSDL, there are 2 operation names "get-ResultByUsn" and "getSubjectMarks" at time 't1'.

Figure 1. Sample WSDL file of result web service at time t1

```
<definitions>
  <service>
    <portType>
        <operation name=”GetResultByUsn”
          .......
          .......
        </operation>
        <operation name=”GetSubjectMarks”>
          .......
          .......
        </operation>
      </portType>
    </service>
  </definition>
```

Figure 2. Sample WSDL of the same result service at time t2

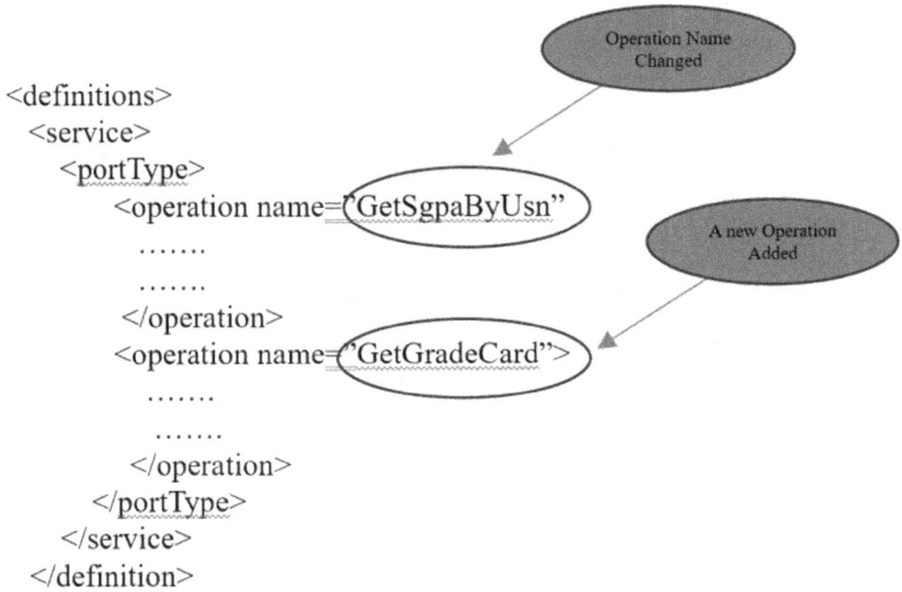

Change of WSDL file contents in Figure 2 shows, existing operation "GetResult-ByUsn"is modified as "getSgpaByUsn" and a new operation name is added. This indicates necessity of dynamic composition plan which need to be done at run time.

This system considers contents such as courses, assignment, curriculum and interactions such as assessment of learner, progress of learner, and user management. The stakeholders of this system are teachers, programmers & technical users. Teachers or Web service provider should publish their Web services & system library will have repository of published Web Services. The user will request for required information which will be directed to search system & available services' WSDL files from service library are directed to Integration/composition system. Before considering the Web services for composition, security aspect needs to be considered for maintaining integrity and confidentiality of data transfer between service provider and service consumer.

From the Web services of service library, multiple composition plans will be designed and shown to the user who selects required composition plan & dynamic composition takes place & result will be returned to end user. Integration of available services to frame required LMS during runtime & generation of multiple composition plan are research issues which require an AI technique & suitable algorithm. Apriori algorithm is an AI based technique used in this article.

RELATED WORK

Existing system (Moodle) contains the data & software related to the LMS. Existing system is centralized server system which consists of functions of learning management system & it is very risky to manage the server in this hot geographic area

Agnès F and Moulay Driss (2019) focussed on dynamic composition with "SMARTROAD" case study which is meant for composing of smart vehicle driving services according to the context. The developers of services are provided with necessary inputs to process the context. Here availability, network traffic & data dependencies of the services are main 3 factors need to be considered for service execution. The generated data during events of "SMARTROAD" are collected & developers will get trained with these data to handle the events. QOS factors are considered to recommend the services & system performance is analysed. For user business interaction, OWL-S files which are based on SLA are advertised in the UDDI registry

Given that block chain is used for semantic Web service composition & Web services involved in composition are provided by several organizations (Sridevi S. et al 2021). Here agreement between provider and consumer is encoded using block chain and also to broadcast the transactions blockchain is used. Smart contract is used to avoid the selection of unpleasant Web service & to ensure Quality of service regarding efficient, trust and secured Web services.

Rathod et al (2016) informed to use AI planning with GOAL based constraint driven Web service composition. One Web services composition is called another Web service composition which called as nested composition and uses WSBPEL or WSMO. Optimal solution for "travel scheduling" case study is performed using an AI technique. Providing of departure location, time, destination and user constraint to AI planner with hotel options will discovers services from RESTRegistry. The discovered services are based on quality and if services are not available then new value added services are generated based on available services.

Sebastián et al (2020) in their work pre-condition and post condition parameters are used to compose Web services. Metrics used for composition are composition time, automation level & adaption level by authors (M. Garriga et al 2016). (Hssina and Badr et al 2014) also focussed on creation of e-learning Web service using distributed client / server architecture with the help of WSDL, UDDI and SOAP.

Gleeson, Gerard and C. Pahl (2008) are used Grid technologies to share courseware & LMS is used to store & manage the learning content & thus by repeated use & sharing of courseware. Reusability, loose coupling, Distributed Nature is advantages of Web Services compared to Web Applications. Rick Strahl (2015) written methods/functions to access database of FoxPro Using OLEDB driver, they have implemented in Visual studio .NET. Helper classes of Westwind. Utilities .NET library provides a simple data access layer. They suggested to use ADO.NET data libraries to access the data.

S. Zhang et al (2015) proved that Swarm intelligence technique is resulted into favourable results in scalability, efficiency and performance. For deadlock avoidance & safety features in Web service composition, Petri nets are used. Petri nets are highly recommendable in-service Composition which requires input/output compatibility and exceptional paths. But there are few drawbacks in this system such as mapping work flow patterns & synchronization in high-level Petri nets.

Marinela Mircea (2012) discussed about storing distributed contents requires publishing of the service in distributed environment using open-source tools such as Java is very helpful. Authors of "Janus Wrapper" which is existing Technology given that it is very difficult task to a create Virtual Learning Environment. The LeAP project in Tasmania is the main successful implementation of a service-oriented project and very rare example of service-oriented VLE.

Homa et al (2014) focussed on a new mathematical based evaluation for service composition by providing security aspect is proposed by authors. An Analytic Hierarchy Process (AHP) is decision-making technique which is adopted based on multiple criteria. Results of this research is analysed statistically for correctness and efficiency of results.

Slaimi et al (2013) given that horizontal & vertical composition is performed by authors based on Ontology which is nothing but OVWSC (Ontology based Web Service Composition). In this work it is given about Domain services ontology which is a process to suggest rules for automatically selecting Web services for generating abstract workflow.

AI techniques provide a solid background for semantic Web service composition by the theoretical works, such as the Causal Link Matrix (CLM) given by Lécué F and Léger A (2006). Web service composition constituted by a formal theoretical model accommodating CLM which is an AI planning technique. All causal relations between semantic Web services are computed by CLM and these pre-computed parameters are utilized to formulate valid compositions. But there are a smaller number of implementation and experimental results. Hence conclusions cannot be drawn about its scalability.

Guillermo R (2016) provided information about number of research work carried out in Web Service composition with AI techniques. Different techniques are presented in both conference and journal papers. It is shown in their result that 37.5% of research work carried out using AI planning, 12.5% of research work carried out in the composition of Web services using Propositional logic and 20.5% of research work carried out using Genetic Algorithms etc.

Benefits of using AI is to predict the next set of operations in E-Learning system and for pre-fetching the same for faster access. There also some drawback in this system, such as storing datasets related remote Web services, pre-fetching huge size of WSDL files and user choice volatility in choosing the E-learning operations.

METHODOLOGY

Existing researches broken down the centralized applications of E-learning into standalone applications and then these are accessed as Web services. Existing software can be reused for developing standard based educational services with the help of SOA.

Steps required includes (1) Storing learning content in a distributed fashion indicates registering the services in library of services with an interface. and (2) dynamically composing the E-learning contents when necessary or appropriate according to user requirement.

Deploying E-learning Webservices

Brief Outline of entire system is given in Figure 3.

Figure 3. Outline of the system

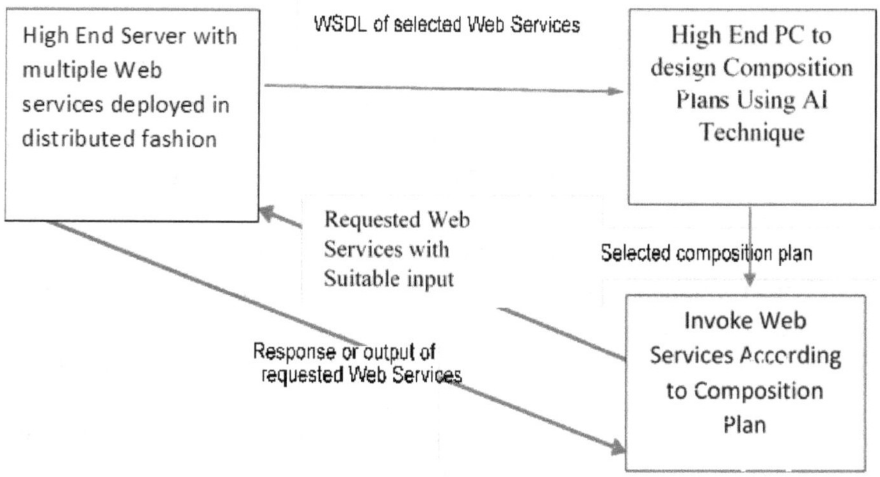

Faculties in remote location created their teaching- learning services and published it. Then the WSDL is generated and parameters of these WSDL is used to integrate the Webservices. The approach to integration of Web services is given in Figure 4.

Architecture of Dynamic Composition of Learning Management Web Services

Figure 4. Architecture of e-learning system and its composition

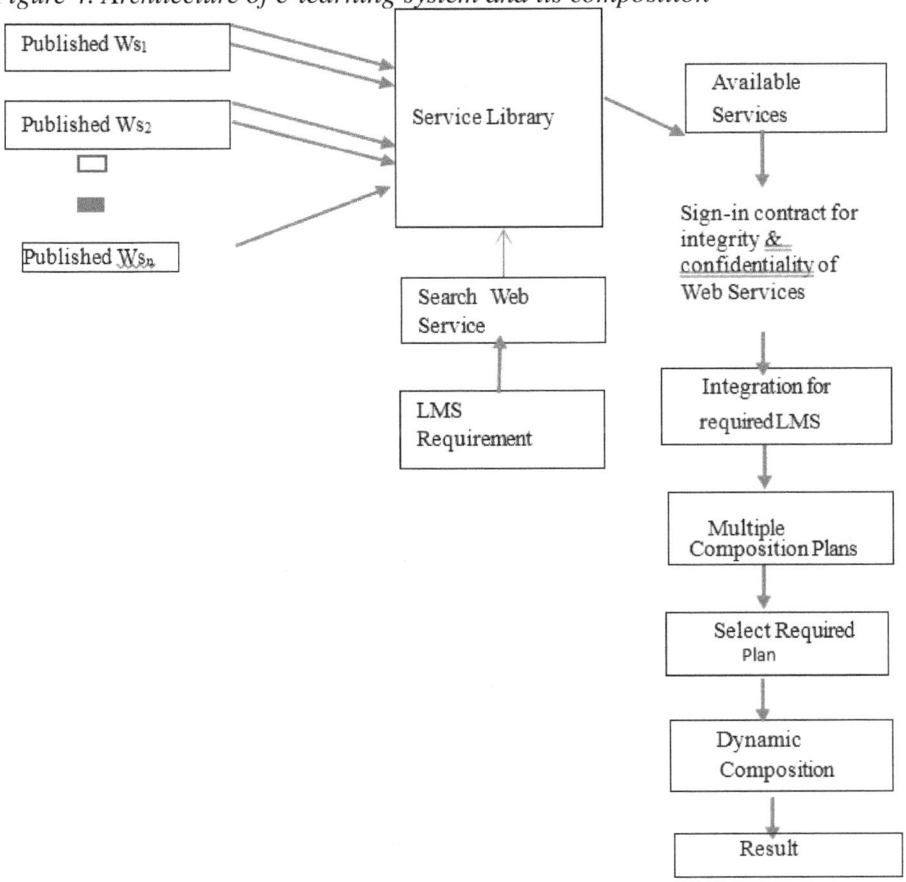

Integration of required LMS Using an AI Technique

LMS is a composed system of the distributed Web services and user may need any information which is combination of different operations. Which operations are needed to be composed for which requirement? This question will be answered through proper training of the composition plan system. According to literature survey, 100% effective composition algorithms are not available still now. Therefore, this research is focussed on composing services of LMS to satisfy user request dynamically. An Artificial Intelligence technique includes training the system with existing composition plans with available services with maximum number of possible compositions and developing a suitable algorithm to create required suitable composition plan.

- Dynamic Content Optimization: While CDNs are typically known for caching static content (like images and scripts), modern CDNs also optimize dynamic content delivery. They can cache and serve dynamically generated content intelligently, reducing server load and improving response times.
- Content Pre-fetching and Predictive Caching: Predictive algorithms and machine learning models can anticipate user actions or content needs based on historical data. Pre-fetching and caching content that is likely to be requested can significantly reduce latency by having the content ready before it's needed.
- Overall, the logic behind dynamic content optimization revolves around finding a balance between generating personalized, frequently changing content dynamically while leveraging caching, fragmentation, compression, and adaptive techniques to optimize the delivery process. This ensures a faster, more responsive, and personalized user experience, even for content that is inherently dynamic and constantly changing.
- Content-Based Filtering: Recommends methods similar to those a user has interacted with based on attributes or characteristics of the methods. Content-based filtering is a recommendation system technique that predicts what content a user might like based on the characteristics and features of methods they have already shown interest in. The logic behind content-based filtering to predict the next content is explained with Apriori algorithm.

An approach for dynamic composition using content-based filtering is given in Figure 5.

Figure 5 Steps involved in web service integration

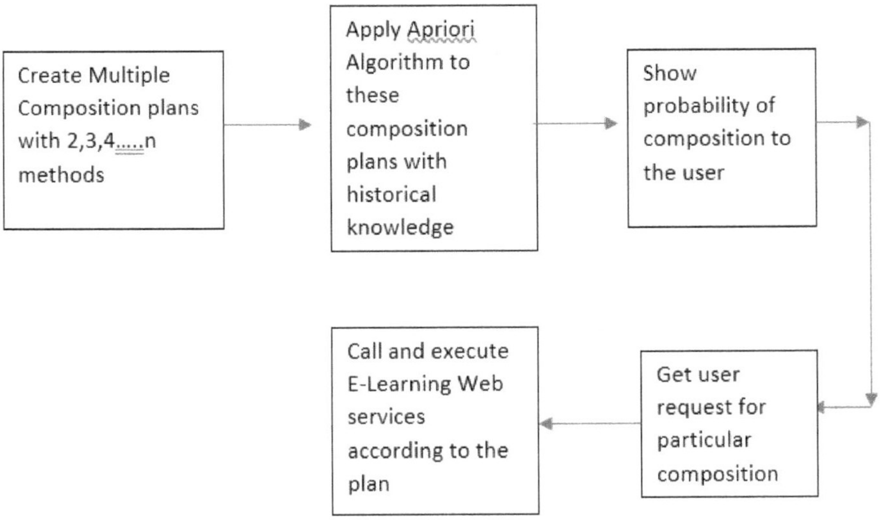

- Dynamic Web Services Integration: Within this decentralized architecture, various Web services can be integrated to enhance the functionality and features of the e-learning platform. During runtime, according to the requirement, Web services need to be called passing output of the previous Web service as the input to the required Web service. This needs understanding of the port types and parameters. A machine learning approach to do this is given in Figure 6 and explained in detail.

Figure 6. Overview of machine learning approach for dynamic composition

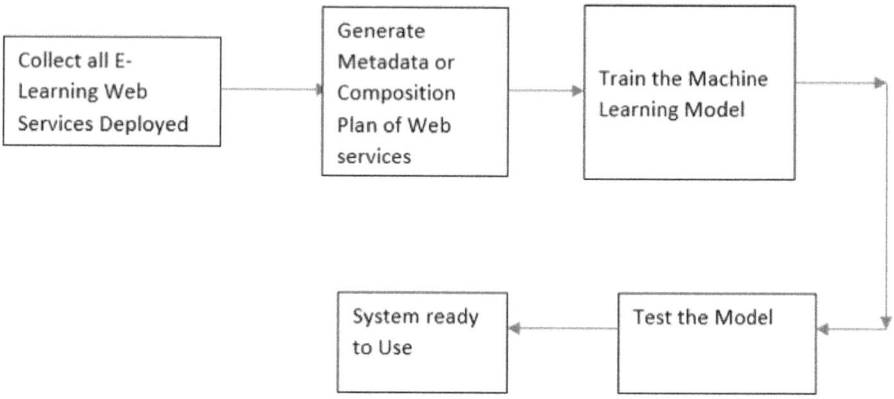

- Collection of E-Learning Web services: WSDL of each service is used to get link of deployed Web services and their all details including type of results returned.
- Generating Composition plan of all methods: This includes methods which has appropriate output and which can be fed into input of required methods.
- Training the model: This includes training the learning model with all possible composition plans for a particular user request. Usage of Apriori algorithm for pruning the in-frequent methods and joining the frequent methods.
- Testing the model: Giving appropriate request for LMS service which displays possible composition plans and fed into service caller system for runtime execution.
- System readiness: Executed Webservices results will be outputted to the user as the result.
- E-Learning Service Representation: Each service in E-learning system is represented using WSDL(Web Service Description Language). WSDL indicates Service name, operation/method names, their portTypes defined by number of parameters, parameters' types and type of return values. These features could include metadata like genre, keywords, tags, text descriptions, or other relevant properties specific to the methods.

For an example, GetSubjectMarks→GetTotalMarks→GetGrade are three methods which are composed sequentially. Here GetSubjectMarks' operation output is given as input to GetTotalMarks and output of "GetTotalMarks" method is given as input to GetGrade method. Similarly for other methods possible association rules are framed and trained to the model using Apriory algorithm as given in Figure 5.

Figure 7. Possible association of e-learning methods

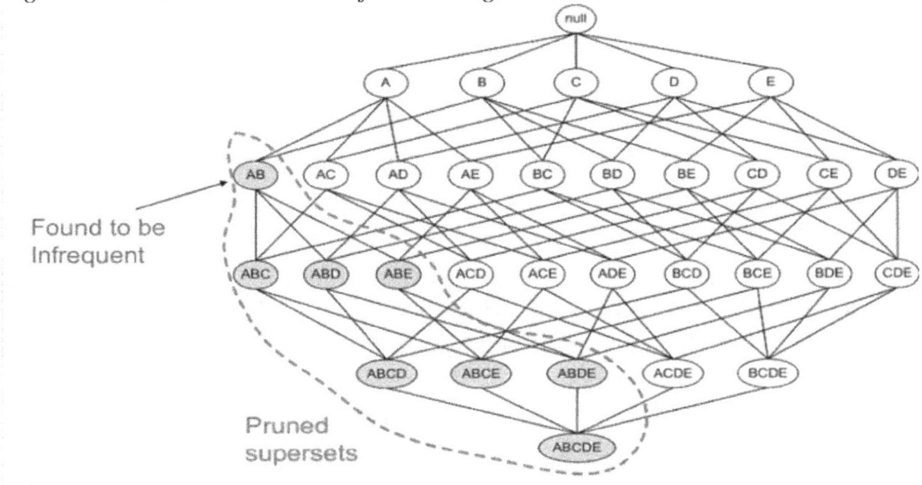

Using association rule of possible methods, this system generated multiple composition plans and Apriori algorithm by chonny (2020) is applied to find frequently generated requests and details are given here.

At the beginning support and confidence of the user request is calculated as given in equation 1 and 2.

$$\textbf{Support(M)} = \frac{\textbf{Number of requests containing the Method(M)}}{\textbf{Total Number of Requests}}$$

$$\textbf{Confidence(M)} = \frac{\textbf{Number of requests containing the Method(M and N)}}{\textbf{Total Number of Requests contains M}}$$

Apriori Algorithm
L1={frequest 1- requests}
For (k=2;L_{k-1} !=0;k++) do begin
C_k=apriori-gen($L_{k-1)}$
for each request t∈ D do begin
C_t=subset(Ck,t)
For each candidate c∈C_t do
c.count++
end
L_k={ c ∈C_k | c.count>=minsup}

End
Answer=$\cup_k L_k$

- Here **Lk:** frequent k-methods, satisfy minimum support
- **Ck:** candidate k-methods, possible frequent k-methods
- 'D' is the dataset of possible composition plans of all available methods

Apriori algorithm follows bottom-up approach where candidates generated by self-joining. The subset indicates possible composition of all the methods and infrequent subsets are pruned. The process is repeated until no more composed subsets can be derived from the data.

- Use k-1 methods to generate k method sets
- Getting C[k] by joining L[k-1] and L[k-1]
- Prune C[k] with subset testing
- Generate L[k] by extracting the methods in C[k] that satisfy minSup

Usability and User Experience Design

Designing for usability and user experience (UX) in a multi-platform system is a complex but essential task to ensure a seamless and consistent user journey across different devices. Here are some key strategies and best practices:

Understand the User experience: User opinion is surveyed to get information about in which context and platform the user interacts with the system. Conducted user research to understand the context in which users interacted with the system on different platforms. Their motivation and goals are used to get Personas and Scenarios which is understood by user personas and scenarios to represent typical users and their goals, motivations, and behaviours on each platform are understood. User interface experience and behaviour focussed on the consistent visual elements like, typography, colours, icons and components across all platforms. It is understood that user responsive techniques which implemented with adaptive design principles to tailor the experience to more optimized design is followed. Native guidelines are followed to provide familiar and intuitive experience and which provide platform-specific features for interactions. To do consistent navigation, clear information architecture ensured logical and easy to navigate with clear labelling and categorization.

Lazy loading and code splitting: To improve performance, through fast load time lazy loading technique is used with images for improving initial load time and performance. Code splitting techniques are used to minimize the number of HTTP requests by combining files. High contrast fonts which are scalable are used to design user interfaces. This application is tested with variety of browsers to identify and fix compatibility issues. To identify pain points, usability testing is conducted through real users on different platforms. User feedback is taken to improve the user satisfaction and also content management is done for easy updates and maintenance.

Implementation

E-learning Web services are collected from remote locations which are implemented either using Java or .Net platform. WSDL files of remote Web services are collected and processed to get signature of these remote methods. WSDL files are implemented using WSDL helper classes as described in this section.

At the beginning WSDLHelper class is imported and object of this class is created. During creation of the object location of WSDL file of Web services is passed as parameters to the constructors of the class. Then various methods of this classes are called to parse and get useful information from WSDL files.

Let us consider weather service is stored in the Web service "http://webservicex .net/globalweather.asmx". To get WSDL detail of this web service it is need to download WSDL file. At the beginning WSDLHelper object parses WSDL definition and stores portTypes with details of existing operations. Through GetOperations method of WSDLHelper class object, operation element will be extracted with following statement by Sumathi and Niranjan (2015, 2018).

OperationName=Searchops.get(count).getName() statement.

operationCount= WSDLHelper.getInMessageParts(Searchops.get(count))

Once count of operations and operation name is got, it is needed to get input and output of the operations. This information required to populate the web services tuple. For each user request, what will be next Web service required depends on output of the executed service and same technique is used to generate composition plan.

This article used Python for implementing Apriori algorithm. Sample python code is given here.

```
def apriori(frequent_operations, minimum_support, minimum_confidence):
def get_frequent_itemsets(candidates, frequent_operations, minimum_support):
operation_counts = {}
for operation in frequent_operations:
for request_set in candidates:
if request_set.issubset(frequent_operations):
if request_set not in request_set _counts:
request_set _count[request_set] = 1
else:
request_set _count [request_set] += 1
```

return { request_set: count for request_set, count in request_set _counts.items() if count >= minimum_support}

In this code sample frequent operations gives frequent set of operations requested by the user. Candidates gives previous requested operations. If any requested operations matches previous operation in frequent set of operations, then next operation is fetched by the associated operation using Union rule.

RESULT

It is shown in Figure 8 that candidate generation takes seconds of time to find possible composable methods by interpreting WSDL of each service. In Figure 9 time taken to find the support of each composition plan and pruning the in-frequent compositions is shown. Once the required support of frequent requests found, pruning takes less time. After training the system with possible composition plans, execution of services takes less time and shown in Figure 10.

Figure 8. Time taken for each candidate generation in Apriori algorithm

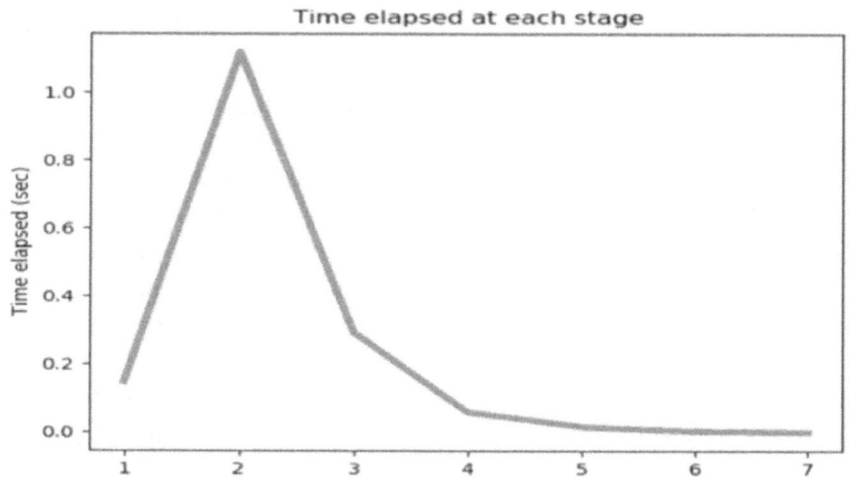

Figure 9. Time taken for pruning and counting support

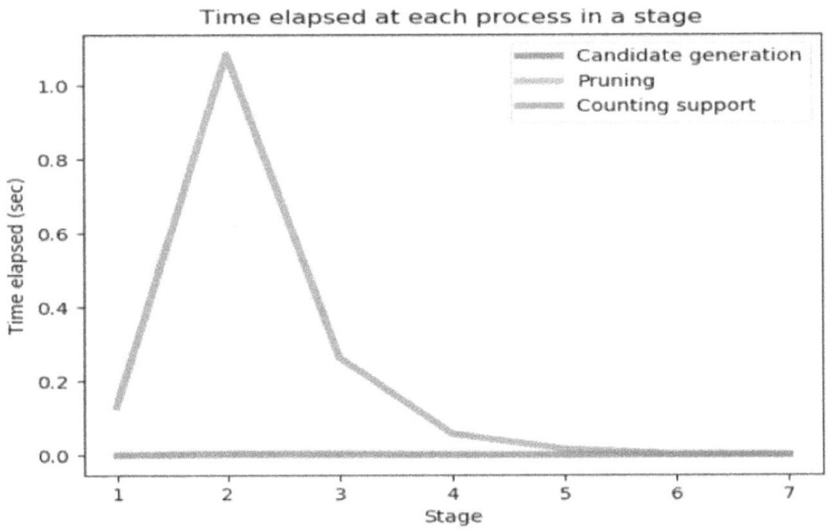

In Figure 10, it is shown the retrieval performance training the system with 200 and .300 methods. Performance factors are calculated as given in equation 3,4,5,6 and 7.

Accuracy=(TP+TN)/(TP+TN+FP+FN) (3)

Recall=TP/(TP+FN)

(4)

Score =TN/(TN+FP)

(5)

Precision=TP/(TP+FP)

(6)

F-Measure=2*(P*R)/(P+R) (7)

During testing the system, it is found that performance is improved for model trained with 300 methods compared with 200 methods.

Figure 10. Performance of retrieval model

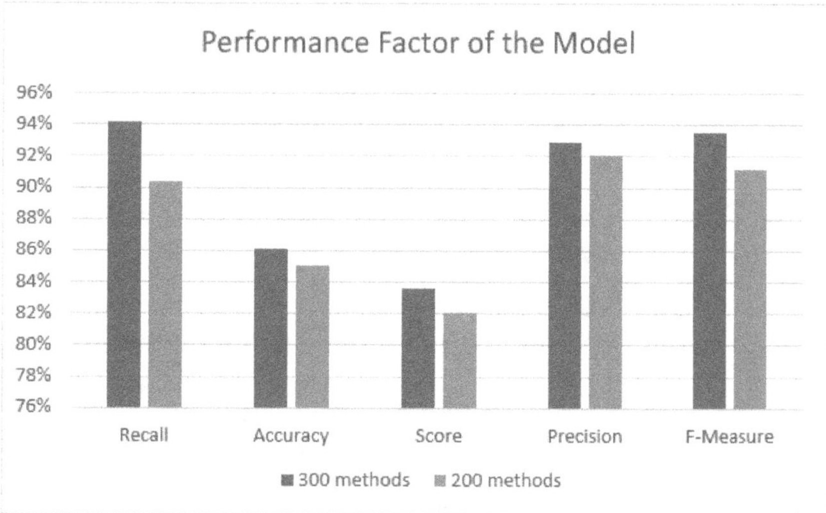

Figure 11. Learning Management System

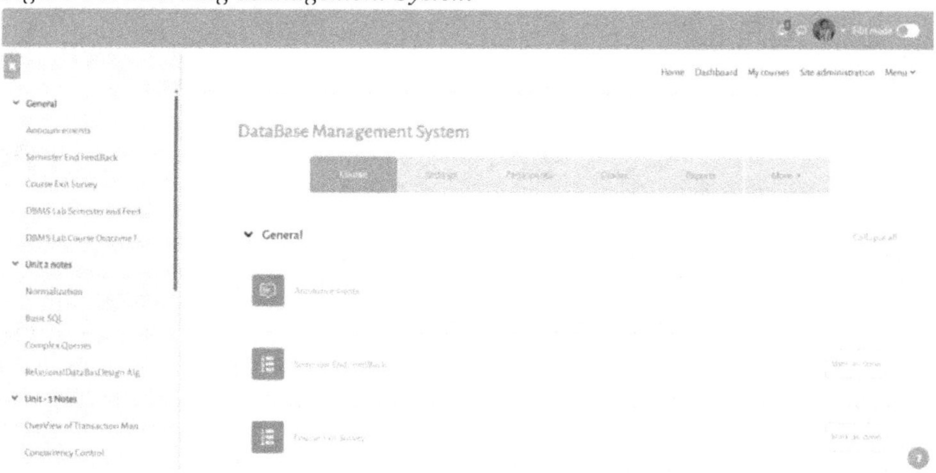

In the background of this system, integration of Web services is performed by combining the Web services of different platform. But user needs an attractive interface. Figure 11 shows attractive interface and also feedback of the user who used this system which is calculated in deciding user experience in with this system.

ANALYSIS

Advantage of Web services compared to Web Application is Web application is centralized and designed to known outcome. But Web services are distributed in nature and designed to return a service upon user requirement. Web applications will give outcome which is designed for known requirements. But composed Web services will give outcome which is not known at design time and are dynamic in nature.

Web applications cannot interact dynamically in runtime with each other and Web Services can be composed dynamically.

Educational Web Services need to be deployed properly and can be composed during run-Time. For example, output of student information can be fetched to library information system Web services. Different users function or services can be reused to get one integrated system. Another main advantage of Distributed Web Services compared to centralized services are Reusability, distributed, composition is involved, load balance and less resource usage.

Dynamic composition method is innovative and not solved accurately with 100 percent accuracy. But compared to static composition, dynamic composition is more useful. BPEL model is used for static composition, but there is no such tool available for dynamic composition of Web services. Therefore the proposed system plays vital rule in integrating multi-platform E-learning Web services.

CONCLUSION

According to literature review, existing works focussed on different methods to perform dynamic Web service composition by considering QOS properties. Through literature review it is observed that to address all the problems of dynamic composition no system been developed yet. The proposed system focussed on integrating the distributed learning management services in contrast to centralized system. Usage of AI technique will focus on giving a suitable solution to address the dynamic composition problem. In Apriori algorithm, every time it is required to scan with frequently requested data sets and more time is taken to generate candidate methods according to number of available methods. Currently the proposed system works with existing freely available Web services and also some Web services are created for practical implementation. While it is required to consider QOS parameters of the services and also ethical clearance is required for using some appropriate Web services. In the future work to overcome this problem quality and ethical issues are considered.

REFERENCES

Chonyy. (2022). Apriori — Association Rule Mining In-depth Explanation and Python Implementation Towards Data Science, https://towardsdatascience.com /apriori-association-rule-mining -explanation-and-python-implementation-290b42afdfc6

Front, A., & Rahmani, M. D. (2019). A context-aware recommendation-based system for service, composition in smart environments. *Service Oriented Computing and Applications*, 341–355.

Garriga, M., Flores, A., Cechich, A., & Zunino, A. (2015). Web service composition mechanisms: A review. *IETE Technical Review*, 32(5), 1–8. DOI: 10.1080/02564602.2015.1019942

Gleeson & Pahl. (2008). Service-based Grid Architectures to support the Virtualization of Learning Technology Systems.

Hssina, B. (2014). Web services at the service of e-learning platforms. *International Journal of Innovation and Applied Studies*, 7(4), 1574–1581. https://west-wind.com/presentations/creatingandconsumingfoxprowebserviceswithdotnet.pdf

Lécué, F., & Léger, A. (2006). A Formal Model for Semantic Web Service Composition. In Lecture Notes in Computer Science: Vol. 4273. *The Semantic Web - ISWC* (pp. 385–398). Springer.

Mircea, M. (2012). SOA adoption in higher education: A practical guide to service-oriented virtual learning environment. *Procedia: Social and Behavioral Sciences*, 31, 218–223. DOI: 10.1016/j.sbspro.2011.12.045

Movahednejad, H., Ibrahim, S. B., Sharifi, M., Selamat, H. B., Lashkari, A. H., & Sayed, G. H. T. (2014). Novel Security Conscious Evaluation Criteria for Web Service Composition. Research Journal of Applied Sciences, Engineering and Technology, 7(4), 673-695.

Qusay, I. (2018). Web Applications And Web Services: A Comparative Study. *Science Journal of University of Zakho*, 6(1), 35. Advance online publication. DOI: 10.25271/2018.6.1.375

Rathod, D., Parikh, S., & Dahiya, M. S. (2016), Goal-Based Constraint Driven Dynamic RESTful Web Service Composition Using AI Techniques. In Proceedings of International Conference on ICT for Sustainable Development. Advances in Intelligent Systems and Computing, vol 408. Springer. DOI: 10.1007/978-981-10-0129-1_77

Rodrigues, G., Soria, A., & Campo, M. (2015). AI-based web service composition: A review. *IETE Technical Review*, 33(4), 1–8. DOI: 10.1080/02564602.2015.1110061

Slaimi, F. (2014). Ontology based vertical web service composition. *Int. J. Knowl. Based Intell. Eng. Syst.*, 18, 1–12.

Sridevi, S., Karpagam, G. R., Vinoth Kumar, B., & Uma Maheswari, J. (2021), Investigation on Blockchain Technology for Web Service Composition: A Case Study. International Journal of Web Services Research 18(1). DOI: 10.1109/ICATCCT.2015.7456981

Strahl. (2015). Converting Foxpro to Web Services. Southwest Fox 2015.

Sumathi & Chiplunkar. (2018). Populating Parameters of Web Services by Automatic Composition Using Search Precision and WSDL Weight Matrix. IJCSE. .DOI: 10.1504/IJCSE.2016.10007953

Vallejos, S., Leonardo, D. R. A., Rodríguez, G., Berdun, L., & Toscani, R. (2020). Preference-Based AI Planning for Web Service Composition. IEEE Latin America Transactions, 18(11).

Zhang, S., Lee, C., Chan, H., Choy, K., & Wu, Z. (2015). Swarm intelligence applied in green logistics: A literature review. *Engineering Applications of Artificial Intelligence*, 37, 154–169. DOI: 10.1016/j.engappai.2014.09.007

Chapter 8
Human Resource Development (HRD) Strategies for Emerging Entrepreneurship:
Leveraging UX Design for Sustainable Digital Growth

R. Somasundaram
https://orcid.org/0000-0002-0377-9094
Department of Management Studies, Kongu Engineering College, Perundurai, India

Saurabh Chandra
https://orcid.org/0000-0003-4172-9968
School of Law, Bennett University, India

J. Tamilarasu
Department of Management Studies, Nandha Engineering College (Autonomous), Erode, India

Archana M. Kinagi
https://orcid.org/0009-0001-5185-7974
Department of MBA (Women), Sharnbasva University, Kalaburagi, India

Shreevamshi Naveen
Department of Management Studies, Dayananda Sagar College of Engineering, Bengaluru, India

DOI: 10.4018/979-8-3693-2337-3.ch008

ABSTRACT

This chapter explores the strategic use of HRD for sustainable growth in emerging entrepreneurial ventures focusing on UX designs, highlighting the challenge of building agile teams in competitive digital markets, founded by innovators. By integrating HRD practices with UX design principles, startups can enhance creativity, improve collaboration, and focus on customer-centered product development. The chapter aims to enhance the company's vision through talent acquisition, continuous learning, and team empowerment, while incorporating UX methodologies for intuitive, user-centered digital solutions. Connecting HRD and UX design will lead to faster innovation, better alignment of business goals and user needs, promoting long-term growth and sustaining digital change. This chapter suggests that strategic HRD and thoughtful UX design can significantly enhance the competitive advantage of emerging startups in the digital era.

INTRODUCTION

In today's fast changing environment of entrepreneurship, the early stages of a startup's venture bring both opportunity and risk. It is the world in which highly competitive and ever-changing startups play a very important role in their survival and growth, the ability to adapt and innovate. In this context, there are two rather critical factors in the successful development of an emerging business: Human Resource Development (HRD) and User Experience (UX) design. This chapter approaches and establishes the interconnectedness of both disciplines and how they can be strategically leveraged to drive sustainable digital growth in emerging startups(Borriraklert & Kiattisin, 2021).

Human resource development is defined as those processes and strategies that focus on the growth and development of an organization's human capital. In the context of a startup framework, HRD is central because it is the talent of a startup that produces products and services that can innovate, create, and scale in competitive markets. Unlike established corporations, startups face the challenge of beginning to build teams from scratch in an environment characterized by limited resources and a high degree of uncertainty. Recruitment, staff development, and talent retention are critical capabilities, and hence HRD strategies that could account for the distinct needs of a startup must be designed with flexibility, creativity, and agility being some of the paramount needs(MacDonald, 2019). Founders and entrepreneurs learn the importance of investing in the human resources early and how the power behind the teams could make or break their business ventures.

In the digital age, parallel to Human Resource Development is the concept of User Experience or UX design. User Experience design is the activity of creating products and services that use both technology and interaction design elements for meaningful, relevant, and intuitive experiences of users. If customers have limitless choices digitally, then quality of experience often makes the difference between a startup and others. It becomes an essential quality in order to attract and retain customers for startups. A well-designed product, aligned with the needs of users, helps build a loyal customer base and establishes competitive advantages in the marketplace. Poor UX will badly trigger frustration and negative comments on social media too, which could turn out to be drivers for failure in an already volatile startup context(Yerram et al., 2019).

The intersection of HRD and UX design has always presented an interesting and rather somewhat underexplored avenue for almost all startups. While these disciplines are often considered separately, even their integration takes the huge potential of a startup to great positive levels for sustainable growth. Approaches under HRD which impact stimulating creativity, collaboration, and continuous learning may directly support the development of innovative, user-centered products. UX design can prove to provide valuable inputs to the HR team in terms of what skills and competencies are required for making the process of product development better. Through aligned efforts from HRD and UX, startups can create an innovative culture where employees are empowered to think critically, solve problems, and create products that can meet business goals as well as user needs(Lermen et al., 2023).

HRD is among the last priority items in emerging entrepreneurship-ideas like product development or customer acquisition. However, a view of this kind can be short sighted in that successful startups rely not only on the people but the people themselves. A balanced team with just the right mix of skills, experience, and mindset will make all the difference. Effective HRD can therefore move from this recruitment and training; it can also develop an environment in which employees are motivated to their best contribution. These include providing opportunities for professional growth, fostering open communication, and encouraging innovation. Where resources are often limited, HRD is the area in which investment in a startup can make the largest difference in the face of change for keeping a business agile and competitive(Park et al., 2018).

One of the critical elements of HRD in a startup is talent acquisition. For any startup, attracting talent strategically is the top priority since the wrong hire can seriously derail the progress of the startup. New startups usually rely on the most creative and cost-effective means because large corporations have a great many recruitment teams and all other resources at their beck and call. This may involve strategic use of one's network, leveraging social media, or building an employer brand that rings in with potential candidates. However, talent acquisition is not the beginning (Park et al., 2018). Having the right people on board a startup is only the first step; they must quickly start to build their employees' skills and capabilities. Continuous learning and development are now essential. The particular industry in which most startups operate within is very fast-moving and requires rapid technological change. The employees must be able to adapt to new tools and technologies besides the changing needs of the market. HRD strategies should, therefore, provide avenues for such adaptability. This may take forms such as formal training programs, mentoring, or on-the-job experiences. Offering employees such opportunities will greatly affect the team in terms of innovating and solving complex problems(Park et al., 2018).

Another part of HRD for startups is empowering teams. Empowered employees assume ownership of their work; they present creative ideas and are willing to go beyond limits to help the company achieve success. Start-ups have flat structures of organization, and a culture of experimentation; thus, they are very well placed to empower the teams. Ideally, the founders and the leaders of the start-ups must focus on creating an environment where employees feel trusted enough to take decisions, to experiment, and figure out new ideas. This empowerment should be supplemented by clear vision and goals along with the right resources and support mechanisms in favor of the employee to succeed (Malik et al., 2023).

While HRD focuses attention on the development of company team members, UX design, by contrast, is outwardly customer and end-user focused on the products or services developed within a startup. Still, there is an obvious connection between them. Startups invested in HRD strategies that promote the culture of creativity and innovation are more likely to build functional and delightful user experiences in their products and services. In short, UX design really boils down to understanding user needs, behaviors, and preferences and designing products that meet those needs in intuitive and meaningful ways. A product with good UX is something which feels intuitive, solves a real problem, and then evokes positive emotions in the user. Achieving this kind of design requires lots of understanding of the user, which can only be achieved through research, testing, and iteration (Evans, 2014).

ligning HRD and UX design strategies in startups can create a feedback loop to support both employee development and product innovation. For example, the information gained from a UX designer in terms of user behavior, preference, and pain points may feed into HRD work to create and equip staff with skills to tackle such needs. Similarly, as HRD works to instill the culture of collaboration and cross-functional teamwork, the processes of design-to-be-developed may well be seamless with designers, developers, and product managers all working together toward more effective UX designing and built solutions that are properly user-centered. Integration of HRD and UX design can finally lead to products that not only serve users' needs but also surprise them with better expected results, further driving customer loyalty and business growth (Øvad & Larsen, 2015).

This chapter has represented the importance of Human Resource Development and User Experience design as critical components of a startup's strategy for sustainable digital growth. This encompasses ensuring proper talent, skills, and culture that exist to drive innovation, growth, and achievement in the startup environment while UX design focuses on creating meaningful and intuitive products that meet users' needs. While this does not necessarily mean the two disciplines have to collide, such integral integration will definitely enhance the ability of startups to innovate, compete, and scale in increasingly competitive digital competition. The remaining chapters will talk about specific HRD strategies, principles of UX design, and what a startup can practically do to harness synergy opportunities in HRD and UX toward long-term success(Simsek Caglar et al., 2022).

Scope: This chapter will explore the nexus of Human Resource Development (HRD) and User Experience (UX) design for novel starts. The scope includes strategies on how to acquire talent, continuous learning, empowerment of the team, and the role of UX in creating intuitive, user-centered experiences. The present chapter is intended to be a departure point for practical insights about how startups might ensure digital growth, innovation, and competitive advantage in markets constantly in evolution- all with a special focus on the synergy of HRD and UX.

Objectives: The major objectives of this chapter are to provide insights on how an emerging startup can strategically utilize human resource development and user experience design for sustainable digital growth. The chapter shall look into actionable strategies that could help startups create an agile, innovative team through strategies relating to talent acquisition, continuous learning, and team empowerment through HRD. This chapter attempts to demonstrate how UX design may be applied within the creation of user-centred products leading to increased customer satisfaction. Simultaneously, the integration of HRD and UX design can help new startups with innovation, enhanced development of product elements, and survival in the digital platform.

BACKGROUND: HUMAN RESOURCE DEVELOPMENT (HRD) FOR STARTUPS

Human resource development is among the most significant aspects of configuration within the new entrepreneurial landscape, largely defining organizational culture, team dynamics, and innovation. The strategies developed aim at building up creativity and cooperation in bad resource conditions, volatile market situations, and the demand for agility found in startups. This identifies the most important HRD concepts and principles, powerful talent acquisition and retention strategies, continuous learning and development initiatives, and so on, and the need to empower agile teams and leadership development(Apraiz et al., 2023). Figure 1 provides a comprehensive overview of the HRD lifecycle in startups, emphasizing the interconnectedness of various HRD stages.

Figure 1. Main stages of Human Resource Development (HRD) for startups

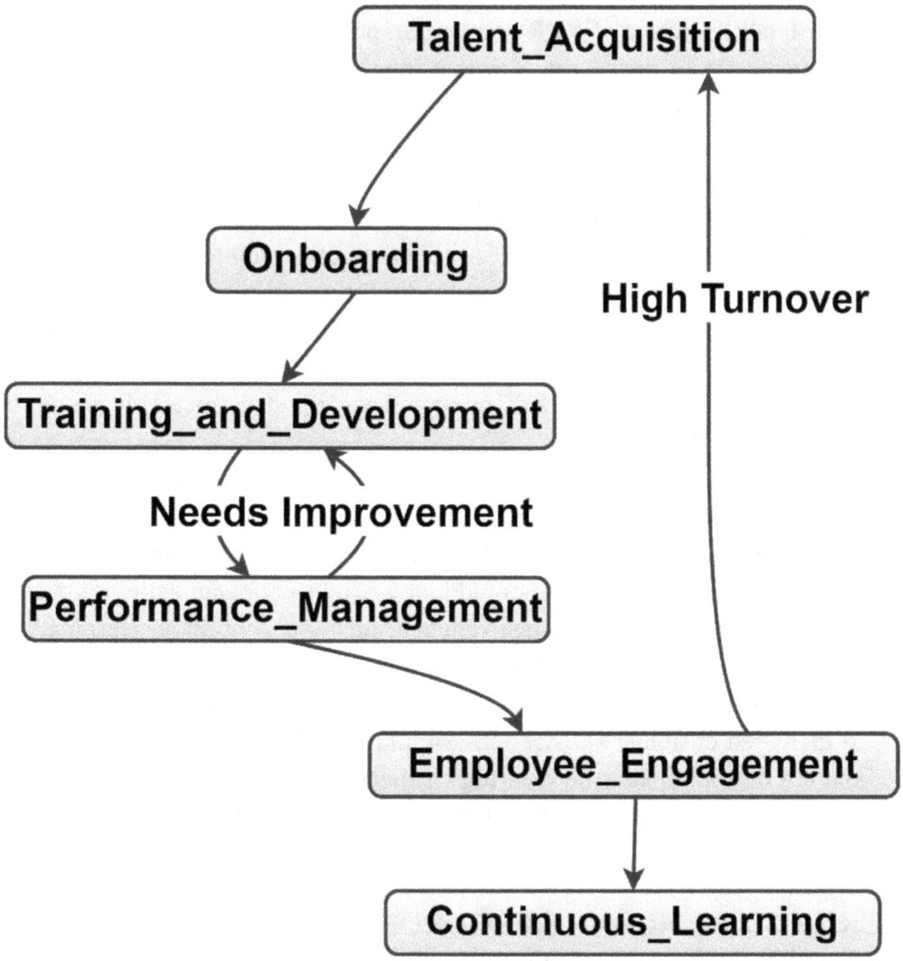

HRD Concepts and Principles

Human Resource Development refers to a set of practices focused on developing employees' skills and knowledge competencies within an organization. In other words, HRD involves the implementation of principles such as alignment to the organizational goals, the engagement of employees, and a culture that encourages and propagates continuous improvement. For startups, given their value for innovation and agility, the strategies must establish a flexible framework for the achievement of quick adaptation and responsiveness(Gomathi et al., 2023).

The concept of lifelong learning denotes this kind of continuous acquisition of the skills and knowledge that are very relevant throughout one's work life. This principle highly relates to startups, since the rapid developments within the technologies and market tendencies demand better response across departments in a startup. HRD initiatives, therefore, should be aimed at growing a growth mindset in individuals and creating the willingness to challenge, learn from feedback, and show signs of resiliency when faced with setbacks(Boopathi, 2024; S & Gopi, 2024).

On the other hand, effective HRD should ensure it utilizes mechanisms that enable employees to comment on any issues or suggestions that strike them as relevant to them so that there is ownership and commitment with the organization. This will, therefore, create a conducive atmosphere to promote the review of morale and retention levels of a startup. In a nutshell, the tenets of HRD are basic components of achieving a productive workforce because their goals encompass the vision and goals of the startup.

Talent Acquisition and Retention for Emerging Startups

Talent acquisition is one of the most significant components of HRD for emerging startups, as the wrong team can break or make the fledgling company. In effect, the nature of a startup, regardless of the industry in question, does involve competition with established organizations when recruiting the best talent available, making it incumbent on the organization to strategize how to find the best talent. An effective talent acquisition strategy for a startup should be built around developing a compelling employer brand that means something to the potential candidates. This is about expressing the mission, values, and culture of the startup in such a way that speaks to the self-motivation of individuals who want to have meaningful and impactful work experience(Gomathi et al., 2023).

Leverage social media, professional networks, and industry events to attract talent and promote unique offerings to the target talents, as well as build a referral programme encouraging current employees to recommend possible candidates.

This ups the chances of getting the right candidate and fosters a collaborative and trustworthy environment in the team.

Retention is as important for start-ups also, especially when the turnover rate may be very high and affects operations and growth. Start-ups must be able to create a positive work environment that should engage employees and ensure that they feel satisfied with their work. They can accomplish this through competitive compensation packages and opportunities in professional development, and through recognition programs that celebrate employee performance. There also needs to be open communication and transparency where employees are able to feel connected to the aims and progress of the organization.

Another retention strategy would be to provide the employees with an ownership stake in the outcome of the startup. Through equity or profit-sharing that reflects employees' stake in the next phase of the venture, employees are reminded to make investments in the company's future. In this way, through the creation of interest alignment between individual and organizational, the startup would have a committed workforce ready to work and push the business forward.

Continuous Learning and Development Strategies

Continuous learning and development is the integral essence of HRD in the present scenario, since employees in startups are always required to face new challenges and embrace opportunities. The structured approach to learning should include formal and informal development initiatives in a startup. Formal training may assume the character of essential capabilities and mastery of knowledge for the employees, whereas more informal learning opportunities—like mentoring, coaching, and peer-to-peer knowledge sharing—can develop collaboration and strengthen team dynamics(Timms, 2021).

Encouraging experimentation and risk-taking can help in the building of a culture for experimentation, one of the very effective strategies of continuous learning. Startups need to create an environment where employees are never left uncomfortable while trying a new idea, learning from failures, and iterating on work. It not only enhances individual growth but also contributes to the agility of the organization and the overall innovation capacity.

In addition, a quality onboarding process for start-ups would avail continuous learning from day one, and thus always keeps new employees learning. Thus, an all-inclusive onboarding program involves an orientation program, education on company policies and procedures as well as giving a chance to new joiners to make acquaintances with the colleagues. This way, employee onboarding investment by start-ups ensures that the fresh team member feels valued and empowered to contribute to the growth of the organization quickly.

Feedback and performance reviews are crucial for learning and development. Startups must adopt a culture that promotes a lot of feedback between managers and employees continuously. Constructive feedback should help individuals know what skills to build or improve, and what ones to leverage to eventually grow strength. All performance reviews, in any case, must be connected with individual development plans comprising clearly defined goals and opportunities for growth, holding the individual accountable for making a difference.

Agile Enabling Teams and Leadership Skills Development

What an effective empowering of agile teams the HRD in startups requires, considering that for such ventures of primary importance are flexibility and responsiveness. Efficient coordination between members characterizes agile teams, as well as openness toward changing circumstances and their ability to produce results in a very fast environment. Such a culture of autonomy and trust will empower such teams, bestowing upon individuals freedom and relegating to them work being done and decisions made without too much oversight(Zaki & Islam, 2021).

It can be acquired through delegation of authority where leaders empower team members with the execution and decision-making authority for some of the responsibilities. It boosts not only motivation but also innovation as employees are more likely to come up with creative solutions when they feel owning their work. Facilitate cross-functional collaboration in a startup since teams learn from one another across disciplines hence adopting a holistic approach in solving problems.

Leadership development is the other significant aspect of HRD for startups since leaders should drive teams and support a culture of innovativeness. A startup needs to invest in training leadership functions of the emerging leaders so that they have the ability to inspire, motivate, and empower others to achieve outcomes. Such abilities range from training them in communication, conflict resolution, decision making, among many more self-reflection areas on the human resources side for personal growth within the leadership.

Mentorship programs can also play a fruitful leadership role whereby aspiring leaders are paired with accomplished mentors who would guide and nurture them. Startups are therefore able to create relationships that help create leadership pipelines who are capable of navigating the intricacies of the business environment.

HRD is indeed the strongest impetus for success of emerging startups. Understanding the concepts and principles of HRD will lay a strong foundation for growth and innovation through proper talent acquisition and retention strategies, continuous learning and development, agile teams, and leadership empowerment. Startups that take the right stance in HRD will find it easier to attract top talent, increase collaboration, and achieve sustainable digital growth by winning in a changing competitive landscape. The strategic HRD measures adopted by the startup would help empower the employees and infuse innovation so that these lead to enhancing the satisfaction levels of employees, while creating worthwhile benefits for all success factors of the organization.

EXPLORING UX DESIGN IN THE STARTUP ECOSYSTEM

User Experience is now a key element to be implemented in achieving effective products and services within today's digital arena, especially in startups. In fact, to starters that operate under time constraints and other heavy restrictions of resources and competition, effective UX design can hence play a major role in dictating their level of success. This section explores the central tenets of UX design, the critical role it plays in developing digital products, and its stand in regards to company objectives(Foo & Turner, 2019). The importance of User Experience (UX) design in the startup ecosystem is highlighted in Figure 2.

Figure 2. Importance of User Experience (UX) design in the startup ecosystem

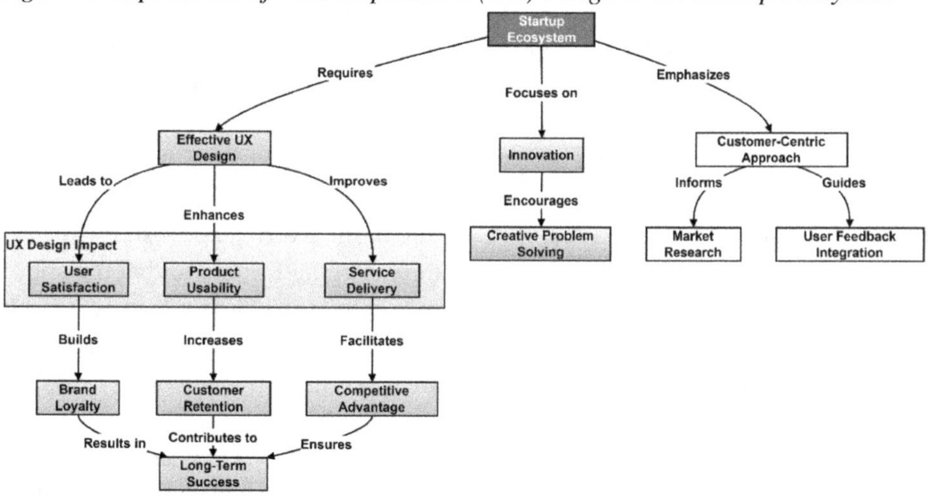

Core Principles of UX design

At the heart of a good UX design are its several core principles on which rests the entire process of delivering user-centered products. They are usability, accessibility, desirability, and user engagement.

An important factor of usability is that the products designed should be simple and intuitive to work with. A perfectly designed product does not have a steep learning curve. Therefore, it enables the users to get the task done. Performing usability testing as early as possible in the design process empowers the startups to recognize their pain points and iterate on their designs according to the feedback from the users.

Accessibility ensures that products are usable by people from all walks of life, ranges, and disabilities. Therefore, this principle supports inclusion, bringing the idea of accessibility to startups while designing, thus catering to a large audience. Incorporating accessibility features like compatibility with screen readers and adjustable text sizes showcase the sense of social responsibility while increasing possible user groups.

Desirability is the emotional connect of an end-user with a product. For example, a desirable product does not exactly engage users on an emotional level but does give loyalty and repeat usage. Improving the desirability aspect can be done by startups by considering aesthetics, branding, and user-centric storytelling appealing to users' needs and desires.

User Engagement: It builds products that engage and retain users through sustainable interaction. Some of the features include gamification, personalization, social sharing, among others. Engaged users are most likely to turn into brand ambassadors. They will then join forces with organic growth through word-of-mouth referrals.

Stick tightly to these core principles and you are on your way to building experiences that people care about, thereby leading to customer satisfaction and loyalty.

UX Role in Digital Product Development

It plays a very crucial role in the whole lifecycle of digital product development. Right from conceptual ideation of what is going to be developed to even after the launch, post-release testing, and evaluation, UX informs decisions that can result in either success or failure for the product(Foo & Turner, 2019).

Research and Discovery: It is the starting point of UX design, where it attempts to understand the needs, behaviors, and pain points of its target audience by startups. Techniques used include surveys, interviews, usability testing, and more that give great insights to inform the design process. One would be able to identify the needs of the users and target accordingly the product to be developed to solve a specific problem as a matter of relevance and usefulness.

Prototyping and Testing: With the research insight in hand, a firm will then proceed into prototyping. In this phase, either low-fidelity wireframes or even high-fidelity interactive prototypes are developed. The prototyped designs are used for repeated testing and improvement based on user feedback. Such processes during prototyping help in setting up usability testing for pinpointing flaws in design that would make the final product more user-friendly with less variation from what is expected by the users.

Design Implementation Once the prototypes are finalized, they move toward the design implementation phase. This involves visual design elements, interaction patterns, and finalization of content. In this phase, collaboration is needed between UX designers, developers, and product managers to ensure that the final product achieves equilibrium in terms of user needs satisfaction and technical feasibility.

Post-Launch Evaluation The UX design process does not stop at launch but goes into post-launch assessment. The collection of user feedback, use data analysis, and A/B testing will give a startup workable ideas on how to improvise the product for better user experiences. In this respect, startups are responsive to changes in markets as well as their users' needs over time.

For a startup, it's a world where agility is the key and rapid iteration is part of the package. So, the integration of UX design with the product development cycle can make it easier for streamlined workflows, and this could improve the outcome easily. Thus, a startup may differentiate itself from crowded markets while creating products that impact the desired audience in more significant ways.

UX Design and Business Objectives

To get the best out of UX design, therefore, there is a need for startups to ensure that their overall design efforts focus on the core as business goals. Such integration would instigate a wholeist approach where in user needs and strategic business goals collaborate(Hoogervorst et al., 2002).

Understand Business Objectives: At the beginning, startups define the business objectives and determine the key performance indicators that make sense for the success of such a venture. User retention, increase in conversion rates, or brand loyalty-all these objectives give a very powerful framework for the UX efforts of a business.

It would mean that a user-centric business strategy puts the needs of a user at the center of decision-making processes. The startups should find how UX can contribute to the achievement of business goals. For example, if their aim is the increase in sales, then UX design might be concentrated on the purchaser process-to minimize friction and maximize conversion.

Balancing Business Priorities with User Needs: In attempting to align UX design with business goals, startups have to find a balance between user needs and organizational priorities. Feedback sessions and usability testing with users can bring out areas of conflict where business goals are in tension with a good user experience. Startups must be in a position to make judicious trade-offs that are well aligned to user satisfaction as business goals are achieved.

Creating a UX Measurement Framework. A measurement framework will help the startup measure if the impact of UX design has been met towards business goals through key metrics such as user engagement, satisfaction, and conversion. Such tools include analytic software, user feedback surveys, and heatmaps.

The synergy that would really help both user experience and organizational performance of the startups is when UX design is appropriately aligned with business goals. A well-executed UX strategy has user satisfaction, enhances better conversion rates, and leads to sustainable growth.

UX design is the thin line that makes all the difference in the dynamic startup ecosystem with regard to how a start-up would be able to design impactful products and maintain a relationship with users for an extended time. On the basis of core principles like usability, accessibility, desirability, and user engagement, the relevant product for the target audience can be produced by the start-up. In addition, UX design provides integration in the product development lifecycle by focusing on the fulfillment of needs of users from research to post-launch review.

Ultimately, business goals and UX design must be in tandem for best returns from efforts in design. Startups, which do integration of UX into their strategy well, will not only maximize user satisfaction but also support organizational growth in such a highly competitive landscape. By investing in UX design as a strategic priority, startups can create experiences that build loyalty, engagement, and sustainable success in the digital age.

LEVERAGING UX DESIGN FOR SUSTAINABLE DIGITAL GROWTH

It is a very powerful tool for achievement in sustainable growth if Human Resource Development policies can get integrated into User Experience design in rapidly evolving digital startup landscapes. The union between HRD initiatives and UX principles helps in innovation, increases engagement of employees within a company, and inspires user-centered products that resonate within the marketplace. This chapter explores the synergies between HRD strategies and UX design in improvements in employee creativity and collaboration, culminating in the design of effective, user-centered products(Kantamneni, 2022). The UX design in Figure 3 is a combination of UX and HRD.

Figure 3. UX design with integrated Human Resource Development (HRD)

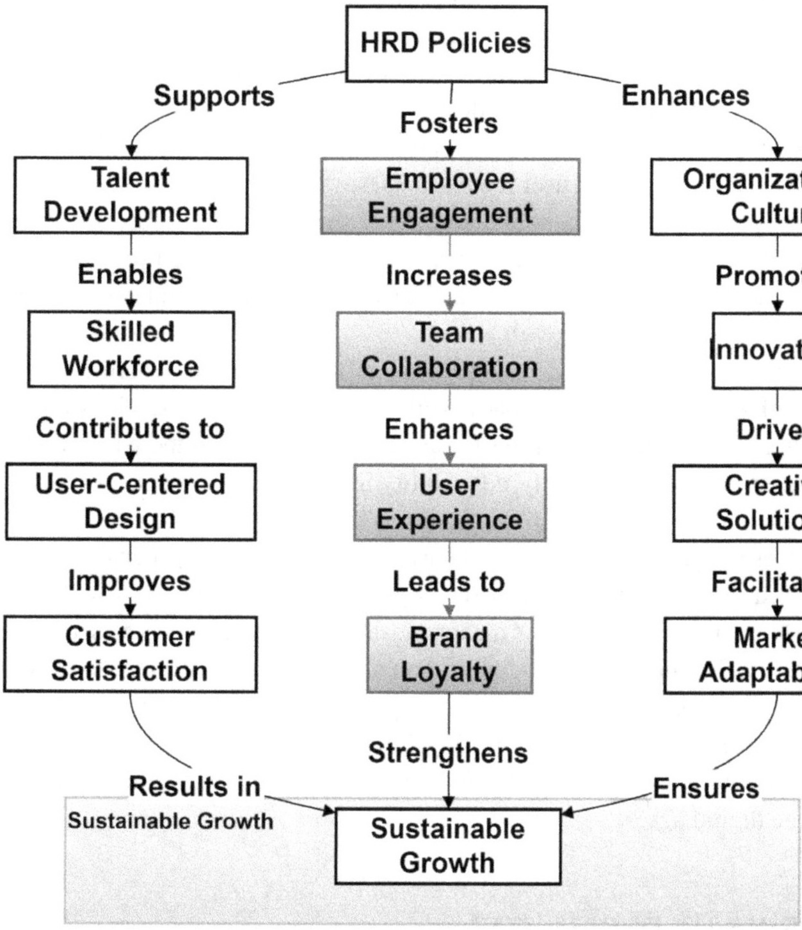

Combining HRD Strategies with UX Design

This is regarded as combining some human resource development strategies with UX design ideas, an integral step towards creating a work environment through which employees are productive and innovative in new business ventures. By considering employees as internal users, the implementation of UX design principles is possible on matters that give a better workplace experience, therefore better business outcomes(Sundberg, 2015).

Understanding Employee Needs: To a large extent, just as in conducting user research is the beginning of the UX design, understanding the needs of employees will work as the foundation for the successful realization of HRD. Surveys, interviews, or focus groups could be used as methodologies to seek information about the employees' experience, preference, and pain points. It will inform the approach strategies used in HRD in the aim to make it a more engaging and supportive work environment for people

Using UX design principles, startups can create HR programs that have the employee experience as the core of the service. That means they should be able to have intuitive onboarding processes and have professional development opportunities beneficial towards catering to the needs of each worker, such as flexible work arrangements. Once designed in this manner, the very HR systems will work for enhancing job satisfaction, retention, and loyalty.

Innovation Culture: Integrating UX design with HRD helps an enterprise create innovation culture in the startups. The cross-functional collaboration and open communication can eliminate silos through the sharing of ideas and create team thinkers by facilitating the ideas on the workshops and brainstorming sessions, which are on design thinking.

Continuous Improvement Loops through Feedback: Just as UX design may demand iterative testing and feedback, similarly, HRD strategies should employ mechanisms for continuous improvement. Regular check-ins, performance evaluation, and streams of feedback help an organization measure the effectiveness of its HRD initiative. The ability to be responsive to the input generated from employees helps a startup evaluate its strategy so as to fit the needs of a more increasingly evolving workforce.

Improving Creativity and Collaboration at the Employee Level using UX

Creativity and collaboration will characterize successful startups focused on market distinctiveness; therefore, UX design can be a catalyst for these forces in the workplace(Evans, 2014).

Creation of Collaboration Spaces: The nature of designing both physical and digital workspace affects the collaboration among the employees. The collaborative workspaces incorporation through promoting interaction between employees can give an atmosphere through which ideas flow freely. Open layouts, shared resources, and technology-enabled collaboration tools can enable more employees' interaction towards creativity.

Using UX Tools for Team Engagement There are numerous UX tools and methodologies that startups can use in order to ensure more engagement among the teams and stronger collaboration. Techniques like user journey mapping, empathy mapping, and design sprints help teams visualize what user experiences could exist there and what opportunities lie in such experiences for innovation. Such collaborative activities foster creative solutions to problems as well as team dynamics.

Encouraging Diverse Perspectives: A diverse workforce brings in many perspectives, which can be creative and innovative. Startups need to focus on being proactive in diversity and inclusion within the team by valuing the backgrounds, experiences, and skill sets that differ from one another. Only then can organizations utilize diverse thinking for creative solutions to enhance creative power.

Engaging Productive Imagination: Companies may engage their employees in productive imagination by recognizing and rewarding their innovative efforts. The companies may design recognition policies such as awarding individual rewards for individual success and recognition of team success to create an environment where imagination is encouraged and rewarded. More opportunities to workers in popularizing their ideas and innovations will also develop a feeling of ownership and pride.

Providing Products Centered on Users for Market Satisfaction

Lastly, in this combination of HRD strategies and UX design, the end result will be products that are user-centric, then resonate with the target audience and drive market success. Aligning employee and user needs helps startups build products not only for meeting market requirements but also to create loyal customers(Lund, 2011; Sundberg, 2015).

User Research and Empathy: User research is where startups must start with their product development. It is a way to understand the needs, behaviors, and pain points of the users, so an organization can create something that solves real problems. Techniques that include usability testing, surveys, and focus groups provide meaningful input into making design decisions in alignment with user expectations.

Iterative Design Process: This might be one very typical UX design feature-implementing iterative design process within a product developed by these startups. This will involve developing prototypes, testing them with users, and then iterating on that insight based on feedback from the users. Thus, the startups refine their products to better meet user needs. It's both product quality enhancement and very fast adjustment according to the market.

Interactions Between Teams: This will actually require excellent collaboration between UX designers, product managers, and developers to be effective. Cross-functional teams can determine a number of areas of diversity to make sure that a decision made during the design process falls in line with the business goals while keeping focus on what the user needs. It stands for a great example through proper communication and feedback loops between the team members.

Measuring Success through User Engagement: User-centered products will be measured using metrics that show success in terms of engaging and satisfying users. Since startups can now track the KPIs, such as user retention rates, conversion rates, and customer feedback, a more well-defined sense of what works and what does not will come into view regarding products and how they find a reaction in users. Regular monitoring and adjustment of the user experience will form a reliable recipe for winning in the marketplace over the long term.

This happens only when the opportunity of UX design for sustainable digital growth is brought together with HRD strategies while keeping in mind its user-centered principles. Only then can the startups create an all-encompassing approach to innovation, characterized by employee needs, creativity, and collaborations - and built on the experience of the users - with a view to accelerating successful product development. Thus, the alignment of HRD and UX design will not only enhance employee engagement and satisfaction but also aid the products resulting from such organizations to better cater to the needs and expectations of the users to sustain further growth within a competitive digital landscape.

HRD AND UX SYNERGY: DRIVING INNOVATION AND GROWTH

This defines the alignment of HRD and UX in the modern business environment, mainly for startups, where mutual benefits in innovation as well as long-term growth can be achieved. This chapter discusses how the alignment of HRD initiatives with UX design principles could advance a customer-centric culture, stimulate innovation, and have a radical impact on long-term growth and sustainability in business concerning their digital capacities(Hoogervorst et al., 2002; Koloszár et al., 2024). Figure 4 illustrates the effective combination of Human Resource Development (HRD) and User Experience (UX) in driving innovation and growth for startups.

Figure 4. Synergy between Human Resource Development (HRD) and User Experience (UX) in driving innovation and growth for startups

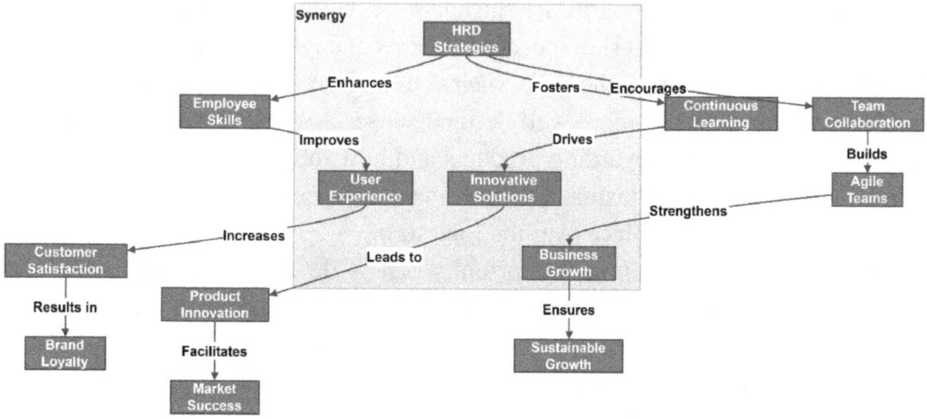

Strategic Alignment Between HRD and UX for Startups

Shared Vision and Objectives: Success of the startup rests upon a common vision for HRD and UX. Shared aims are set out that align with employee development and direct user satisfaction, which in turn culminates in coordination. This way, by setting HRD initiatives in tandem with the UX goals, every individual member will be all aware of his own bit toward achieving the aim of offering value to the customers. This sense of purpose builds excitement and engagement throughout the organization.

Cross-functional Collaboration: The integration of HRD and UX cuts across organizational silos. In essence, cross-functional collaboration brings on board the teams from HR, UX designers, and product managers to develop innovative solutions for people. Collaboration through brainstorming sessions, design thinking workshops, brainstorming, and more ensures that fresh ideas are generated to resonate with employees as well as with customers.

Training and development: The best way in which start-ups can align HRD with UX is by acquiring training and development programs that emphasize the importance of user experience. This is because a skill where employees learn UX research, design thinking, and customer empathy will increase productivity in delivering user-centered products. Therefore, a training program that highlights an understanding of building some user needs will enable the workforce to implement UX principles into their daily work.

Feedback Mechanisms: Creating feedback loops between these factors is an excellent way to maintain alignment. Consistent assessments for both employee engagement as well as user experience can reflect where progress can be made. Some of the types of tools which can be leveraged include employee satisfaction surveys, user testing and analytics analysis to show a company where their strategies are weak and adjust through data to improve employee satisfaction as well as user experience.

Creating a Customer-Centric Culture Through UX

Empathy and Understanding: Customer-centric culture starts from empathy. Startups have to understand the needs, preferences, and behaviors of users profoundly. This demands HRD initiatives that enable employees to interact directly with customers through user interviews, support channels, or community outreach. That fosters empathy, allowing every employee of the startup to feel responsible for improving the user experience.

Innovation through User-Centered Design: Principles of UX design: The focus, under the principles, is on user-centered approaches. When organisational culture is infused with UX practices, it can then motivate a startup to innovation. Challenging employees to think creatively while solving the problem of a user leads to creating an innovative solution that makes for uniqueness in the marketplace of the business. Innovation does not only provide solutions to customers' needs but can also be a source for new streams of revenue and business models.

Recognition of contribution from users: The best way to develop a customer-centric culture would be by acknowledging and celebrating the contribution of the users. Shifting focus on user feedback and telling stories about users would be great ways to concentrate on features in product development, largely driven by user input. It is an act that gives the user a sense of belonging and loyalty with a startup while emphasizing on the most crucial input that the startup depends upon.

Agility and Responsiveness: Start-ups have an agile mindset that enables them to be responsive to changing customer needs. The appropriate HRD strategies required will be the strengthening of employees to adapt and innovate in real time. A work environment has to be flexible to allow for the sprint of experiments and risks through experimentation, in order to stay ahead of changing trends in the marketplace and then to ensure long-term business growth and digital sustainability.

It further develops employee engagement and retention. It not only benefits the customer but also has a tremendous impact on the engagement and retention levels of the employees. When employees believe that their development corresponds to user needs, they become naturally motivated and satisfied in their job roles. High employee engagement translates to lower rates of turnovers, and a powerful culture of loyalty and commitment is developed with less recruitment and training.

Increased Customer Satisfaction and Loyalty: A customer-centric approach taken through effective HRD and UX strategies increase customer satisfaction. If people feel that their needs are placed first, they tend to be loyal to the brand. Happy customers drive repeat business and positive word-of-mouth referral ability and higher lifetime value of the customer, all of which contribute to long-term business growth.

Sustainable business practices: The integration of HRD and UX motivates startups to embrace sustainable business operation. Knowing the user's need and the feedback of the users, proper decisions can be made that may provide considerations toward ethical requirements, environmental excellence, and social responsibility. By doing so, sustainability would not only meet the needs of socially aware customers but also make the startup stand accountable as a responsible industry leader.

The Benefits of HRD and UX Integration: Data-Driven Decision Making Startups that put more significance on user research or employee feedback will utilize data analytics for strategy formulation in their focus. From the study of performance metrics and behavior, startups will arrive at the trend, optimize processes, and make strategical adjustments in enhancing both employee performance and user satisfaction(Revathi et al., 2024).

The synergy between Human Resource Development and User Experience is actually one of the most important drivers for innovation and growth in terms of creating a startup. Developing a customer-centric culture is paramount in a startup, which then enables HRD initiatives to be strategically aligned with UX principles to really enhance creativity and engage employees towards sustainable business success. Emphasis on empathy, collaboration, and data-driven decision-making will not only meet customer needs but will help to put startups in an excellent position for long-term growth and digital sustainability in the highly competitive marketplace. This integration would allow for a step forward into the depths of the digital territory while encouraging a culture of innovation that propels them forward.

Figure 5. Challenges and opportunities that arise from integrating Human Resource Development (HRD) and User Experience (UX) in startups

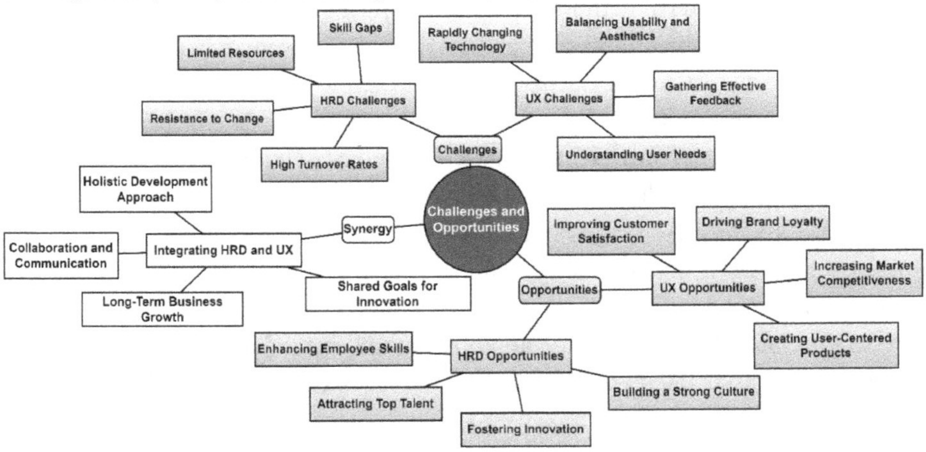

CHALLENGES AND OPPORTUNITIES

With the evolving character of startups, a syncretic worldview about HRD and UX brings in both challenges and opportunities; hence it becomes very very important for entrepreneurs who wish to take from their teams the maximum efficiencies to believe in and understand the concepts (Apraiz et al., 2023; Mustafa & Karimi, 2021; Zaki & Islam, 2021). The figure 5 demonstrates the potential challenges and opportunities associated with integrating Human Resource Development (HRD) and User Experience (UX) in startups.

Common Challenges of HRD and UX Confronted by Startups

Resource Constraint: In most startups, a small budget and few workers characterize the company. It would be challenging for the company to put in place the overall HRD and UX strategy. The resources would prevent proper training, UX research, and user-centered design principles. Such constraints lead to skill development among employees being limited and the products subsequently failing to meet the expectations of the users(Agrawal et al., 2024; Boopathi, 2024; Ravisankar et al., 2024).

Cultural Resistance: Building the kind of culture that prides itself with HRD and UX in a startup environment valuing speed and agility is tough. Employees resist changes in already established practices or feel overwhelmed by new expectations based on user-centered approaches. More immediate business goals probably will outweigh longer-term development plans for the founding teams leading to neglect of both employee as well as user needs.

To balance short-term with long-term goals further, a startup usually keeps the focus on short-term objectives, such as rapid growth or product launch. It may ultimately lose its investments in Human Resource Development and User Experience, which are more visionary and require commitment over a longer period of time. A workforce that is not sufficiently trained to innovate and evolve as the company expands may be the result of a lack of this balance.

Varied Skill Sets: As startups scale, they experience an integration challenge in terms of the diversity of skill sets among the team members. The various UX competencies of various team members happen to be a very complicated issue for HRD initiatives. There may be no apparent understanding related to roles and responsibilities associated with UX design and research, resulting in inefficiencies and misunderstandings.

Keeping Track of Rapid Technological Changes: The digital landscape is always evolving, and it is almost impossible for a startup to be aware of the trends, tools, and methodologies needed to support UX design. HRD programs need to change frequently so that employees update their skills and knowledge. Lack of adaptation leads to outdated practices and is then a hindrance to competitiveness.

Prosperity and Innovation Outlook

Cross-Disciplinary Collaboration: This is one of the interesting points in which HRD and UX really come to mainstream to create opportunities for cross-disciplinary collaboration. The kind of environment that start-ups can create can bring the HR and UX practitioners together to improve the employee experience and user interaction at large. From here, innovation begins to start in furthering solutions that both provide employee satisfaction as well as engaging user involvement(Naveeenkumar et al., 2024; Ravisankar et al., 2024).

Employee Empowerment - Emphasis on empowering employees through HRD initiatives, which also encourage innovation. Ability building skill development, mentorship and leadership training provide the flagship activities that can help in the development of an incredibly competent and motivated workforce ready to contribute ideas and improvements to UX design processes.

User-Centered Product Development. With UX behind the startup, it makes the development of user-centered products a responsibility of the system, thereby ensuring greater customer satisfaction and loyalty. Employee contributors for UX research and design make it easier for startups to use this knowledge to develop solutions that attract target audiences. It is through this user-centricity that differentiates startups in competitive markets, catapulting them into sustainable growth.

Improvement in the HRD Strategy of Startups by Using Emerging Technology The strategic use of any emerging technology, like e-learning platforms, virtual reality, or artificial intelligence, assists in improving the HRD strategy of the startups. Since they are cost-effective and scalable tools, they are highly effective for employee training on methodologies and principles of UX. With the usage of the latest technology, startups can evolve an immersive learning experience that helps in the development and retention of skills.

Agility to respond to feedback is just one of the benefits of startups. Agility can be translated to make swift adjustments according to feedback from employees and users. With proper mechanisms in place, one may drive insights that inform HRD and UX strategies in a way that allows constant improvement. Responding this quickly may lead to better practices or products, hence forming the base of culture for innovation.

Future Trends in HRD and UX for Entrepreneurship

Data-Driven Decisions. With the increased accessibility of data analytics tools, it has become indispensable for most startups to draw insights from data into informing HRD and UX strategies. It then makes companies make appropriate decisions through the analytics of employee performance metrics as well as user behavior analytics, thus improving outcomes in these two areas(Boopathi, 2024; Pasumarthy et al., 2024).

Emphasis would be laid on Emotional Intelligence: EI is likely to emerge as the overall head of effective teamwork and user experiences in future HRD initiatives. It would lead employees to understand and manage emotions, hence enhancing collaboration, improving communication, and a deeper connection with their users.

Integration of Artificial Intelligence: AI will be the integrated mainstream in both HRD and UX. It will enable automation, personalization, and learning experiences for employees. In UX design, AI would hone the interaction with the user with predictive analytics and personalized recommendation for the content.

The norm of sustainability is fast becoming an imperative requirement that will influence HRD and UX strategies at all levels. Startups will start taking proactive approaches to building sustainability into all operations-from development into products designed and conceived. That can solve what consumers are looking for-the responsible business practice nature-but will also attract those more talent-minded toward a firm that is a responsible and sustainable way to do business.

Remote and hybrid work models. Remote and hybrid work environments will place new demands on training programs and UX design. Startups should come up with training plans and UX strategies that fit the diverse lifestyle of employees; it must make users experience the best with the same effect, be it from a remote or any hybrid workplace.

While HRD and UX-related challenges are present for startups, they in fact open a wide variety of possibilities for growth and innovation. As awareness of these challenges, will enable capturing opportunities, adding to a synergistic environment, which fosters both employee development and user satisfaction, the way ahead in entrepreneurship will thus require focus on trends in HRD and UX-a sustained success and products will only be realized when resonating with the users.

CONCLUSION

HRD would complement UX but is more urgent in the dynamic context of emerging startups to foster sustainable growth. This chapter has traced how HRD strategy can be well aligned with UX design principles to ensure many takeoffs for innovation, to actually build and connect the culture, and thus finally lead toward user-centered products that meet market demands.

Because resource constraints, cultural resistance, and the necessity of acquiring a diverse array of skills exist in this case, the above issues should be addressed through strategic planning and a commitment to continuous learning. The best way to realize an agile and creative workforce that can successfully handle the complexities of the digital landscape is by investing in employee development and empowering teams. On the other hand, the user-centric approach of product development points toward a very critical need-to-know basis of user needs and which should be integrated into the design process for proper understanding of the needs of users. This not only increases the satisfaction of customers but also builds loyalty as well as creates brand advocacy.

Expected trends in the future of HRD and UX in startups include data-driven decision-making, new importance of emotional intelligence, and the role of AI. Shaping the future in all these senses, the most promising startup will be best prepared in competition within the growing fierceness of the market -that which makes these trends, above all, shifting its focus toward a customer-centric culture. All in all, it shows how such synergy between HRD and UX can be a great catalyst for innovation and thus for long-lasting business success. With this synergy, startups will make sustainable pathways to growth that not only bring about employee engagement but deliver outstanding user experience, hence a long-lasting impact in the digital economy.

REFERENCES

Agrawal, A. V., Bakkiyaraj, M., Das, S., Reddy, C. M. S., Kiran, P. B. N., & Boopathi, S. (2024). Digital Strategies for Modern Workplaces and Business Through Artificial Intelligence Techniques. In *Multidisciplinary Applications of Extended Reality for Human Experience* (pp. 231–258). IGI Global. DOI: 10.4018/979-8-3693-2432-5.ch011

Apraiz, A., Lasa, G., & Mazmela, M. (2023). Evaluation of user experience in human–robot interaction: A systematic literature review. *International Journal of Social Robotics*, 15(2), 187–210. DOI: 10.1007/s12369-022-00957-z

Boopathi, S. (2024). Digital HR Implementation for Business Growth in Industrial 5.0. In *Convergence of Human Resources Technologies and Industry 5.0* (pp. 1–22). IGI Global. DOI: 10.4018/979-8-3693-1343-5.ch001

Borriraklert, A., & Kiattisin, S. (2021). User experience design (UXD) competency model: Identifying well-rounded proficiency for user experience designers in the digital age. *Archives of Design Research*, 34(3), 61–79. DOI: 10.15187/adr.2021.08.34.3.61

Evans, P. (2014). Exploring the relationship between discourse and a practice perspective on HRD in a virtual environment. *Human Resource Development International*, 17(2), 183–202. DOI: 10.1080/13678868.2014.886889

Foo, H. Y., & Turner, J. J. (2019). Entrepreneurial learning'-the role of university led business incubators and mentors in equipping graduates with the necessary skills set for Industry 4.0. *International Journal of Education. Psychology and Counseling*, 4(30), 283–298.

Gomathi, S., Rajeswari, A., & Kadry, S. (2023). Emerging HR practices—Digital upskilling: A strategic way of talent management and engagement. In *Disruptive artificial intelligence and sustainable human resource management* (pp. 51–63). River Publishers. DOI: 10.1201/9781032622743-4

Hoogervorst, J. A., Koopman, P. L., & van der Flier, H. (2002). Human resource strategy for the new ICT-driven business context. *International Journal of Human Resource Management*, 13(8), 1245–1265. DOI: 10.1080/09585190210149501

Kantamneni, S. (2022). *User Experience Design: A Practical Playbook to Fuel Business Growth*. John Wiley & Sons.

Koloszár, L., Bednárik, É., Erdős, F., Thinakaran, R., & Takáts, A. (2024). User experience testing methods: Conclusions from the literature. *Edelweiss Applied Science and Technology*, 8(5), 1400–1412. DOI: 10.55214/25768484.v8i5.1843

Lermen, F. H., de Moura, P. K., Bertoni, V. B., Graciano, P., & Tortorella, G. L. (2023). Does maturity level influence the use of Agile UX methods by digital startups? Evaluating design thinking, lean startup, and lean user experience. *Information and Software Technology*, 154, 107107. DOI: 10.1016/j.infsof.2022.107107

Lund, A. (2011). *User experience management: Essential skills for leading effective UX teams*. Elsevier.

MacDonald, C. M. (2019). User experience (UX) capacity-building: A conceptual model and research agenda. *Proceedings of the 2019 on Designing Interactive Systems Conference*, 187–200. DOI: 10.1145/3322276.3322346

Malik, A., Budhwar, P., & Mohan, H., & NR, S. (. (2023). Employee experience–the missing link for engaging employees: Insights from an MNE's AI-based HR ecosystem. *Human Resource Management*, 62(1), 97–115. DOI: 10.1002/hrm.22133

Mustafa, A. S., & Karimi, K. (2021). Enhancing gamified online learning user experience (UX): A systematic literature review of recent trends. *Human-Computer Interaction and Beyond-Part*, I, 74–99. DOI: 10.2174/9789814998819121010007

Naveeenkumar, N., Rallapalli, S., Sasikala, K., Priya, P. V., Husain, J., & Boopathi, S. (2024). Enhancing Consumer Behavior and Experience Through AI-Driven Insights Optimization. In *AI Impacts in Digital Consumer Behavior* (pp. 1–35). IGI Global. DOI: 10.4018/979-8-3693-1918-5.ch001

Øvad, T., & Larsen, L. B. (2015). The prevalence of UX design in agile development processes in industry. *2015 Agile Conference*, 40–49. DOI: 10.1109/Agile.2015.13

Park, S., Jeong, S., & Ju, B. (2018). Employee learning and development in virtual HRD: Focusing on MOOCs in the workplace. *Industrial and Commercial Training*, 50(5), 261–271. DOI: 10.1108/ICT-03-2018-0030

Pasumarthy, R., Mohammed, S., Laxman, V., Krishnamoorthy, V., Durga, S., & Boopathi, S. (2024). Digital Transformation in Developing Economies: Forecasting Trends, Impact, and Challenges in Industry 5.0. In *Convergence of Human Resources Technologies and Industry 5.0* (pp. 47–68). IGI Global. DOI: 10.4018/979-8-3693-1343-5.ch003

Ravisankar, A., Shanthi, A., Lavanya, S., Ramaratnam, M., Krishnamoorthy, V., & Boopathi, S. (2024). Harnessing 6G for Consumer-Centric Business Strategies Across Electronic Industries. In *AI Impacts in Digital Consumer Behavior* (pp. 241–270). IGI Global.

Revathi, S., Babu, M., Rajkumar, N., Meti, V. K. V., Kandavalli, S. R., & Boopathi, S. (2024). Unleashing the Future Potential of 4D Printing: Exploring Applications in Wearable Technology, Robotics, Energy, Transportation, and Fashion. In *Human-Centered Approaches in Industry 5.0: Human-Machine Interaction, Virtual Reality Training, and Customer Sentiment Analysis* (pp. 131–153). IGI Global.

S, B., & Gopi, S. (2024). Crafting Effective HR Strategies for the Modern Workplace: Navigating the Digital Frontier. In *Convergence of Human Resources Technologies and Industry 5.0* (pp. 23–46). IGI Global. DOI: 10.4018/979-8-3693-1343-5.ch002

Simsek Caglar, P., Roto, V., & Vainio, T. (2022). User experience research in the work context: Maps, gaps and agenda. *Proceedings of the ACM on Human-Computer Interaction, 6*(CSCW1), 1–28. DOI: 10.1145/3512979

Sundberg, H.-R. (2015). *The role of user experience in a business-to-business context.*

Timms, P. (2021). *Transformational HR: How human resources can create value and impact business strategy*. Kogan Page Publishers.

Yerram, S. R., Mallipeddi, S. R., Varghese, A., & Sandu, A. K. (2019). Human-Centered Software Development: Integrating User Experience (UX) Design and Agile Methodologies for Enhanced Product Quality. *Asian Journal of Humanity. Art and Literature*, 6(2), 203–218. DOI: 10.18034/ajhal.v6i2.732

Zaki, T., & Islam, M. N. (2021). Neurological and physiological measures to evaluate the usability and user-experience (UX) of information systems: A systematic literature review. *Computer Science Review*, 40, 100375. DOI: 10.1016/j.cosrev.2021.100375

KEY TERMS AND DEFINITIONS

Artificial Intelligence (AI): AI refers to the processes of imitation of human intelligent activities by computer systems. Such processes include learning, which involves acquiring information and setting rules for utilizing that information, reasoning through use of rules in getting to approximate or definite conclusions, and self-correction. For HR and UX, AI can be utilized in data analysis, improving user interaction, and even decision-making processes.

EI End: EI is the capability of an individual to discern, understand, and control his or her own emotions and also the emotions of others. High EI functions ability helps a person find his or her way in social complexities and make personal decisions that bring in positive results. In the workplace, EI plays a great role concerning effective communication, teamwork, and leadership.

Human Resource Development (HRD): HRD is the framework of enabling employees to grow in their personal as well as organizationally based skills, knowledge, and competencies. This encompasses various types of training, career development, performance management, coaching, and mentoring to improve individual and organizational performance.

Human Resources (HR): HR Generally represents the department of an organization in charge of employing human resource management processes. These may include hiring, recruiting, training, performance appraisal, and other employee benefits. The HR develops the culture of the company and also ensures compliance with labor laws.

KPI: KPIs are measurable values that demonstrate how effectively an organization is achieving key business objectives. Organizations use KPIs for monitoring their success in terms of meeting targets. Among the common KPIs for HR, the following would be on the list: employee turnover rate, training completion rate, and employee satisfaction scores.

User Experience (UX): UX is the overall ability of interaction between the end-user and the company, its services, and its products with which they are presented. It zeroes in on the holistic enhancement of usability, accessibility, and pleasure furnished in the user-product interaction. Good UX design aims for the fulfillment of needs by the user and their satisfaction through intuitive design and functionality.

Chapter 9
A Framework for Age Estimation Using Facial Features:
A Comprehensive Survey

A. Annie Micheal
Department of Computer Science and Engineering, Sathyabama Institute of Science and technology, Kanchipuram, India

B. U. Anu Barathi
Department of Computer Science and Engineering, Sathyabama Institute of Science and technology, Kanchipuram, India

A. Ancy Micheal
Department of School of Computer Science and Engineering, Vellore Institute of Technology (Chennai Campus), Chengalpattu, India

Essakki Raja T.
Department of Computer Science and Engineering with Data Science, Sathyabama Institute of Science and Technology, Kancheepuram, India

ABSTRACT

In human age estimation, an exact age or age group is assigned automatically to a given facial image. Due to changes in facial features caused by wrinkles and muscle sag with the increase in age, age estimation becomes difficult and complex. Variability in facial expressions, illumination conditions, environment, pose, plastic surgery, occlusion, image quality, and facial makeup gives rise to some of the challenges that affect the accuracy of age estimation. With the newly developing real-time and

DOI: 10.4018/979-8-3693-2337-3.ch009

age-related applications, there is an increasing demand for more accurate estimation of age. Several methodologies have been developed by researchers to handle this requirement. The work reported here represents an exhaustive survey on face age estimation. Discussed here are five major models of age image representation and various age learning algorithms, a review of the existing aging databases has been made, and the latest state-of-the-art methods for the estimation of age are summarized.

INTRODUCTION

The human face is a repository of information on individual characteristics, including age, facial expression, ethnicity, gender, identity, emotion, and pose. Recently, facial age estimation has become one of the most active topics of research due to its increasing number of real-world applications, including human-computer interaction, biometric systems, surveillance, targeted advertisement, commercial development, demographic studies, and content-based indexing and searching. It refers to the process of assigning an age or age group to an image of a face. The age range in the image could be actual age, appearance age, and perceived age. The actual age would mean the amount of year one has lived since birth, the chronological age (Othmani et al., 2020).

The Appearance age bases on one's look. Perceived age is the estimated age derived by a computer algorithm from the individual's appearance. Three particular features now highlight the process of facial aging. Inevitable and uncontrollable aging: The process of aging is slow, irreversible, and cannot be consciously accelerated or retarded. Personalized aging profile: Everybody ages uniquely, differentially internal to genetic influences in combination with exogenous variables such as lifestyle, disease processes, along with the ambient surroundings. Temporal aging pattern: Facial variations at any particular age determine the structure of older faces, not younger ones. The two major stages in which aging of human faces can be divided are: from birth to adulthood and from adulthood onwards to old age (Moyse, 2014).

Craniofacial growth greatly alters the shape and form of the human face from early childhood, when it is more circular in form, to the oval structure characteristic of adulthood. The changes accompanying the development of the cranium are rather dramatic; going forward, there is a backward sloping of the forehead and a reduction in its size provide more space on the cranium. To compensate for these changes, other features such as the ears, nose, eyes, and mouth, become larger and fill in these spaces between them. Furthermore, the cheeks become elongated and larger while the chin becomes more prominent or protruded. For the most part, though, facial skin itself does not change much during its early stages of growth (Shirode & Handore, 2016).

When the individual enters old age from adulthood, changes, or more accurately aging, of the skin becomes the most obvious and noticeable change. It is a phase when textural changes are most apparent, such as wrinkle formation, sagging of the skin, and loss of muscle tone. This would be the manifestation of under-eye puffiness or bags, drooping of the cheeks, less robust musculature, wrinkle formation, double chin appearance, and the gradual development of freckles and age spots. Whereas these factors tend to alter the general outline of the face, it is usually not as radical when compared to earlier stages in one's life because aging tends to act more on the skin and patterns of the underlying tissue (Kavita & Chhillar, 2022).

Background: Facial age estimation has become a key area in computer vision, thanks to improvements in machine learning and image processing technologies. Accurate determination of a person's age from facial images presents quite a wide range of applications in security, marketing, and personalized services, among others. The challenges in this field are changing facial expressions, different lighting conditions, and cosmetic use that might change the facial look of a person. Researchers are more concerned with the refinement of algorithms to obtain accuracy and reliability using large datasets with complex models. With the advancement in technology, the application of facial age estimation into practical systems further expands, opening new avenues and solutions in various industries.

Scope: The scope of facial age estimation involves developing and implementing a method or algorithm that can effectively estimate the age of an individual by correctly analyzing his or her facial images. This not only encompasses variabilities introduced by facial expressions, lighting conditions, and cosmetic changes but also the use of different techniques in the improvement of prediction accuracy, ranging from classical image processing methods to deep models. It is a wide area that extends further to integrating these technologies into real-world applications such as biometric verification, targeted advertising, and personalized user experience. By capitalizing on several sources of data and imaginative algorithms, the research space has striven to increase both accuracy and domain applicability for age estimation systems.

Objectives: Research on estimating facial age primarily focuses on devising proficient techniques that could rightly estimate an individual's age from their face. This is done by increasing the ability of age prediction algorithms by modeling various challenges that may be involved, such as facial expression, lighting conditions, and image quality. They try to enhance robustness of the algorithm by analyzing and incorporating a wide variety in terms of facial features and aging patterns. The aim goes further in using such fine-tuned techniques in real-world applications, such as biometric systems, online marketing based on individual preference, and forensic applications. In this regard, it contributes to practical requirements and gives impetus to the advancement of computer vision.

Figure 1. Craniofacial growth model at different age periods

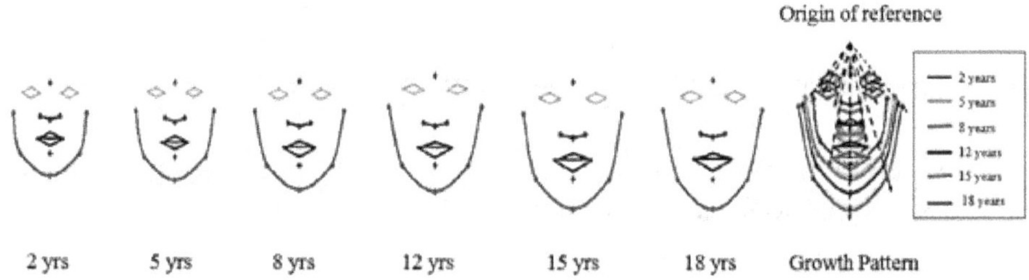

Figure 2. Facial age changes from 3-100 years

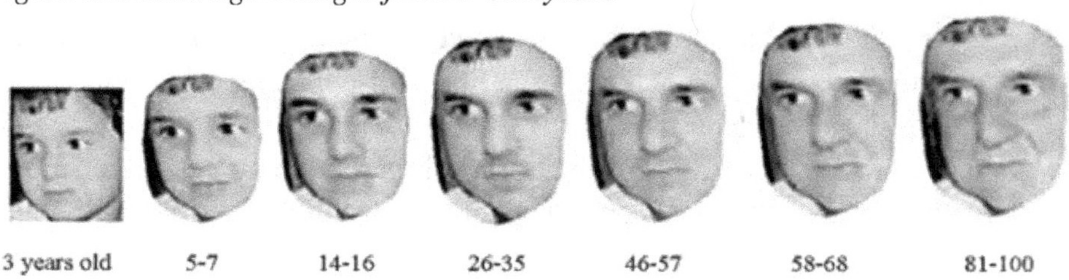

AGING DATABASES FOR AGE ESTIMATION AND GENDER CLASSIFICATION

One significant task in the study of face age estimation is to construct a comprehensive aging database. High-quality datasets with precise labels of age are required in both the training and testing of machine learning models for accurate prediction of age. The images can be sourced from users or downloaded from free Internet repositories. While free image availability on the internet has enabled such datasets, it is important to obtain good quality chronometric image series in order to ensure that an aging database is reliable and large-scale. Presented below is a summary of some of the widely used aging databases each having special characteristics and challenges (Alkaabi et al., 2020; Koruga et al., 2011; Onifade & Akinyemi, 2015). Figures 1 and 2 illustrate the significant change in craniofacial growth from birth to adulthood. The Craniofacial Growth Model shows changes in facial age from 3-100 years.

Figure 3. Various states and transitions involved in working with such databases

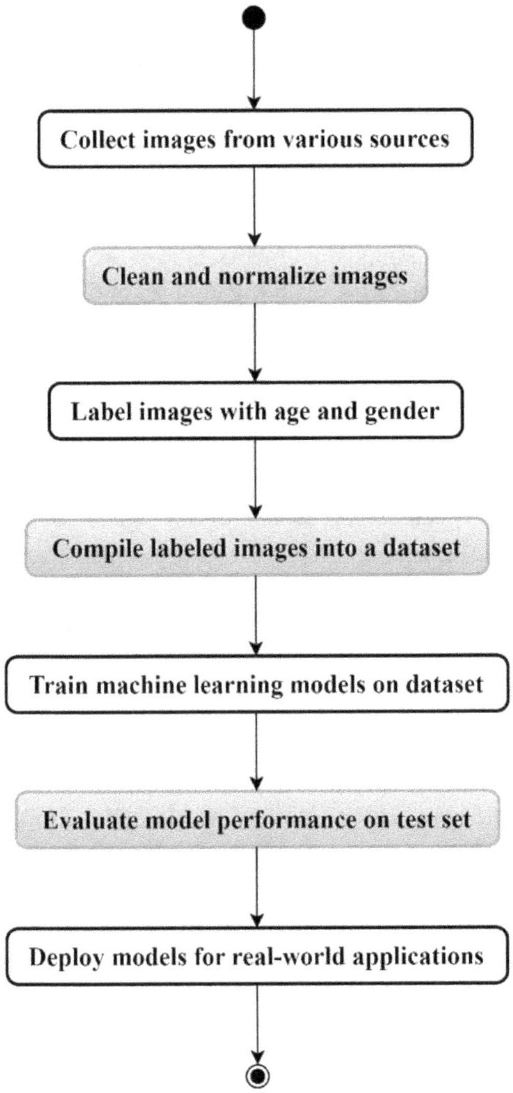

The process of creating an aging database involves collecting, preprocessing, annotation, dataset construction, training machine learning models, evaluating their performance, and deploying the models in real-world applications. Figure 3 provides a comprehensive understanding of the process.

Aging Database of Face and Gesture Recognition Research Network (FG-NET)

Another popular source for the estimation of facial age is the FG-NET Aging Database. The dataset includes 1,002 face images taken from 82 subjects aged 0-69 years. Peculiar features are the great diversity of its subjects and the inclusion of people from different races. About 50% of this dataset consists of subjects below the age of 13 years, which makes it an important resource for the study of younger age-related changes of the face. The dataset consists of RGB and grayscale images, shot from photographs or scanned documents. Due to the fact that pictures are taken with cameras, and sometimes with scanning devices of different quality, resolution might be different. The FG-NET database also introduces pose, illumination, and facial expression changes, further complicating the estimation process. Each image in the FG-NET database has been hand-annotated with 68 face landmarks, adding more information that can be further used in the feature extraction of the face. Besides the images, the dataset contains metadata such as age, gender, whether the subject is wearing spectacles, presence of a mustache or beard, and head pose around the vertical and horizontal axes. Despite extensive annotation, one major weakness with the FG-NET dataset is that it contains relatively few images per subject, which may limit its usefulness for training models requiring large-scale data (Koruga et al., 2011).

The Audience Database

The Audience Database is more modern and includes 26,000 images for 2,284 subjects; this dataset is large as compared to FG-NET. Images in this database were obtained from Flickr.com, and most of them were taken by iPhones or other smart-phones. It adds other challenges into the dataset, as the quality of the smartphone images may vary quite a lot regarding the conditions under which the photos were taken (Han et al., 2013). What makes the Audience Database challenging is that it encompasses highly varied factors such as noise, illumination variation, and pose variation, all of which real-world environments would include. Such variability is hard to generalize by machine learning models but closer to the environments in which age estimation models are likely to be deployed. All have been manually tagged with gender and age, while other metadata such as image tags, additional pictures, and related text are provided where available. Such rich annotation further extends the applicability of this dataset to a wide range of age estimation tasks.

FERET Database

FERET is one of the oldest and best-established resources in face recognition research. It was collected between 1993 and 1996; the base includes 1,199 subjects with face images. Within two days, a total of 15 sessions were carried out by capturing images under variable lighting conditions, scales, poses, and facial expressions. Diversity like this adds to making this dataset highly suitable for the evaluation of age estimation models with respect to real-world variability. In all, the FERET database consists of 14,126 images that have been divided into three sets: the Gallery set, Duplicate I probe set, and Duplicate II probe set. Out of these, the Gallery set contains 1,196 frontal images while the Duplicate I and Duplicate II probe sets contain 722 and 234 images, respectively. These probe sets are certainly useful to assess the performance of models when there is a time difference between training and testing image collection. For instance, the time difference between images in Duplicate II can vary from 540 to 1,031 days, which will be useful as a benchmark to test models in a longitudinal manner (Hu et al., 2016).

MORPH Database

Another popular resource available for age estimation and other face-based biometric applications is the database entitled MORPH. MORPH was developed by the Face Aging Group of the University of North Carolina and has two parts: MORPH Album 1 and MORPH Album 2. Album 1 contains 1,724 digitized images of 515 subjects in the age range from 15 to 68. Album 2 is much bigger, with more than 55,000 images taken from 13,618 subjects aged between 16 and 77 (Hu et al., 2016).

The two albums in the MORPH database are richly described in metadata, such as gender, race, date of birth, acquisition date, facial hair, glasses, weight, height, and ethnicity. This is one of the richest resources available thus far for studying how different factors contribute to the aging process. In particular, the size of its subject pool and age span of MORPH Album 2 are particularly well-suited for training deep learning models, which often require extensive data to do much of anything.

CVL Database (Center for Vital Longevity)

CVL database by Meredith Minear, Denise Park at the University of Michigan provides a smaller but more focused set of face images. The data falls into three categories: 308 profile images in the first category, 580 neutral face color and

159 grayscale images in the second, and 258 images of the same faces displaying emotions like anger, happiness, sadness, and surprise make up the third category. Subjects in the CVL database are aged between 18 and 94, from different racial backgrounds. Age can be figured out from the filenames, while the folder structure has information about gender and category. While the CVL dataset may be smaller in comparison with other aging datasets, with the focus on emotional expressions and both color and grayscale images, it is an enriching source for researchers in the area of interaction between emotional states and aging (Shejul et al., 2017).

CACD: Cross Age Celebrity Database

The Cross-Age Celebrity Database represents, up to now, the largest publicly available cross-age face dataset, and it was compiled by Chen et al. It includes 163,446 images of 2,000 celebrities, with photographs taken between 2004 and 2013. The age range was from 16 to 62 years, and their exact age can be calculated by subtracting the date of birth from the year in which a given photograph was taken. What was unique in CACD was that it had used Google Image search to collect its images, in this case depending on celebrity names and specific years as search keywords. As in the case of "Emma Watson 2004", this could yield a result of images taken in that particular year when the actress would have appeared at public events or film stills. That this method not only ensures a large variety in the images but also makes CACD, in its own right, unique for studying how facial features change over time for individuals in the public eye. Although the dataset is not as bound by metadata compared to others, its size and focus on cross-age variations make it invaluable for training deep learning models for age estimation (Silvia & Supangkat, 2020).

Yamaha Gender and Age (YGA) Database: In essence, the YGA database has been developed for the application of gender classification and age estimation from facial images. Gathered by Yamaha, this database was intended to be used in human-machine interaction research, especially for research that required the features of age and gender to be essential. Despite the fact that the YGA database is useful-the gender is well-represented and there is a large range of age groups-the limited availability of the database resulted in less usage of the database in many large-scale studies(Atallah et al., 2018).

Waseda Human-Computer Interaction Technology Database: WITDB: WIT-DB is one of the richest resources in regard to research on human-computer interaction. There are several modalities in that database: face images, audio recordings, motion data which can be utilized for age and gender classification. The facial images are well-labeled in this dataset; hence, this dataset is pretty much suitable for the training of robust age and gender classifiers since it was collected under controlled conditions. The dataset has different lightening conditions, as well as different facial expressions and poses (Rhodes, 2009).

Iranian Face Database [IFDB]: IFDB was developed to alleviate the imbalance of datasets that are usually representative of the Middle East population in the study of Facial Analysis. This dataset includes high-resolution images of Iranian subjects, and their age labels range from childhood to old age. The metadata provided in IFDB, other than age, is gender and different facial expressions. This database is useful for studying how well age estimation algorithms perform across races due to its focus on one particular ethnic group (ELKarazle et al., 2022).

3D Morphable Database: The database contains 3D face scans that can be used for generating age-progression and age-estimation models based on both shape and texture. This dataset is unique in that this 3D nature can handle variants of pose and lighting conditions. Further, the dataset includes annotation for facial landmarks, which makes it very versatile for experimenting with 3D-based face recognition models(Gift et al., 2024; Palaniappan et al., 2023; Senthil et al., 2023).

Kyaw's Web-Collected Database: The web-collected database of Kyaw consists of a large-scale dataset collected from scraped images off the web. Images in this database were, therefore, taken in unconstrained environments and expose the models to real-world challenges like light variations, pose variability, and so forth. Both age and gender labels will be included in the dataset so that a more robust model can be built by the researchers in diverse environments. However, due to the web-based collection method, inconsistencies in labeling and image quality are found (Huerta et al., 2015).

Ni's Web-Collected Database: Ni's web-collected dataset is similar in composition to that of Kyaw, containing images of faces gathered from sundry sources on the Internet. This dataset collection aims at creating a more varied composition for the purpose of classification based on age and gender. Facial expressions, poses, and lighting conditions include a wide range, making this an exceptionally versatile resource with which to train a deep learning model. In this regard, however, it shares some similarity with other datasets that have been collected from the Web, where noise in the data is an issue as a result of inconsistency in quality and labeling of the images (Abhulimen & Ogunti, 2021).

Gallagher's Web-Collected Database: The database by Gallagher is formed from a collection of images from public web sources and social media. It mainly finds its application in age classification tasks, with varieties of subjects across different age ranges. Indeed, this dataset has widely been adopted in the evaluation study about the robustness of age-estimation algorithms. Again, though it's good in diversity, it has inconsistencies of pose and light condition and image quality which increase the model training challenge.

AI & R Asian Face Database: The AI & R Asian Face Database covers only facial images of Asian individuals for those insufficiently represented in the facial databases, many of which have a dominant global face recognition dataset. This dataset provides that vital material for those models needing balanced ethnic representation. This contains extensive age groups, ranging from childhood to old age, and is thus very suitable for age progression studies. The whole collection is done in a controlled manner to ensure quality with correct labels on age and gender classes(Pitchai et al., 2024; Srinivas et al., 2023).

Burt's Caucasian Face Database: Burt's Caucasian Face Database was developed to study Caucasian facial perception. The images in this database are well-tagged, and the age and gender labels are accurate. It's useful when one wants quality pictures to analyze the face of the subject, but the subjects are of only one type, Caucasians, which makes it restrictive if one looks to test models for generalization across ethnicities.

Lotus Hill Research Institute (LHI) Database: One of the largest databases of facial images, the Lotus Hill Research Institute, or LHI, is focused on age estimation and gender classification model building. It is one of the most varied LHI databases due to the inclusion of different races and age groups. It includes detailed annotation for every image, such as the marking of facial landmarks and lighting conditions, which are helpful in developing models tolerant to variation in these factors.

Productive Aging Lab Face or PAL Database: From the perspective of aging and variations in facial features, the PAL database covers a wide range of high-resolution images of different individuals from various age groups, mostly of older adults. This makes it very effective for research on the changes in facial features brought on by age and for improving the age estimation algorithms on older populations.

FRGC - Face Recognition Grand Challenge Database: FRGC was developed as a part of a challenge in an effort to push the state of the art in face recognition further. It is a large database with more than 50,000 images, representing a wide age range from 0 to 80 years. The dataset includes both frontal face images under controlled lighting and those captured outdoors under less controlled conditions. Each subject's image is annotated with age and gender, and therefore this dataset will be useful for age and gender classification purposes.

UIUC-IFP Database: The UIUC-IFP dataset covers an age-diverse database that ranges from very broad age groups. Furthermore, it is very different in a way that it creates and constructs very robust models for age estimation. It is one of the best in terms of analyses for time-varying changes to facial features because the dataset consists of multiple images taken from the same subjects over a few years. Examples of available annotations in this dataset include landmarks on faces, illumination, and pose variations, making this dataset one of the most comprehensive datasets for research focused on age and gender classification tasks.

Asian Face Age Database (AFAD): The AFAD dataset involves Asian face images prepared for age estimation tasks. It includes a wide range of subjects from very young children to older adults, with both teenagers and young adults being very heavily represented. The dataset is well-annotated with highly accurate age labels based on the year the image was taken. AFAD is a great resource for building models that are better suited for the population in Asia and find the lack of diversity many face datasets have on a global level.

AmI-Face Database: The AmI-Face is a dataset that includes facial images from subjects operating in various realistic environments, including home and workplace settings. This dataset is best utilized for ambient intelligence applications wherein age and gender classification are used to personalize the user experience. Many different ages are represented, ranging from children to older adults. Each environment may capture metadata regarding the scenario of capture, including lighting and camera angles.

AgeDB Database: AgeDB is a large-scale face image dataset designed for the specific task of age estimation. Images of individuals from a wide range of age groups are maintained, along with their accurate age labels based on the year images were taken. One of the key characteristics of AgeDB pertains to its diversity: shots with individuals from various ethnic backgrounds, in different pose variations, and exhibiting different facial expressions. Large and diverse data is important for deep learning models that are to be used in different applications with high accuracy, hence it sees wide usage as a dataset.

It is one of the largest public datasets for age and gender classification. The IMDb-WIKI database contains more than 500,000 celebrity face images along with their age and gender labels based on the publicly available information on IMDb and Wikipedia. The dataset is highly diverse in nature since the images are captured under a variety of settings and lighting conditions. This makes IMDb-WIKI one of the favorite choices for the training of large-scale deep learning models because of its size and diversity.

APPA-REAL Database: The APPA-REAL database was developed to satisfy the demand for real-world images concerning age estimation tasks. It includes photos of individuals in unconstrained settings, including public places and social meetings. The dataset consists of credible age labels with respect to the particular year a photograph was taken, thus being quite helpful in developing models required for generalizing to real life scenarios.

UTKFace Database: The UTKFace database contains images of individuals from a wide range of age groups, with accurate age labels regarding gender and ethnicity. In fact, the dataset is so diverse that it contains images of people from a wide variety of ethnic backgrounds and of different ages. UTKFace is widely used for age estimation and gender classification tasks, and well-labeled images are a great source for training deep learning models.

Figure 4. Various applications of facial age estimation

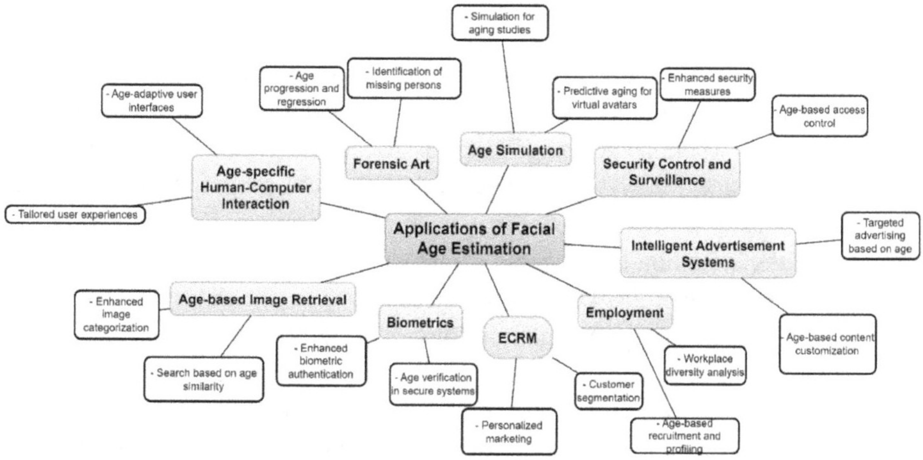

APPLICATIONS OF FACIAL AGE ESTIMATION

While in the nascent stage, with continuous research and improvement in the field of machine learning, computer vision, and artificial intelligence, face age estimation began finding its place as an integral tool in a variety of real-life applications. The art of estimating the age of an individual correctly from facial features has come a long way in serving security and surveillance to marketing and customer management with value. Unlike identity-based recognition systems focusing on matching the face against specific individuals, age estimation models emphasize probable age ranges of a subject with respect to visible cues in the face. As we are going to discuss, various application areas apply age estimation as a critical module(Angulu et al., 2018; Fu et al., 2010; Huerta et al., 2015; Panis & Lanitis, 2015; Shejul et al.,

2017; Shekhawat & Rathor, 2020). Figure 4 illustrates the application of facial age estimation technology across various industries and domains.

1. Age-Based Retrieval for Image Faces

Age-based facial image retrieval issues a query based on specified age criteria to a database of facial images. It will help in cases involving age as a major distinctive characteristic, such as missing persons or historical records. For instance, the police may want to fetch from the database images belonging to subjects of a certain age group in order to find their targets or missing persons. Besides, age-specific retrieval supports solutions for digital image archives, where pictures made in a certain period or having targets of a particular age group are the ones to be retrieved. For example, such a scenario might be desired while doing some genealogical study or searching images for certain characters in a movie. Clearly, being able to automatically retrieve images by age will provide a strong tool for structuring and filtering large image databases.

2. Forensic Art

The technology of the estimation of facial age is of extreme importance for forensic art. These methods are vital in cases involving missing children, elderly individuals with cognitive impairments, or suspects who have been on the run from the law for several years. The age estimation software would ultimately enable forensic artists to enhance the image of a person as he or she would appear after some time has lapsed. This technology helps in building images that denote the natural aging phenomena of wrinkles, sagging skin, and graying hair. It helps police forces distribute updated images of missing persons or fugitives more effectively.

3. Electronic Customer Relationship Management (ECRM)

Facial age estimation is also very important in developing the functions and capabilities of Electronic Customer Relationship Management systems. The algorithms for estimating the age can be used to have businesses tailor their offerings and services according to given age groups. This could be age estimation at the entrance of retail, offering appropriate promotions to customers through digital kiosks or mobile apps. With this, it allows companies to understand the different age demographics in their customer base and can thus bring refinement into their marketing strategies, product placements, and user experience(Naveeenkumar et al., 2024; Ravisankar et al., 2024). This also finds its application in online platforms, where websites or apps would change their interface or offering of content with respect to the estimated age of the user for greater personalization and engagement.

4. Security Control and Surveillance

Facial age estimation finds paramount importance in security control and surveillance systems. Cameras with installed facial recognition deployed in public places, transportation centers, and government facilities embody algorithms for age estimation. Security systems can easily identify anomalies or suspicious behavior based on age-related criteria by estimating the approximate age of individuals in real time. For instance, places with alcohol sold will be able to find people who look underage and inform the security personnel. Similarly, on the grounds of age-restricted access to certain areas like casinos, nightclubs, or adult-themed websites, age estimation is employed(Agrawal et al., 2023; Nanda et al., 2024; Puranik et al., 2024).

In more sophisticated applications, age estimation incorporates other biometric information, such as gait or voice recognition, to build more robust profiles of individuals for surveillance. It is more convenient when law enforcement agencies have to pursue suspects whose looks will change with time but whose age bracket would likely be a continuous feature.

Age-specific HCI designs user interfaces and experiences based on the estimated age of the user. This becomes incredibly important in industries, such as healthcare, where an elderly patient would be shown a much more simplified, accessible interface. On another end, education tools for children could take much advantage of interfaces designed to match stages in their development. Age estimation will dynamically adjust these interfaces to suit the user's cognitive and physical abilities.

6. Age Simulation

Age simulation refers to a process that uses technology in the facial age estimation of portraying the after-effects brought about by aging on a person's face and features over a period of time. This may find applications in various fields such as medical, cosmetics, and entertainment. The cosmetic industry may use age simulation, for instance, to view what skincare products or cosmetic surgery would result in. Medical professionals might use it to show patients how aging could affect them due to certain lifestyle choices, such as smoking, exposure to the sun, or lack of proper rest. Simulation software for age allows a person to see what changes their facial features may go through after some time; this can be a very compelling factor in leading a healthier lifestyle.

Simulation of age in the entertainment arena is where one would employ realistic aging of actors in movies and TV serials. That way, the production crew can portray actors' character aging without too much fuss over makeup and prosthetics, and this will also ensure smooth transitions over different periods of time in storytelling.

7. Biometrics

Facial age estimation forms a useful extension to biometric identification systems, which operate on physiological and behavioral traits to verify identity. Age estimation can, therefore, be an alternative to mainstream biometrics where the need for precise identification is not required in controlling access to services with age restrictions or to content that needs to be restricted to users of certain ages. For example, facial age estimation instead of fingerprint or retinal scan can facilitate systems where age becomes the determinant-the access permit could be for purchasing alcohol, viewing online contents that might be banned due to age restrictions, or participating in events at specific ages. Besides, age estimation biometrics are important in combating fraud in scenarios of online age verification, whereby individuals may attempt to declare the wrong age for unauthorized access. These algorithms provide an added layer of security that verifies the user's age against the information provided, hence reducing the risk of fraud(Sengeni et al., 2023).

8. Employment

Other sectors for which age estimates relevant to decisions on appointments are those that require certain levels of physical health and maturity. For example, employers in military or police forces may want assurance that candidates fall within a specific age bracket for particular tasks. At the same time, age estimation allows verifying the age of various individuals in those particular industries where the limits of age exist, like modeling, acting, or sports. The technologies will also play a crucial role in preventing age-based discrimination at the time of recruitment. While classifying the automatic age of an applicant, companies can keep their recruitment process unbiased and free from any intentional or unintentional ageism. This helps in maintaining transparency and legitimacy in the hiring process in harmony with labor laws regarding age discrimination.

Facial age estimation represents an important key to intelligent advertisement systems; their ads will be dynamically tailored based on viewers' demographic characteristics. This is an opportunity for retailers and marketers to use this technology to show age-appropriate advertisements in public spaces, including shopping malls, digital billboards, or smart kiosks. It could be targeted at older people to promote retirement plans or anti-age products, while the younger audience would see sportswear or ads for tech gadgets. Such a possibility to serve targeted ads, based on the viewer's estimated age, can considerably enhance the efficiency of marketing campaigns and make shopping more personalized.

The estimation of facial age can help e-commerce companies personalize the online shopping experience for consumers by manipulating product recommendations according to perceived age groups. In such a way, brands can get closer to customers and increase their conversion rate by offering to customers products which would correspond to the age-related needs of their clients.

Facial age estimation technology is one of the fastest-growing technologies and finds its application in almost every sector. Applications range from security and surveillance to intelligent advertisement systems, all driven by age estimation in a manner that boosts efficiency, personalization, and security. The versatility within the technology of age estimation renders it ever relevant in newer industries as more come forward to realize the benefits of integrating age-based insights into their operations. Owing to the further modernization of machine learning and artificial intelligence, even more sophisticated applications are bound to emerge, making facial age estimation literally indispensable in the modern world.

AGE ESTIMATION STUDIES

Facial age estimation has become a growing field of study in computer vision, where one tries to develop techniques that are more accurate in predicting an individual's age from their facial features. This challenge is complex and requires one to come up with robust feature extraction techniques, careful feature selection, and sophisticated learning models. This section will elaborate on the most critical aspects contributing to the success of facial age estimation. Figure 5 presents a structured overview of the facial age estimation process, outlining the objectives and obstacles to enhance accuracy (Han et al., 2013; Kavita & Chhillar, 2022; Koruga et al., 2011; Moyse, 2014; Shirode & Handore, 2016).

Figure 5. Facial age estimation in computer vision

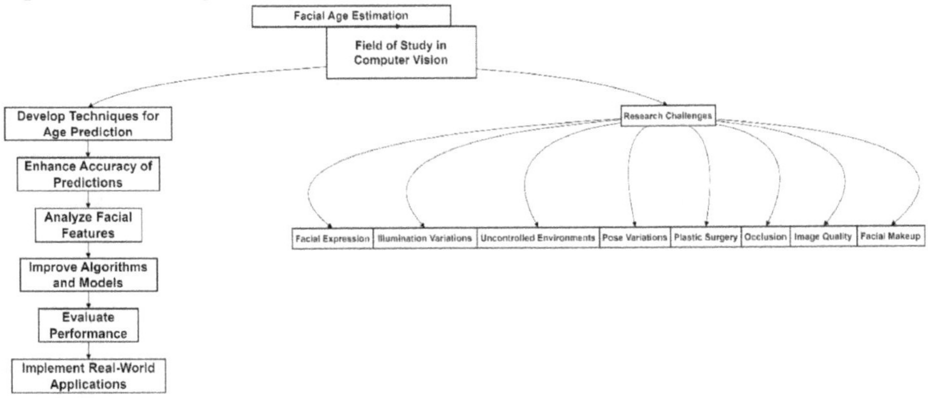

Feature Extraction Techniques

Feature extraction is the quintessential step that determines the performance of the age estimation model because the correct facial attributes are identified, changing with age. These can be segregated broadly into two important classes of algorithms: shape-based and texture-based.

Shape-Based Algorithms: These shape-based algorithms emphasize the detection of the geometrical structure of the face, such as facial landmarks and contours that, with time, due to craniofacial growth or due to aging, go through changes. Key facial landmarks consider the position of eyes, nose, mouth, and chin, each providing the basis for understanding facial geometry.

There is a recession on the forehead, expansion of cheekbones, and protrusion of the chin that happen with age. In shape-based methods, these facial landmarks are extracted and measure the proportion, distances, and angles of the face that correspondingly change with aging. Active shape models or ASMs, and active appearance models known as AAMs are based on a few shape-based techniques. These approaches predict age by making use of statistical models of facial shape variation. In ASMs, the method aligns a set of pre-set landmarks of the face to the subject's face and adjusts those points in order to minimize error in matching facial shape. AAMs extend this approach by modeling the facial appearance as well and use both shape and texture features for age prediction. Such a shape-based algorithm's accuracy largely depends upon the precision with which landmark detection is performed. Such precision could easily be compromised in cases of pose variation, occlusion, or even facial expressions. However, despite all the hindrances, shape-based features provide essential information toward age estimation, particularly when combined with other methods.

Texture-Based Algorithms: These algorithms usually take as input the texture of the skin, which changes drastically when a person begins to age. Wrinkles, fine lines, and roughness of skin texture are important features that give significant information about the age of an individual. This textural feature can be captured by various image processing techniques. The normal features extraction techniques based on textural features include LBP, Gabor filters, and DCT. LBP descriptors have gained a lot of popularity in facial age estimation due to their effectiveness in the capture of micro-level skin texture variations. This approach works by converting an input image into a binary pattern based on the relative intensities of neighboring pixels. Further, these patterns go ahead to describe the texture for different facial regions, thereby capturing the details that include wrinkles and skin tone variations-characteristic of aging.

Gabor filters are used for extracting multi-scale and multi-orientation texture features. These filters detect changes in the skin at different resolutions and orientations, hence being useful in the detection of directional properties of wrinkles and other aging-related texture changes. Texture-based algorithms are somewhat good at capturing subtle facial aging details, but such algorithms easily fall prey to changes brought about by lighting conditions or image quality. Many age estimation methods currently perform better when integrating both shape-based and texture-based algorithms.

Feature Selection in Age Estimation

In age estimation, after feature extraction from facial images, informative features should be selected. Feature selection can be regarded as the process of dimensionality reduction, selecting information attributes that provide significant contribution to precision in age prediction. It will help in preventing overfitting of the model and reducing computational complexity of learning.

Some of the feature selection techniques in age estimation include the PCA, LDA, and GA. PCA is widely applied to reduce dimensionality from shape-based and texture-based features by finding a set of uncorrelated variables or principal components that capture most of the variance in data. Conversely, LDA works to find the optimum low-dimensional feature space that maximizes the separability between different age groups. Other methods of age estimation include feature selection using Genetic Algorithms. These algorithms use evolutionary principles in the search for an optimal subset of features that maximizes age prediction accuracy. GAs iteratively evaluate different feature subsets and evolve the selection process over generations, with gradual model performance improvement. Feature selection depends on the type of features extracted from an image and the complexity of the dataset. Wholesome feature selection improves model generalization, ensuring that only the most relevant information is considered for age prediction.

Learning Models for Age Estimation

After feature extraction and feature selection, a learning model must be trained to predict the age of an individual from the selected features. The learning model for age estimation can be grossly divided into two categories, classification, and prediction-based models.

Classification Models: In these approaches, age estimation is considered as a multi-class classification problem where each age or age group is taken as a different class. The model is trained to classify a facial image into one of those predefined age classes. The general approaches for classification in age estimation have included the use of Support Vector Machines, Random Forests, and Convolutional Neural Networks. Support Vector Machines have been extensively applied to age estimation tasks due to their robustness against high-dimensional data and their ability to identify the optimal separating hyperplane between distinct age classes. That in itself means that SVMs will work for small and medium-sized datasets, but their performance on large-scale age estimation may be problematic.

Another popular classification method comprises the random forests, which also involve an ensemble of decision trees for making predictions. Each of the trees in the forest is trained on a random subset of the data, and the final age prediction is made through averaging predictions over all trees. Random Forests are robust to overfitting and perform well in scenarios with noisy data or complex feature spaces. Facial age estimation has been carried out by CNN-based architectures in recent years. CNNs automatically learn a hierarchical representation of features from the raw pixel data of facial images that capture both shape and texture features. CNNs and other deep learning models have increased age estimation accuracy, especially when large datasets are available to perform training.

Predictive Models

In contrast, predictive models treat age estimation as a kind of regression problem, where the goal is to predict the exact numerical age of an individual. For such a task, the most commonly used methods are linear regression, Gaussian processes, and deep neural networks. The linear regression model predicts age by fitting a linear relationship between the selected features and the target age values. While simple and easy to implement, linear regression may not capture the complex nonlinear relationships between facial features and aging patterns(Anitha et al., 2023; Palaniappan et al., 2023; Senthil et al., 2023).

Gaussian Processes: it allows for more flexible regression, where a nonlinear relationship between the features and the age can be modeled. These models can estimate the probability distribution of the predicted age, thus providing not only the estimate of the age but also the uncertainty of this prediction. Deep learning-based regression models have gained much popularity for age estimation in recent works, such as fully connected neural networks or CNNs. Such models learn complex nonlinear mappings between facial features and age, hence becoming very effective to predict the exact age of an individual.

Age estimation can be viewed as a complex process involving several steps: feature extraction, selection, and learning model training. Shape-based and texture-based algorithms form the basis of capturing facial features, while classification and predictive models offer different methods of age prediction. A combination of the appropriate techniques and models develops an accurate age estimation to support a wide range of real-world applications, including security and healthcare.

Figure 6. (a-e) Comparative analysis of age estimation techniques

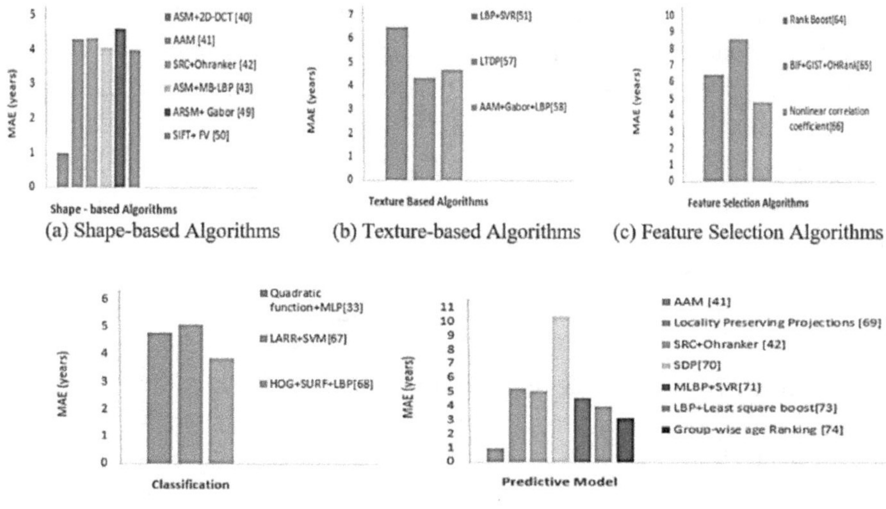

(a) Shape-based Algorithms (b) Texture-based Algorithms (c) Feature Selection Algorithms

(d) Classification Model (e) Predictive model

Figure 6 illustrates techniques and models used in studies on age estimation. Each part of this figure corresponds to a part of the process, from the feature extraction techniques that may be shape-based and texture-based algorithms, the selection methods, and up to the learning models, which are divided into classification and predictive models (Abhulimen & Ogunti, 2021; Al-Shannaq & Elrefaei, 2019; ELKarazle et al., 2022; Punyani et al., 2020; Rhodes, 2009; Silvia & Supangkat, 2020). Each section is discussed in detail as follows:

(a) Shape-based Algorithms

The shape-based methods dwell on the geometric features extraction of the face, which are highly relevant for age estimation in view of the structural changes in facial landmarks related to age. These methods usually work based on landmark detectors like eyes, nose, mouth, and chin, followed by measures of distances, angles, and proportions between them. With increasing age, some facial features change in a pretty predictable fashion. For example, the jaw line is not as well-defined, the volume of the cheeks becomes depleted, and the area around the socket of the eye starts to protrude. Shape-based methods modulate such an effect by estimating the facial structure across time. The two most usual implementations in this category are Active Shape Models and Active Appearance Models. ASMs focus on the exact fitting of facial landmarks, while AAMs include shape and appearance information to obtain a proper age estimate.

(b) Texture-based Algorithms

Part (b) illustrates texture-based algorithms, which concentrate on the skin texture that varies significantly with age. As one gets older, one's skin becomes coarser, develops wrinkles, and undergoes changes in pigmentation. Features of texture will be representative of this type of change by examining pixel patterns in face images. The LBP method will encode the texture of an image based on the relative intensity of the neighboring pixels and is one of the most used methods based on texture. Gabor filters and DCT feature extraction are also widely used for multi-scale and multi-orientation texture features, helping to identify wrinkle patterns and skin smoothness. These work effectively in finding fine-grained details of facial aging and often are combined with shape-based features for better accuracy.

(c) Feature selection Algorithms

The feature selection will be based on all the extracted shape-based and texture-based features as shown in part (c). Feature selection would reduce the dimensionality of data with an efficient and correct learning model. Some traditionally used techniques include Principal Component Analysis (PCA), Linear Discriminant Analysis (LDA), and Genetic Algorithms (GA). Whereas PCA reduces dimensionality by selecting the most important components within the data, LDA ensures maximum separation between age classes. Genetic Algorithms are an optimization technique that selects features through a mimic of natural selection in search of the optimum subset of features that best predict the age. In this way, these techniques eliminate redundancies or irrelevancies that empower model performance.

(d) Classification Model

Classification models replace the age estimation problem with the problem of multi-class classification where the age groups are predefined such as 20-30, 30-40 and so on. Some popular techniques which are generally used include Support Vector Machines, Random Forests, and Convolutional Neural Networks. While SVMs are suited to high-dimensional data to find the optimal hyperplane separating different age classes, Random Forests are robust to noisy data in that an image will be classified based on the output of multiple decision trees. Recently, CNNs have emerged as the most popular approach since they automatically learn features hierarchically from raw pixel data, thus they're pretty appropriate for the face recognition and age classification tasks.

(e) Predictive Model

Predictive models in age estimation deal with the problem as a regression problem, where the correct numerical age of an individual is predicted. Models usually learn to predict continuous values with the objective of eventually classifying them into one of many discrete classes of age.

Linear regression is the simplest approach, wherein it is assumed that the relationship between facial features and age is linear. However, since aging depends on complex nonlinear patterns, more sophisticated techniques have been Gaussian Processes and deep learning-based regression models. Gaussian Processes provide a probabilistic framework: they provide age estimates together with the associated uncertainties. Deep learning-based regression models can predict exact age with high accuracy by learning nonlinear mappings between features and age using fully connected neural networks.

CONCLUSION

Age estimation is a process of determining the real age or age group of an individual using his/her biometric features. In the current era, age estimation plays a significant role. We have presented a comprehensive overview of age estimate algorithms using face images, which have grown in popularity in recent decades as a result of their prospective real-world applications in numerous emerging fields. Different real-life applications for age estimation are explained. A comprehensive survey of various aging databases has been presented. We have discussed feature extraction, feature selection techniques, and the types of age learning algorithms. The design of an age estimation system necessitates careful extraction and selection of the facial features in order to effectively estimate the age. In addition, we have discussed a complete overview of current state-of-the-art techniques for age estimation using face images.

REFERENCES

Abhulimen, O., & Ogunti, E. (2021). Facial age estimation using deep learning: A review. *Methods (San Diego, Calif.)*, 8(5).

Agrawal, A. V., Magulur, L. P., Priya, S. G., Kaur, A., Singh, G., & Boopathi, S. (2023). Smart Precision Agriculture Using IoT and WSN. In *Handbook of Research on Data Science and Cybersecurity Innovations in Industry 4.0 Technologies* (pp. 524–541). IGI Global. DOI: 10.4018/978-1-6684-8145-5.ch026

Al-Shannaq, A. S., & Elrefaei, L. A. (2019). Comprehensive analysis of the literature for age estimation from facial images. *IEEE Access : Practical Innovations, Open Solutions*, 7, 93229–93249. DOI: 10.1109/ACCESS.2019.2927825

Alkaabi, S., Yussof, S., Al-Khateeb, H., Ahmadi-Assalemi, G., & Epiphaniou, G. (2020). Deep convolutional neural networks for forensic age estimation: A review. *Cyber Defence in the Age of AI, Smart Societies and Augmented Humanity*, 375–395.

Angulu, R., Tapamo, J. R., & Adewumi, A. O. (2018). Age estimation via face images: A survey. *EURASIP Journal on Image and Video Processing*, 2018(1), 1–35. DOI: 10.1186/s13640-018-0278-6

Anitha, C., Komala, C., Vivekanand, C. V., Lalitha, S., & Boopathi, S. (2023). Artificial Intelligence driven security model for Internet of Medical Things (IoMT). *IEEE Explore*, 1–7.

Atallah, R. R., Kamsin, A., Ismail, M. A., Abdelrahman, S. A., & Zerdoumi, S. (2018). Face recognition and age estimation implications of changes in facial features: A critical review study. *IEEE Access : Practical Innovations, Open Solutions*, 6, 28290–28304. DOI: 10.1109/ACCESS.2018.2836924

ELKarazle, K., Raman, V., & Then, P. (2022). Facial age estimation using machine learning techniques: An overview. *Big Data and Cognitive Computing*, 6(4), 128. DOI: 10.3390/bdcc6040128

Fu, Y., Guo, G., & Huang, T. S. (2010). Age synthesis and estimation via faces: A survey. *IEEE Transactions on Pattern Analysis and Machine Intelligence*, 32(11), 1955–1976. DOI: 10.1109/TPAMI.2010.36 PMID: 20847387

Gift, M. D. M., Senthil, T. S., Hasan, D. S., Alagarraja, K., Jayaseelan, P., & Boopathi, S. (2024). Additive Manufacturing and 3D Printing Innovations: Revolutionizing Industry 5.0. In *Technological Advancements in Data Processing for Next Generation Intelligent Systems* (pp. 255–287). IGI Global. DOI: 10.4018/979-8-3693-0968-1.ch010

Han, H., Otto, C., & Jain, A. K. (2013). Age estimation from face images: Human vs. Machine performance. *2013 International Conference on Biometrics (ICB)*, 1–8. DOI: 10.1109/ICB.2013.6613022

Hu, Z., Wen, Y., Wang, J., Wang, M., Hong, R., & Yan, S. (2016). Facial age estimation with age difference. *IEEE Transactions on Image Processing*, 26(7), 3087–3097. DOI: 10.1109/TIP.2016.2633868 PMID: 27913345

Huerta, I., Fernández, C., Segura, C., Hernando, J., & Prati, A. (2015). A deep analysis on age estimation. *Pattern Recognition Letters*, 68, 239–249. DOI: 10.1016/j.patrec.2015.06.006

Kavita, K., & Chhillar, R. S. (2022). Human face recognition and age estimation with machine learning: A critical review and future perspective. *International Journal of Electrical and Computer Engineering Systems*, 13(10), 945–952. DOI: 10.32985/ijeces.13.10.9

Koruga, P., Ševa, J., & Bača, M. (2011). A Review of Face Recognition Algorithms and Their Application in Age Estimation. *Proceedings of the 22nd Central European Conference on Information and Intelligent Systems.*

Moyse, E. (2014). Age estimation from faces and voices: A review. *Psychologica Belgica*, 54(3), 255–265. DOI: 10.5334/pb.aq

Nanda, A. K., Sharma, A., Augustine, P. J., Cyril, B. R., Kiran, V., & Sampath, B. (2024). Securing Cloud Infrastructure in IaaS and PaaS Environments. In *Improving Security, Privacy, and Trust in Cloud Computing* (pp. 1–33). IGI Global. DOI: 10.4018/979-8-3693-1431-9.ch001

Naveeenkumar, N., Rallapalli, S., Sasikala, K., Priya, P. V., Husain, J., & Boopathi, S. (2024). Enhancing Consumer Behavior and Experience Through AI-Driven Insights Optimization. In *AI Impacts in Digital Consumer Behavior* (pp. 1–35). IGI Global. DOI: 10.4018/979-8-3693-1918-5.ch001

Onifade, O. F., & Akinyemi, D. J. (2015). A review on the suitability of machine learning approaches to facial age estimation. *International Journal of Modern Education and Computer Science*, 7(12), 17–28. DOI: 10.5815/ijmecs.2015.12.03

Othmani, A., Taleb, A. R., Abdelkawy, H., & Hadid, A. (2020). Age estimation from faces using deep learning: A comparative analysis. *Computer Vision and Image Understanding*, 196, 102961. DOI: 10.1016/j.cviu.2020.102961

Palaniappan, M., Tirlangi, S., Mohamed, M. J. S., Moorthy, R. S., Valeti, S. V., & Boopathi, S. (2023). Fused Deposition Modelling of Polylactic Acid (PLA)-Based Polymer Composites: A Case Study. In *Development, Properties, and Industrial Applications of 3D Printed Polymer Composites* (pp. 66–85). IGI Global.

Panis, G., & Lanitis, A. (2015). An overview of research activities in facial age estimation using the FG-NET aging database. *Computer Vision-ECCV 2014 Workshops: Zurich, Switzerland, September 6-7 and 12, 2014. Proceedings*, 13(Part II), 737–750.

Pitchai, R., Guru, K. V., Gandhi, J. N., Komala, C. R., Kumar, J. R. D., & Boopathi, S. (2024). Fog Computing-Integrated ML-Based Framework and Solutions for Intelligent Systems: Digital Healthcare Applications. In *Technological Advancements in Data Processing for Next Generation Intelligent Systems* (pp. 196–224). IGI Global. DOI: 10.4018/979-8-3693-0968-1.ch008

Punyani, P., Gupta, R., & Kumar, A. (2020). Neural networks for facial age estimation: A survey on recent advances. *Artificial Intelligence Review*, 53(5), 3299–3347. DOI: 10.1007/s10462-019-09765-w

Puranik, T. A., Shaik, N., Vankudoth, R., Kolhe, M. R., Yadav, N., & Boopathi, S. (2024). Study on Harmonizing Human-Robot (Drone) Collaboration: Navigating Seamless Interactions in Collaborative Environments. In *Cybersecurity Issues and Challenges in the Drone Industry* (pp. 1–26). IGI Global.

Ravisankar, A., Shanthi, A., Lavanya, S., Ramaratnam, M., Krishnamoorthy, V., & Boopathi, S. (2024). Harnessing 6G for Consumer-Centric Business Strategies Across Electronic Industries. In *AI Impacts in Digital Consumer Behavior* (pp. 241–270). IGI Global.

Rhodes, M. G. (2009). Age estimation of faces: A review. *Applied Cognitive Psychology*, 23(1), 1–12. DOI: 10.1002/acp.1442

Sengeni, D., Padmapriya, G., Imambi, S. S., Suganthi, D., Suri, A., & Boopathi, S. (2023). Biomedical waste handling method using artificial intelligence techniques. In *Handbook of Research on Safe Disposal Methods of Municipal Solid Wastes for a Sustainable Environment* (pp. 306–323). IGI Global. DOI: 10.4018/978-1-6684-8117-2.ch022

Senthil, T., Puviyarasan, M., Babu, S. R., Surakasi, R., Sampath, B., & Associates. (2023). Industrial Robot-Integrated Fused Deposition Modelling for the 3D Printing Process. In *Development, Properties, and Industrial Applications of 3D Printed Polymer Composites* (pp. 188–210). IGI Global.

Shejul, A. A., Kinage, K. S., & Reddy, B. E. (2017). Comprehensive review on facial based human age estimation. *2017 International Conference on Energy, Communication, Data Analytics and Soft Computing (ICECDS)*, 3211–3216. DOI: 10.1109/ICECDS.2017.8390049

Shekhawat, H. S., & Rathor, H. S. (2020). Impacts of change in facial features on age estimation and face identification: A review. *Smart Systems and IoT: Innovations in Computing:Proceeding of SSIC 2019*, 801–812.

Shirode, P., & Handore, S. (2016). Estimation of age from human facial features. *2016 3rd International Conference on Computing for Sustainable Global Development (INDIACom)*, 2098–2103.

Silvia, S., & Supangkat, S. H. (2020). A literature review on facial age estimation researches. *2020 International Conference on ICT for Smart Society (ICISS)*, 1–6. DOI: 10.1109/ICISS50791.2020.9307606

Srinivas, B., Maguluri, L. P., Naidu, K. V., Reddy, L. C. S., Deivakani, M., & Boopathi, S. (2023). Architecture and Framework for Interfacing Cloud-Enabled Robots. In *Handbook of Research on Data Science and Cybersecurity Innovations in Industry 4.0 Technologies* (pp. 542–560). IGI Global. DOI: 10.4018/978-1-6684-8145-5.ch027

KEY TERMS AND DEFINITIONS

AAM: Active Appearance Models, combining shape and texture for object recognition.

AFAD: Asian Face Age Dataset, used for age estimation in facial recognition.

AI: Artificial Intelligence, the simulation of human intelligence in machines, often used in image analysis.

APPA: Aged People's Appearance dataset, for studying aging effects on facial features.

ASM: Active Shape Models, statistical models used for facial feature localization.

CACD: CelebA Attribute Dataset, used for training facial recognition models.

CNN: Convolutional Neural Network, a deep learning architecture commonly used for image analysis.

CVL: Computer Vision Lab, a research facility focusing on image processing and computer vision technologies.

DB: Database, a structured collection of data, often used for storing images.

DCT: Discrete Cosine Transform, a technique used in image compression.

ELK: Elasticsearch, Logstash, and Kibana; a stack for searching and analyzing large data sets, including images.

FERET: Facial Recognition Technology database, a benchmark for facial recognition algorithms.

FG: Foreground, the primary subject of an image, often distinguished from the background.

FRGC: Face Recognition Grand Challenge, a large-scale facial recognition dataset.

GA: Genetic Algorithm, a search heuristic for optimizing problems.

HCI: Human-Computer Interaction, studying how people interact with computers, including image interfaces.

IFDB: Image Feature Database, a collection of image features for analysis.

IFP: Image Feature Points, specific points in an image used for analysis.

II: Image Indexing, the process of organizing and retrieving images based on metadata.

IMD: Image Metadata, data that describes various attributes of an image.

LBP: Local Binary Patterns, a feature descriptor used in image processing.

LDA: Linear Discriminant Analysis, used for feature extraction and classification.

LHI: Local Histogram Equalization, a technique for enhancing image contrast.

MORPH: Morphology, a technique in image processing for analyzing shapes within images.

NET: Neural Network, a computational model inspired by the human brain, used in deep learning.

PAL: Palette-based Image, an image representation using a limited set of colors.

PCA: Principal Component Analysis, a method for reducing dimensionality in datasets.

REAL: Realistic image dataset for benchmarking algorithms.

RGB: Red, Green, Blue; a color model used for digital images where colors are created by combining these three primary colors.

SVM: Support Vector Machine, a supervised learning model for classification tasks.

TV: Total Variation, a method for image denoising.

UIUC: University of Illinois at Urbana-Champaign, known for research in computer vision.

UTKF: University of Texas at Killeen's Facial Dataset, used for recognition research.

WIKI: Wikipedia, a free online encyclopedia often used as a resource for definitions.

WIT: Web Image Tagging, the practice of labeling images online for better searchability.

YGA: Young's Gaussian Approximation, a technique in image processing for enhancing image features.

Chapter 10
Innovative System Using Artificial Intelligence and Robotics for Fire Disaster Management

Komala C. R.
Department of Information Science and Engineering, East Point College of Engineering and Technology, Bengaluru, India

S. Prakash
Department of Information Science and Engineering, East Point College of Engineering and Technology, Bengaluru, India

Yogesh G. S.
Department of Information Science and Engineering, East Point College of Engineering and Technology, Bengaluru, India

T. K. Thivakaran
Department of Information Science and Engineering, East Point College of Engineering and Technology, Bengaluru, India

Nanda Ashwin
Department of Information Science and Engineering, East Point College of Engineering and Technology, Bengaluru, India

ABSTRACT

The chapter discusses how AI and robotics can be developed to enhance fire disaster management systems. The new system applies AI algorithms and robotics approaches to improve early detection, response in real time, and post-disaster analysis. Predictive

DOI: 10.4018/979-8-3693-2337-3.ch010

models using AI algorithms and data from sensors, together with historical fire patterns, result in highly accurate predictions of fire outbreaks. Furthermore, an autonomous robot was used to move quickly to assess and intervene rapidly. These robots scan dangerous environments for hotspots, carry out rescues, and extinguish flames while minimizing human risk and maximizing operational efficiency. Case studies and future research directions highlight technological changes in terms of fire safety and resilience.

INTRODUCTION

The management of fire disaster is a very critical and complex domain demanding continuous innovation. This should keep pace with the constantly evolving threats and technological advances. Meanwhile, conventional tools of the old methods of fire detection and response and recovery, have relied heavily on human intervention and conventional tools that are often greatly inadequate in situations involving big or high-intensity fires. Rising incidences and intensification of the fires as a consequence of urbanization globally, as well as climate change, call for urgent improvement of systems in terms of advanced and efficient approaches. Artificial Intelligence integration with robotics is an innovative way of handling fire disasters with better predictive, responsive, and recovery capabilities (Lee & Chien, 2020).

With the ability to process vast volumes of data and identify intricate patterns, Artificial Intelligence has led to a revolution in various sectors, from healthcare to finance and transport. In fact, its application to fire management is also very promising with an advance system capable of early detection and risk estimation. AI algorithms, including machine learning and deep learning models, can mine information from many sources, such as satellite images and weather reports, in addition to historical records of fire, to predict the outbreak of wildfires with previously unimaginable accuracy. Predictive models allow the authorities to allocate their resources better and prevent fires from spreading when it is possible to gain control over them (Sun et al., 2020).

Robotics adds a physical dimension to fire management. Advanced sensors, cameras, and communication systems enable the deployment of autonomous robots in hazardous areas where human presence would be dangerous or impractical. Fire detection, surveillance, rescue, and firefighting are but just some of the uses for these robots. These robots go through smoky, structurally weakened parts of buildings to analyze and provide focused interventions, thereby greatly reducing the danger that would otherwise exist for human firefighters and increasing overall efficiency in operations (Abid et al., 2021).

Another of the most highly valued benefits of integrating AI and robotics with fire disaster management is situational awareness. Traditional methods are often predicated on one's ability to make the right inputs by viewing the occurrence through manual reporting or visual inspections, which may take some hours. Meanwhile, AI systems can be able to process real-time data from a network of cameras and sensors, and therefore it may give an overview of the developments of the fire (Tan et al., 2021). The real-time analysis gives respondents better decision-making on the use of resources and strategizing and their course correction based on conditions. The use of autonomous robots improves situational awareness with real-time data coming from the fire ground. As they possess high-resolution cameras and thermal sensors, they have made images and data with respect to the behavior of the fire and possible hazards in and around it. They can feed this back to the command centers where the AI systems process it and make suggestions on the decisions and responses to take (Aboualola et al., 2023).

Similarly, AI and robotics create a synergy in fire operations. Autonomous robots can carry diverse firefighting equipment, including water cannons, foam dispensers, and extinguishing agents. They can be programmed to operate at precise and controlled interventions that target the specific parts of the fire to bring about maximum impact while using less water and contributing less damage. This is why precision is valuable when it comes to complex environments, for they may mean fighting in high-rise buildings or industrial facilities, or anything else wherein traditional methods of firefighting are not effective. Besides the operational benefits, AI and robotics also play a great role in making it much easier to handle fire disasters effectively. Extremes of heat and toxic smoke embrace firefighters' struggles with the building collapsing without warning. Humans working as firefighters are protected from hazardous situations while strategic planning and decision-making is concentrated on the side of human firefighters. Robots can work continuously without getting worn out, and they maintain their performance levels even when working for long periods in firefighting operations (Zarghami & Dumrak, 2021).

Another area wherein incredible developments in the field have been seen is the integration of AI with robotics, which also leads to advancements in post-disaster analysis and recovery. After a fire outbreak takes place, the damage thus caused needs to be examined along with the sources of the disaster, and all this being done, the strategies for recovery are put in motion. AI can analyze data from satellite imagery and even from drones, relative to the extent of damage, and produce detailed reports. Doing on-site inspections along with sample collection and providing visual evidence through robotics complements the process. This detailed approach helps understand the impact of the fire and provides feedback for further fire prevention and response strategies (Wilk-Jakubowski et al., 2022).

However, there are also some challenges and considerations associated with the integration of AI and robotics into fire disaster management. There are technical challenges related to ensuring that the robustness and reliability of AI algorithms and robotic systems can be guaranteed in extreme conditions of heat, smoke, and dust. In addition, there are logistical considerations related to the deployment and maintenance of robotic systems in place as well as the integration of AI tools into existing infrastructures of fire management. Ethical and regulatory issues also have to be addressed (Ivić, 2019). The use of AI and robotics in fire management raises immense concerns on data privacy, transparent decision making, and human oversight. It goes without saying that such technologies must be properly deployed as well as in accordance with set standards for public trust and effectiveness to be maintained.

This marks the consolidation of Artificial Intelligence and robotics in a package more holistic than what we know so far, towards an even more advanced step in fire disaster management. Thus, the combination of AI and robotics enhances predictive capabilities, the aspect of situational awareness, and generally enhances the operations of firefighting operations (Choi, 2020). It opens new possibilities for more effective and safer fire response strategies. As research and development evolve on this synergy between AI and robotics, there is promise for even much deeper breakthroughs contributing to a more resilient and adaptable approach to fire disaster management.

Scope

This study focuses on a discussion and analysis of the integration of AI and robotics in the prediction, response, and recovery phases of fire disasters. It addresses the emerging issues related to integration challenges, as well as discussion regarding ethical implications: issues that generally tend to give a comprehensive overview of the transformations that progressively place these innovations in new fire management strategies. It is focused on trends that are currently visible and those that may take root as future directions, with quite potential long-term implications for the practice of fire management.

Objectives

The objectives of incorporating AI and robotics in the management of fire disasters include improving the predictive capabilities, enhancing real-time responses, and optimizing post-disaster recovery processes. With emerging technology, it is intended to reduce the likelihood and severity of fire incidences, achieve high performance levels in an operation, and support more effective and timely recovery processes.

BACKGROUND: ARTIFICIAL INTELLIGENCE IN FIRE DISASTER MANAGEMENT

Figure 1. How Artificial Intelligence (AI) can be used in fire disaster management

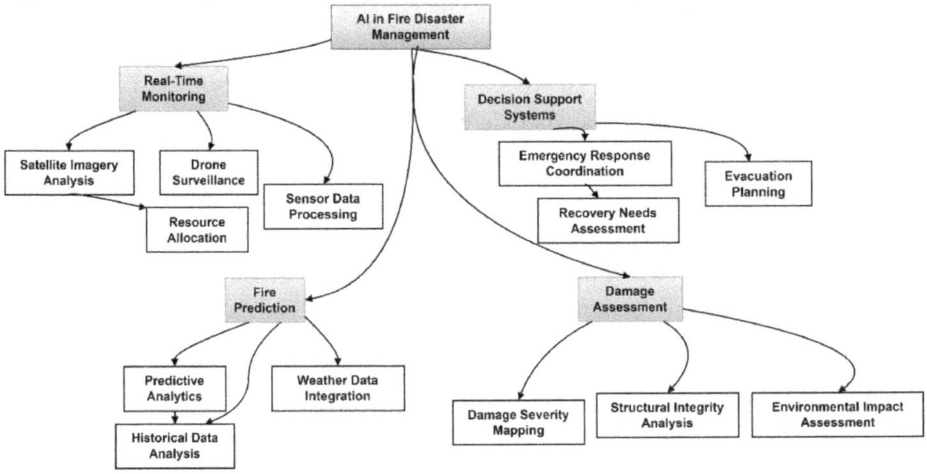

Artificial Intelligence

AI is one branch of computer science whose fundamental objective is to try to make a system into something that can perform most humanly used intelligent tasks. Such tasks include problem-solving, learning, reasoning, and perception. AI systems largely depend on huge technologies such as machine learning (ML), deep learning, natural language processing (NLP), and computer vision. The field of machine learning, which is a sub-class in AI, involves training algorithms on data to be able to recognize patterns and then use them to make predictions or decisions. Deep learning is an advanced class of ML, which in its neural networks form uses more than one layer to break down complicated data structures to extract intricate features(Kankanamge et al., 2021). The figure 1 illustrates the application of Artificial Intelligence (AI) in fire disaster management.

The exploitation of these technologies by AI helps to improve the prediction, detection, and response capabilities in fire disaster management. Using systems based on AI, volumes of data from any source can be analyzed in order to discern patterns or trends that could provide predictive clues about the probability of a fire. With AI, processes that would traditionally be automated can quickly and more precisely lead to decision-making at times when speed and accuracy are critical, such as in fire management.

AI Algorithms and Models for Fire Prediction

Algorithms and models are helpful in predicting and managing fire disasters. Varying types of algorithms such as regression models, classification algorithms, and clustering techniques are used to scan and evaluate the data for predicting risks of fire. Most of the algorithms have specific applications. Consequently, they have various applications with special advantages (AlAli & Alabady, 2022):

Regression models are those models which predict continuous results by using input variables. Using regression models, the probability of a fire will occur can be predicted in fire prediction based on weather conditions, historical fire data, and so on, that depends on the vegetation type. Linear regression, logistic regression, etc., advanced regression techniques can be used to analyze which factors affect fire risks. A classification algorithm classifies data into predefined classes or categories. Classification algorithms in fire management may classify between a high risk zone and a low risk zone by the combination of temperature, humidity, and wind speed among other determinants. Decision trees, SVM, and neural networks can be applied in the classification of data and the prediction of the event of fire incidence. Clustering algorithms group together data that will have most similarities based on the variables of interest. Clustering in fire prediction can be used to identify patterns or clusters of areas at a greater risk of invasion by fires. Therefore, its segmentation can be done with more adequate techniques such as k-means clustering and hierarchical clustering, based on the fire risk factors of particular regions where further prevention can be targeted(Ahamed et al., 2024; Rahamathunnisa et al., 2023).

The training model here entails deep learning, a subcategory of machine learning models that use multilayer neural networks for the assessment of complex information. Two popular types of neural networks are used in developing the fire prediction models: CNNs and RNNs. CNNs have the ability to learn space or spatial hierarchy or spatial data with a practical applicability to detect regions prone to fire, and RNNs learn temporal sequences of data, like weather patterns over time.

AI models are trained upon historical data related to fire incidents, weather conditions, and more relevant variables. Such models train to identify patterns and correlations leading up to the events of fire occurrences. Once the data is adjusted and assessed by the model, it can predict the occurrence of future fires and warn people in advance to mitigate the risks.

Data Sources and Integration

Including various sources of data is one means by which comprehensive risk and behavior of fires can be depicted. Weather Data: Weather conditions are significant in fire risk since they relate to temperature, humidity, wind speed, and precipitation.

Real-time and history on weather data will determine the evolution of fire behavior and potential outbreaks. AI models use this kind of data to determine how current conditions may influence the risk associated with fires (Ofli et al., 2020).

a) Satellite and Aerial Images: Satellite and aerial pictures give broad information on the vegetation cover, land use, and fire spread. Remote sensing technologies such as satellite images, drones, capture high-resolution data that AI models analyze to detect a change in the health of the vegetation, identification of the fire hotspot, and monitoring of the spread of the fire.
b) Historical Fire Data: It is a must, in training the AI models, to have historical data on past fires, such as location, size, intensity, and causes of such incidents. This will help in identifying patterns and trends that result in future fires. Historical data also assesses previous fire management strategies.
c) Geospatial Data: For terrain, vegetation, and other infrastructures, GIS produces spatial data. With the help of GIS data, it can be more effectively mapped out how fire-prone areas exist and which features of terrain may impact fire spread. Therefore, based on GIS data, there is a better ability to plan response strategies well. AI models tend to include GIS data for its integration in order to improve spatial analysis and risk assessments.

Sensor networks, such as weather stations, fire detectors, and IoT devices, provide real-time information about environmental conditions and fire activity. These sensors help in continuous monitoring of fire-prone areas and allow for timely warnings in case of an impending fire. Data integration involves preparation, along with ensuring data homogenization to ensure consistency and accuracy. The AI systems need to be exposed to the greatest diversity of formats of data and sources. Hence, managing and integrating them requires very robust techniques. Data fusion techniques, which integrate information coming from multiple sources, improve the accuracy and reliability of AI predictions.

A summary would therefore come to the conclusion of developing AI in the management of fire disasters by starting the ability of prediction, detection, and even response to any fire-based incident. The integration of data from reports about the weather, satellite images, historical records, and sensor networks allows these AI systems the ability to make invaluable insights and better prepare with a warning preceding any time. In the future, more effective solutions can be made in the management of fire disasters on the basis of new developments in AI and data integration.

ROBOTICS IN FIRE DISASTER MANAGEMENT

Figure 2. Role of robotics in fire disaster management

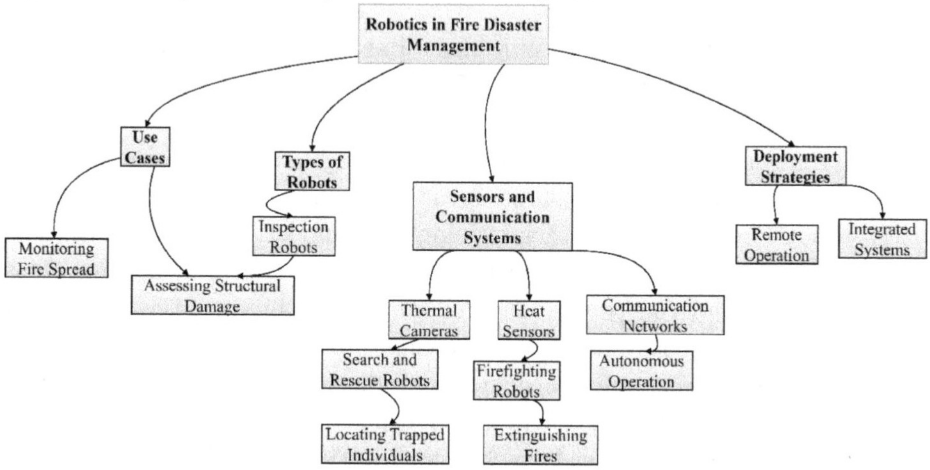

Robotics Technology

Robotics technology basically refers to the design, construction, operation, and use of robots. In relation to the management of fire disasters, robotics is the process of developing machines that can either perform autonomously or semi-autonomously when carrying out various functions. Figure 2 depicts the significant role of robotics in fire disaster management.These robots are fitted with current state-of-the-art technologies such as sensors, actuators, and communication systems to carry out potentially dangerous functions. Important features of robotics technology in relation to fire management are (Maraveas et al., 2021):

The key components used to make robots exhibit movement or manipulation of objects are actuators and motors. Actuation is also to control movement in case of firefighting robot such as driving, climbing stairs, or extending firefighting equipment. In order to enable the robot to navigate challenging terrains, motors drive its wheels or tracks(Mohanty et al., 2023; Pramila et al., 2023; Rahamathunnisa et al., 2023).

a) Power Systems: The power systems of robots used in fire management have to be very strong, so that such robots can function properly and effectively in emergency situations. They are usually composed of high-capacity batteries or other power sources which can keep the robot operative in extended missions.

b) Control Systems: Control systems of robots may be manual, semi-autonomous, or fully autonomous. The advanced control systems with direct preprogrammed instructions or in real time command from human operators will enable a robot to do anything it is designed to do. The AI algorithms decide and execute tasks on their own, and the robots are called autonomous.
c) Durability and Protection: As fire disaster conditions are extremely harsh, robots are designed with these conditions in mind. They are often built from heat-resistant materials, heavily reinforced structures, and casings of protection to withstand high temperatures, smoke, and other debris.

Types of Robots Used in Fire Management

There are numerous types of robots that are used in fire disaster management, each addressed to specific challenges and tasks. Ground-Bot Ground-based robots are those equipped with wheels or tracks and help in moving through rubble and debris. These are used in search and rescue missions, scouting, and fighting fires (Choi, 2020). Examples include:

a) Firefighting Robots: These are often supplied with water canons or foam dispensers to drop fire-suppressing agents on targeted areas. These robots are used in hazardous situations where fires need to be suppressed and human intervention is considered too high-risk.
b) Search and Rescue Robots: These are designed to search through damaged buildings and locate trapped people. They are often equipped with cameras, microphones, and manipulation tools in support of search-and-rescue missions.
c) Drones-Aerial Robots: They are fitted with cameras and sensors that can be used to conduct aerial surveillance and monitoring of a fire scenario. Advantages:
d) Fire Mapping: Drones can acquire high-resolution images and thermal data and map the spread of a fire, assess the spread thereof, and identify hotspots.
e) Real-Time Surveillance: Command centers can receive real-time feeds of video from aerial drones, thus improving situational awareness and guiding efforts on the ground.
f) Underwater Robots: Although used less often, underwater robots are applied under specified scenarios in case of a fire outbreak near water bodies. They can be applied in work like determining water pollution levels or in the laying of equipment that can fight fire within waters.

Sensors and Communication Systems

Sensors and communication systems are crucial elements that add more competencies to robots about the handling of fires (Aboualola et al., 2023; Abraham et al., 2019; Zarghami & Dumrak, 2021).

a) Sensors: There are various sensors on the firefighting robots that assist them in gathering data to carry out their functions. Some of them include the following.
b) Thermal Cameras: This detector scans and senses heat signatures and employs thermal imaging. It enables the robot to see areas where fires are burning hot as well as having hotspots; it can navigate through the smoke-filled setting.
c) Gas Detectors: Also, fitted with this kind of detector, the robots can identify hazardous gases carbon monoxide and methane, which are commonly encountered in fire situations.
d) LIDAR (Light Detection and Ranging): LIDAR sensors generate high-resolution 3D maps of the environment. These allow the robots to find paths to useful locations through rubble and to estimate the integrity of buildings and other structures.
e) Communication Systems: In well-integrated robot operations, communication is essential, especially in highly dynamic and challenging environments. Communication components in the key elements include:
f) Radio Frequency (RF) Communication: RF allows for real-time data transmission between robots and command centers. This is extremely important for remote control, telemetry, and data sharing.
g) Wi-Fi and Cellular Networks: These networks enable high-bandwidth data transfer, so video feeds and sensor data can be forwarded to operators. They are particularly useful in areas where RF communication may be limited.

Deployment Strategies and Use Cases

The deployment of robots in fire disaster management is strategically planned and coordinated with the following aims (Fan et al., 2021):

a) Pre-Deployment Plan: The fire management teams deploy the robot before the actual fire event to position them in high-risk fire-prone areas or to be equipped for rapid deployments. This ensures that the robots are fully functional, fully charged, and equipt with all necessary sensors.

b) Real-Time Deployment: The robots are deployed according to real-time needs and conditions in the event of an active fire. They are sent to areas that may be too impossible for human firefighters, or they assist in obtaining critical information that may inform response actions.
c) Post-Fire Analysis: Robots can be used in post-disaster assessment and recovery after a fire. These machines can survey the affected areas, determine damage, and collect data to inform future fire management strategies.

Case Studies

a) Urban Fires: This is applicable in urban areas where robots are used to cross narrow alleys and skyscrapers. They can provide real-time situational awareness, assist the firefighting effort, and perform a search and rescue job.
b) Industrial Fires: Robots in industrial facilities can be utilized as equipped with special firefighting equipment and deal with hazardous materials, thus extinguishing fires in a resultant environment that has poisonous fumes or an explosive risk.
c) Wildfire Management: Big Wildfires Mapping and Monitoring Aerial Drones Ground-based robots Possibly establishing firebreaks, delivery of fire retardants and assistance in evacuation.

In robotics technology, several robots with highly sophisticated sensors and communication systems have emerged as an innovative mechanism for fire disaster management. These are tactfully deployed by firefighting teams to enhance their operational capabilities, improve safety, and respond better to complex fire situations. The future benefits would indeed lie in the continued development of robotics technology, with its significant enhancement of more effective disaster response strategies and management.

Figure 3. Integration of AI and robotics in fire disaster management

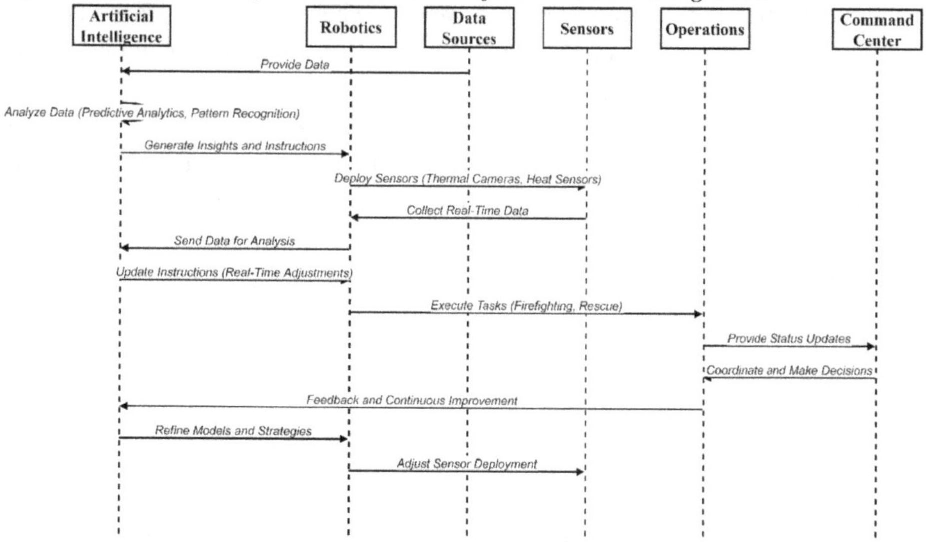

INTEGRATION OF AI AND ROBOTICS

The merger of AI and robotics is one revolutionary advancement in managing fire disasters because the merging of two modern avenues, AI and robotics, will be able to strengthen each other toward maximizing the given efficiencies and effectiveness for operational proficiency. Its synergy uses AI advanced capability in processing data, as well as the capabilities of robotics in physical play on the threats as a whole with a fire disaster. By integrating AI and robotics, fire management systems can achieve unprecedented levels of situational awareness, real-time data analysis, and autonomous operations to ultimately improve response times and safety outcomes (Damaševičius et al., 2023). The integration of AI and robotics in fire disaster management ensures a seamless flow of information and decision-making processes, as illustrated in Figure 3.

Combination of AI and Robotics

The synergies between AI and robotics are instrumental in the transformation of fire disaster management. Algorithms formed from AI provide the necessary cognitive capabilities required for the effective complex decision-making system, whereas the robotic system offers physical capabilities to carry out physically demanding and risky undertakings. It creates an interaction whereby AI systems guide robotic actions on the basis of real-time data and where robots provide sensory input and physical execution necessary for effective disaster response (Velev & Zlateva, 2023).

AI enhances robotics through the possibility of higher-order algorithms processing large data packets from disparate sources, such as sensors and cameras. For instance, the AI can assess patterns of fire behavior and predict spots likely to be a hotspot so that robots can be stationed accordingly. On the other hand, robotics enhances AI in terms of accuracy, real-time information, and the quality of input information for AI systems to enhance predictive and decision-making processes. This mutual improvement ensures that not only do the robots run on AI, but also they provide great information in enriching the models of AI over time.

Enhancing Situational Awareness

Situational awareness is the core concept in fire disaster management as it refers to knowing the current condition of the environment and predicting the future conditions. The integration of AI with robotics highly improves the situational awareness since it collects information in detail, analyzes it, and presents it in graphic and visual forms (Zhang et al., 2022).

Installing various sensors like thermal cameras, gas detectors, and LIDAR atop the robotic systems collects fire data in as much detail as possible from the fire environment. AI-based algorithms crunch all this data to contribute to actionable insights. For example, with thermal imaging data from robots, AI models can detect heat signatures and predict fire spread patterns. Such information will help fire management teams make informed decisions about resource allocation and evacuation strategies. Integration with AI and robotics will thus bring real-time situational awareness through the steady stream of updates regarding fire conditions. Aerially, drones with AI can monitor large grounds, giving a bird's eye view of the advancing fire. On the ground, robots will be able to navigate through smoke and debris for on-the-ground observations. This integration of sources of data creates a comprehensive picture of the fire situation to coordinate response more effectively.

Real-Time Data Analysis and Decision-Making

Real-time data analysis and decision-making are vital in the high-stakes environment of fire disaster management. The integration of AI and robotics makes it possible to process vast data on a very fast basis to provide real-time and precise decision-making. Artificial intelligence algorithms process information coming from sensors as well as robots in order to identify trends, anomalies, or emerging threats. For instance, AI can use real-time weather data, intensity measurements of fire, and historical fire patterns to predict what the behavior of a fire would be. With this predictive capability, fire management teams can forecast their trend toward change, thereby having the possibility of proactively taking steps that prevent change or even alter the direction in desirable ways (Velev & Zlateva, 2023).

This function of robotics is being shared with the offering of instant on-the-ground data. Ground robots can report information that is first-hand in nature, which includes direct conditions of fires, structural damage, and other hazards. Drones available in the air can provide 24/7 monitoring and can also grant access to critical information to the command center faster. The combination of real-time data from the robots and AI analysis helps in taking the correct decisions of fire management based on the present accurate information.

Self-Sustained Firefighting and Rescue Operations

With the coming in of AI and robotics, the autonomous firefighting and rescue operations can be fully employed to limit interference by human elements in hazardous conditions and improve the operational efficiency. Using autonomous robots powered by AI, tasks like putting out the fires to executing search and rescue activities can be carried out by them with very little interference from humans. Autonomous work in hazardous environments with human access inability. Thus, such robots can be programmed to roam through smoke-filled areas to look for hotspots of fire and inject water or foam to extinguish the flames. AI algorithms will keep on guiding these robots to make decisions in real-time based on the conditions around the environment and the behavior of the fire (Ivić, 2019).

Autonomous robots with AI will fly through smashed buildings or toxic environments during search and rescue operations to look for and rescue people entangled in the rubble. They would use sensors to detect life signs such as heat or movement and algorithms that follow their AI to give rescue efforts priority or coordinate with the human responders to ensure operations of rescue. It not only makes fire fighting and rescue more efficient but also safer, since it reduces the risk to human fire fighters. Taking on the most dangerous tasks gives human teams a chance to concentrate on strategic decision-making and coordination.

Integration of AI and robotics into fire disaster management is a significant advancement in technological capability. Coupled with AI and robotics, it ensures heightened situational awareness, enabling real-time data analysis and decision-making and complete autonomous firefighting and rescue operations. It further gives a boost toward executing a more effective and efficient response to fire disasters, ultimately improving safety outcomes and operational effectiveness. This portends an even brighter future in the evolution and application of AI and robotics to transform fire disaster management, with emerging solutions to always-evolving challenges of fire emergencies.

OPERATIONAL BENEFITS AND CHALLENGES

Apart from great in-house operational benefits such as safety and efficiency of fire disaster management, artificial intelligence and robotics have several technical and logistical challenges that must be met in order to realize their full potential. Understand both the advantages and the obstacles associated with these technologies is crucial so that their application in fire management may be optimized (Benis et al., 2018; Muhammad et al., 2018). The integration of AI and robotics in fire disaster management offers both operational advantages and challenges, as illustrated in Figure 4.

Figure 4. Operational benefits and challenges of integrating artificial intelligence (AI) and robotics in fire disaster management

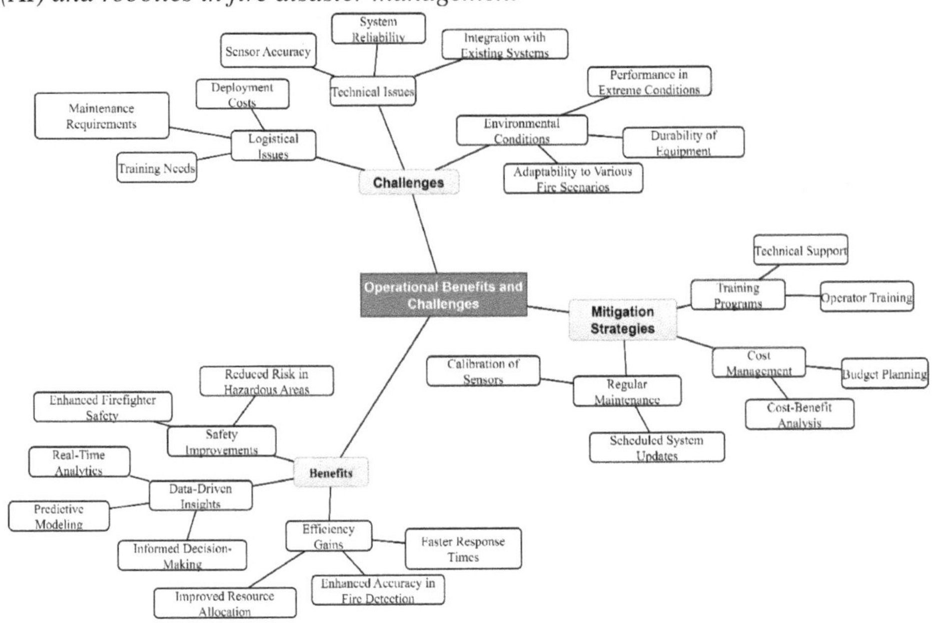

Improvements on Safety and Efficiency

AI/robotics complements the safety and efficiency of fire disaster management. The largest advantages include the ability to conduct dangerous area operations in which humans cannot afford to stay or enter for any period. For example, autonomous firefighting robots can be programmed to go into smoke-filled buildings, walk through rubble, douse fires, and so on, without risking human lives. This impacts the exposure of firefighters to risky situations and improves general safety(Ahamed et al., 2024; Sekhar et al., 2024; Teja et al., 2024).

There is also a notable increase in the efficiency of use through the use of AI and robotics. Mass quantities of data are processed very rapidly, and insights are brought to bear in real-time decision-making and resource allocation with the help of AI algorithms. Robotics, which incorporate advanced sensors, can rapidly search for victims, map the fire boundaries, and distribute extinguishing agents much more quickly and precisely than in the past. It is through this automation of the tasks that the response time is quickened. This also allows for better coordination and delivery of the fire management in a more efficient manner.

Drones cover the aerial surveillance, while ground robots will cover the operations on the grounds with multicomprehensive areas being covered. This multi-faceted approach enhances the team's situational awareness by quickening the response and decision-making that affects the fire management team.

Technical and Logistical Challenges

However, there are various technical and logistical challenges to the integration of AI with robotics in fire disaster management. Development and maintenance of the communication system free from failures represent a significant challenge. The operations of robots and AI systems have to be coordinated with the human parties participating in the fire disaster management process. In fires, broken physical infrastructures stand for possible smoke and heat destructions, which often would compromise the communication networks. Therefore, a significant technical challenge comes in the form of ensuring that robots are able to maintain reliable communication and transmit data in such conditions(Puranik et al., 2024; Srinivas et al., 2023; Venkateswaran et al., 2024).

Another challenge relates to the design and programming of autonomous systems that can properly work well in very unstable or ever-changing environments, like conditions during fires. Fire conditions do change quickly in short periods, and so does the necessary requirement that robots be equipped with AI algorithms that could adjust in real-time with such changes. The development of robust algorithms that can handle variability and uncertainty of fire scenarios is very complex and requires continuous refining and testing.

Logistical challenges also confront deployed and maintained robotic systems. Firefighting robots must be transported, deployed, and serviced in difficult environments. It involves some logistical tasks to ensure that robots are available and operationally ready when they are needed. In addition, the integration of robotics into established fire management workflows will necessitate training for personnel and revising standard operating procedures, which is time-consuming and resource-intensive.

Reliability and Robustness in Extreme Conditions

Reliability and robustness of the AI and robotics system play an important role in the successful application of such systems in the management of fire disasters. Environments where the structures are burning are hostile, with extreme conditions of high temperatures, smoke, and structural instability. Robots and AI systems must be designed to withstand these conditions and operate reliably under stress (Velev & Zlateva, 2023).

Robustness in ground-based robots basically means that they should be able to go through debris, resist heat, and not get affected by falling objects. These are often designed with fire-resistant materials and robust structures to withstand the fire environment. But with even such precautions, there will always be a risk of some mechanical failure or sensor malfunctioning at extremely high conditions.

Although aerial drones are less susceptible to debris, they still entail some problems associated with them, such as maintaining steady flight in strong winds and the transmission of data through smoke and other obstructions. Ensuring such systems to be reliable would require exhausting tests and the development of technologies that can cope with environmental stressors.

It requires decision-making processes to be robust by building autonomous robots. Algorithms that power autonomous robots must be capable of dealing with incomplete or noisy data while basing decisions on it accurately in the limited information. Great challenges will include the development of AI able to sustain high performance under uncertainty and conditions that keep changing.

Generally, the integration of AI and robotics in the management of fire disasters gives much operational advantage, such as safety and effectiveness. However, to address the technical and logistic challenges such as reliable communication, adaptable algorithms, and the system, the effectiveness of these technologies has to be maximized. As a result, the AI and robotics will continue advancing to further enhance their scope on fire management that results in effective and safe responses to fire disasters.

POST-DISASTER ANALYSIS AND RECOVERY

The evaluation and recovery processes after a fire disaster will prove to be very crucial in determining the damage, aiding recovery, and shedding light on potential future prevention strategies. The application of AI and robotics has dramatically improved these processes by providing advanced tools for damage assessment reporting and analysis. This chapter focuses on how AI and robotics assist in post-disaster analysis and recovery and presents lessons learned and potential avenues for improvement in the future(Aboualola et al., 2023; Damaševičius et al., 2023).

AI in Post-Disaster Damage Assessment and Reporting

AI is also indispensable in post-fire damage assessment and reporting. Within a short period following a fire, damage needs to be evaluated rapidly and accurately to determine the extent of damage, prioritize recovery efforts, and provide an estimate for the costs of repair. AI has the potential to analyze damage from diverse data sources, which includes machine learning and computer vision-based systems.

One of the more important applications of AI in damage assessment is based on the use of analysis from aerial imagery captured by drones or satellites. AI algorithms can process high-resolution images and identify damage to structures, infrastructure, and natural landscapes in quantity. These algorithms are trained to recognize patterns associated with fire damage, such as structural collapse, charring, and scorched vegetation. Through automating heavy imagery data analysis, AI speeds up evaluations and cuts the need for human inspection. AI also strengthens reporting by creating a comprehensive damage report as well as illustration work products, including heatmaps, damage severity maps, and statistical summaries of the impact effects. Such detailed, well-organized reporting supports key decision-makers with resource allocation and coordination towards recovery.

Robotics Contributions to Post-Fire Analysis

Robots contribute extensively to post-fire analysis, for instance providing crucial ground-based data and performing tasks that will be quite tricky for human responders. Currently, ground-based robots are fitted with various sensors plus imaging technologies, which enable them to move through environments post-fire to collect critical data (Maheswari et al., 2023; Pramila et al., 2023; Rahamathunnisa et al., 2023).

Important contributions that emerge from robots relate to assessing the structural integrity. Robots can enter partially collapsed buildings where sensors can tell whether other parts of the structure are stable or unstable. They can also determine the condition of infrastructures such as bridges and roads, which are very important information to engineers and to the recovery teams. Robots with environmental sensors can measure residual hazards, such as toxic gases and pollutants. Such information is important for the selection of areas that are safe for reentry and guiding cleanup and decontamination efforts.

Physical samples such as soil and debris can also be collected using robotic systems for further analysis. Secondly, the samples may be analyzed to identify harmful materials or contaminants from the fire, which would be essential in the assessment of environmental impact and public health. This eliminates valuable insights into knowledge gaps that would need further filling of the gaps. The key lessons learned are that AI and robotics should be integrated into existing disaster management workflows. Technology and human responder interaction coordination ensures data collected by the robots and analyzed by AI systems is actionable and supports overall recovery efforts.

Another lesson the organization can take away from this is the necessity to be constantly enhancing the AI algorithms and capabilities of robots. Only through constant training and fine-tuning of AI models will it be possible to manage the variety and complexity of the scenarios that it experiences in a post-disaster setting. In its turn, the technology of robotics needs to develop in addressing potential challenges such as a large amount of instability or hazards in navigating the environment, accuracy of sensors, etc. Advanced sensors and enhanced data analytics would further enable AI and robotics-based post-disaster analysis and recovery. These provide advanced sensory capture, finer resolutions of measurements, and deeper insights into damage patterns and recovery needs. More than that, the scopes for integrative applications of AI and robotics might encompass myriad other technologies, extending from integrating with GIS and IoT platforms. Further integration of those technologies might create an approach to be more integrated and comprehensive in handling the disaster situation, enhancing data sharing and collaboration between different stakeholders.

AI and robotics in post-disaster analysis has changed the game for various reasons, including superior capabilities to assess, report, and be on the ground for searching the damage. This is the point where leveraging technology in teams dealing with disasters improves their response and recovery efforts, making recovery very efficient and effective. With the continued advancement in technology, further development in AI and robotics will make them even more significant during post-disaster analyses, allowing recovery strategies the possibility of more robust and resilient states.

ETHICAL AND REGULATORY CONSIDERATIONS

In integrating Artificial Intelligence and robotics into the management of disasters caused by fire, some transformational benefits may be seen, but it certainly raises significant issues that are both ethical and regulatory. This means embracing these concerns to better ensure that applications for these technologies come out responsibly effective. Specifically, some of these issues pertain to data privacy and security, the transparency of decisions, human oversight, and accountability (Munawar et al., 2022; Wilk-Jakubowski et al., 2022).

Data Privacy and Security

The use of AI and robotics in fire disaster management entails a collection and processing of tremendous data, which can be related to personal or property information. Data privacy and security are therefore essential in building public trust and in legal requirements to operate. Considerations of data privacy are seriously raised by the huge amount of data collected by sensors, drones, and robots, including sensitive details or information pertaining to personal identities or properties and infrastructures. Counter these risks with strong data protection, including encryption, anonymization, and secure data storage practices. Regulators should enforce compliance with legislation such as the GDPR of the European Union and the CCPA of California in order to protect individual rights concerning privacy in the handling of such data.

Another security feature that must be assiduously provided is that the data gathered and transmitted through AI and robotic systems are susceptible to cyberattacks. Safety protocols for the systems require very strict cybersecurity measures, including secure communication channels, frequent software updates, and rigorous access controls. Such a system will ensure data integrity and prevent unauthorized access, thus ensuring reliability in fire management operations and securing sensitive information.

Transparency in Decision-Making

The transparency of the deployment of the decision-making process in the use of AI and robotics systems in the management of fire disasters is very essential. AI algorithms and robotic systems make decisions based on rules and data, so decisions that are arrived at need to have integrity and be justifiable as well. One of the challenges is that some of these AI algorithms are "black boxes": that is, the decision-making process may not be easily understandable to humans. This calls for efforts to be directed at the development of explainable AI models that will allow clear and understandable insights into the decisions reached. Understanding the basis of decisions encourages trust in the technology, but stakeholders must understand the basis behind decisions made within the system.

Transparency over decision-making includes that the criteria followed by AI systems are fair and unbiased. Biases in data or algorithms can lead to discriminatory outcomes, which can cause grave implications in an emergency situation. Mechanisms for detecting and mitigating biases, along with regular reviews of AI models to ensure fairness and accuracy of judgments, are part of the paramount requirement in determining equitable and justifiable decision-making.

Human Oversight and Accountability

Human oversight and liability are what make AI and robotics responsible in fire disaster management. Technologies offering advanced capabilities should complement and build upon human judgment and excellence rather than substitute for it. A good layer of people oversight ensures that the AI and robotic systems used to address fires are monitored and controlled with the due protocols at the operational level. Human operators should be continuously engaged in monitoring how these AI and robotic systems are deployed and operating. This would include setting parameters for system operation, reviewing decision-making processes, and intervening appropriately. Training the operators to understand how to use and manage the system optimally is deemed important, so also is the resolution of any issue arising from it(Koshariya et al., 2023; Mohanty et al., 2023; Senthil et al., 2023).

Accountability also falls in this category, as it always ensures people deploying and utilizing AI and robotics are held accountable for choices and actions. This requires establishment of clear lines of authority and procedures of reporting and handling every problem or failure that may emerge from them. Legal and ethical frameworks should be formulated outlining the standards for accountability and proving there are procedures for handling grievances or misconduct.

In conclusion, addressing the ethical and regulatory considerations of AI and robotics in fire disaster management is well worthwhile. In order to fully exploit such technology, mechanisms to ensure data privacy and security, transparency in decision-making, and effective human oversight and accountability will be necessary. By considering these factors, the dangers of AI and robotics may be justified in minimizing possible destructions brought about by these technologies. In this way, stakeholders may enhance the benefits of these technologies in the event of disaster management and recovery.

Figure 5. Future trends and innovations in fire disaster management

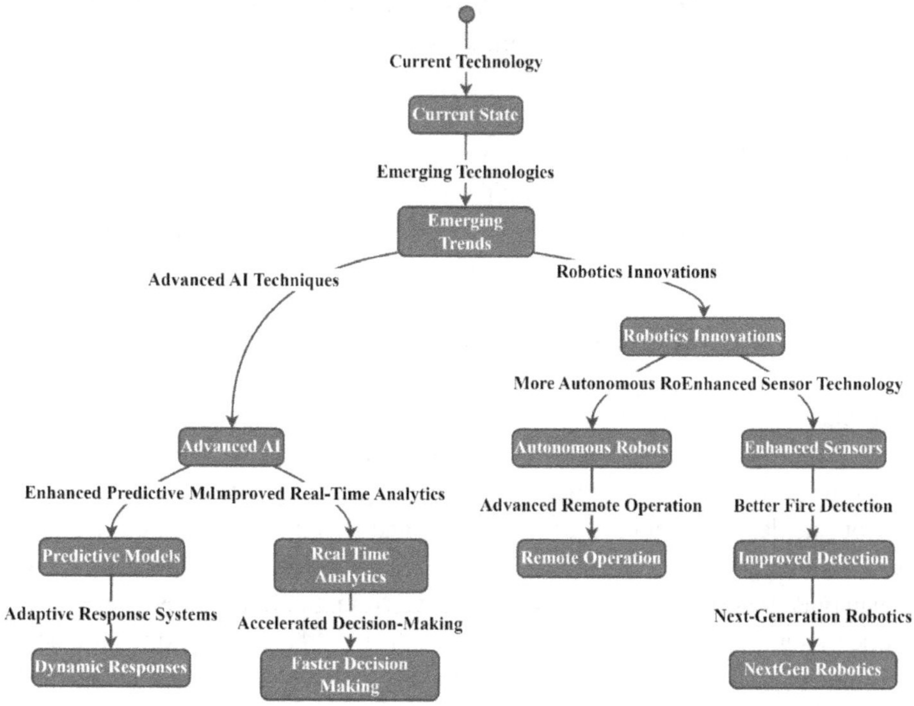

FUTURE TRENDS AND INNOVATIONS

The management landscape of fires is changing fast with the improvement of AI and robotics. New technologies and innovations may be able to enhance the abilities of fire management systems by making them more responsive for difficult fire scenarios. Future trends and innovations in AI and robotics are explored in the subsection as follows: their possible use in future developments and long-term impacts on different strategies related to fire management(Aboualola et al., 2023; Damaševičius et al., 2023; Velev & Zlateva, 2023). Figure 5 illustrates the upcoming trends and innovations in fire disaster management.

Emerging Technologies of Artificial Intelligence and Robotics

Several emerging technologies are set to elevate the game in the fire disaster management space. One of them includes the emergence of sophisticated algorithms in AI based on deep learning and neural networks. By actually analyzing complex patterns in the data coming from various sources, such as satellite images, weather forecasts, and historical fire data, they can help improve predictions and detection related to fires. Advanced predictive models will also send more accurate early warnings, thus improving decision-making when it comes to fire events.

Other promising technologies include robotics, integrated with advanced sensors and communications. Drones, for example, can be equipped with high-resolution cameras, thermal imaging, and LiDAR sensors and would provide detailed, near-to-realtime data on fire behavior and environmental conditions. Ground-based robots, then, with enhanced mobility and environmental sensors, would be able to navigate through debris and hazardous conditions to locate trapped individuals and assess structural damage. Autonomous systems represent another trend in their development. Autonomous firefighting robots are equipped with AI-powered navigation and decision-making capabilities and can work independently in hostile environments. They could potentially perform tasks, including extinguishing fires, deploying fire retardants, or conducting search-and-rescue operations with minimal human involvement.

Room for Further Development

The scope for further research and development in AI and robotics for fire management is large. Improvement of interoperability between different systems and technologies can be done better. Integration of AI algorithms with robotics, drones, and other tools of fire management can facilitate the building of a harmonious and effective response system. Contrasting this, deployment of drones and robots can be guided by analytics from AI-driven models, thus putting them into proper use by harnessing the capabilities of these technologies in a balanced way to support each other(Ahamed et al., 2024; Pramila et al., 2023; Sekhar et al., 2024; Teja et al., 2024).

In machine learning and data analytics, efficiency will be enhanced in processing complex data to allow AI systems' improvements. These will include enhancing fire prediction and behavior analysis models, damage quantification, and damage assessments. Further research in the more complex algorithms and training techniques will further increase precision and reliability of these AI systems. In robotics, the area of materials and design improvement is going to soon foretell a more robust and reliable fire management robot. For instance, heat-resistant and impact-resistant materials would go a long way to enhance the performance of the robots in extreme conditions. Advances in battery technology and energy management would add longer operation durations for autonomous systems, thereby making them perform for even longer periods during emergencies.

Long-Term Impact on Fire Management Strategies

Fire management is going to use artificial intelligence and robotics in ways that will have far-reaching impacts on long-term strategies in tackling fire. It will significantly alter the conducting of operations of fire management. A high point for this development will be the very approach of becoming more proactive and preventive instead of being reactive. Predictive models and early warning systems powered by artificial intelligence of the highest quality will ensure that it becomes possible for fire management teams to acquire information about the risks of fires before they become cases to be dealt with. This proactive approach will have fewer and weaker occurrences of the fire event with lower response costs and less damage.

A robotics and AI integration will mean to have response operations which are both effective and efficient. Real-time data and autonomous systems improve situational awareness and coordination, leading to faster and better responses. With this, it will be easier for the fire management team to protect life and property and natural resources as well. The innovations towards recovery and reconstruction will also be driven by AI and robotics. Their use in post-fire damage assessment and analysis will thus become more accurate, consequently making recovery efforts sharper and more productive. Insights from AI-driven analytics will help determine the most urgent reconstruction needs and resource allocation, thus providing swifter and more effective recovery.

In a nutshell, the future of fire disaster management will have much to change with AI and robotics. New technologies will be used and innovations developed to perfect predictability, improve responses, and increase recovery efforts. Further development in these areas will better enable integration into contemporary processes used in managing fires and, by extension, make it safer, more efficient, and stronger when dealing with fire disasters. Continuous development and application of these technologies will define the future of fire management that is going to provide new opportunities for the safety protection of communities as well as minimizing the impact of fires.

CONCLUSION

The integration of AI and robotics in fire disaster management has significantly improved its effectiveness and efficiency in response and recovery. They indeed provide transformational potential for predicting, managing, and mitigating the risks associated with fires because of such advanced predictive analytics, autonomous systems, and real-time data processing. As discussed, deploying AI and robotics would not only improve situational awareness and operational efficiency but better determine damages and recovery efforts with increased accuracy. However, realizing all these benefits would depend on the resolution of key ethical and regulatory matters, such as data privacy, transparency in decision-making, and oversight by human beings. Future innovations in fire management seem promising and productive because of the development of AI and robotics, which will continue to lead to more proactive strategies and increased strengths in response capabilities. It is to such technologies that the future of fire disaster management will be increasingly entrusted for the protection of lives, property, and the environment from destructive impacts of fire.

REFERENCES

Abid, S. K., Sulaiman, N., Chan, S. W., Nazir, U., Abid, M., Han, H., Ariza-Montes, A., & Vega-Muñoz, A. (2021). Toward an integrated disaster management approach: How artificial intelligence can boost disaster management. *Sustainability (Basel)*, 13(22), 12560. DOI: 10.3390/su132212560

Aboualola, M., Abualsaud, K., Khattab, T., Zorba, N., & Hassanein, H. S. (2023). Edge technologies for disaster management: A survey of social media and artificial intelligence integration. *IEEE Access : Practical Innovations, Open Solutions*, 11, 73782–73802. DOI: 10.1109/ACCESS.2023.3293035

Abraham, L., Biju, S., Biju, F., Jose, J., Kalantri, R., & Rajguru, S. (2019). Swarm robotics in disaster management. *2019 International Conference on Innovative Sustainable Computational Technologies (CISCT)*, 1–5.

Ahamed, B. S., Chakravarthy, K. S., Arputhabalan, J., Sasirekha, K., Prince, R. M. R., Boopathi, S., & Muthuvel, S. (2024). Revolutionizing Friction Stir Welding With AI-Integrated Humanoid Robots. In *Advances in Computational Intelligence and Robotics* (pp. 120–144). IGI Global. DOI: 10.4018/979-8-3693-2399-1.ch005

AlAli, Z. T., & Alabady, S. A. (2022). A survey of disaster management and SAR operations using sensors and supporting techniques. *International Journal of Disaster Risk Reduction*, 82, 103295. DOI: 10.1016/j.ijdrr.2022.103295

Benis, A., Notea, A., & Barkan, R. (2018). Risk and disaster management: From planning and expertise to smart, intelligent, and adaptive systems. In *Building Continents of Knowledge in Oceans of Data: The Future of Co-Created eHealth* (pp. 286–290). IOS Press.

Choi, W. (2020). A study on the intelligent disaster management system based on artificial intelligence. *Journal of the Korean Society of Hazard Mitigation*, 20(1), 127–140. DOI: 10.9798/KOSHAM.2020.20.1.127

Damaševičius, R., Bacanin, N., & Misra, S. (2023). From sensors to safety: Internet of Emergency Services (IoES) for emergency response and disaster management. *Journal of Sensor and Actuator Networks*, 12(3), 41. DOI: 10.3390/jsan12030041

Fan, C., Zhang, C., Yahja, A., & Mostafavi, A. (2021). Disaster City Digital Twin: A vision for integrating artificial and human intelligence for disaster management. *International Journal of Information Management*, 56, 102049. DOI: 10.1016/j.ijinfomgt.2019.102049

Ivić, M. (2019). Artificial intelligence and geospatial analysis in disaster management. *The International Archives of the Photogrammetry, Remote Sensing and Spatial Information Sciences*, 42(W8), 161–166. DOI: 10.5194/isprs-archives-XLII-3-W8-161-2019

Kankanamge, N., Yigitcanlar, T., & Goonetilleke, A. (2021). Public perceptions on artificial intelligence driven disaster management: Evidence from Sydney, Melbourne and Brisbane. *Telematics and Informatics*, 65, 101729. DOI: 10.1016/j.tele.2021.101729

Koshariya, A. K., Khatoon, S., Marathe, A. M., Suba, G. M., Baral, D., & Boopathi, S. (2023). Agricultural Waste Management Systems Using Artificial Intelligence Techniques. In *AI-Enabled Social Robotics in Human Care Services* (pp. 236–258). IGI Global. DOI: 10.4018/978-1-6684-8171-4.ch009

Lee, M.-F. R., & Chien, T.-W. (2020). Artificial intelligence and Internet of Things for robotic disaster response. *2020 International Conference on Advanced Robotics and Intelligent Systems (ARIS)*, 1–6. DOI: 10.1109/ARIS50834.2020.9205794

Maheswari, B. U., Imambi, S. S., Hasan, D., Meenakshi, S., Pratheep, V., & Boopathi, S. (2023). Internet of things and machine learning-integrated smart robotics. In *Global Perspectives on Robotics and Autonomous Systems: Development and Applications* (pp. 240–258). IGI Global. DOI: 10.4018/978-1-6684-7791-5.ch010

Maraveas, C., Loukatos, D., Bartzanas, T., & Arvanitis, K. G. (2021). Applications of artificial intelligence in fire safety of agricultural structures. *Applied Sciences (Basel, Switzerland)*, 11(16), 7716. DOI: 10.3390/app11167716

Mohanty, A., Jothi, B., Jeyasudha, J., Ranjit, P., Isaac, J. S., & Boopathi, S. (2023). Additive Manufacturing Using Robotic Programming. In *AI-Enabled Social Robotics in Human Care Services* (pp. 259–282). IGI Global. DOI: 10.4018/978-1-6684-8171-4.ch010

Muhammad, K., Ahmad, J., & Baik, S. W. (2018). Early fire detection using convolutional neural networks during surveillance for effective disaster management. *Neurocomputing*, 288, 30–42. DOI: 10.1016/j.neucom.2017.04.083

Munawar, H. S., Mojtahedi, M., Hammad, A. W., Kouzani, A., & Mahmud, M. P. (2022). Disruptive technologies as a solution for disaster risk management: A review. *The Science of the Total Environment*, 806, 151351. DOI: 10.1016/j.scitotenv.2021.151351 PMID: 34740667

Ofli, F., Imran, M., & Alam, F. (2020). Using artificial intelligence and social media for disaster response and management: An overview. *AI and Robotics in Disaster Studies*, 63–81.

Pramila, P., Amudha, S., Saravanan, T., Sankar, S. R., Poongothai, E., & Boopathi, S. (2023). Design and Development of Robots for Medical Assistance: An Architectural Approach. In *Contemporary Applications of Data Fusion for Advanced Healthcare Informatics* (pp. 260–282). IGI Global.

Puranik, T. A., Shaik, N., Vankudoth, R., Kolhe, M. R., Yadav, N., & Boopathi, S. (2024). Study on Harmonizing Human-Robot (Drone) Collaboration: Navigating Seamless Interactions in Collaborative Environments. In *Cybersecurity Issues and Challenges in the Drone Industry* (pp. 1–26). IGI Global.

Rahamathunnisa, U., Sudhakar, K., Murugan, T. K., Thivaharan, S., Rajkumar, M., & Boopathi, S. (2023). Cloud Computing Principles for Optimizing Robot Task Offloading Processes. In *AI-Enabled Social Robotics in Human Care Services* (pp. 188–211). IGI Global. DOI: 10.4018/978-1-6684-8171-4.ch007

Sekhar, K. Ch., Ingle, R. B., Banu, E. A., Rinawa, M. L., Prasad, M. M., & Boopathi, S. (2024). Integrating VR and AR for Enhanced Production Systems: Immersive Technologies in Smart Manufacturing. In *Advances in Computational Intelligence and Robotics* (pp. 90–112). IGI Global. DOI: 10.4018/979-8-3693-6806-0.ch005

Senthil, T., Puviyarasan, M., Babu, S. R., Surakasi, R., Sampath, B., & Associates. (2023). Industrial Robot-Integrated Fused Deposition Modelling for the 3D Printing Process. In *Development, Properties, and Industrial Applications of 3D Printed Polymer Composites* (pp. 188–210). IGI Global.

Srinivas, B., Maguluri, L. P., Naidu, K. V., Reddy, L. C. S., Deivakani, M., & Boopathi, S. (2023). Architecture and Framework for Interfacing Cloud-Enabled Robots. In *Handbook of Research on Data Science and Cybersecurity Innovations in Industry 4.0 Technologies* (pp. 542–560). IGI Global. DOI: 10.4018/978-1-6684-8145-5.ch027

Sun, W., Bocchini, P., & Davison, B. D. (2020). Applications of artificial intelligence for disaster management. *Natural Hazards*, 103(3), 2631–2689. DOI: 10.1007/s11069-020-04124-3

Tan, L., Guo, J., Mohanarajah, S., & Zhou, K. (2021). Can we detect trends in natural disaster management with artificial intelligence? A review of modeling practices. *Natural Hazards*, 107(3), 2389–2417. DOI: 10.1007/s11069-020-04429-3

Teja, N. B., Kannagi, V., Chandrashekhar, A., Senthilnathan, T., Pal, T. K., & Boopathi, S. (2024). Impacts of Nano-Materials and Nano Fluids on the Robot Industry and Environments. In *Advances in Computational Intelligence and Robotics* (pp. 171–194). IGI Global. DOI: 10.4018/979-8-3693-5767-5.ch012

Velev, D., & Zlateva, P. (2023). Challenges of artificial intelligence application for disaster risk Management. *The International Archives of the Photogrammetry, Remote Sensing and Spatial Information Sciences*, 48, 387–394. DOI: 10.5194/isprs-archives-XLVIII-M-1-2023-387-2023

Venkateswaran, N., Kunduru, K. R., Ashwin, N., Sundar Ganesh, C. S., Hema, N., & Boopathi, S. (2024). Navigating the Future of Ultra-Smart Computing Cyberspace: Beyond Boundaries. In *Advances in Computational Intelligence and Robotics* (pp. 170–199). IGI Global. DOI: 10.4018/979-8-3693-2399-1.ch007

Wilk-Jakubowski, G., Harabin, R., & Ivanov, S. (2022). Robotics in crisis management: A review. *Technology in Society*, 68, 101935. DOI: 10.1016/j.techsoc.2022.101935

Zarghami, S. A., & Dumrak, J. (2021). Implications of artificial intelligence for bushfire management. *Australian Journal of Emergency Management*, 36(1), 84–91. DOI: 10.47389/36.1.84

Zhang, T., Wang, Z., Zeng, Y., Wu, X., Huang, X., & Xiao, F. (2022). Building artificial-intelligence digital fire (AID-Fire) system: A real-scale demonstration. *Journal of Building Engineering*, 62, 105363. DOI: 10.1016/j.jobe.2022.105363

KEY TERNS AND DEFINITIONS

Artificial Intelligence (AI): The creation and simulation of human intelligence by machines, particularly computer systems, such as learning, reasoning, problem-solving, perception, and understanding language.

California Consumer Privacy Act (CCPA): A state law intended to reinforce privacy rights and consumer protection of California residents, thus inculcating a right to know consumers' personal information gathered about them and its sale.

Convolutional Neural Network (CNN): A class of deep learning models primarily used in processing data that can be formatted in a structured grid, such as images. CNN uses the convolutional layers to automatically detect features, making this model highly effective for image recognition and classification.

Deforestation Detection and Assessment (DAR): Techniques and instruments through which the increment or decrement of forest cover can be detected. Generally, it involves remote sensing data to monitor the level of deforestation and for directing conservation practices.

General Data Protection Regulation or GDPR: This is a European Union regulation, that serves as an instrument that guides data protection and privacy, for any person who resides within the EU or the European Economic Area. Under this regulation, GDPR gives prominence to user consent together with rights on personal data.

Geographic Information System: In GIS, it is an organizational framework used for collecting, managing, and analyzing spatial and geographic data. It integrates the use of the traditional cartography, statistical analysis, and database technology in order to visualize and interpret spatial relationships.

Light Detection and Ranging (LiDAR): A sensing technology that determines distance through illuminating a target with laser light and the subsequent analysis of the reflected light. LiDAR is applied predominantly in topographic mapping, forestry, and environmental monitoring.

Machine Learning (ML): It is an subset of AI that allows systems to learn automatically from experience and improve their performance on a task over time without being explicitly programmed. It involves several algorithms that are trying to find relations or actual patterns in data.

Natural Language Processing (NLP): It is a field of AI in relation to the interaction between computers and humans using natural language. The ability of machines to comprehend, understand, and produce human language in a meaningful way is NLP.

Radio Frequency (RF): Range of electromagnetic frequencies for wireless data transfer. RF technology is applied mainly in communication systems, including radio, television, and wireless networks.

Recurrent Neural Network: It is a type of RNN which is applied to the problems that deal with sequence prediction. Loops help classic architecture retain information from previous inputs inside the networks. This characteristic makes RNN especially useful for jobs like time-series analysis and language modeling.

Support Vector Machine: Support Vector Machine is the supervised algorithm that uses classification or regression task. SVM works according to the finding of the best fit hyperplane which splits apart the data points that belong to different classes in the high-dimensional space.

Chapter 11

Application of Google Earth Engine NDVI Trend to Study Yield of Sugarcane Crop Using Sentinel 2 Data

Malathi Narra
Department of Civil Engineering, Velagapudi Ramakrishna Siddhartha Engineering College (Deemed to be University),, India

Shashidhar Raju Nandhuri
Department of Civil Engineering, Velagapudi Ramakrishna Siddhartha Engineering College (Deemed to be University),, India

Harsha Vardhan Reddy
Department of Civil Engineering, Velagapudi Ramakrishna Siddhartha Engineering College (Deemed to be University),, India

Tejaswini Vallepu
Department of Civil Engineering, Velagapudi Ramakrishna Siddhartha Engineering College (Deemed to be University),, India

Vinay Kumar Gaddam
Department of Civil Engineering, Velagapudi Ramakrishna Siddhartha Engineering College (Deemed to be University),, India

Sai Sumath
Department of Civil Engineering, Velagapudi Ramakrishna Siddhartha Engineering College (Deemed to be University),, India

ABSTRACT

Increasing global food demand and the effects of climate change further indicate a need for proper ways of monitoring crop health. This chapter has demonstrated the importance of normalized difference vegetation index (NDVI) as a non-invasive

DOI: 10.4018/979-8-3693-2337-3.ch011

means of monitoring crop health. A review of the literature indicates that NDVI is useful in determining crop stress, diseases, and performance, especially if considered on a long-term basis. This study is based on sugarcane in Vuyyuru Village, Andhra Pradesh, considering NDVI to analyze crop health for the five-year period of 2018-2022. In this chapter, pre-processing Sentinel satellite imagery through atmospheric correction and image registration was carried out to ensure that data accuracy is ensured. The computation of NDVI values each year involves assessing any patterns or variations that are found in crop health spatially. The work sets out to enhance the understanding of the dynamics in crop health through time, thus giving valued insights for any future agricultural management.

INTRODUCTION

Crop monitoring, in the modern management of agriculture, involves regular observation and evaluation of crops and land during the growing season. It is done with the use of various types of methods, which include those pertaining to satellite imagery, such as that provided by a series of satellites known as the Sentinel series operated by the ESA. Crop monitoring encompasses the timely and precise collection of data related to crop health, growth, and environmental conditions that highlight proper decision-making for farmers and agronomists in order to achieve optimum productivity while minimizing all potential risks and ensuring sustainability of agriculture. Normalized Difference Vegetation Index is one important index derived from satellite imagery, especially those gained by the Sentinel satellites, which have a vital application in the monitoring of crops and agricultural lands (Eisfelder et al., 2023).

The NDVI quantifies vegetation health through comparing near-infrared and red light reflected by plants. With values ranging between -1 and 1, the higher the value, the healthier the vegetation. The NDVI facilitates a range of applications in agriculture. Indeed, NDVI is one of the important indicators in vegetation health for farmers and agronomists in evaluating the health status of crops or vegetations. Therefore, by observing the NDVI value, they are able to observe areas of stress or vitality, which helps them in early intervention against any particular pest, disease, nutrient deficiencies, or water stress. Additionally, monitoring of NDVI through the season will also permit the forecasting of crop yields. GEE is a cloud-based platform developed by the company, capable of analyzing and processing huge volumes of geospatial data (Davis et al., 2023). Various data sets, including those from Sentinel, are provided within Google Earth Engine. To access Google Earth Engine, one needs a Google account. Google Earth Engine has allowed the publishing and sharing of a huge amount of satellite photography datasets, such as Sentinel-1 and Sentinel-2. Sentinel-1 provides optical photography, while Sentinel-2 provides synthetic aperture radar data.

Select the appropriate dataset from among Landsat, Sentinel and Mod is for the image collection. We choose Sentinel database and download the Sentinel-2 satellite images. AOI Selection: Basically, it means that in Google Earth Engine you are allowed to specify an area which you want to analyze. Introduction in a few words only without code: Point of Interest: You are allowed to define an AOI by just specifying one point with latitude and longitude in the degree format (Donovan et al., 2022). An AOI can be defined by specifying the minimum and maximum latitude and longitude coordinates. This generates a rectangular bounding box around the region of interest. Draw on the Map: Google Earth Engine's Code Editor has drawing capabilities. You can draw a shape interactively on the map to define your AOI. This works well in irregularly-shaped areas. Predefined shapes: It also allows predefined geometric shapes like polygons and circles to be supported by Google Earth Engine. You may define the coordinates or the parameters, creating these shapes to specify your AOI (Haerani et al., 2018).

Increasing global food needs, exacerbated even more by unpredictability in climate change, have highlighted efficient and reliable monitoring and management of crop health. Intensive farming methods to meet this need have increasingly underlined the importance of optimum performance from crops. Traditional ways of monitoring and testing crops are useful but are usually unsatisfactory from the viewpoints of scale and accuracy. That's where the use of modern technologies of remote sensing comes into effect, especially NDVI. NDVI refers to powerful imagery taken from both satellite and air that gauges vegetation health and density. The reflectance of light in the red and near-infrared spectra are utilized to obtain a quantitative assessment of the health of plants. Here, high NDVI values range from approximately +1 to depict robust and dense vegetation, whereas low values depict either stressed or sparse vegetation. It is this potential for delineating changes in vegetation health through time that NDVI provides a very useful tool in agricultural management (Maranhão, 2023).

It is for this reason that NDVI is important in monitoring crop health, as the technique is non-invasive and can provide comprehensive data over extensive areas for long periods. Since NDVI captures spectral information from a distance, it bypasses any need to take further measurements on the ground-a very laborous process that could be very limited in scope. This form of remote sensing gives a broad overview of the conditions the crops grow under, hence aiding in the early identification of such problems as diseases, nutritional deficiencies, or stress due to water deficiencies (Sharma, 2018). A large body of literature underlines the utility of NDVI in agriculture. Its application varies from assessing crop stress and diseases to yield forecasting and land cover changes. For instance, NDVI has been used to monitor the effects of environmental stressors such as drought or flooding on the health of crops and the effectiveness of different agricultural methods. It adds more value because the capability of analyzing NDVI data for an extended period enables the researcher and farmer to observe the trend and make informed decisions based on history (de Carvalho et al., 2020).

The present study will present a longitudinal analysis for Vuyyuru Village, Krishna District, Andhra Pradesh, for 2018-2022. Sugarcane has been specifically chosen because of its high economic value and sensitivity to environmental variables. It is done by examining the NDVI values over a five-year period in search of trends and anomalies in crop health to underline the long-term dynamics of sugarcane cultivation. The methodology involved in this approach makes use of Sentinel satellite imagery, which captures the relevant spectral information to be used in computing NDVI. Sentinel satellites are operated by ESA, and their imagery has good resolution and increased coverage compared to others, making it suitable for agricultural monitoring. Other preprocessing steps include atmospheric correction, as would be proper to account for atmospheric interference, image registration to match images from different times and sources, among other processes that ensure the accuracy of the data (Bhunia et al., 2012).

The NDVI values will be calculated for each year and analyzed spatially to outline any trends and anomalies. This longitudinal approach enables an in-depth review of how crop health evolves over time, hence giving insight into the factors that impact crop performance and its resilience. Analysis of such trends will allow this study to contribute to the literature on the dynamics of crop health with useful knowledge in agricultural management and remote sensing. In all, the introduction of NDVI into crop health monitoring raised the bar a notch higher for agricultural practices(Lima Albuquerque Maranhão, 2023). Being able to provide highly detailed, non-invasive assessments over long periods secures its place as an important tool in understanding and managing crop health. Emphasis on a five-year analysis of sugarcane crops in Vuyyuru Village drives home the point that long-term monitoring of crop health is very essential for unraveling the complexities involved in sustainable agricultural operations amidst global challenges.

Objectives

The main aim of the research is to determine, through the use of NDVI, the health of the sugarcane crop in Vuyyuru Village, Andhra Pradesh over a five-year duration from 2018 to 2022. This study will prove that NDVI is a non-destructive tool highly effective in the detection of crops for their health, stress, and diseases. Pre-processing steps applied to Sentinel satellite imagery include atmospheric correction and image registration to ensure data accuracy in the study. Spatial pattern analysis and variation in NDVI values over time have been conducted in this work to understand dynamics in crop health. The results are included on how this information has improved the understanding of long-term trends in crop health that could support and improve future agricultural management strategies and operations.

METHODOLOGY

The critical steps in the analysis of crop health involve the use of NDVI in the processes, from data collection down to the graphical representation, with the use of remote sensing technology and GIS. These means provide a way by which vegetation health can be studied over time in great detail, therefore yielding useful insights into the dynamics of crops and environmental impacts.

Data collection is the first step in analyzing NDVI. Satellite images from NASA's EOSDIS or other satellite data providers are acquired for each year of the decade that compose the study area. Such imagery is used because it carries the required spectral information needed to estimate NDVI. Commonly, the imagery shall contain bands representing NIR and R wavelengths, essential components in the accurate computation of NDVI. Effective monitoring and analysis require high-resolution, consistent, and accurate access to satellite data(Guha et al., 2019). Where NIR is the reflectance in the NearInfrared band, and R is the reflectance in the Red band. This equation is the difference between the reflectance of the NIR and Red bands, divided by their sum. High NDVI values correspond with healthy and dense vegetation, whereas low values would indicate stressed or sparser vegetation. Correct computation of NDVI depends on correct reflectance measurements; therefore, quality satellite imagery has a major effect on the reliability of the results.

- Data Collection: Satellite imagery covering the study area for each year over the decade was acquired. These images are usually available from sources like NASA's Earth Observing System Data and Information System (EOSDIS) or other satellite providers.
- NDVI Calculation: The NDVI formula is calculated using the Near-Infrared (NIR) and Red (R) bands of the satellite imagery: NDVI=NIR+R/ NIR−R where NIR is the reflectance in the Near-Infrared band and R is the reflectance in the red band.
- Data Analysis: NDVI values were extracted from each processed image for the same area of interest. These values were then organized chronologically to analyze the trends over the decade.
- Graphical Representation: The NDVI trends over the decade were graphically represented using a line plot. The x-axis represents the years, and the y-

axis represents the NDVI values. Each point on the graph corresponds to the NDVI value for a specific year, allowing for a visual assessment of vegetation changes.

The work involves the extraction of NDVI values from each processed image that corresponds to the same area of interest. Once NDVI values are computed for each year's image, they are organized chronologically. This chronological organization allows trend analysis over the decade, enabling the identification of patterns and variations in vegetation health. It helps in understanding in detail how the health of the crop has evolved overtime and can reveal trends like the cycles of season, long-term decline, or vegetation health improvement (García Cárdenas et al., 2018). This is a major step whereby one visualizes the NDVI trend. The NDVI values over the decade are graphically represented using a line plot. In the plot, the years of interest are taken on the x-axis, while the NDVI values are on the y-axis. Each point of the graph corresponds to the NDVI value for that particular year, thus enabling clear visualization of vegetation changes. It is a great avenue through which easy interpretation of trends can be represented while detailing periods of deterioration or improvement of crop health rather quickly.

Implementation

Steps to perform crop mapping in QGIS:
Step-1: Downloading the satellite images of the ROI.
Step-2: Creation of new raster layer
Step-3: Stacking of images to get the entire ROI. Step-4: Merging of the added layers
Step-5: De-selecting all the layers expect merged layer
Step-6: Selection of properties option to know average NDVI values of each layer
Step-7: Now copy all the results into the excel sheet.
Step-8: Draw the graph corresponding to the NDVI and the months

Implementation with regard to crop mapping and NDVI analysis involves the use of GIS software such as QGIS(Bisanzio et al., 2014). Steps involved in QGIS include:

- These are satellite images with ROI captured in the whole time of study, including relevant spectral bands for NDVI calculation.
- In QGIS software, a new raster layer is created to house these satellite images. In this step, the downloaded images are imported into the GIS software.
- After the removal of noises from the image dataset, it undergoes stacking for the visualization of all aspects of the ROI. During the process of stacking,

several images are combined into a single composite image representative of many images, which is very essential for the study of temporal changes.

- The different layers are merged into a single composite layer after stacking. In this stage, all the temporal data is compiled into one layer in order to simplify the analysis.
- The objective of de-selecting all layers other than the one that was merged is to ensure clarity and preciseness in the analysis. This is a step to ensure that focus is retained on the combined dataset.
- To determine the average value of NDVI values for each layer, the properties option in QGIS is selected. The application functions to summarize NDVI values for respective periods.
- The results are copied onto an Excel sheet, showing the NDVI values for each year. This is important for further data analysis and manipulation outside the GIS environment.

A graph in Excel is then created to plot the NDVI values against months or years. An Excel graph of this represents further analysis, allowing the visualizing and interpretation of trends with ease.

Generally, NDVI analysis combined advanced technology of remote sensing with the use of GIS for applications pertaining to the monitoring and assessment of crop health over a continuous period of time. By following such a process, researchers and practitioners can develop some useful insights from vegetation dynamics that would be helpful in agricultural management practices for improving crop health monitoring and management strategy.

DOWNLOADING THE SATELLITE IMAGES OF THE ROI

Acquisition of high-quality satellite imagery is the first and most important step for any remote sensing analysis, including all types of NDVI studies. It forms the base through which the Normalized Difference Vegetation Index computation can be done with subsequent analysis on vegetation health across different periods. Downloading satellite images is a complex process and requires careful attention to a number of key factors to ensure that data acquired is appropriate for reliable analysis(Diaz de Carvalho et al., 2020; Garcia-Garcia et al., 2021).

Identifying the Source of Satellite Imagery

The first step in downloading satellite images is to identify reliable sources that provide the necessary data. Major space agencies, as well as major commercial satellite providers, make access to satellite imagery available(Boopathi et al., 2023; Boopathi & Kanike, 2023; Das et al., 2024). The major sources that are usually used include:

- NASA's Earth Observing System Data and Information System: The EOSDIS provides access to the massive volumes of satellite imagery from several missions, such as those generated by Landsat and MODIS. For vegetation studies, such data is very useful due to their long-time history and high spatial resolution.
- The ESA's Copernicus Programme Sentinel satellites have the capability to provide high-resolution imagery with frequent revisit times. For example, Sentinel-2 provides multispectral images highly utilized for NDVI calculation.
- US Geological Survey: The USGS Earth Explorer portal is another very useful resource, which also gives access to imagery from the Landsat satellites and other remote sensing datasets. Some satellites in this series have been orbiting since the early 1970s creating an outstanding record for historical and trend analyses.
- Commercial Providers: Companies like DigitalGlobe and GeoIQ provide high-resolution imagery. For more specialized data, they could be reached out to. While this is often associated with a price tag, these services may ensure even better quality and additional features.

Choosing the Correct Imagery

Once the data source is identified, selecting the proper images is the next phase. Some key considerations are

- Temporal Scale: The images should capture the full temporal scale of interest. For example, in studies that assess change over time in many years, like in longitudinal analyses, such as an NDVI study over ten years, images should be taken at regular intervals-for example, annually-to generate valid results about temporal trends.
- Resolution: Image resolution is a critical factor to consider due to its impact on output detail and quality. High-resolution images carry more information

but, more often than not, come with larger file sizes and heightened computing needs.

- Spectral Bands: In the computation of NDVI, it is important that the imagery carries both NIR and Red bands. Ensure that the imagery to be used for such computation does have these spectral bands for proper NDVI computation.
- Cloud Cover: Select images with least cloud cover; this may obstruct the view of the ground and hence impact the accuracy in NDVI computations. Most of the data providers provide information on statistics relating to cloud cover to help make the best choice.

Downloading the Images

Once one has selected the imagery of choice, the process of downloading includes:

- Creating an Account: This involves signing up with the data provider in order to access their download interface. User accounts may be mandated by certain providers before accessing their data.
- Definition of the Region of Interest: Use the tools of the provider to determine the area in which your interest applies. This involves outlining a polygon over the region of interest or typing out the coordinates directly to download imagery that best represents the location of interest.
- Selection of Image Files: Based on the time frame and resolution identified, the concrete image files to be downloaded need to be selected. Most providers allow downloading in bulk by selecting multiple images.
- Download and Store the Data: Initiate the download. It may take a considerable amount of time; the size can be really huge. Store files in an organized way on your local system or on cloud storage for easy access during the analysis phase.
- Data Format and Compatibility: Verify that the downloaded files are in a format compatible with post-processing. Standardized formats such as GeoTIFF or HDF are widely supported by remote sensing and GIS software.

Post-Download Preparation

After download, it is necessary to prepare the images for analysis: quality checking, performing any correction that might be required-for example, atmospheric correction-and ensuring that the images are correctly aligned and registered for accurate computation of NDVI.

In other words, downloading satellite images over the ROI is one of the most critical initial steps in any remote sensing analysis. High-quality imagery from reliable sources can be selected and acquired by researchers to ensure that the NDVI calculation and further analysis based on the derived data are done using accurate and comprehensive data.

Implementation

Choose a platform based on the accuracy and clarity of the photos you desire. Satellite photos can be downloaded from a variety of paid and open sources. In order to obtain the necessary satellite photos, we are going to use the Google Earth Engine, also known as (GEE). To get started, create an account on the website and open the code editor. The screen that appears when opening Google Earth Engine is shown below. Then obtain the images of the area required by selecting the region of interest commonly known as (ROI). The latitudes and longitudes are stated in the code, the region of interest (ROI) need not be specified. Download the images for every 15 days of the month. Since according to NRSC the crop day is defined for every 15 days. Download 2 images for every month by changing the days in the code. similarly download all the images for a year that is 24 images per year for the consecutive 5 years(Mwinuka et al., 2022; Tucker et al., 2020). In the months of rainy season pls make a note on cloud pixel percentage, generally we prefer 5%. But in rainy season it should be less than 30% for good results. All the images should be in tiff format. Download all the images to the google drive for the easy access further

Details of Study Area

Figure 1. (a) Screen page of google earth engine website, (b) providing code to google earth engine, (c) satellite image of area of study in GEE, (d) coordinates and total area of study area

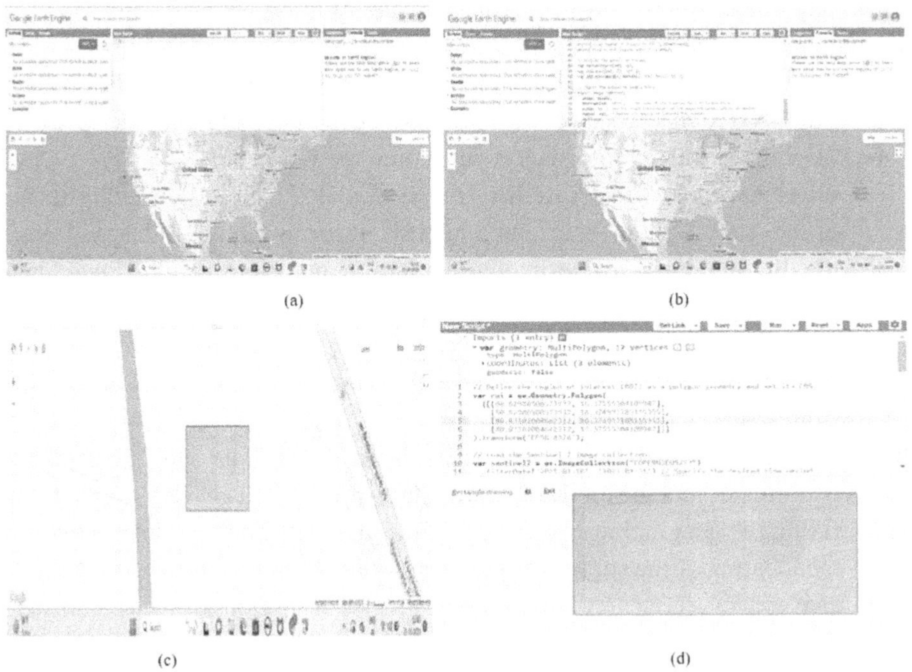

Total number of pixels in ROI: 150N
Area of ROI (square meters) `: 150N
8011.980500422226

Figure 1 (a), (b),(c), and (d) outlines some of the main steps for satellite image analysis using GEE along with some general points of the platform's evolution. Four-panel overview, one pane at a time. The code for image downloading is shown in Appendex.

a) **Screen Page of Google Earth Engine Website:** The below panel is the screen display when the website opens in GEE. This page is used as the landing page for users to gain access to the resources and tools available in GEE. It has an easy-to-use user interface that enables the user to initiate projects, view various data sets, and access different functionalities within. On the dashboard are options to view satellite images and run analyses and scripts. The "Code Editor" button is really easy to see; it's the interface where you would actually insert and execute your own scripts.

b) **Coding in Google Earth Engine:** The second window here shows how a user provides code in the GEE Code Editor. This is the code editor to which users write and run their code in JavaScript to perform their analysis of satellite imagery and any other type of geospatial analysis they want to do. The common code would involve the import of satellite data, regions of interest, and an analytical function applied to the data. This step is crucial as it ensures that the analysis is customized to meet the needs of the study, such as through the calculation of NDVI or the extraction of specific vegetation metrics.

   (c) **GEE Area of Study Satellite Image:** Panel (c) shows a satellite image of the study area as represented in GEE. It forms the input that will drive the different analyses desired herein into their various results. Such high-resolution imagery allows for great perspective, with sufficient detail to allow the observation and assessment of the spatial features of this area, like land cover, vegetation, and other manifestations of change as observable from space.

   (d) **Coordinates and Total Area of Study Area:** The last panel presents the coordinates and the total area of the study region. This is very important in fixing the geographical boundary of the analysis. The coordinates will fix the location of the study area precisely, while the measurement of the total area conveys the scale of the analysis. Precise definitions of such parameters ensure that the analyses are focused and relevant to the specific geographic region of interest.

Creation of New Raster Layer

Install the QGIS software of the latest version. Since the downloaded images are analyzed in the QGIS software. The screen after opening the QGIS software is shown in the figure below. Among the options present in the qgis select the layer on the header side of screen and then add layers and then add raster layer. Raster layers are used to input multispectral satellite imagery, capturing different bands of light, into QGIS. The NDVI raster layer provides a valuable tool for decision-making in agriculture, forestry, and environmental management by identifying areas of interest for further investigation or intervention.

Figure 2. (a) Screen page of QGIS software, selection of raster layer for input of images

(a)

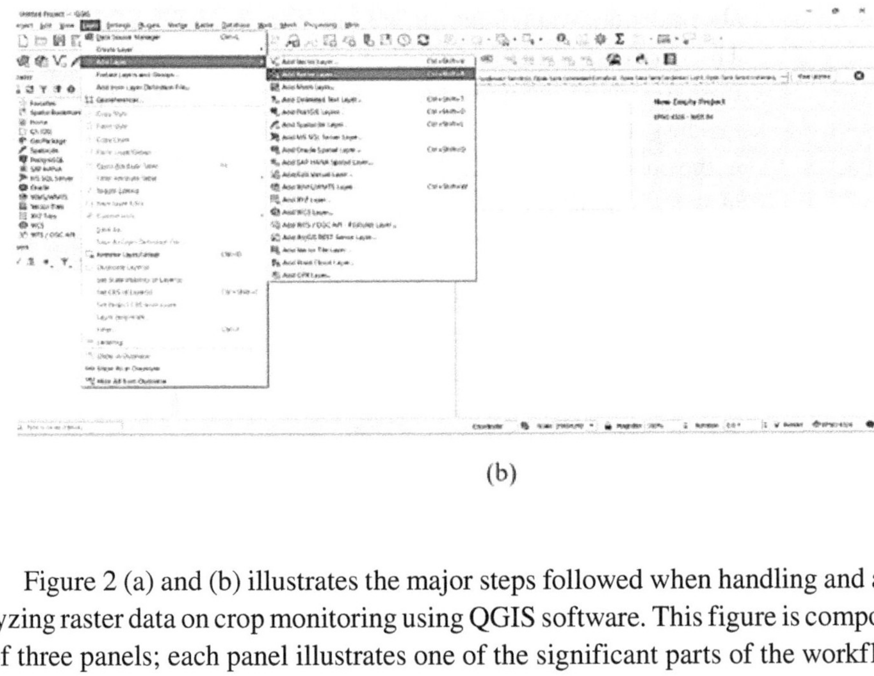

(b)

Figure 2 (a) and (b) illustrates the major steps followed when handling and analyzing raster data on crop monitoring using QGIS software. This figure is composed of three panels; each panel illustrates one of the significant parts of the workflow:

a) Screen Page of QGIS Software: The first panel provides a snapshot of the interface of QGIS software. QGIS is a free and open-source geographic information system used to spatially analyze and map data. This screen page explains the main parts that constitute the QGIS workspace: the menu bar, toolbars, and map canvas. The latter is the area where the spatial data are viewed and manipulated, while on its side there is the so-called Layers Panel, managing the several data layers present in the workspace. Among the capabilities one will find useful in this interface are adding layers, editing, and doing some spatial analysis.

(b) Selecting a Raster Layer to Input Images: Panel (b) shows how to choose a raster layer to input in QGIS. Raster layers are spatial data represented in either pixel or grid form and play an important role in the analysis of satellite images or other remote sensing data. Here, the user imports and selects the desired raster layers, such as NDVI value layers or raw satellite imagery. The interface typically possesses choices that enable browsing and loading of image files, ensuring correct data addition to the project. This selection is very important in order to make certain that proper analysis is carried out on relevant imagery, as well as proper alignment of data layers with the study area.

Stacking of Images to get the Entire ROI: Stacking of the images signifies the inserting the images one above the above of all 24 images in a year. Stacking helps all the images to insert correctly one above the above in order to find the average NDVI of the image. The inserting of the images should be in the correct order either from top to bottom or bottom to top of the months in the year. For the easy access create a folder contain all the images in the order in the computer. This make the relief from confusion of images are in order or not.

Figure 3. (a) Inserting of images of crop in raster layer, (b) output image of crop in raster layer

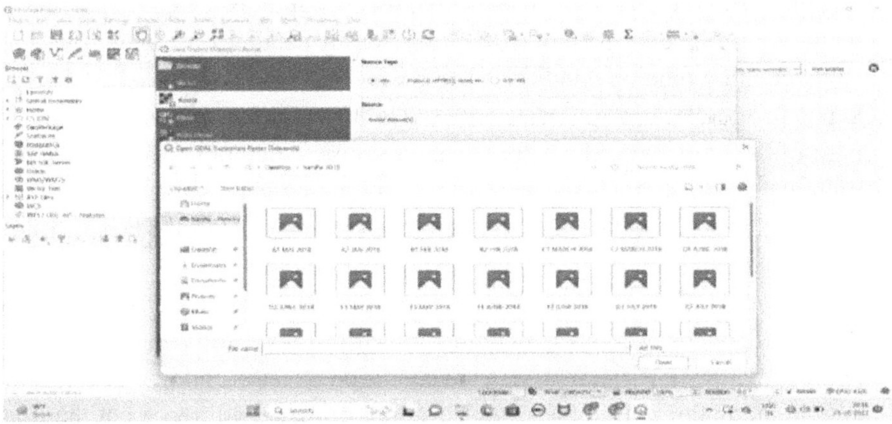

(a)

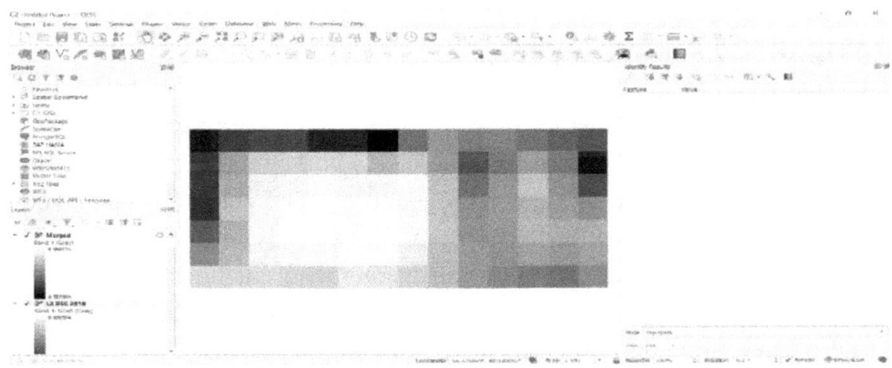

(b)

Figure 3 (a) and (b) illustrates how images are inserted in a QGIS raster layer. This might be one of the important steps for maintaining and analyzing the spatial data during the crop monitoring process

(a) Insertion of Images of Crop in Raster Layer: QGIS allows users to view raster data using the "Layer" menu or "Browser Panel." Users can add spatial data layers, including rasters, by selecting "Add Raster Layer" or similar from the menu. They can browse their computer or network storage for raster image files, such as GeoTIFF, JPEG, and PNG format, which contain pixelated information representing the study area. Once the file is found, the user can select it and click "Open" or "Add" to add it to the QGIS workspace. The raster layer displays in the map canvas, showing the spatial distribution of crop data features like cover and health. Users can also check image alignment and properties, such as the coordinate reference system and spatial resolution, to ensure the image integrates with the rest of the data. This process captures the entire process of integrating raster images into a QGIS project for detailed spatial analysis and insight creation on crop conditions and monitoring.

(b) Output Image of Crop in Raster Layer: The last panel provides the resultant image of the crop inside the output raster layer. This output image is a result of different analytical processes that have been run on the input raster layers. For example, this could show NDVI values of the crop calculated and hence visualize the health and condition of the vegetation. This final image, as projected on the map canvas, shall allow the user to interpret and further analyze the results. Color gradients or overlays may represent various levels of vegetation health, therefore making it easier to assess the condition of crops and find general patterns or anomalies within the data. This output image will represent the final visual output of data analysis done in QGIS.

Merging of the Added Layers

The pixels of the study area i.e. 84 as mentioned in Figure 4 are merged in all images one above the another. if any of the pixels in the images are missing then they don't merge. this helps to know there is mistake and correction can be done easily. the proper merging helps to determine the avg ndvi of all the pixels This merging process is particularly useful when dealing with satellite imagery or other raster datasets with multiple bands. It allows you to create a single, composite image for easier visualization and analysis. Keep in mind that the success of the merge depends on the compatibility of the input raster layers in terms of spatial resolution, extent, and band configuration.

Figure 4. Merging of the added layers

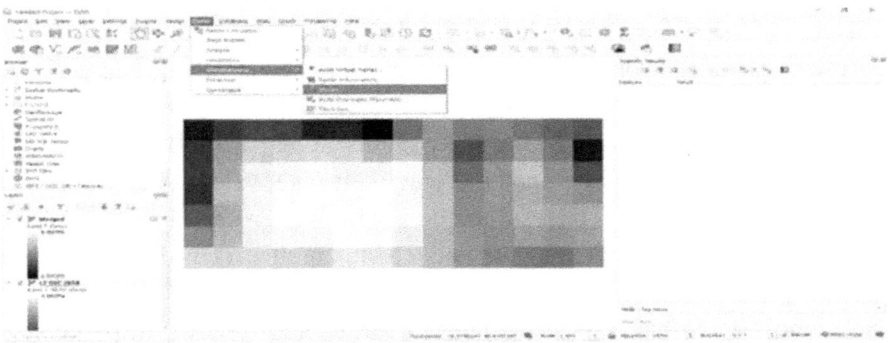

(a) Merging of Total 24 Images in a Year using the Merge Tool

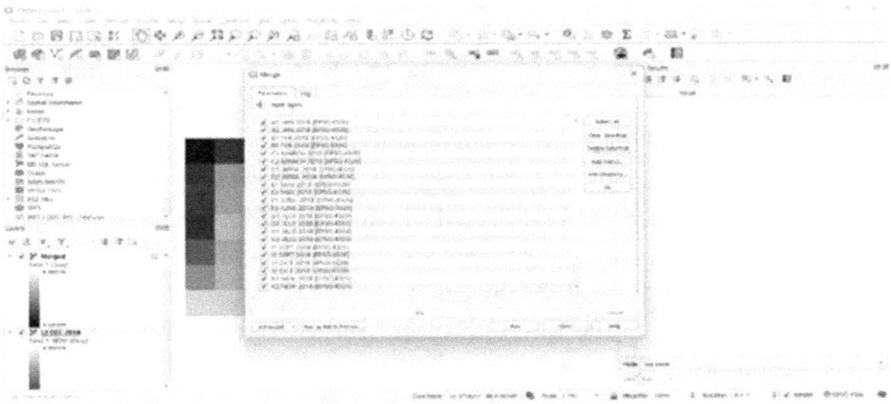

(b) Selection of all 24 Images in a Year in an Order

Figure 4 (a) and (b) illustrates the merge multiple raster images in QGIS. This step is quite important toward the development of a coherent dataset from disparate images. The process is quite helpful when one has to handle more than one image captured within a year for temporal change analysis or when data has to be aggregated for summarised assessments.

(a) Merging of Total 24 Images in a Year using the Merge Tool: Panel (a) illustrates how merging can be performed within QGIS for 24 different images into a single composite image using the Merge Tool. This tool offers the potential to process several raster datasets into one seamless layer. This process is useful when combining data that was captured at different times-for example, monthly images or images from multiple dates in the year. To initiate this in QGIS, the "Raster" menu is opened, followed by "Miscellaneous," then "Merge." The Merge Tool window pops up, and the user will be prompted to select the input layers, in this case, the 24 raster images representing parts of the year. It does this by selecting those layers and merging their pixel values to come up with one unified raster layer. The resulting output from the merge maintains spatial characteristics of each of the input images to comprehensively depict the status of the crop during each year.

(b) Selecting All 24 Images in a Year in an Order: Panel (b) shows the progress of selecting and setting the order of the 24 images prior to merging. This requires proper selection and ordering to capture the temporal order in which data was obtained. In QGIS, this translates to opening the "Merge" dialogue and manually adding each raster image in order. Typically, users select images either from the Layers Panel or directly from the file system and manage them in such a way that if the images represent different time points in chronological order, then this is respected. Accordingly, switching the order of these images allows the user to easily control how the merged layer will represent change through time so that in your final composite, this progression or variation in crop conditions through the year is accurately reflected. Having identified and ordered the images in this way, the user will perform the merge, resulting in one raster layer with data combined from all 24 images.

De-selecting all the Layers Expect Merged Layer: After merging all the images, a new layer of merged image are formed specify a name for it. deselect all the 24 images from the merged layers, then only the merged layer is specified on the screen with all the pixels of 24 images merging together which makes the calculation of ndvi very easy, at the left corner we can see the total layers including merged layer. The demerging should be done there by clicking on the tick box.

Figure 5 .Output of the image after merging of all images of crop

Figure 5 illustrates resulting output image of all individual crop images merged together. This composite raster layer merges information from multiple images into a single, unified look at the crops across the time period considered. The result is a fully integrated display of temporal variations and general health conditions in one combined layer.

SELECTION OF PROPERTIES OPTION TO KNOW AVG NDVI VALUES OF EACH LAYER

While dealing with hundreds and thousands of satellite images, the calculation of NDVI becomes utterly unworkable and time-consuming by hand. Therefore, it is imperative to use GIS software in order to automate as much of this process as possible. A very good way could be by taking advantage of the built-in functions of GIS, such as QGIS, which considerably helps in the calculation and, consequently, analysis of NDVI values (Shahfahad et al., 2020; Tucker et al., 2020). How to find out the average NDVI values for each layer using the "Properties" option in QGIS, considering that one always has to deal with more than one image, is explained here step by step.

Automating NDVI Calculation and Analysis

Preparing and Merging of Satellite Images

Before calculating the average values of NDVI, make sure that the satellite images are correctly processed and merged into one layer, including:

- Downloading of Satellite Images: Obtain the satellite images for the entire duration of the study from any trusted source, each containing Near-Infrared and Red spectral bands.
- Import Images in QGIS: Import images in QGIS one by one as raster layers.
- Layer Stacking and Merging: A new raster layer is to be created by stacking the images. This will merge all the temporal data into one composite layer for easier analyses thereafter. Make sure that all images are stitched using the QGIS toolset for stack and merge layers.

Automatic Calculation of NDVI

Once merged, QGIS will be able to automate the calculation of NDVI across all the layers. The formula behind NDVI is buried inside the processing tools.

- Opening Raster Calculator: Open the Raster Calculator tool in QGIS. This is the tool you will use to perform mathematical operations on raster layers and to calculate the NDVI.
- Input NDVI Formula: Now input the NDVI formula into the Raster Calculator. The formula you will use is:

$$\mathbf{NDVI} = (\mathbf{NIR} + \mathbf{R})/(\mathbf{NIR} - \mathbf{R}) \quad (1)$$

where NIR is abbreviation of the Near-Infrared band and R stands for the Red band. Note that you must select the appropriate bands from the raster layers in this expression.

- Compute NDVI Layer: Click Run to obtain a new NDVI raster layer. It will contain NDVI values per each pixel, reflecting the health of the vegetation.

Selecting the Properties Option for Average NDVI Values

In order to compute the average of NDVI values per each layer follow these:

Name the Merged NDVI Layer: Include a full descriptive name for the new NDVI layer so you can identify it later.

Accessing Layer Properties

- Right-Click the Layer: In the Layers panel, right-click the merged NDVI layer.

- Select 'Properties': Click 'Properties' from the context menu to open the Layer Properties dialog box.

Click Information Tab:

- Open the Information Tab: In the Layer Properties dialog click on the 'Information' tab. The tab provides several statistics and metadata of the raster layer. View Statistical Information: In the 'Information' tab, several important statistics will be viewed. Among them the minimum, maximum, mean and standard deviation of NDVI values of the whole layer can be read. Record Average NDVI Values.
- Note the Average NDVI: In the statistical data identify the average NDVI value. This is the mean NDVI of all the pixels in the layer, and it gives a summary of the vegetation condition over the study area.
- Record Data: If you have more than one NDVI layer for different time periods, or images write down the average NDVI values for each layer.

Analyzing and Using NDVI Data

Now, taking the mean values into consideration for NDVI, you proceed further with the analysis.

- Temporal Analysis: Now, it will be possible to compare the average NDVI values between different layers to draw inferences regarding changes in vegetation health on a temporal scale. Such a comparison may result in some sort of trend, such as improved/deteriorated health of crops at a particular point in time.
- Graphical representation: Plot graphs or charts to represent temporal changes in average NDVI values. That way, one could visualize the temporal dynamics in crop health and thus establish a pattern or anomaly.
- Reporting and Decision Making: Analyzed data are used for informed decisions on crop management, policy-making, or further research. The average values of NDVI can be used to depict the health status of crops, therefore guiding on necessary interventions or management strategies.

Troubleshooting and Quality Checks

When doing these, make sure that:

- Data Accuracy: Satellite images are well aligned and the NDVI calculation is accurate. If wrong band selection or any other error in the processing has taken place, one may get unreliable values of NDVI.
- Consistency Across Layers: Consistency of the value of NDVI in different layers prove that merging and calculation of values have taken place rightly.
- Regular Updates: Periodically update the satellite images of the ongoing projects and re-calculate the values of NDVI in order to keep the information updated and accurate.

The calculation and analysis of average NDVI values in QGIS are based on merging satellite images, automating the NDVI calculation, and tapping into properties tools in the software for statistics extraction. This approach streamlines the analysis, letting the user perform big data sets in an effective way and derive valuable insights from the trend of vegetation health over time.

Since the calculation of ndvi for total 120 images by formula method as mentioned above is impossible and takes time. In the code itself the bands for calculation of ndvi and the formula is mentioned the output of the image itself gives the avg ndvi of each pixel.to determine the avg ndvi of layers. right on the name given to the merged images and then go to the properties and then to the information it gives the avg ndvi of all the pixels present in the layer. note all the ndvi values.

EXAMPLE OF OUTPUT NDVI VALUES

Now Copy all the Results into the Excel Sheet for all the five consecutive years from 2018 to 2022, follow the same steps mentioned above and determine the avg ndvi similarly for all the five years. Insert the values of ndvi for 5 years in the excel sheet for drawing the graph of ndvi and the months of corresponding years (Barka et al., 2019; Diaz de Carvalho et al., 2020; Garcia-Garcia et al., 2021). Figure 6 illustrates two aspects of the NDVI analysis over five consecutive years (2018 to 2022):

(a) Arithmetic Line Graphs for Consecutive 5 Years: This panel shows a line graph depicting the NDVI trends across the five-year period. Each line represents the NDVI values for a specific year, allowing for a visual comparison of vegetation health changes over time. The x-axis denotes the years, while the y-axis displays the NDVI values, highlighting variations and trends in crop health.
(b) NDVI Results for Consecutive 5 Years in Excel Sheet: This panel displays the NDVI data in an Excel sheet format. It provides a tabular summary of the NDVI values calculated for each year, facilitating detailed numerical analysis and comparison.

Figure 6. Output NDVI values: five years (2018 to 2022)

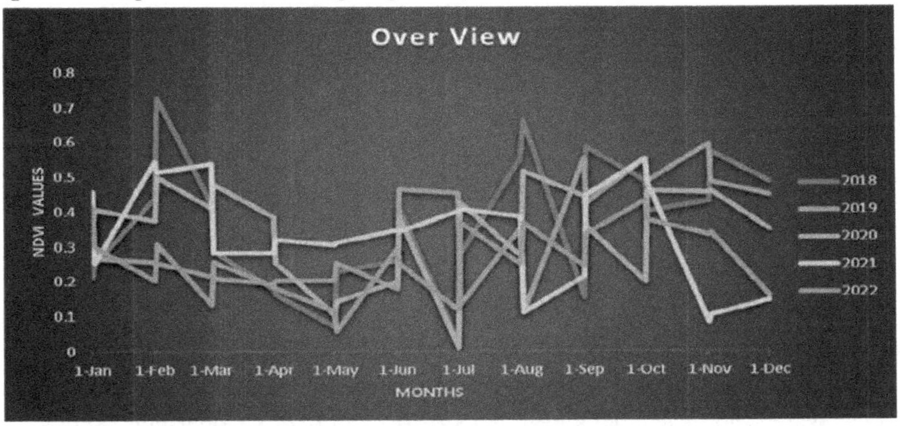

(a) Arithmetic Line Graphs for Consecutive 5 Years

1	Months	2018	2019	2020	2021	2022
2	1-Jan	0.21343	0.4388	0.3475	0.4564	0.4121
3	2-Jan	0.25185	0.2674	0.4079	0.2532	0.3009
4	1-Feb	0.42816	0.2564	0.3734	0.544	0.2028
5	2-Feb	0.726	0.2543	0.4981	0.5113	0.3064
6	1-Mar	0.4204	0.2138	0.4103	0.5361	0.133
7	2-Mar	0.2876	0.2081	0.4791	0.2815	0.2566
8	1-Apr	0.1779	0.1922	0.3843	0.2855	0.1854
9	2-Apr	0.1616	0.2025	0.2529	0.3204	0.179
10	1-May	0.0712	0.2027	0.1044	0.3057	0.1152
11	2-May	0.2268	0.2524	0.142	0.3123	0.0577
12	1-Jun	0.2591	0.1766	0.2	0.3474	0.2951
13	2-Jun	0.411	0.4643	0.3845	0.3425	0.25184
14	1-Jul	0.0203	0.4518	0.0088	0.40164	0.1177
15	2-Jul	0.27844	0.1328	0.4242	0.4073	0.3691
16	1-Aug	0.5503	0.3515	0.2725	0.3858	0.2499
17	2-Aug	0.65944	0.1123	0.5157	0.1093	0.3671
18	1-Sep	0.15243	0.5523	0.4425	0.2126	0.241
19	2-Sep	0.5838	0.4227	0.3572	0.4464	0.3364
20	1-Oct	0.4849	0.5494	0.1979	0.5506	0.433
21	2-Oct	0.4001	0.48447	0.4584	0.4841	0.37512
22	1-Nov	0.4299	0.5935	0.4542	0.081	0.3334
23	2-Nov	0.57022	0.4864	0.4592	0.1036	0.3414
24	1-Dec	0.4854	0.4473	0.3486	0.1471	0.1562
25	2-Dec	0.62766	0.3913	0.2563	0.4117	0.23522

(b) NDVI Results for Consecutive 5 Years in Excel Sheet

FUTURE ADVANCEMENTS IN REMOTE SENSING AND NDVI ANALYSIS

As the remote-sensing field develops further, future technologies and methodologies hold great promise for enhancing the capabilities and wider range of applications of NDVI analysis. Such development is bound to provide more accurate, timely, and detailed information on vegetation health with which better management and conservation practices can be effectively implemented. Let's delve into the major areas where new advancements are foreseen to make critical differences (Davis et al., 2023; Eisfelder et al., 2023; Lima Albuquerque Maranhão, 2023; Maranhão, 2023).

Improved Satellite Sensor Technologies

In the future, satellite sensor technologies will continue to generate imagery with increased resolutions and accuracies. Currently, a new generation of sensors featuring improved spectral and spatial resolutions are under development that will allow the discrimination of vegetation types at finer resolutions, while enabling more accurate measurements regarding the health of vegetation (Pachiappan et al., 2024; Rahamathunnisa et al., 2024). Future satellite missions, such as NASA's Surface Water and Ocean Topography (SWOT) and ESA's Copernicus Sentinel-3 for example, will allow better capabilities in monitoring most of the environmental variables listed above. These contribute to an enhanced NDVI calculation because they have data in even finer detail, thus enabling subtle changes in vegetation health and stress that may be captured poorly or missed by coarser-resolution imagery.

Multi-Source Data Integration

Multi-source data integration will comprehensively enhance the accuracy and reliability of NDVI analysis. Integrating data from several sources creates a far more whole-scale view of the dynamics in vegetation. Drones with high-resolution multispectral sensors provide imagery at finer resolutions compared to satellites. The options are also there for ground-based sensors that monitor the soil moisture and nutrient level in a location. In this way, combining different data sources, the various data sources enable the researcher and practitioner to arrive at a far more sophisticated understanding of vegetation health and stressors.

Improved Data Processing and Analytics

In fact, with the advancement in data processing and analytics, handling increasing volume and complex data acquired from remote sensing will be very useful. Advanced machine learning algorithms and techniques in AI will allow for sophisticated analysis of NDVI data. The AI-driven models themselves will automatically identify meaningful patterns out of large datasets, hence helping in vegetation stress detection and changes over time. This will also be enabled by cloud computing technologies, which store and process huge volumes of satellite imagery in real time for analysis and decision-making.

Higher Temporal Resolution

Higher temporal resolution of satellite observation will provide more frequent and timely information concerning vegetation health. Though current satellite missions offer periodic snapshots of vegetation conditions, future development in this trend is likely to feature higher temporal resolution. For example, newly deployed constellations with higher revisit times will further enhance capacity for continuous vegetation health monitoring to deliver more timely and actionable insights. This is particularly useful in tracking seasonal changes, early signs of stress, and responding to environmental changes more effectively.

Integration with Climate Models

Integration of NDVI data into climate models will yield information on the impact of climate change on vegetation health. Future development will involve the application of remote sensing data in conjunction with projected climate change to study variable temperatures, shifting rainfall, and anomalies in extreme weather events as they pertain to vegetation. Such integration allows foresight into risk and vulnerability that proactive management can reduce in crops and natural vegetation regarding changing climates.

Real-Time Monitoring

Real-time monitoring is going to revolutionize NDVI analysis and change the immediate way one views vegetation health. Advances in satellite technology and data transmission will facilitate near-real-time updates of vegetation conditions, thus enabling immediate responses to emerging issues. This capability will be especially useful for agricultural management, disaster response, and environmental conservation, where timely information is critical to effective decision-making.

Increased Accessibility and User Engagement

It will further enhance the accessibility of NDVI data and engage the participation of an increased circle of users in their use. It will be ensured that user-friendly platforms and tools develop better access to NDVI data and make interpretation easier for farmers, researchers, and policy-makers. Enhanced visualization tools, dashboards, and mobile applications will make it easier to engage users and speed up decision-making at various levels. Further, democratization of access to remote-sensing data allows local communities and stakeholders to be more effective in managing their environments.

Improvement in Data Fusion Techniques

Approaches of data fusion, which will integrate NDVI with other RS-indices and datasets, will lead to more informative results about the health status of vegetation. For example, the integration of NDVI with data on soil properties, land use, and vegetation type will allow for the refined analysis of conditions in vegetation. It would be more holistic and hence increase the identification of a specific stressor in order to manage vegetation more effectively(Agrawal et al., 2023; Pramila et al., 2023).

Data Privacy and Security

Accordingly, data privacy and security issues will increasingly have to be taken into consideration in the future while advances in remote-sensing technologies continue to evolve. Ensuring sensitive data is secure and data usage is conformed to privacy laws and regulations will be crucial in order to uphold trust and integrity in remote sensing applications. Future developments will be essentially characterized by upgraded, intensified security measures and protocols in safeguarding data and ensuring responsible use(Rahamathunnisa et al., 2023; Srinivas et al., 2023).

The consequence, in turn, is the ability for NDVI analysis and remote sensing to create a bright outlook for fostering our perception of vegetation health. This enables new insights driven by improved satellite sensor technologies, the combining of data from multiple sources, advance processing of data, and near real-time monitoring. The application of such advances will better position researchers, practitioners, and policy-makers toward effective management and the conservation of vegetation, mitigating climate change impacts on vegetation, and ensuring sustainable agriculture.

CONCLUSION

The interpretation of NDVI trends over a five-year period using Sentinel satellite data provided a nuanced perspective on the temporal evolution of crop health and productivity changes. The yield of the crop is more in the year 2021 compared to other years. Through the systematic tracking of vegetation indices, on can detect changes cyclical patterns. The graph is decreasing for months April to May and July to august every year. These helps to detect anomalies, and anticipate potential challenges, thereby facilitating proactive measures to optimize resource allocation, mitigate risks, and promote resilience in agricultural systems.

The synthesis of NDVI trends spanning five years through Sentinel satellite monitoring underscores the utility of remote sensing technology in crop assessment and management. The consistent monitoring of NDVI values allows for the identification of seasonal patterns, growth trends, and potential stressors, enabling stakeholders to implement targeted interventions and optimize agricultural practices for enhanced productivity and resilience.

REFERENCES

Agrawal, A. V., Magulur, L. P., Priya, S. G., Kaur, A., Singh, G., & Boopathi, S. (2023). Smart Precision Agriculture Using IoT and WSN. In *Handbook of Research on Data Science and Cybersecurity Innovations in Industry 4.0 Technologies* (pp. 524–541). IGI Global. DOI: 10.4018/978-1-6684-8145-5.ch026

Barka, I., Bucha, T., Molnár, T., Móricz, N., Somogyi, Z., & Koreň, M. (2019). Suitability of MODIS-based NDVI index for forest monitoring and its seasonal applications in Central Europe. *Lesnícky Casopis*, 65(3–4), 206–217. DOI: 10.2478/forj-2019-0020

Bhunia, G. S., Kesari, S., Chatterjee, N., Mandal, R., Kumar, V., & Das, P. (2012). Seasonal relationship between normalized difference vegetation index and abundance of the Phlebotomus kala-azar vector in an endemic focus in Bihar, India. *Geospatial Health*, 7(1), 51–62. DOI: 10.4081/gh.2012.104 PMID: 23242680

Bisanzio, D., Amore, G., Ragagli, C., Tomassone, L., Bertolotti, L., & Mannelli, A. (2014). Temporal variations in the usefulness of normalized difference vegetation index as a predictor for Ixodes ricinus (Acari: Ixodidae) in a Borrelia lusitaniae focus in Tuscany, central Italy. *Journal of Medical Entomology*, 45(3), 547–555. DOI: 10.1093/jmedent/45.3.547 PMID: 18533451

Boopathi, S., & Kanike, U. K. (2023). Applications of Artificial Intelligent and Machine Learning Techniques in Image Processing. In *Handbook of Research on Thrust Technologies' Effect on Image Processing* (pp. 151–173). IGI Global. DOI: 10.4018/978-1-6684-8618-4.ch010

Boopathi, S., Pandey, B. K., & Pandey, D. (2023). Advances in Artificial Intelligence for Image Processing: Techniques, Applications, and Optimization. In *Handbook of Research on Thrust Technologies' Effect on Image Processing* (pp. 73–95). IGI Global.

Das, P., Ramapraba, P., Seethalakshmi, K., Mary, M. A., Karthick, S., & Sampath, B. (2024). Sustainable Advanced Techniques for Enhancing the Image Process. In *Fostering Cross-Industry Sustainability With Intelligent Technologies* (pp. 350–374). IGI Global. DOI: 10.4018/979-8-3693-1638-2.ch022

Davis, Z., Nesbitt, L., Guhn, M., & van den Bosch, M. (2023). Assessing changes in urban vegetation using Normalised Difference Vegetation Index (NDVI) for epidemiological studies. *Urban Forestry & Urban Greening*, 88, 128080. DOI: 10.1016/j.ufug.2023.128080 de Carvalho, L. F. D., Amado, T. J. C., Sobrinho, J. C., de Paula Amaral, L., Pott, L. P., Piccin, M., & Pedron, V. F. (2020). Nutritional status of corn plants estimated through different vegetation indices in the growth stages. *Revista Engenharia Na Agricultura-REVENG, 28*(Contínua), 255–264.

Diaz de Carvalho, L. F., Carneiro Amado, T. J., Cardoso Sobrinho, J., de Paula Amaral, L., Pierre Pott, L., Piccin, M., & Freitas Pedron, V. (2020). Nutritional status of corn plants estimated through different vegetation indices in the growth stages. *Engenharia na Agricultura*, 28(1), 255–264. DOI: 10.13083/reveng.v28i.8564

Donovan, G. H., Gatziolis, D., Derrien, M., Michael, Y. L., Prestemon, J. P., & Douwes, J. (2022). Shortcomings of the normalized difference vegetation index as an exposure metric. *Nature Plants*, 8(6), 617–622. DOI: 10.1038/s41477-022-01170-6 PMID: 35697731

Eisfelder, C., Asam, S., Hirner, A., Reiners, P., Holzwarth, S., Bachmann, M., Gessner, U., Dietz, A., Huth, J., Bachofer, F., & Kuenzer, C. (2023). Seasonal Vegetation Trends for Europe over 30 Years from a Novel Normalised Difference Vegetation Index (NDVI) Time-Series—The TIMELINE NDVI Product. *Remote Sensing (Basel)*, 15(14), 3616. DOI: 10.3390/rs15143616

García Cárdenas, D. A., Ramón Valencia, J. A., Alzate Velásquez, D. F., & Palacios Gonzalez, J. R. (2018). Dynamics of the indices NDVI and GNDVI in a rice growing in its reproduction phase from multi-spectral aerial images taken by drones. *International Conference of ICT for Adapting Agriculture to Climate Change*, 106–119.

Garcia-Garcia, D., la Rosa, X. R., Bedoya, D. G., & Schrevens, E. (2021). Linear mixed model analysis of NDVI-based canopy coverage, extracted from sequential UAV multispectral imagery of an open field tomato irrigation experiment. *Computers and Electronics in Agriculture*, 189, 106399. DOI: 10.1016/j.compag.2021.106399

Guha, S., Govil, H., & Diwan, P. (2019). Analytical study of seasonal variability in land surface temperature with normalized difference vegetation index, normalized difference water index, normalized difference built-up index, and normalized multiband drought index. *Journal of Applied Remote Sensing*, 13(2), 024518–024518.

Haerani, H., Apan, A., & Basnet, B. (2018). Mapping of peanut crops in Queensland, Australia, using time-series PROBA-V 100-m normalized difference vegetation index imagery. *Journal of Applied Remote Sensing*, 12(3), 036005–036005. DOI: 10.1117/1.JRS.12.036005

Lima Albuquerque Maranhão, R. (2023). *Assessing Normalized Difference Vegetation Index (NDVI) data to estimate winter wheat yields and analyze winter wheat by homogeneous subregions at field scale in Kansas* [PhD Thesis].

Maranhão, R. L. A. (2023). *Assessing Normalized Difference Vegetation Index (NDVI) Data to Estimate Winter Wheat Yields and Analyze Winter Wheat by Homogeneous Subregions at Field Scale in Kansas*. Kansas State University.

Mwinuka, P. R., Mourice, S. K., Mbungu, W. B., Mbilinyi, B. P., Tumbo, S. D., & Schmitter, P. (2022). UAV-based multispectral vegetation indices for assessing the interactive effects of water and nitrogen in irrigated horticultural crops production under tropical sub-humid conditions: A case of African eggplant. *Agricultural Water Management*, 266, 107516. DOI: 10.1016/j.agwat.2022.107516

Pachiappan, K., Anitha, K., Pitchai, R., Sangeetha, S., Satyanarayana, T., & Boopathi, S. (2024). Intelligent Machines, IoT, and AI in Revolutionizing Agriculture for Water Processing. In *Handbook of Research on AI and ML for Intelligent Machines and Systems* (pp. 374–399). IGI Global.

Pramila, P., Amudha, S., Saravanan, T., Sankar, S. R., Poongothai, E., & Boopathi, S. (2023). Design and Development of Robots for Medical Assistance: An Architectural Approach. In *Contemporary Applications of Data Fusion for Advanced Healthcare Informatics* (pp. 260–282). IGI Global.

Rahamathunnisa, U., Subhashini, P., Aancy, H. M., Meenakshi, S., & Boopathi, S. (2023). Solutions for Software Requirement Risks Using Artificial Intelligence Techniques. In *Handbook of Research on Data Science and Cybersecurity Innovations in Industry 4.0 Technologies* (pp. 45–64). IGI Global.

Rahamathunnisa, U., Sudhakar, K., Padhi, S., Bhattacharya, S., Shashibhushan, G., & Boopathi, S. (2024). Sustainable Energy Generation From Waste Water: IoT Integrated Technologies. In *Adoption and Use of Technology Tools and Services by Economically Disadvantaged Communities: Implications for Growth and Sustainability* (pp. 225–256). IGI Global.

Shahfahad, K., Kumari, B., Tayyab, M., Ahmed, I. A., Baig, M. R. I., Khan, M. F., & Rahman, A. (2020). Longitudinal study of land surface temperature (LST) using mono-and split-window algorithms and its relationship with NDVI and NDBI over selected metro cities of India. *Arabian Journal of Geosciences*, 13(19), 1–19. DOI: 10.1007/s12517-020-06068-1

Sharma, I. (2018). *Modeling of land surface temperature (LST) and normalized difference vegetation index (NDVI) in Nepal: 2000-2015* [PhD Thesis]. Prince of Songkla University.

Srinivas, B., Maguluri, L. P., Naidu, K. V., Reddy, L. C. S., Deivakani, M., & Boopathi, S. (2023). Architecture and Framework for Interfacing Cloud-Enabled Robots. In *Handbook of Research on Data Science and Cybersecurity Innovations in Industry 4.0 Technologies* (pp. 542–560). IGI Global. DOI: 10.4018/978-1-6684-8145-5.ch027

Tucker, R., Callaham, J. A., Zeidler, C., Paul, A.-L., & Ferl, R. J. (2020). NDVI imaging within space exploration plant growth modules–A case study from EDEN ISS Antarctica. *Life Sciences in Space Research*, 26, 1–9. DOI: 10.1016/j.lssr.2020.03.006 PMID: 32718674

KEY TERMS AND DEFINITIONS

AI: Artificial Intelligence.
AOI: Area of Interest.
EOSDIS: Earth Observing System Data and Information System.
ESA: European Space Agency.
GEE: Google Earth Engine.
GIS: Geographic Information System.
HDF: Hierarchical Data Format.
IQ: Intelligence Quotient.
JPEG: Joint Photographic Experts Group.
MODIS: Moderate Resolution Imaging Spectroradiometer.
NASA: National Aeronautics and Space Administration.
NDVI: Normalized Difference Vegetation Index.
NIR: Near-Infrared.
NRSC: National Remote Sensing Centre.
OUTPUT: Output (results or data produced by a process).
PNG: Portable Network Graphics.
QGIS: Quantum Geographic Information System.
ROI: Region of Interest.
RS: Remote Sensing.
SWOT: Strengths, Weaknesses, Opportunities, Threats (analysis framework).
TIFF: Tagged Image File Format.
US: United States.
USGS: United States Geological Survey.
VALUES: Data or numerical results.

APPENDIX I: CODE FOR IMAGE DOWNLOADING

```
// Load the Sentinel-2 image collection.
var roi = ee.Geometry.Rectangle([80.85, 16.75, 80.95, 16.85]);
var sentinel2 = ee.Image Collection ("COPERNICUS/S2")
.filterDate('2022-01-16', '2022-01-31')
// Specify the desired time period.
.filterBounds (Map.getBounds(true))
// Filter by the current map view.
.filterMetadata('CLOUDY_PIXEL_PERCENTAGE','less_than', 5);
// Define a function to calculate NDVI. function calculateNDVI(image) { return image.normalized Difference(['B8', 'B4']). rename('NDVI');
}
// Map the NDVI calculation function over the image collection. var ndviCollection = sentinel2. Map (calculateNDVI);
// Function to add NDVI as a band to each image in the collection. function addNDVIBand(image) {
return image.addBands(calculateNDVI(image));
}
// Map the addNDVIBand function over the image collection to add the NDVI band. var ndviCollection WithBands = sentinel2.map (addNDVIBand);
// Clip the NDVI image to the region of interest.
var ndviROI = ndviCollection WithBands .map (function(image) { return image.clip(roi);
});
// Visualization parameters for NDVI.
var ndviVis = {min: -1, max: 1, palette: ['red', 'yellow', 'green']};
// Create a mosaic of NDVI images for the ROI. var mosaic = ndviROI.select('NDVI').mosaic();
// Display the mosaic on the map. Map.centerObject(roi, 18); Map.addLayer (roi,{},'ROI'); Map.addLayer (mosaic, ndviVis, 'NDVI Mosaic ROI');
// Print the image collection information. print('Sentinel-2 Image Collection:', sentinel2);
```

```
// Export the mosaic to Google Drive. Export.image.toDrive({
image: mosaic, description: 'ndvi', // The name of the exported
file on Google Drive.
  scale: 10, // Set the scale (resolution) of the exported
image, adjust as needed. region: roi, // Define the region of
interest for export.
  maxPixels: 1e13 // Set the maximum number of pixels for the
export, adjust as needed.
  });
  // Convert the ROI to a feature (assuming the ROI is a sin-
gle geometry) var roiFeature = ee.Feature(roi);
  // Create a Feature Collection with the ROI feature
  var roiFeatureCollection = ee.Feature ollection ([roiFea-
ture]);
  Export.table. toDrive({
  collection: roiFeature Collection,
  description: 'ROI_Shapefile', // Change to your desired de-
scription folder: 'ROI', // Change to the name of the folder
you want to create in Google Drive fileNamePrefix: 'ROI_Shape-
file',
  fileFormat: 'SHP'
  });
```

Compilation of References

Abhulimen, O., & Ogunti, E. (2021). Facial age estimation using deep learning: A review. *Methods (San Diego, Calif.)*, 8(5).

Abid, S. K., Sulaiman, N., Chan, S. W., Nazir, U., Abid, M., Han, H., Ariza-Montes, A., & Vega-Muñoz, A. (2021). Toward an integrated disaster management approach: How artificial intelligence can boost disaster management. *Sustainability (Basel)*, 13(22), 12560. DOI: 10.3390/su132212560

Aboualola, M., Abualsaud, K., Khattab, T., Zorba, N., & Hassanein, H. S. (2023). Edge technologies for disaster management: A survey of social media and artificial intelligence integration. *IEEE Access : Practical Innovations, Open Solutions*, 11, 73782–73802. DOI: 10.1109/ACCESS.2023.3293035

Abraham, L., Biju, S., Biju, F., Jose, J., Kalantri, R., & Rajguru, S. (2019). Swarm robotics in disaster management. *2019 International Conference on Innovative Sustainable Computational Technologies (CISCT)*, 1–5.

Adomavicius, G., & Tuzhilin, A. (2005). Toward the Next Generation of Recommender Systems: A Survey of the State-of-the-Art and Possible Extensions. *IEEE Transactions on Knowledge and Data Engineering*, 17(6), 734–749. DOI: 10.1109/TKDE.2005.99

Agrawal, A. V., Bakkiyaraj, M., Das, S., Reddy, C. M. S., Kiran, P. B. N., & Boopathi, S. (2024). Digital Strategies for Modern Workplaces and Business Through Artificial Intelligence Techniques. In *Multidisciplinary Applications of Extended Reality for Human Experience* (pp. 231–258). IGI Global. DOI: 10.4018/979-8-3693-2432-5.ch011

Agrawal, A. V., Magulur, L. P., Priya, S. G., Kaur, A., Singh, G., & Boopathi, S. (2023). Smart Precision Agriculture Using IoT and WSN. In *Handbook of Research on Data Science and Cybersecurity Innovations in Industry 4.0 Technologies* (pp. 524–541). IGI Global. DOI: 10.4018/978-1-6684-8145-5.ch026

Ahamed, B. S., Chakravarthy, K. S., Arputhabalan, J., Sasirekha, K., Prince, R. M. R., Boopathi, S., & Muthuvel, S. (2024). Revolutionizing Friction Stir Welding With AI-Integrated Humanoid Robots. In *Advances in Computational Intelligence and Robotics* (pp. 120–144). IGI Global. DOI: 10.4018/979-8-3693-2399-1.ch005

Ahmetovic, D., Fedorovych, K., Voeikau, O., & Babbitt, C. (2019). Deep learning for automatically detecting manual web accessibility issues. Paper presented at the 2019 Seventh International Conference on Learning Representations (ICLR), New Orleans, LA, USA. DOI: 10.48550/arXiv.1908.11815

Akinrinola, N. O., Okoye, C., Ofodile, N. O. C., & Ugochukwu, E. (2024). Navigating and reviewing ethical dilemmas in AI development: Strategies for transparency, fairness, and accountability. *GSC Advanced Research and Reviews*, 18(3), 50–58. DOI: 10.30574/gscarr.2024.18.3.0088

AlAli, Z. T., & Alabady, S. A. (2022). A survey of disaster management and SAR operations using sensors and supporting techniques. *International Journal of Disaster Risk Reduction*, 82, 103295. DOI: 10.1016/j.ijdrr.2022.103295

Albert, W., & Tullis, T. (2013). *Measuring the user experience: Collecting, analyzing, and presenting usability metrics*. Newnes.

Alhammad, M. M., & Moreno, A. M. (2022). *Integrating user experience into Agile | Proceedings of the ACM/IEEE 44th International Conference on Software Engineering: Software Engineering Education and Training*. https://dl.acm.org/doi/abs/10.1145/3510456.3514156

Alikanioti, D., Yannakoudakis, H., & Rei, M. (2016). Semantic Refinement in NLP. *Neural Computation*, 22(2), 145–160.

Alikaniotis, D., Yannakoudakis, H., & Rei, M. (2016). Automatic text scoring using neural networks. *Proc. 54th Annu. Meeting Assoc. Computational Linguistics*, 1, 715–725.

Alkaabi, S., Yussof, S., Al-Khateeb, H., Ahmadi-Assalemi, G., & Epiphaniou, G. (2020). Deep convolutional neural networks for forensic age estimation: A review. *Cyber Defence in the Age of AI, Smart Societies and Augmented Humanity*, 375–395.

Alqudah, M. K., Razali, R., Alqudah, M. K., Dalaien, A., Alabool, H. M., & Alkhazaleh, H. A. (2023). A grounded theory of selecting lean and agile practices for software development. *Journal of Software (Malden, MA)*, 36(4), e2539. Advance online publication. DOI: 10.1002/smr.2539

Al-Shannaq, A. S., & Elrefaei, L. A. (2019). Comprehensive analysis of the literature for age estimation from facial images. *IEEE Access : Practical Innovations, Open Solutions*, 7, 93229–93249. DOI: 10.1109/ACCESS.2019.2927825

AlShorman, O., AlShorman, B., Alkhassaweneh, M., & Alkahtani, F. (2020). A review of internet of medical things (IoMT)-based remote health monitoring through wearable sensors: A case study for diabetic patients. *Indonesian Journal of Electrical Engineering and Computer Science*, 20(1), 414–422. DOI: 10.11591/ijeecs.v20.i1.pp414-422

Al-Turjman, F., Nawaz, M. H., & Ulusar, U. D. (2020). Intelligence in the Internet of Medical Things era: A systematic review of current and future trends. *Computer Communications*, 150, 644–660. DOI: 10.1016/j.comcom.2019.12.030

Amershi, S., Weld, D., Vorvoreanu, M., Fourney, A., Nushi, B., Collisson, P., & Horvitz, E. (2019). Guidelines for human-AI interaction. In *Proceedings of the 2019 CHI Conference on Human Factors in Computing Systems* (pp. 1-13). DOI: 10.1145/3290605.3300233

Amoako-Gyampah, K. (2007). Perceived usefulness, user involvement and behavioral intention: An empirical study of ERP implementation. *Computers in Human Behavior*, 23(3), 1232–1248. DOI: 10.1016/j.chb.2004.12.002

Angulu, R., Tapamo, J. R., & Adewumi, A. O. (2018). Age estimation via face images: A survey. *EURASIP Journal on Image and Video Processing*, 2018(1), 1–35. DOI: 10.1186/s13640-018-0278-6

Anitha, C., Komala, C., Vivekanand, C. V., Lalitha, S., & Boopathi, S. (2023). Artificial Intelligence driven security model for Internet of Medical Things (IoMT). *IEEE Explore*, 1–7.

Apple. (2023). Differential privacy overview. https://www.apple.com/privacy/docs/Differential_Privacy_Overview.pdf

Apraiz, A., Lasa, G., & Mazmela, M. (2023). Evaluation of user experience in human–robot interaction: A systematic literature review. *International Journal of Social Robotics*, 15(2), 187–210. DOI: 10.1007/s12369-022-00957-z

Ardiny, H., & Khanmirza, E. (2018, October). The role of AR and VR technologies in education developments: opportunities and challenges. In 2018 6th rsi international conference on robotics and mechatronics (icrom) (pp. 482-487). IEEE. DOI: 10.1109/ICRoM.2018.8657615

Ashfaq, Z., Rafay, A., Mumtaz, R., Zaidi, S. M. H., Saleem, H., Zaidi, S. A. R., Mumtaz, S., & Haque, A. (2022). A review of enabling technologies for Internet of Medical Things (IoMT) Ecosystem. *Ain Shams Engineering Journal*, 13(4), 101660. DOI: 10.1016/j.asej.2021.101660

Atallah, R. R., Kamsin, A., Ismail, M. A., Abdelrahman, S. A., & Zerdoumi, S. (2018). Face recognition and age estimation implications of changes in facial features: A critical review study. *IEEE Access : Practical Innovations, Open Solutions*, 6, 28290–28304. DOI: 10.1109/ACCESS.2018.2836924

Azevedo, D., Ramelot, J., Legay, A., & Kieffer, S. (2024). With or Without U(sers): A Journey to Integrate UX Activities in Cybersecurity. *Lecture Notes in Computer Science*, 14728, 212–231. DOI: 10.1007/978-3-031-61379-1_14

Azuma, R. T. (1997). A Survey of Augmented Reality. *Presence (Cambridge, Mass.)*, 6(4), 355–385. DOI: 10.1162/pres.1997.6.4.355

Ba, J. L., Kiros, J. R., & Hinton, G. E. (2016). Layer normalization. arXiv:1607.06450.

Bajaj, R., Bhat, S., Chakravarthy, S., Chand, S., Iyer, S., Panakkat, A., & Sawant, K. (2020). AI at Amazon: Solving for customer-obsession. *Communications of the ACM*, 63(12), 57–63. DOI: 10.1145/3417988

Barka, I., Bucha, T., Molnár, T., Móricz, N., Somogyi, Z., & Koreň, M. (2019). Suitability of MODIS-based NDVI index for forest monitoring and its seasonal applications in Central Europe. *Lesnícky Casopis*, 65(3–4), 206–217. DOI: 10.2478/forj-2019-0020

Barros, L., Tam, C., & Varajão, J. (2024). Agile software development projects – unveiling the human-related critical success factors. *Information and Software Technology*, 107432, 107432. Advance online publication. DOI: 10.1016/j.infsof.2024.107432

Bayesteh, A. (2024). Agile-Based Optimized Planning and Scheduling Methodology for Multiple Scattered Projects. *ERA*. https://doi.org/doi:10.7939/r3-sywn-m748

Beattie, A., Lacey, C., & Caudwell, C. (2019). "It's like the Wild West": User Experience (UX) Designers on Ethics and Privacy in Aotearoa New Zealand. *Design and Culture*. Advance online publication. 10.1080V17547075.2023.2211391

Becker, N., Chalkiadakis, M., Eidetog, H., Gezer, D., Wikler, J. H., & Wahlström, R. (2022). Automatic adaptation of web applications for mobile devices using artificial intelligence. *IEEE Access : Practical Innovations, Open Solutions*, 10, 10397–10411. DOI: 10.1109/ACCESS.2022.3143342

Ben Dhaou, I., Ebrahimi, M., Ben Ammar, M., Bouattour, G., & Kanoun, O. (2021). Edge devices for internet of medical things: Technologies, techniques, and implementation. *Electronics (Basel)*, 10(17), 2104. DOI: 10.3390/electronics10172104

Benis, A., Notea, A., & Barkan, R. (2018). Risk and disaster management: From planning and expertise to smart, intelligent, and adaptive systems. In *Building Continents of Knowledge in Oceans of Data: The Future of Co-Created eHealth* (pp. 286–290). IOS Press.

Beyer, H., & Holtzblatt, K. (1998). *Contextual Design: Defining Customer-Centered Systems*. Morgan Kaufmann.

Bhunia, G. S., Kesari, S., Chatterjee, N., Mandal, R., Kumar, V., & Das, P. (2012). Seasonal relationship between normalized difference vegetation index and abundance of the Phlebotomus kala-azar vector in an endemic focus in Bihar, India. *Geospatial Health*, 7(1), 51–62. DOI: 10.4081/gh.2012.104 PMID: 23242680

Billinghurst, M., Clark, A., & Lee, G. (2015). *A Survey of Augmented Reality. Foundations and Trends® in Human*–Computer. *Interaction*, 8(2-3), 73–272.

Bisanzio, D., Amore, G., Ragagli, C., Tomassone, L., Bertolotti, L., & Mannelli, A. (2014). Temporal variations in the usefulness of normalized difference vegetation index as a predictor for Ixodes ricinus (Acari: Ixodidae) in a Borrelia lusitaniae focus in Tuscany, central Italy. *Journal of Medical Entomology*, 45(3), 547–555. DOI: 10.1093/jmedent/45.3.547 PMID: 18533451

Blomberg, J., Burrell, M., & Guest, G. (2003). An ethnographic approach to design. *Handbook of Human-Computer Interaction, 964-986.*

Boopathi, S. (2024). Digital HR Implementation for Business Growth in Industrial 5.0. In *Convergence of Human Resources Technologies and Industry 5.0* (pp. 1–22). IGI Global. DOI: 10.4018/979-8-3693-1343-5.ch001

Boopathi, S., Pandey, B. K., & Pandey, D. (2023). Advances in Artificial Intelligence for Image Processing: Techniques, Applications, and Optimization. In *Handbook of Research on Thrust Technologies' Effect on Image Processing* (pp. 73–95). IGI Global.

Boopathi, S., & Kanike, U. K. (2023). Applications of Artificial Intelligent and Machine Learning Techniques in Image Processing. In *Handbook of Research on Thrust Technologies' Effect on Image Processing* (pp. 151–173). IGI Global. DOI: 10.4018/978-1-6684-8618-4.ch010

Borodin, Y., Bigham, J. P., Dausch, G., & Ramakrishnan, I. V. (2010). *More than Meets the Eye: A Survey of Screen-Reader Browsing Strategies.Proceedings of the 2010 International Cross-Disciplinary Conference on Web Accessibility (W4A), 1-10.* DOI: 10.1145/1805986.1806005

Borriraklert, A., & Kiattisin, S. (2021). User experience design (UXD) competency model: Identifying well-rounded proficiency for user experience designers in the digital age. *Archives of Design Research*, 34(3), 61–79. DOI: 10.15187/adr.2021.08.34.3.61

Bransford, J. D., Brown, A. L., & Cocking, R. R. (2000). *How People Learn: Brain, Mind, Experience, and School.* National Academy Press.

Brooke, J. (1996). *SUS: A quick and dirty usability scale. In P. W. Jordan, B. Thomas, B. A. Weerdmeester, & I. L. McClelland (Eds.), Usability Evaluation in Industry (pp. 189-194). CRC Press.*

Brownlee, J. (2021). What is natural language processing? Machine Learning Mastery. https://machinelearningmastery.com/what-is-natural-language-processing/

Bryman, A. (2016). *Social Research Methods* (5th ed.). Oxford University Press.

Bryson, J. J., Diamantis, M. E., & Grant, T. D. (2017). Of, for, and by the People: The Legal Lacuna *of Synthetic Persons.Artificial Intelligence and Law*, 25(3), 273–291. DOI: 10.1007/s10506-017-9214-9

Buie, E., & Murray, D. (Eds.). (2012). *Usability in Government Systems: User Experience Design for Citizens and Public Servants.* Morgan Kaufmann.

Chen, Y., Wang, X., Yang, J., Wu, Z., Chen, Y., & Peng, Y. (2024). *A Multi-Platform Compatible Remote Control based on Gesture Recognition Algorithm.* DOI: 10.1109/EEBDA60612.2024.10485976

Cheung, R., & Vogel, D. (2013). Predicting user acceptance of collaborative technologies: An extension of the technology acceptance model for e-learning. *Computers and Education/Computers & Education, 63*, 160–175. DOI: 10.1016/j.compedu.2012.12.003

Choi, H., & Kang, H. (2020). The study on the development of artificial intelligence education program for design students. *International Journal of Technology and Design Education*, 30(6), 1085–1101. DOI: 10.1007/s10798-019-09554-y

Choi, W. (2020). A study on the intelligent disaster management system based on artificial intelligence. *Journal of the Korean Society of Hazard Mitigation*, 20(1), 127–140. DOI: 10.9798/KOSHAM.2020.20.1.127

Chonyy. (2022). Apriori — Association Rule Mining In-depth Explanation and Python Implementation Towards Data Science, https://towardsdatascience.com /apriori-association-rule-mining -explanation-and-python-implementation-290b42afdfc6

Collado, J. A., Mora, P. S., & Parham, E. (2024). A guerrilla usability lab with free software | Interactions. In *Interactions*. https://dl.acm.org/doi/abs/10.1145/2451856 .2451871

Conati, C., Aleven, V., Guzman, E., & Cen, H. (2020). Predicting student mindtracing behaviour to help teach skills better. In *International Conference on Artificial Intelligence in Education* (pp. 144-155). Springer. DOI: 10.1007/978-3-030-52237-7_12

Cornide-Reyes, H., Duran, C., Baltierra, S., Silva-Aravena, F., & Morales, J. (2024a). Improving UX in Digital Transformation Projects Through Lean Principles. *Lecture Notes in Computer Science*, 14703, 161–178. DOI: 10.1007/978-3-031-61281-7_11

Crichton, G., Perera, S., Fleming, D., Acharya, P., Tahmuras, V., Church, L., & Dengel, A. (2018). AI-assisted privacy note coding at scale: Methodology and challenges. *Journal of the American Medical Informatics Association : JAMIA*, 25(10), 1339–1351. DOI: 10.1093/jamia/ocy124 PMID: 30010902

Cross, R., & Prusak, L. (2002). The people who make organizations go - or stop. *Harvard Business Review*, 80(6), 104–112. DOI: 10.20529/IJME.2018.041002 PMID: 12048992

Dahlbäck, N., Jönsson, A., & Ahrenberg, L. (1993). Wizard of Oz studies: Why and how. *Knowledge-Based Systems*, 6(4), 258–266. DOI: 10.1016/0950-7051(93)90017-N

Damaševičius, R., Bacanin, N., & Misra, S. (2023). From sensors to safety: Internet of Emergency Services (IoES) for emergency response and disaster management. *Journal of Sensor and Actuator Networks*, 12(3), 41. DOI: 10.3390/jsan12030041

Das, P., Ramapraba, P., Seethalakshmi, K., Mary, M. A., Karthick, S., & Sampath, B. (2024). Sustainable Advanced Techniques for Enhancing the Image Process. In *Fostering Cross-Industry Sustainability With Intelligent Technologies* (pp. 350–374). IGI Global. DOI: 10.4018/979-8-3693-1638-2.ch022

Davidson, J., Liebald, B., Liu, J., Nandy, P., Van Vleet, T., Gargi, U., & Sampath, D. (2010). The YouTube Video Recommendation System. *Proceedings of the Fourth ACM Conference on Recommender Systems,* 293-296. DOI: 10.1145/1864708.1864770

Davis, Z., Nesbitt, L., Guhn, M., & van den Bosch, M. (2023). Assessing changes in urban vegetation using Normalised Difference Vegetation Index (NDVI) for epidemiological studies. *Urban Forestry & Urban Greening*, 88, 128080. DOI: 10.1016/j.ufug.2023.128080

de Carvalho, L. F. D., Amado, T. J. C., Sobrinho, J. C., de Paula Amaral, L., Pott, L. P., Piccin, M., & Pedron, V. F. (2020). Nutritional status of corn plants estimated through different vegetation indices in the growth stages. *Revista Engenharia Na Agricultura-REVENG, 28*(Contínua), 255–264.

De Jong, T., Linn, M. C., & Zacharia, Z. C. (2013). Physical and virtual laboratories in science and engineering education. *Science*, 340(6130), 305–308. DOI: 10.1126/science.1230579 PMID: 23599479

Desmet, P., & Hekkert, P. (2007). Framework of product experience. *International Journal of Design*, 1(1), 57–66.

Devlin, J. (2019). BERT: Pre-training of Deep Bidirectional Transformers. *Language Processing Journal*, 40(3), 287–296.

Devlin, J., Chang, M.-W., Lee, K., & Toutanova, K. (2019). *BERT: Pre-training of deep bidirectional transformers for language understanding. Journal of Language Processing, 40(3), 287-296.*

Diakopoulos, N. (2016). Accountability in algorithmic decision making. *Communications of the ACM*, 59(2), 56–62. DOI: 10.1145/2844110

Diaz de Carvalho, L. F., Carneiro Amado, T. J., Cardoso Sobrinho, J., de Paula Amaral, L., Pierre Pott, L., Piccin, M., & Freitas Pedron, V. (2020). Nutritional status of corn plants estimated through different vegetation indices in the growth stages. *Engenharia na Agricultura*, 28(1), 255–264. DOI: 10.13083/reveng.v28i.8564

Diplom-Ingenieur, Yilmaz, C., & Hanbury, A. (2022). *Merging the Gap Between Automated and Human Centered Usability Testing DIPLOMARBEIT zur Erlangung des akademischen Grades Software Engineering & Internet Computing*. https://web.archive.org/web/20221004124754id_/https://repositum.tuwien.at/bitstream/20.500.12708/81158/1/Yilmaz Can OEzguer - 2022 - Merging the Gap Between Automated and Human Centered...pdf

Diro, A. A., & Chilamkurti, N. (2018). Distributed attack detection scheme using deep learning approach for Internet of Things. *Future Generation Computer Systems*, 82, 761–768. DOI: 10.1016/j.future.2017.08.043

Dobashi, K., Ho, C. P., Fulford, C. P., & Lin, M.-F. G. (2019). *A Heat Map Generation to Visualize Engagement in Classes Using Moodle Learning Logs*. DOI: 10.1109/INCIT.2019.8912068

Domingos, P. (2015). *The Master Algorithm: How the Quest for the Ultimate Learning Machine Will Remake Our World*. Basic Books.

Donovan, G. H., Gatziolis, D., Derrien, M., Michael, Y. L., Prestemon, J. P., & Douwes, J. (2022). Shortcomings of the normalized difference vegetation index as an exposure metric. *Nature Plants*, 8(6), 617–622. DOI: 10.1038/s41477-022-01170-6 PMID: 35697731

Dove, G. (2019). Reframing design at the intersection of UX and AI. In *Proceedings of the 2019 CHI Conference on Human Factors in Computing Systems* (pp. 1-6). DOI: 10.1145/3290607.3312782

Dove, G., Halskov, K., Forlizzi, J., & Zimmerman, J. (2017, May). UX design innovation: Challenges for working with machine learning as a design material. In *Proceedings of the 2017 chi conference on human factors in computing systems*(pp. 278-288). DOI: 10.1145/3025453.3025739

Drissi, S., & Amirat, A. (2016). An adaptive e-learning system based on student's learning styles: An empirical study. *International Journal of Distance Education Technologies*, 14(3), 34–51. DOI: 10.4018/IJDET.2016070103

Dzikovska, M. O.SemEval-2013 task 7: The joint student response analysis and 8th recognizing textual entailment challenge. *Proc. 2nd Joint Conf. Lexical Comput. Semantics*, 2, 263–274.

Eisfelder, C., Asam, S., Hirner, A., Reiners, P., Holzwarth, S., Bachmann, M., Gessner, U., Dietz, A., Huth, J., Bachofer, F., & Kuenzer, C. (2023). Seasonal Vegetation Trends for Europe over 30 Years from a Novel Normalised Difference Vegetation Index (NDVI) Time-Series—The TIMELINE NDVI Product. *Remote Sensing (Basel)*, 15(14), 3616. DOI: 10.3390/rs15143616

ELKarazle, K., Raman, V., & Then, P. (2022). Facial age estimation using machine learning techniques: An overview. *Big Data and Cognitive Computing*, 6(4), 128. DOI: 10.3390/bdcc6040128

Engberg, T. (2024). Optimizing Developer Experience: Component Playground Integration in Software Development. In *DIVA*. https://www.diva-portal.org/smash/record.jsf?pid=diva2%3A1864501&dswid=-6087

Ericsson, K. A., & Simon, H. A. (1993). *Protocol Analysis: Verbal Reports as Data*. MIT Press. DOI: 10.7551/mitpress/5657.001.0001

Evans, P. (2014). Exploring the relationship between discourse and a practice perspective on HRD in a virtual environment. *Human Resource Development International*, 17(2), 183–202. DOI: 10.1080/13678868.2014.886889

Fahim, K. E., Kalinaki, K., & Shafik, W. (2024). Electronic Devices in the Artificial Intelligence of the Internet of Medical Things (AIoMT). In *Handbook of Security and Privacy of AI-Enabled Healthcare Systems and Internet of Medical Things* (pp. 41–62). CRC Press.

Familoni, N. B. T., & Babatunde, O. (2024). User experience (UX) design in medical products: theoretical foundations and development best practices. *Engineering Science & Tecnology Journal*, 5(3), 1125–1148. DOI: 10.51594/estj.v5i3.975

Fan, C., Zhang, C., Yahja, A., & Mostafavi, A. (2021). Disaster City Digital Twin: A vision for integrating artificial and human intelligence for disaster management. *International Journal of Information Management*, 56, 102049. DOI: 10.1016/j.ijinfomgt.2019.102049

Fernandez-Viña, R., López-Moreno, A., & Gómez-Pulido, J. A. (2021). An AI-based approach to automated image description for visually impaired people. *Sensors (Basel)*, 21(14), 4679. DOI: 10.3390/s21144679 PMID: 34300418

Fleury, S., & Chaniaud, N. (2024). Multi-user centered design: Acceptance, user experience, user research and user testing. *Theoretical Issues in Ergonomics Science*, 25(2), 209–224. Advance online publication. DOI: 10.1080/1463922X.2023.2166623

Foo, H. Y., & Turner, J. J. (2019). Entrepreneurial learning'-the role of university led business incubators and mentors in equipping graduates with the necessary skills set for Industry 4.0. *International Journal of Education. Psychology and Counseling*, 4(30), 283–298.

Fornell, C., Johnson, M. D., Anderson, E. W., Cha, J., & Bryant, B. E. (1996). The American Customer Satisfaction Index: Nature, purpose, and findings. *Journal of Marketing*, 60(4), 7–18. DOI: 10.1177/002224299606000403

Front, A., & Rahmani, M. D. (2019). A context-aware recommendation-based system for service, composition in smart environments. *Service Oriented Computing and Applications*, 341–355.

Fu, Y., Guo, G., & Huang, T. S. (2010). Age synthesis and estimation via faces: A survey. *IEEE Transactions on Pattern Analysis and Machine Intelligence*, 32(11), 1955–1976. DOI: 10.1109/TPAMI.2010.36 PMID: 20847387

Gan, Q., Liu, Z., Liu, T., Zhao, Y., & Chai, Y. (2023). Design and user experience analysis of AR intelligent virtual agents on smartphones. *Cognitive Systems Research*, 78, 33–47. DOI: 10.1016/j.cogsys.2022.11.007

García Cárdenas, D. A., Ramón Valencia, J. A., Alzate Velásquez, D. F., & Palacios Gonzalez, J. R. (2018). Dynamics of the indices NDVI and GNDVI in a rice growing in its reproduction phase from multi-spectral aerial images taken by drones. *International Conference of ICT for Adapting Agriculture to Climate Change*, 106–119.

Garcia-Garcia, D., la Rosa, X. R., Bedoya, D. G., & Schrevens, E. (2021). Linear mixed model analysis of NDVI-based canopy coverage, extracted from sequential UAV multispectral imagery of an open field tomato irrigation experiment. *Computers and Electronics in Agriculture*, 189, 106399. DOI: 10.1016/j.compag.2021.106399

Garriga, M., Flores, A., Cechich, A., & Zunino, A. (2015). Web service composition mechanisms: A review. *IETE Technical Review*, 32(5), 1–8. DOI: 10.1080/02564602.2015.1019942

Ghubaish, A., Salman, T., Zolanvari, M., Unal, D., Al-Ali, A., & Jain, R. (2020). Recent advances in the internet-of-medical-things (IoMT) systems security. *IEEE Internet of Things Journal*, 8(11), 8707–8718. DOI: 10.1109/JIOT.2020.3045653

Gideon, N., Adewunmi, N. A., Jacks, S., & Ajala, A. (2024). Conceptualizing communication efficiency in energy sector project management: The role of digital tools and agile practices. *Engineering Science & Tecnology Journal*, 5(4), 1487–1501. DOI: 10.51594/estj.v5i4.1078

Gift, M. D. M., Senthil, T. S., Hasan, D. S., Alagarraja, K., Jayaseelan, P., & Boopathi, S. (2024). Additive Manufacturing and 3D Printing Innovations: Revolutionizing Industry 5.0. In *Technological Advancements in Data Processing for Next Generation Intelligent Systems* (pp. 255–287). IGI Global. DOI: 10.4018/979-8-3693-0968-1.ch010

Glady, J. B. P., D'Souza, S. M., Priya, A. P., Amuthachenthiru, K., Vikram, G., & Boopathi, S. (2024). A Study on AI-ML-Driven Optimizing Energy Distribution and Sustainable Agriculture for Environmental Conservation. In *Harnessing High-Performance Computing and AI for Environmental Sustainability* (pp. 1–27). IGI Global., DOI: 10.4018/979-8-3693-1794-5.ch001

Gleeson & Pahl. (2008). Service-based Grid Architectures to support the Virtualization of Learning Technology Systems.

Gomathi, S., Rajeswari, A., & Kadry, S. (2023). Emerging HR practices—Digital upskilling: A strategic way of talent management and engagement. In *Disruptive artificial intelligence and sustainable human resource management* (pp. 51–63). River Publishers. DOI: 10.1201/9781032622743-4

Gomez-Uribe, C. A., & Hunt, N. (2016). The Netflix recommender system: Algorithms, business value, and innovation. *ACM Transactions on Management Information Systems*, 6(4), 1–19. DOI: 10.1145/2843948

Google. (2022). Flutter: Build apps for any screen. https://flutter.dev/

Gopal, M., Lurdhumary, J., Bathrinath, S., Priya, A. P., Sarojwal, A., & Boopathi, S. (2024). Energy Harvesting and Smart Highways for Sustainable Transportation Infrastructure: Revolutionizing Roads Using Nanotechnology. In *Principles and Applications in Speed Sensing and Energy Harvesting for Smart Roads* (pp. 136–165). IGI Global. DOI: 10.4018/978-1-6684-9214-7.ch005

Gowri, N. V., Dwivedi, J. N., Krishnaveni, K., Boopathi, S., Palaniappan, M., & Medikondu, N. R. (2023). Experimental investigation and multi-objective optimization of eco-friendly near-dry electrical discharge machining of shape memory alloy using Cu/SiC/Gr composite electrode. *Environmental Science and Pollution Research International*, 30(49), 1–19. DOI: 10.1007/s11356-023-26983-6 PMID: 37126160

Guerrero-Ulloa, G., Rodríguez-Domínguez, C., & Hornos, M. J. (2023). Agile Methodologies Applied to the Development of Internet of Things (IoT)-Based Systems: A Review. *Sensors (Basel)*, 23(2), 790. DOI: 10.3390/s23020790 PMID: 36679594

Guha, S., Govil, H., & Diwan, P. (2019). Analytical study of seasonal variability in land surface temperature with normalized difference vegetation index, normalized difference water index, normalized difference built-up index, and normalized multiband drought index. *Journal of Applied Remote Sensing*, 13(2), 024518–024518.

Hackett, S., & Parmanto, B. (2005). A longitudinal evaluation of accessibility: Higher education websites. *Internet Research*, 15(3), 281–294. DOI: 10.1108/10662240510602690

Hackos, J. T., & Redish, J. C. (1998). *User and Task Analysis for Interface Design*. Wiley.

Haerani, H., Apan, A., & Basnet, B. (2018). Mapping of peanut crops in Queensland, Australia, using time-series PROBA-V 100-m normalized difference vegetation index imagery. *Journal of Applied Remote Sensing*, 12(3), 036005–036005. DOI: 10.1117/1.JRS.12.036005

Haghi, M., Thurow, K., & Stoll, R. (2017). Wearable devices in medical internet of things: Scientific research and commercially available devices. *Healthcare Informatics Research*, 23(1), 4–15. DOI: 10.4258/hir.2017.23.1.4 PMID: 28261526

Hailpern, J., Liu, Y., Moore, D., Marques, D., & Gaspar, J. (2021). AI-enabled conversational agents for improved user experience. In *Human-Computer Interaction. Design Practice in Contemporary Societies* (pp. 555–566). Springer. DOI: 10.1007/978-3-030-77752-2_38

Han, H., Otto, C., & Jain, A. K. (2013). Age estimation from face images: Human vs. Machine performance. *2013 International Conference on Biometrics (ICB)*, 1–8. DOI: 10.1109/ICB.2013.6613022

Hanumanthakari, S., Gift, M. M., Kanimozhi, K., Bhavani, M. D., Bamane, K. D., & Boopathi, S. (2023). Biomining Method to Extract Metal Components Using Computer-Printed Circuit Board E-Waste. In *Handbook of Research on Safe Disposal Methods of Municipal Solid Wastes for a Sustainable Environment* (pp. 123–141). IGI Global. DOI: 10.4018/978-1-6684-8117-2.ch010

Harte, R., Glynn, L., Rodríguez-Molinero, A., Baker, P. M. A., Scharf, T., Quinlan, L. R., & ÓLaighin, G. (2017). A Human-Centered Design Methodology to Enhance the Usability, Human Factors, and User Experience of Connected Health Systems: A Three-Phase Methodology. *JMIR Human Factors*, 4(1), e8–e8. DOI: 10.2196/humanfactors.5443 PMID: 28302594

Hartson, R., & Pyla, P. S. (2012). *The UX Book: Process and guidelines for ensuring a quality user experience*. Elsevier.

Hartson, R., & Pyla, P. S. (2012). *The UX Book: Process and Guidelines for Ensuring a Quality User Experience*. Morgan Kaufmann.

Hartson, R., & Pyla, P. S. (2018). *The UX book: Agile UX design for a quality user experience*. Morgan Kaufmann.

Hassenzahl, M., & Tractinsky, N. (2006). User experience - a research agenda. *Behaviour & Information Technology*, 25(2), 91–97. DOI: 10.1080/01449290500330331

Hattie, J. (2009). *Visible Learning: A Synthesis of Over 800 Meta-Analyses Relating to Achievement*. Routledge.

Hed Zetterström, M., & Johansson, I. (2024). *Operationalizing UX Practices : Embedding Accessibility into Agile B2B Software Development*. https://www.diva-portal.org/smash/record.jsf?pid=diva2%3A1875940&dswid=7869

Heilman, M., & Madnani, N. (2013). ETS: Domain adaptation and stacking for short answer scoring. *Proc. Joint Conf. Lexical Comput. Semantics*, 2, 275–279.

Henry, S. L., Abou-Zahra, S., & Brewer, J. (2014). *The role of accessibility in a universal web. Journal of Inclusive Design in the* Built *Environment, 1(1), 5-20.*

Herendy, C. (2020). Using Traditional Research Methods in Contemporary UX Surveying. *Lecture Notes in Computer Science*, 12423, 123–132. DOI: 10.1007/978-3-030-60114-0_8

Hinderks, A., José, F., Escalona, M. J., & Thomaschewski, J. (2024). Requirements for User Experience Management - A Tertiary Study. *Unir.Net*. https://doi.org/DOI: 1989-1660

Hoogervorst, J. A., Koopman, P. L., & van der Flier, H. (2002). Human resource strategy for the new ICT-driven business context. *International Journal of Human Resource Management*, 13(8), 1245–1265. DOI: 10.1080/09585190210149501

Hoy, M. B. (2018). Alexa, Siri, Cortana, and More: An Introduction to Voice Assistants. *Medical Reference Services Quarterly*, 37(1), 81–88. DOI: 10.1080/02763869.2018.1404391 PMID: 29327988

Hsi, S., Ma, J., Allen, A., Sikes, K., & Alexander, M. (2007). From "Guerrilla" Methods to Structured Evaluations: Examples of Formative Web Design from the Exploratorium's Evidence and Mind Projects. In *Museums & Web*. https://citeseerx.ist.psu.edu/document?repid=rep1&type=pdf&doi=ad8e5a9e1d047952f820633e558b2aee5cbad6a8

Hssina, B. (2014). Web services at the service of e-learning platforms. *International Journal of Innovation and Applied Studies*, 7(4), 1574–1581. https://west-wind.com/presentations/creatingandconsumingfoxprowebserviceswithdotnet.pdf

Huang, X., Zou, D., Cheng, G., & Xie, H. (2021). A systematic review of AR and VR enhanced language learning. *Sustainability (Basel)*, 13(9), 4639. DOI: 10.3390/su13094639

Huerta, I., Fernández, C., Segura, C., Hernando, J., & Prati, A. (2015). A deep analysis on age estimation. *Pattern Recognition Letters*, 68, 239–249. DOI: 10.1016/j.patrec.2015.06.006

Hussain, Z., Babe, M., Saravanan, S., Srimathy, G., Roopa, H., & Boopathi, S. (2023). Optimizing Biomass-to-Biofuel Conversion: IoT and AI Integration for Enhanced Efficiency and Sustainability. In *Circular Economy Implementation for Sustainability in the Built Environment* (pp. 191–214). IGI Global.

Huynh, K., Benarivo, J., Da Xuan, C., Sharma, G. G., Kang, J., Madugalla, A., & Grundy, J. (2021). *Improving Human-Centric Software Defect Evaluation*. Reporting, and Fixing. DOI: 10.1109/COMPSAC51774.2021.00064

Hu, Z., Wen, Y., Wang, J., Wang, M., Hong, R., & Yan, S. (2016). Facial age estimation with age difference. *IEEE Transactions on Image Processing*, 26(7), 3087–3097. DOI: 10.1109/TIP.2016.2633868 PMID: 27913345

IBM. (2021). Watson Studio: Accelerate AI deployment and increase operational trust. https://www.ibm.com/cloud/watson-studio

IBM. (2022). AI for API integration and modernization. https://www.ibm.com/cloud/api-integration-modernization

Isomursu, M., Sirotkin, A., Voltti, P., & Halonen, M. (2012). *User Experience Design Goes Agile in Lean Transformation -- A Case Study*. DOI: 10.1109/Agile.2012.10

Ivić, M. (2019). Artificial intelligence and geospatial analysis in disaster management. *The International Archives of the Photogrammetry, Remote Sensing and Spatial Information Sciences*, 42(W8), 161–166. DOI: 10.5194/isprs-archives-XLII-3-W8-161-2019

Jacob, R. J., & Karn, K. S. (2003). *Eye tracking in human-computer interaction and usability research: Ready to deliver the promises. In J. Hyona, R. Radach, & H. Deubel (Eds.), The Mind's Eye: Cognitive and Applied Aspects of Eye Movement Research (pp. 573-605). Elsevier Science.*

Jacobson, A., & Sandin, F. (2019). Personalized music recommendations at Spotify. *Communications of the ACM*, 62(11), 75–80. DOI: 10.1145/3358492

Janardhana, K., Singh, V., Singh, S. N., Babu, T. R., Bano, S., & Boopathi, S. (2023). Utilization Process for Electronic Waste in Eco-Friendly Concrete: Experimental Study. In *Sustainable Approaches and Strategies for E-Waste Management and Utilization* (pp. 204–223). IGI Global.

Jeong, D. H., Jeong, B. K., & Ji, S. Y. (2024). *Understanding Semantic User Interactions in Visualization*. DOI: 10.20944/preprints202404.2019.v1

Jiang, D., Zhang, C., Cui, L., & Chuah, M. C. (2022). Privacy-preserving machine learning: Threats, models, and techniques. *IEEE Internet of Things Journal*, 9(20), 19668–19687. DOI: 10.1109/JIOT.2022.3164936

Jobin, A., Ienca, M., & Vayena, E. (2019). The global landscape of AI ethics guidelines. *Nature Machine Intelligence*, 1(9), 389–399. DOI: 10.1038/s42256-019-0088-2

Jorge-Botana, G., Luzon, J. M., Gomez-Veiga, I., & Cordero, M. (2015). Automated LSA assessment of summaries in distance education: Some variables to be considered. *Journal of Educational Computing Research*, 52(3), 341–364. DOI: 10.1177/0735633115571930

Kakhi, K., Alizadehsani, R., Kabir, H. D., Khosravi, A., Nahavandi, S., & Acharya, U. R. (2022a). The internet of medical things and artificial intelligence: Trends, challenges, and opportunities. *Biocybernetics and Biomedical Engineering*, 42(3), 749–771. DOI: 10.1016/j.bbe.2022.05.008

Kale, S. (2020). The rise of augmented reality (AR) and virtual reality (VR) technologies in the era of AI. *International Journal of Innovation and Applied Studies*, 30(3), 705–710.

Kankanamge, N., Yigitcanlar, T., & Goonetilleke, A. (2021). Public perceptions on artificial intelligence driven disaster management: Evidence from Sydney, Melbourne and Brisbane. *Telematics and Informatics*, 65, 101729. DOI: 10.1016/j.tele.2021.101729

Kantamneni, S. (2022). *User Experience Design: A Practical Playbook to Fuel Business Growth.* John Wiley & Sons.

Kaptein, M., Markopoulos, P., de Ruyter, B., & Aarts, E. (2015). Personalizing persuasive technologies: Explicit and implicit personalization using persuasion profiles. *International Journal of Human-Computer Studies*, 77, 38–51. DOI: 10.1016/j.ijhcs.2015.01.004

Katsaris, I., & Vidakis, N. (2021). Adaptive e-learning systems through learning styles: A review of the literature. *Adv. Mobile Learn. Educ. Res.*, 1(2), 124–145. DOI: 10.25082/AMLER.2021.02.007

Kavita, K., & Chhillar, R. S. (2022). Human face recognition and age estimation with machine learning: A critical review and future perspective. *International Journal of Electrical and Computer Engineering Systems*, 13(10), 945–952. DOI: 10.32985/ijeces.13.10.9

Keating, G., Guest, D., Konertz, A., Padovani, N., & Villa, A. (2011). Designing the AR experience: Tools and tips for mobile augmented reality UX design. In Design, User Experience, and Usability. Theory, Methods, Tools and Practice: First International Conference, DUXU 2011, Held as Part of HCI International 2011, Orlando, FL, USA, July 9-14, 2011 *Proceedings*, 1(Part II), 135–141.

Kelly, B., Sloan, D., Phipps, L., Petrie, H., & Hamilton, F. (2005). *Forcing Standardization or Accommodating Diversity? A Framework for Applying the WCAG in the Real World. Proceedings of the 2005 International Cross-Disciplinary Workshop on Web Accessibility (W4A), 46-54.*

Khare, R., Chinnasamy, A., Shashibhushan, G., Suresh Kumar, P., Hemalatha, R., & Boopathi, S. (2024). Energy Cascade Conversion System and Energy-Efficient Infrastructure: Experimentation, Results, Discussion, and Case Studies. In *Advances in Environmental Engineering and Green Technologies* (pp. 115–139). IGI Global. DOI: 10.4018/979-8-3693-0492-1.ch006

Khodeir, N. (2021, April). Bi-GRU urgent classification for MOOC discussion forums based on BERT. *IEEE Access : Practical Innovations, Open Solutions*, 9(1), 58243–58255. DOI: 10.1109/ACCESS.2021.3072734

Klebbe, R., Steinert, A., & Müller-Werdan, U. (2019). Wearables for older adults: requirements, design, and user experience. Perspectives on Wearable Enhanced Learning (WELL) Current Trends, Research, and Practice, 313-332.

Klemmer, S. R., Hartmann, B., & Takayama, L. (2006). How Bodies Matter: Five Themes for Interaction Design. *Proceedings of the 6th Conference on Designing Interactive Systems (DIS),* 140-149. DOI: 10.1145/1142405.1142429

Kobialka, P., Tarifa, S. L. T., Bergersen, G. R., & Johnsen, E. B. (2024). User journey games: Automating user-centric analysis. *Software & Systems Modeling*, 23(3), 605–624. Advance online publication. DOI: 10.1007/s10270-024-01148-2

Kohavi, R., Longbotham, R., Sommerfield, D., & Henne, R. M. (2009). Controlled experiments on the web: Survey and practical guide. *Data Mining and Knowledge Discovery*, 18(1), 140–181. DOI: 10.1007/s10618-008-0114-1

Kolko, J. (2012). Wicked Problems: Problems Worth Solving. *Interactions (New York, N.Y.)*, 19(5), 28–34.

Koloszár, L., Bednárik, É., Erdős, F., Thinakaran, R., & Takáts, A. (2024). User experience testing methods: Conclusions from the literature. *Edelweiss Applied Science and Technology*, 8(5), 1400–1412. DOI: 10.55214/25768484.v8i5.1843

Konidena, B. K., Malaiyappan, J. N. A., & Tadimarri, A. (2024). Ethical Considerations in the Development and Deployment of AI Systems. *European Journal of Technology*, 8(2), 41–53. DOI: 10.47672/ejt.1890

Koponen, T. (2018). Weighing Ultralight, User interface evaluation of a mobile photo editing application. In *Aalto.fi*. https://aaltodoc.aalto.fi/items/00842ee0-1a76-4081-bd1e-e541f9dd8c2e

Koruga, P., Ševa, J., & Bača, M. (2011). A Review of Face Recognition Algorithms and Their Application in Age Estimation. *Proceedings of the 22nd Central European Conference on Information and Intelligent Systems.*

Koshariya, A. K., Khatoon, S., Marathe, A. M., Suba, G. M., Baral, D., & Boopathi, S. (2023). Agricultural Waste Management Systems Using Artificial Intelligence Techniques. In *AI-Enabled Social Robotics in Human Care Services* (pp. 236–258). IGI Global. DOI: 10.4018/978-1-6684-8171-4.ch009

Kous, D., Ma, X., Zangerle, E., & Gennari, R. (2020). Assistive technologies for enhancing accessibility and inclusion: A position paper from the AAATE Accessibility and Active Aging Working Group. *Disability and Rehabilitation. Assistive Technology*, 15(5), 521–527. DOI: 10.1080/17483107.2020.1752606 PMID: 30985225

Krug, S. (2014). *Don't Make Me Think, Revisited: A Common Sense Approach to Web Usability* (3rd ed.). New Riders.

Kujala, S., Roto, V., Väänänen-Vainio-Mattila, K., Karapanos, E., & Sinnelä, A. (2011). UX Curve: A method for evaluating long-term user experience. *Interacting with Computers*, 23(5), 473–483. DOI: 10.1016/j.intcom.2011.06.005

Kumar, P. (2021). Low-Resource Settings in AI-Driven Education. *Educational Data Science*, 28(3), 89–101.

Kumar, S., Chakrabarti, S., & Roy, S. (2017). Earth movers distance pooling over Siamese LSTMs for automatic short answer grading. *Proc. Int. Joint Conf. Artif. Intell.*, 2046–2052.

Kuniavsky, M. (2010). *Smart things: ubiquitous computing user experience design.* Elsevier.

Kusuma, W. A., Jantan, A. H., Admodisastro, N. I., & Norowi, N. (2024). Elevated Novice Developer Productivity and Self-efficacy by Promoting UX Journey in Software Requirement Elicitation. *JOIV : International Journal on Informatics Visualization*, 8(1), 401. Advance online publication. DOI: 10.62527/joiv.8.1.2171

Laurillard, D. (2012). *Teaching as a Design Science: Building Pedagogical Patterns for Learning and Technology*. Routledge.

Law, E. L. C., Van Schaik, P., & Roto, V. (2014). Attitudes towards user experience (UX) measurement. *International Journal of Human-Computer Studies*, 72(6), 526–541. DOI: 10.1016/j.ijhcs.2013.09.006

Law, E. L.-C., & Van Schaik, P. (2010). Modelling user experience–An agenda for research and practice. *Interacting with Computers*, 22(5), 313–322. DOI: 10.1016/j.intcom.2010.04.006

Lazar, J., Goldstein, D. F., & Taylor, A. (2015). *Ensuring Digital Accessibility through Process and Policy.* Morgan Kaufmann.

Lazar, J., Feng, J. H., & Hochheiser, H. (2017). *Research methods in human-computer interaction.* Morgan Kaufmann.

Lécué, F., & Léger, A. (2006). A Formal Model for Semantic Web Service Composition. In Lecture Notes in Computer Science: Vol. 4273. *The Semantic Web - ISWC* (pp. 385–398). Springer.

Lécué, F., Lind, L., Burns, C., Zysset, P., Mashburn, E., & Mironov, D. (2022). Explainable and transparent AI: A holistic approach. Explainable AI: Interpreting. *Explaining and Visualizing Deep Learning*, 11, 1–18. DOI: 10.1007/978-3-031-04083-2_1

Lee, M.-F. R., & Chien, T.-W. (2020). Artificial intelligence and Internet of Things for robotic disaster response. *2020 International Conference on Advanced Robotics and Intelligent Systems (ARIS)*, 1–6. DOI: 10.1109/ARIS50834.2020.9205794

Lee, S. (2023). Optimizing AI Models for Efficiency. *Computers & Education*, 15(4), 233–245.

Lei, H., Lai, W., Feaster, W., & Chang, A. C. (2024). Artificial intelligence and agile project management. *Elsevier EBooks*, 401–405, 401–405. Advance online publication. DOI: 10.1016/B978-0-323-90534-3.00016-0

Lemon, K. N., & Verhoef, P. C. (2016). Understanding customer experience throughout the customer journey. *Journal of Marketing*, 80(6), 69–96. DOI: 10.1509/jm.15.0420

Leon, C., & Anna, F. (2020). Investigating transformers for automatic short answer grading. *Proc. Int. Conf. Artif. Intell. Educ.*, 43–48.

Leong, V., Raheel, K., Sim, J. Y., Kacker, K., Karlaftis, V. M., Vassiliu, C., Kalaivanan, K., Chen, A., Robbins, T. W., Sahakian, B. J., & Kourtzi, Z. (2022). A New Remote Guided Method for Supervised Web-Based Cognitive Testing to Ensure High-Quality Data: Development and Usability Study. *JMIR. Journal of Medical Internet Research. Journal of Medical Internet Research*, 24(1), e28368–e28368. DOI: 10.2196/28368 PMID: 34989691

Lermen, F. H., de Moura, P. K., Bertoni, V. B., Graciano, P., & Tortorella, G. L. (2023). Does maturity level influence the use of Agile UX methods by digital startups? Evaluating design thinking, lean startup, and lean user experience. *Information and Software Technology*, 154, 107107. DOI: 10.1016/j.infsof.2022.107107

Levin, M. (2014). *Designing multi-device experiences: An ecosystem approach to user experiences across devices*. O'Reilly Media, Inc.

Lewin, C. (2022). Building a culture of continuous learning for user experience professionals. *Interaction*, 29(1), 36–40. DOI: 10.1145/3505837

Li, X., Xu, B., Teng, Y., Ren, Y. T., & Hu, Z. M. (2014, August). Comparative research of AR and VR technology based on user experience. In 2014 International Conference on Management Science & Engineering 21th Annual Conference Proceedings (pp. 1820-1827). IEEE. DOI: 10.1109/ICMSE.2014.6930456

Liao, W. X., Zeng, B., Yin, X. W., & Wei, P. F. (2021). An improved aspect category sentiment analysis model for text sentiment analysis based on RoBERTa. *Applied Intelligence*, 51(6), 3522–3533. DOI: 10.1007/s10489-020-01964-1

Lima Albuquerque Maranhão, R. (2023). *Assessing Normalized Difference Vegetation Index (NDVI) data to estimate winter wheat yields and analyze winter wheat by homogeneous subregions at field scale in Kansas* [PhD Thesis].

Lind, G., & Mishchenko, M. (2024). Not So Agile. *Apress EBooks*, 155–172. DOI: 10.1007/979-8-8688-0187-7_10

Liu, B. (2020). *Sentiment analysis: Mining opinions, sentiments, and emotions*. Cambridge University Press. DOI: 10.1017/9781108639286

Liu, T., Ding, W., Wang, Z., Tang, J., Huang, G., & Liu, Z. (2019). Automatic short answer grading via multiway attention networks. *Proc. Int. Conf. Artif. Intell. Educ.*, 169–173. DOI: 10.1007/978-3-030-23207-8_32

Liu, Y.RoBERTa: A robustly optimized BERT pretraining approach. arXiv:1907.11692v1.

Li, Z., & Guo, H. (2021). Artificial intelligence and internet of things towards intelligent manufacturing: A review. *IEEE Access : Practical Innovations, Open Solutions*, 9, 45796–45814. DOI: 10.1109/ACCESS.2021.3066883

Löfblom, J. (2017). Defining user experience principles for developing health and fitness wearables and smartwatches.

Luger, E., & Sellen, A. (2016). *"Like Having a Really Bad PA": The Gulf Between User Expectation and Experience of Conversational Agents. Proceedings of the 2016 CHI Conference on Human Factors in Computing Systems (CHI), 5286-5297.*

Lund, A. (2011). *User experience management: Essential skills for leading effective UX teams*. Elsevier.

MacDonald, C. M. (2019). User experience (UX) capacity-building: A conceptual model and research agenda. *Proceedings of the 2019 on Designing Interactive Systems Conference*, 187–200. DOI: 10.1145/3322276.3322346

Magistretti, S., & Trabucchi, D. (2024). Agile-as-a-tool and agile-as-a-culture: A comprehensive review of agile approaches adopting contingency and configuration theories. *Review of Managerial Science*. Advance online publication. DOI: 10.1007/s11846-024-00745-1

Maheswari, B. U., Imambi, S. S., Hasan, D., Meenakshi, S., Pratheep, V., & Boopathi, S. (2023). Internet of things and machine learning-integrated smart robotics. In *Global Perspectives on Robotics and Autonomous Systems: Development and Applications* (pp. 240–258). IGI Global. DOI: 10.4018/978-1-6684-7791-5.ch010

Malik, A., Budhwar, P., & Mohan, H., & NR, S. (. (2023). Employee experience–the missing link for engaging employees: Insights from an MNE's AI-based HR ecosystem. *Human Resource Management*, 62(1), 97–115. DOI: 10.1002/hrm.22133

Mankoff, J., Fait, H., & Tran, T. (2005). Is Your Web Page Accessible? A Comparative Study of Methods for Assessing Web Page Accessibility for the Blind. *Proceedings of the SIGCHI Conference on Human Factors in Computing Systems,* 41-50. DOI: 10.1145/1054972.1054979

Mannay, D., & Pauwels, L. (2024). The SAGE Handbook of Visual Research Methods. https://www.torrossa.com/en/resources/an/5018807#page=334

Maranhão, R. L. A. (2023). *Assessing Normalized Difference Vegetation Index (NDVI) Data to Estimate Winter Wheat Yields and Analyze Winter Wheat by Homogeneous Subregions at Field Scale in Kansas*. Kansas State University.

Maraveas, C., Loukatos, D., Bartzanas, T., & Arvanitis, K. G. (2021). Applications of artificial intelligence in fire safety of agricultural structures. *Applied Sciences (Basel, Switzerland)*, 11(16), 7716. DOI: 10.3390/app11167716

Martinelli, S., Lopes, L., & Zaina, L. (2024). UX Research practices related to Long-Term UX: A Systematic Literature Review. *Information and Software Technology*, 107431, 107431. Advance online publication. DOI: 10.1016/j.infsof.2024.107431

Marvaniya, S., Saha, S., Dhamecha, T. I., Flotz, P., Sindhgatta, R., & Sengupta, B. (2018). Creating scoring rubric from representative student answers for improved short answer grading. Proc. 27th ACM Int. Conf. Inf. Knowl. Manage., 993–1002. DOI: 10.1145/3269206.3271755

McInerney, J., & Smyth, B. (2020). Recommender Systems: A Deep Learning Perspective. *Journal of Artificial Intelligence Research*, 69, 1–53.

McKenna, A. F., Kellam, N. N., & Carroll, D. R. (2011). Assessing learning outcomes from the perspectives of designers. *International Journal of Engineering Education*, 27(3), 578–588.

McKinney, S. M. (2020). Predictive personalization: Predicting user traits from text for personalized systems. *Frontiers in Big Data*, 3, 9. DOI: 10.3389/fdata.2020.00009

Meckenstock, J.-N. (2024). Shedding Light on the Dark Side – A Systematic Literature Review of the Issues in Agile Software Development Methodology Use. *Journal of Systems and Software/˜The œJournal of Systems and Software, 211*, 111966. DOI: 10.1016/j.jss.2024.111966

Mehrabi, N., Morstatter, F., Saxena, N., Lerman, K., & Galstyan, A. (2021). A survey on bias and fairness in machine learning. *ACM Computing Surveys*, 54(6), 1–35. DOI: 10.1145/3457607

Meingast, M. (2016). *Agile and UX: The Road to Integration The Challenges of the UX Practitioner in an Agile Environment - Melissa Meingast, Timothy Ballew, Rochelle Edwards, Eric Nordquist, Christopher Sader, Danielle Smith, 2013*. https://journals.sagepub.com/doi/abs/10.1177/1541931213571224

Mircea, M. (2012). SOA adoption in higher education: A practical guide to service-oriented virtual learning environment. *Procedia: Social and Behavioral Sciences*, 31, 218–223. DOI: 10.1016/j.sbspro.2011.12.045

Mishra, P., & Singh, G. (2023). Internet of medical things healthcare for sustainable smart cities: Current status and future prospects. *Applied Sciences (Basel, Switzerland)*, 13(15), 8869. DOI: 10.3390/app13158869

Mohanraj, G., Krishna, K. S., Lakshmi, B. S., Vijayalakshmi, A., Pramila, P. V., & Boopathi, S. (2024). Optimizing Trust and Security in Healthcare 4.0: Human Factors in Lightweight Secured IoMT Ecosystems. In *Lightweight Digital Trust Architectures in the Internet of Medical Things (IoMT)* (pp. 52–72). IGI Global. DOI: 10.4018/979-8-3693-2109-6.ch004

Mohanty, A., Venkateswaran, N., Ranjit, P., Tripathi, M. A., & Boopathi, S. (2023). Innovative Strategy for Profitable Automobile Industries: Working Capital Management. In *Handbook of Research on Designing Sustainable Supply Chains to Achieve a Circular Economy* (pp. 412–428). IGI Global.

Mohler, M., Bunescu, R., & Mihalcea, R. (2011). Learning to grade short answer questions using semantic similarity measures and dependency graph alignments. Proc. Annu. Meeting Assoc. Comput. Linguistics, Hum. Lang. Technol., 752–762.

Moran, K., Viyovic, V., Bandara, C., Gordon, M., Nguyen, C. D., Hill, C., & Singer, J. (2021). Automating UI design migration to support web app evolution. *IEEE Transactions on Software Engineering*. Advance online publication. DOI: 10.1109/TSE.2021.3076790

Morley, J., Floridi, L., Kinsey, L., & Elhalal, A. (2021). From what to how: An initial review of publicly available AI ethics tools, methods and research to translate principles into practices. *Science and Engineering Ethics*, 27(2), 1–28. DOI: 10.1007/s11948-021-00300-8 PMID: 31828533

Movahednejad, H., Ibrahim, S. B., Sharifi, M., Selamat, H. B., Lashkari, A. H., & Sayed, G. H. T. (2014). Novel Security Conscious Evaluation Criteria for Web Service Composition. Research Journal of Applied Sciences, Engineering and Technology, 7(4), 673-695.

Moyse, E. (2014). Age estimation from faces and voices: A review. *Psychologica Belgica*, 54(3), 255–265. DOI: 10.5334/pb.aq

Muhammad, K., Ahmad, J., & Baik, S. W. (2018). Early fire detection using convolutional neural networks during surveillance for effective disaster management. *Neurocomputing*, 288, 30–42. DOI: 10.1016/j.neucom.2017.04.083

Munawar, H. S., Mojtahedi, M., Hammad, A. W., Kouzani, A., & Mahmud, M. P. (2022). Disruptive technologies as a solution for disaster risk management: A review. *The Science of the Total Environment*, 806, 151351. DOI: 10.1016/j.scitotenv.2021.151351 PMID: 34740667

Mustafa, A. S., & Karimi, K. (2021). Enhancing gamified online learning user experience (UX): A systematic literature review of recent trends. *Human-Computer Interaction and Beyond-Part*, I, 74–99. DOI: 10.2174/97898149988191210100007

Mwinuka, P. R., Mourice, S. K., Mbungu, W. B., Mbilinyi, B. P., Tumbo, S. D., & Schmitter, P. (2022). UAV-based multispectral vegetation indices for assessing the interactive effects of water and nitrogen in irrigated horticultural crops production under tropical sub-humid conditions: A case of African eggplant. *Agricultural Water Management*, 266, 107516. DOI: 10.1016/j.agwat.2022.107516

Nanda, A. K., Sharma, A., Augustine, P. J., Cyril, B. R., Kiran, V., & Sampath, B. (2024). Securing Cloud Infrastructure in IaaS and PaaS Environments. In *Improving Security, Privacy, and Trust in Cloud Computing* (pp. 1–33). IGI Global. DOI: 10.4018/979-8-3693-1431-9.ch001

Natarajan, T., & Pichai, S. (2024). Behaviour-Driven Development and Metrics Framework for Enhanced Agile Practices in Scrum Teams. *Information and Software Technology*, 170, 107435. DOI: 10.1016/j.infsof.2024.107435

Naveeenkumar, N., Rallapalli, S., Sasikala, K., Priya, P. V., Husain, J., & Boopathi, S. (2024). Enhancing Consumer Behavior and Experience Through AI-Driven Insights Optimization. In *AI Impacts in Digital Consumer Behavior* (pp. 1–35). IGI Global. DOI: 10.4018/979-8-3693-1918-5.ch001

Neumann, O., Kirklies, P.-C., & Schott, C. (2023). Adopting agile in government: A comparative case study. *Public Management Review*. Advance online publication. 10.1080V14719037.2024.2354776

Nguyen, A. T., Nguyen, T. T. D., Al-Zubaidi, R., Nguyen, H. A., & Nguyen, H. V. (2021). A comprehensive survey of code translation from high-level program models to blockchain bytecodes. *ACM Computing Surveys*, 54(2), 1–37. DOI: 10.1145/3409555

Nguyen, D., De Mulder, Y., Van Rotterdam, P., & De Jong, R. (2019). Behavior prediction: Definition and problem space analysis. *IEEE Access : Practical Innovations, Open Solutions*, 7, 163239–163261. DOI: 10.1109/ACCESS.2019.2952286

Nguyen, M. T., Le, D. T., & Le, L. (2021). Transformers-based information extraction with limited data for domain-specific business documents. *Engineering Applications of Artificial Intelligence*, 97, 104100. DOI: 10.1016/j.engappai.2020.104100

Nielsen, J. (1994). *Enhancing the explanatory power of usability heuristics. Proceedings of the SIGCHI Conference* on *Human Factors in Computing Systems, 152-158.*

Nielsen, J. (1993). *Usability Engineering*. Academic Press. DOI: 10.1016/B978-0-08-052029-2.50007-3

Nielsen, J. (1994). Enhancing the explanatory power of usability heuristics. In *Proceedings of the SIGCHI Conference on Human Factors in Computing Systems* (pp. 152-158). DOI: 10.1145/191666.191729

Nielsen, J. (2001). *First Rule of Usability?* Don't Listen to Users. Jakob Nielsen's Alertbox. Nielsen Norman Group.

Nielsen, J., & Molich, R. (1990). Heuristic Evaluation of User Interfaces. *Proceedings of the SIGCHI Conference on Human Factors in Computing Systems,* 249-256.

Nike. (2021). Nike's commitment to AI ethics. https://nike.app.box.com/v/aiprinciplesreport

Niknejad, N., Ismail, W. B., Mardani, A., Liao, H., & Ghani, I. (2020). A comprehensive overview of smart wearables: The state of the art literature, recent advances, and future challenges. *Engineering Applications of Artificial Intelligence*, 90, 103529. DOI: 10.1016/j.engappai.2020.103529

Noorollah, N., & Ayoubi, R. (2021). Toward iterative and continuous user experience development. In *User Experience Design for the Internet of Things* (pp. 97–119). Springer., DOI: 10.1007/978-3-030-72288-0_5

Norman, D. A., & Draper, S. W. (Eds.). (1986). *User-Centered System Design: New Perspectives* on Human-Computer Interaction. Lawrence Erlbaum Associates.

Norman, D. A. (2004). *Emotional Design: Why We Love (or Hate) Everyday Things*. Basic Books.

Norman, D. A. (2013). *The Design of Everyday Things (Revised and Expanded Edition)*. Basic Books.

Norman, D. A. (2013). *The Design of Everyday Things: Revised and Expanded Edition*. Basic Books.

Norman, D. A. (2013). *The design of everyday things: Revised and expanded edition*. Constellation Books.

Norman, D. A., & Draper, S. W. (1986). *User centered system design. New perspectives on human-computer interaction*. L. Erlbaum Associates Inc. DOI: 10.1201/b15703

Norman, D., & Stappers, P. J. (2015). DesignX: Complex socio-technical systems. She Ji. *The Journal of Design, Economics, and Innovation*, 1(2), 83–94. DOI: 10.1016/j.sheji.2016.01.002

Novick, T. (2021). Inclusive design at Microsoft. Microsoft Design. https://www.microsoft.com/design/inclusive

Nurmuradov, D., & Bryce, R. (2017). Caret-HM: recording and replaying Android user sessions with heat map generation using UI state clustering. Proceedings of the 26th ACM SIGSOFT International Symposium on Software Testing and Analysis. https://dl.acm.org/doi/abs/10.1145/3092703.3098231

O'Brien, H. L., & Toms, E. G. (2010). The development and evaluation of a survey to measure user engagement. *Journal of the American Society for Information Science and Technology*, 61(1), 50–69. DOI: 10.1002/asi.21229

Ofli, F., Imran, M., & Alam, F. (2020). Using artificial intelligence and social media for disaster response and management: An overview. *AI and Robotics in Disaster Studies*, 63–81.

Okano, Y., Kudoh, T., Le Minh, Q., Abe, A., O'Brien, C., & Kitagawa, H. (2021). Bayesian intelligent access control. AI for Data Privacy and Security (AI4DPS) Workshop. *IJCAI (United States).*

Oladapo, N., Ejiga, H., Okeke, D., & Akinoso, E. (2024). Conceptualizing agile development in digital transformations: Theoretical foundations and practical applications. *Engineering Science & Tecnology Journal*, 5(4), 1524–1541. DOI: 10.51594/estj.v5i4.1080

Olorunsogo, N. T., Adekunle, N., Okolo, A., & Babawarun, N. O. (2024). Ethical considerations in AI-enhanced medical decision support systems: A review. *World Journal of Advanced Engineering Technology and Sciences*, 11(1), 329–336. DOI: 10.30574/wjaets.2024.11.1.0061

Olsson, T., Lagerstam, E., Kärkkäinen, T., & Väänänen-Vainio-Mattila, K. (2013). Expected user experience of mobile augmented reality services: A user study in the context of shopping centres. *Personal and Ubiquitous Computing*, 17(2), 287–304. DOI: 10.1007/s00779-011-0494-x

Onifade, O. F., & Akinyemi, D. J. (2015). A review on the suitability of machine learning approaches to facial age estimation. *International Journal of Modern Education and Computer Science*, 7(12), 17–28. DOI: 10.5815/ijmecs.2015.12.03

Ormeño, E., & Pinciroli, F. (2024). Systematic Mapping Protocol — UX Design role in software development process. In *arXiv.org*. https://arxiv.org/abs/2402.13143

Osasona, N. F., Amoo, N. O. O., Atadoga, N. A., Abrahams, O., Farayola, N. O. A., & Samson, B. (2024). Reviewing the ethical implications of AI in decision making processes. *International Journal of Management & Entrepreneurship Research*, 6(2), 322–335. DOI: 10.51594/ijmer.v6i2.773

Othman, M. K., & Anuar, N. N. (2024). A Comprehensive User Experience Analysis of Cultural Heritage Progressive Web App Using a Hybrid UEQ-IPA Approach | Journal on Computing and Cultural Heritage. In *ACM Journal on Computing and Cultural Heritage*. https://dl.acm.org/doi/abs/10.1145/3647998

Othmani, A., Taleb, A. R., Abdelkawy, H., & Hadid, A. (2020). Age estimation from faces using deep learning: A comparative analysis. *Computer Vision and Image Understanding*, 196, 102961. DOI: 10.1016/j.cviu.2020.102961

Øvad, T., & Larsen, L. B. (2015). The prevalence of UX design in agile development processes in industry. *2015 Agile Conference*, 40–49. DOI: 10.1109/Agile.2015.13

Pachiappan, K., Anitha, K., Pitchai, R., Sangeetha, S., Satyanarayana, T., & Boopathi, S. (2024). Intelligent Machines, IoT, and AI in Revolutionizing Agriculture for Water Processing. In *Handbook of Research on AI and ML for Intelligent Machines and Systems* (pp. 374–399). IGI Global.

Palaniappan, M., Tirlangi, S., Mohamed, M. J. S., Moorthy, R. S., Valeti, S. V., & Boopathi, S. (2023). Fused Deposition Modelling of Polylactic Acid (PLA)-Based Polymer Composites: A Case Study. In *Development, Properties, and Industrial Applications of 3D Printed Polymer Composites* (pp. 66–85). IGI Global.

Panis, G., & Lanitis, A. (2015). An overview of research activities in facial age estimation using the FG-NET aging database. *Computer Vision-ECCV 2014 Workshops: Zurich, Switzerland, September 6-7 and 12, 2014. Proceedings*, 13(Part II), 737–750.

Park, S., Jeong, S., & Ju, B. (2018). Employee learning and development in virtual HRD: Focusing on MOOCs in the workplace. *Industrial and Commercial Training*, 50(5), 261–271. DOI: 10.1108/ICT-03-2018-0030

Pasumarthy, R., Mohammed, S., Laxman, V., Krishnamoorthy, V., Durga, S., & Boopathi, S. (2024). Digital Transformation in Developing Economies: Forecasting Trends, Impact, and Challenges in Industry 5.0. In *Convergence of Human Resources Technologies and Industry 5.0* (pp. 47–68). IGI Global. DOI: 10.4018/979-8-3693-1343-5.ch003

Persson, H., Åhman, H., Yngling, A. A., & Gulliksen, J. (2015). Universal design, inclusive design, accessible design, design for all: Different concepts—one goal? On the concept of accessibility—historical, methodological and philosophical aspects. *Universal Access in the Information Society*, 14(4), 505–526. DOI: 10.1007/s10209-014-0358-z

Pillay, N., & Wing, J. (2019). *Agile UX: Integrating good UX development practices in Agile*. DOI: 10.1109/ICTAS.2019.8703607

Pitchai, R., Guru, K. V., Gandhi, J. N., Komala, C. R., Kumar, J. R. D., & Boopathi, S. (2024). Fog Computing-Integrated ML-Based Framework and Solutions for Intelligent Systems: Digital Healthcare Applications. In *Technological Advancements in Data Processing for Next Generation Intelligent Systems* (pp. 196–224). IGI Global. DOI: 10.4018/979-8-3693-0968-1.ch008

Polson, P. G., Lewis, C., Rieman, J., & Wharton, C. (1992). Cognitive walkthroughs: A method for theory-based evaluation of user interfaces. *International Journal of Man-Machine Studies*, 36(5), 741–773. DOI: 10.1016/0020-7373(92)90039-N

Poole, A., & Ball, L. J. (2006). Eye tracking in HCI and usability research. *Encyclopedia of Human-Computer Interaction, 211-219.* DOI: 10.4018/978-1-59140-562-7.ch034

Porcelli, L., Mastroianni, M., Ficco, M., & Palmieri, F. (2024). A User-Centered Privacy Policy Management System for Automatic Consent on Cookie Banners. *Computers*, 13(2), 43. DOI: 10.3390/computers13020043

Porcheron, M., Fischer, J. E., & Sharples, S. (2017). *"Do Animals Have Accents?": Talking with* Agents *in Multi-Party Conversation.Proceedings of the 2017 ACM Conference on Computer Supported Cooperative Work and Social Computing (CSCW),207-219.*

Pramila, P., Amudha, S., Saravanan, T., Sankar, S. R., Poongothai, E., & Boopathi, S. (2023). Design and Development of Robots for Medical Assistance: An Architectural Approach. In *Contemporary Applications of Data Fusion for Advanced Healthcare Informatics* (pp. 260–282). IGI Global.

Prasad, M. S. C., Dhanalakshmi, M., Mohan, M., Somasundaram, B., Valarmathi, R., & Boopathi, S. (2024). Machine Learning-Integrated Sustainable Engineering and Energy Systems: Innovations at the Nexus. In *Harnessing High-Performance Computing and AI for Environmental Sustainability* (pp. 74–98). IGI Global. DOI: 10.4018/979-8-3693-1794-5.ch004

Procreator. (2024). *5 remarkable UX design case studies (2024 insights). https://procreator.design*

Punyani, P., Gupta, R., & Kumar, A. (2020). Neural networks for facial age estimation: A survey on recent advances. *Artificial Intelligence Review*, 53(5), 3299–3347. DOI: 10.1007/s10462-019-09765-w

Puranik, T. A., Shaik, N., Vankudoth, R., Kolhe, M. R., Yadav, N., & Boopathi, S. (2024). Study on Harmonizing Human-Robot (Drone) Collaboration: Navigating Seamless Interactions in Collaborative Environments. In *Cybersecurity Issues and Challenges in the Drone Industry* (pp. 1–26). IGI Global.

Puspitasari, I., Nuzulita, N., & Hsiao, C.-S. (2024). Agile User-Centered Design Framework to Support the Development of E-Health for Patient Education. *Studies in Computational Intelligence*, 131–144. DOI: 10.1007/978-3-031-57037-7_10

Qureshi, F., & Krishnan, S. (2018). Wearable hardware design for the internet of medical things (IoMT). *Sensors (Basel)*, 18(11), 3812. DOI: 10.3390/s18113812 PMID: 30405026

Qusay, I. (2018). Web Applications And Web Services: A Comparative Study. *Science Journal of University of Zakho*, 6(1), 35. Advance online publication. DOI: 10.25271/2018.6.1.375

Rahamathunnisa, U., Sudhakar, K., Padhi, S., Bhattacharya, S., Shashibhushan, G., & Boopathi, S. (2024). Sustainable Energy Generation From Waste Water: IoT Integrated Technologies. In *Adoption and Use of Technology Tools and Services by Economically Disadvantaged Communities: Implications for Growth and Sustainability* (pp. 225–256). IGI Global.

Rampolla, J., & Kipper, G. (2012). *Augmented reality: An emerging technologies guide to AR*. Elsevier.

Rathnayake, B., & Lanka, S. (2019). *Crowd-sourced user experience evaluation and adaptation for a personalized user interface*. http://dl.lib.uom.lk/bitstream/handle/123/16005/TH4009.pdf?sequence=2

Rathod, D., Parikh, S., & Dahiya, M. S. (2016), Goal-Based Constraint Driven Dynamic RESTful Web Service Composition Using AI Techniques. In Proceedings of International Conference on ICT for Sustainable Development. Advances in Intelligent Systems and Computing, vol 408. Springer. DOI: 10.1007/978-981-10-0129-1_77

Ravisankar, A., Shanthi, A., Lavanya, S., Ramaratnam, M., Krishnamoorthy, V., & Boopathi, S. (2024). Harnessing 6G for Consumer-Centric Business Strategies Across Electronic Industries. In *AI Impacts in Digital Consumer Behavior* (pp. 241–270). IGI Global.

Reeves, T. C., & Hedberg, J. G. (2003). *Interactive Learning Systems Evaluation*. Educational Technology Publications.

Reichheld, F. F. (2003). The One Number You Need to Grow. *Harvard Business Review*, 81(12), 46–54. PMID: 14712543

Resnick, M., & Silverman, B. (2005). Some reflections on designing construction kits for kids. *Proceedings of the 2005 conference on Interaction design and children*, 117-122. DOI: 10.1145/1109540.1109556

Revathi, S., Babu, M., Rajkumar, N., Meti, V. K. V., Kandavalli, S. R., & Boopathi, S. (2024). Unleashing the Future Potential of 4D Printing: Exploring Applications in Wearable Technology, Robotics, Energy, Transportation, and Fashion. In *Human-Centered Approaches in Industry 5.0: Human-Machine Interaction, Virtual Reality Training, and Customer Sentiment Analysis* (pp. 131–153). IGI Global.

Revuze. (2023). Revuze: AI-driven product analytics. https://revuze.it/

Rhodes, M. G. (2009). Age estimation of faces: A review. *Applied Cognitive Psychology*, 23(1), 1–12. DOI: 10.1002/acp.1442

Riordan, B., Horbach, A., Cahill, A., Zesch, T., & Chong, M. L. (2017). *Investigating neural architectures for short answer scoring. Proc. 12th Workshop Innov.* Use NLP Building Educ. Appl.

Ritonummi, S., Siitonen, V., Salo, M., & Henri, P. (2022). Exploring barriers that prevent employees from experiencing flow in the software industry | Emerald Insight. *Journal of Workplace Learning*, 36(3), 223–238. DOI: 10.1108/JWL-11-2022-0146

Rittel, H. W., & Webber, M. M. (1973). Dilemmas in a general theory of planning. *Policy Sciences*, 4(2), 155–169. DOI: 10.1007/BF01405730

Robson, C. (2016). *Real World Research* (4th ed.). Wiley.

Rodrigues, G., Soria, A., & Campo, M. (2015). AI-based web service composition: A review. *IETE Technical Review*, 33(4), 1–8. DOI: 10.1080/02564602.2015.1110061

Roto, V., Law, E., Vermeeren, A., & Hoonhout, J. (Eds.). (2011). User Experience White Paper: *Bringing Clarity to the Concept of User Experience. Retrieved from-* https://www.allaboutux.org/uxwhitepaper

Rowland, C., Goodman, E., Charlier, M., Light, A., & Lui, A. (2015). *Designing connected products: UX for the consumer Internet of Things*. O'Reilly Media, Inc.

S, B., & Gopi, S. (2024). Crafting Effective HR Strategies for the Modern Workplace: Navigating the Digital Frontier. In *Convergence of Human Resources Technologies and Industry 5.0* (pp. 23–46). IGI Global. DOI: 10.4018/979-8-3693-1343-5.ch002

Saha, S., Dhamecha, T. I., Marvaniya, S., Sindhgatta, R., & Sengupta, B. (2018). Sentence level or token level features for automatic short answer grading? Use both. *Proc. Int. Conf. Artif. Intell. Educ.*, 503–517. DOI: 10.1007/978-3-319-93843-1_37

Sahu, A., & Bhowmick, P. K. (2020, January–March). Feature engineering and ensemble-based approach for improving automatic short-answer grading performance. *IEEE Transactions on Learning Technologies*, 13(1), 77–90. DOI: 10.1109/TLT.2019.2897997

Salam, A. (2024). Internet of things for sustainable human health. In *Internet of Things for Sustainable Community Development: Wireless Communications, Sensing, and Systems* (pp. 217–242). Springer. DOI: 10.1007/978-3-031-62162-8_7

Salminen, J., Jung, S.-G., & Jansen, B. (2022). Developing Persona Analytics Towards Persona Science. Proceedings of the 27th International Conference on Intelligent User Interfaces. https://dl.acm.org/doi/abs/10.1145/3490099.3511144

Sa, M. (2024). User-centered data access control techniques for secure and privacy-aware mobile systems. *Figshare*. DOI: 10.25394/PGS.26069632.v1

Saravanan, S., Khare, R., Umamaheswari, K., Khare, S., Krishne Gowda, B. S., & Boopathi, S. (2024). AI and ML Adaptive Smart-Grid Energy Management Systems: Exploring Advanced Innovations. In *Principles and Applications in Speed Sensing and Energy Harvesting for Smart Roads* (pp. 166–196). IGI Global. DOI: 10.4018/978-1-6684-9214-7.ch006

Sarkar, C., Soderston, C., Klementiev, D., & Bell, E. (2010). Remote Automated User Testing: First Steps toward a General-Purpose Tool. *Studies in Computational Intelligence*, 37–50. DOI: 10.1007/978-3-642-13273-5_3

Sauro, J., & Lewis, J. R. (2016). *Quantifying the User Experience: Practical Statistics for User Research*. Morgan Kaufmann.

Savolainen, O. (2010). User experience design in open source development: Approaches to usability work in the Moodle community. *Tuni.Fi*. https://doi.org/https://trepo.tuni.fi/handle/10024/81866

Schmutz, S., Sonderegger, A., & Sauer, J. (2016). Implementing Recommendations from Web Accessibility Guidelines: A Comparative Study of Web Designers' Perspectives. *International Journal of Human-Computer Studies*, 97, 160–168.

Sculley, D., Holt, G., Golovin, D., Davydov, E., Phillips, T., Ebner, D., . . . Dennison, D. (2015). Machine learning: The high interest credit card of technical debt. In SE4ML: Software Engineering for Machine Learning (NIPS 2015 Workshop).

Sekhar, K. Ch., Ingle, R. B., Banu, E. A., Rinawa, M. L., Prasad, M. M., & Boopathi, S. (2024). Integrating VR and AR for Enhanced Production Systems: Immersive Technologies in Smart Manufacturing. In *Advances in Computational Intelligence and Robotics* (pp. 90–112). IGI Global. DOI: 10.4018/979-8-3693-6806-0.ch005

Selwyn, N. (2011). *Education and the Digital: What the Research Tells Us*. Routledge.

Selwyn, N. (2016). *Education and Technology: Key Issues and Debates* (2nd ed.). Bloomsbury Academic.

Senthil, T., Puviyarasan, M., Babu, S. R., Surakasi, R., Sampath, B., & Associates. (2023). Industrial Robot-Integrated Fused Deposition Modelling for the 3D Printing Process. In *Development, Properties, and Industrial Applications of 3D Printed Polymer Composites* (pp. 188–210). IGI Global.

Seuzen, N., Gorban, A. N., Levesley, J., & Mirkes, E. M. (2020). Automatic short answer grading and feedback using text mining methods. Procedia Comput. Sci., 169, 726–743. DOI: 10.1016/j.procs.2020.02.171

Seuzen, N. (2020). Text Mining in Automated Grading. *Journal of Educational Measurement*, 39(3), 213–229.

Shahfahad, K., Kumari, B., Tayyab, M., Ahmed, I. A., Baig, M. R. I., Khan, M. F., & Rahman, A. (2020). Longitudinal study of land surface temperature (LST) using mono-and split-window algorithms and its relationship with NDVI and NDBI over selected metro cities of India. *Arabian Journal of Geosciences*, 13(19), 1–19. DOI: 10.1007/s12517-020-06068-1

Shah, V., & Khang, A. (2023). Internet of medical things (IoMT) driving the digital transformation of the healthcare sector. In *Data-centric AI solutions and emerging technologies in the healthcare ecosystem* (pp. 15–26). CRC Press. DOI: 10.1201/9781003356189-2

Sharma, A., & Nayyar, V. (2024). Ethical Marketing and Sustainable Development Goals. *Advances in Marketing, Customer Relationship Management, and e-Services Book Series*, 83–91. DOI: 10.4018/979-8-3693-2215-4.ch007

Sharma, I. (2018). *Modeling of land surface temperature (LST) and normalized difference vegetation index (NDVI) in Nepal: 2000-2015* [PhD Thesis]. Prince of Songkla University.

Shejul, A. A., Kinage, K. S., & Reddy, B. E. (2017). Comprehensive review on facial based human age estimation. *2017 International Conference on Energy, Communication, Data Analytics and Soft Computing (ICECDS)*, 3211–3216. DOI: 10.1109/ICECDS.2017.8390049

Shekhawat, H. S., & Rathor, H. S. (2020). Impacts of change in facial features on age estimation and face identification: A review. *Smart Systems and IoT: Innovations in Computing:Proceeding of SSIC 2019*, 801–812.

Shin, D., & Hwang, Y. (2017). Integrated acceptance and sustainability evaluation of Internet of Medical Things: A dual-level analysis. *Internet Research*, 27(5), 1227–1254. DOI: 10.1108/IntR-07-2016-0200

Shirode, P., & Handore, S. (2016). Estimation of age from human facial features. *2016 3rd International Conference on Computing for Sustainable Global Development (INDIACom)*, 2098–2103.

Shumaker, R., & George, C. (2016). Mobile computing trends: Insights from case studies. In Mobile Computing and Wireless Networks: Concepts, Methodologies, Tools, and Applications (pp. 176-189). IGI Global. DOI: 10.4018/978-1-4666-8751-6.ch012

Shu, W., Cai, K., & Xiong, N. N. (2021a). Research on strong agile response task scheduling optimization enhancement with optimal resource usage in green cloud computing. *Future Generation Computer Systems*, 124, 12–20. DOI: 10.1016/j.future.2021.05.012

Silvia, S., & Supangkat, S. H. (2020). A literature review on facial age estimation researches. *2020 International Conference on ICT for Smart Society (ICISS)*, 1–6. DOI: 10.1109/ICISS50791.2020.9307606

Simsek Caglar, P., Roto, V., & Vainio, T. (2022). User experience research in the work context: Maps, gaps and agenda. *Proceedings of the ACM on Human-Computer Interaction, 6*(CSCW1), 1–28. DOI: 10.1145/3512979

Sinha, S. R., Park, Y., Sinha, S. R., & Park, Y. (2017). Developing and Improving User Experiences. Building an Effective IoT Ecosystem for Your Business, 201-224.

Slaimi, F. (2014). Ontology based vertical web service composition. *Int. J. Knowl. Based Intell. Eng. Syst.*, 18, 1–12.

Smith, G. G., Haworth, R., & Zitnik, S. (2020). Computer science meets education: Natural language processing for automatic grading of open-ended questions ineBooks. *Journal of Educational Computing Research*, 58(7), 1227–1255. DOI: 10.1177/0735633120927486

Smith, J., & Doe, A. (2022). Advances in AI for Education. *Journal of Educational Technology*, 45(2), 123–135.

Sommer, J. (2024). Predictive value of card sorting on browsing performance and user satisfaction - University of Twente Student Theses. *Utwente.Nl.* https://doi.org/https://purl.utwente.nl/essays/62420

Song, Wen, Xiao, & Park. (2021). Semantics perception and refinement network for aspect-based sentiment analysis. Knowl.-Based Syst., 214.

Sreedhar, P. S. S., Sujay, V., Rani, M. R., Melita, L., Reshma, S., & Boopathi, S. (2024). Impacts of 5G Machine Learning Techniques on Telemedicine and Social Media Professional Connection in Healthcare. In *Advances in Medical Technologies and Clinical Practice* (pp. 209–234). IGI Global. DOI: 10.4018/979-8-3693-1934-5.ch012

Sridevi, S., Karpagam, G. R., Vinoth Kumar, B., & Uma Maheswari, J. (2021), Investigation on Blockchain Technology for Web Service Composition: A Case Study. International Journal of Web Services Research 18(1). DOI: 10.1109/ICATCCT.2015.7456981

Srivastava, J., Routray, S., Ahmad, S., & Waris, M. M. (2022). [Retracted] Internet of Medical Things (IoMT)-Based Smart Healthcare System: Trends and Progress. *Computational Intelligence and Neuroscience*, 2022(1), 7218113. PMID: 35880061

St. Jean, B. (2014). Devising and implementing a card-sorting technique for a longitudinal investigation of the information behavior of people with type 2 diabetes. *Library & Information Science Research*, 36(1), 16–26. DOI: 10.1016/j.lisr.2013.10.002

Starbucks. (2022). Starbucks modernization: How AI is brewing a better experience. https://stories.starbucks.com/stories/2022/how-ai-is-brewing-a-better-starbucks-experience/

Stelvaga, A., & Fortin, C. (2017). Design principles of wearables systems: an IoT approach. In DS 87-3 Proceedings of the 21st International Conference on Engineering Design (ICED 17) Vol 3: Product, Services and Systems Design, Vancouver, Canada, 21-25.08. 2017 (pp. 419-428).

Strahl. (2015). Converting Foxpro to Web Services. Southwest Fox 2015.

Subha, S., Inbamalar, T., Komala, C., Suresh, L. R., Boopathi, S., & Alaskar, K. (2023). A Remote Health Care Monitoring system using internet of medical things (IoMT). *IEEE Explore*, 1–6.

Sullivan, S. (2016). *Designing for wearables: Effective UX for current and future devices*. O'Reilly Media, Inc.

Sultan, M. A., Salazar, C., & Sumner, T. (2016). Fast and easy short answer grading with high accuracy. Proc. Conf. North Amer. Chapter Assoc. Comput. Linguistics, Hum. Lang. Technol., 1070–1075. DOI: 10.18653/v1/N16-1123

Sumathi & Chiplunkar. (2018). Populating Parameters of Web Services by Automatic Composition Using Search Precision and WSDL Weight Matrix. IJCSE. .DOI: 10.1504/IJCSE.2016.10007953

Sundberg, H.-R. (2015). *The role of user experience in a business-to-business context.*

Sung, C., Dhamecha, T. I., & Mukhi, N. (2019). Improving short answer grading using transformer-based pre-training. *Proc. Conf. Artif. Intell. Educ.*, 469–481. DOI: 10.1007/978-3-030-23204-7_39

Sun, W., Bocchini, P., & Davison, B. D. (2020). Applications of artificial intelligence for disaster management. *Natural Hazards*, 103(3), 2631–2689. DOI: 10.1007/s11069-020-04124-3

Talipu, A. (2021). Research and development of a remote usability testing platform for better user experience. *Univpm.It.* https://doi.org/manual

Tan, H., Wang, C., Duan, Q., Lu, Y., & Li, R. (2020a). Automatic short answer grading by encoding student responses via a graph convolutional network. *Interactive Learning Environments*, 2020, 1–15.

Tan, H., Wang, C., Duan, Q., Lu, Y., & Li, R. (2020b). Enhancing Grading Precision with GCNs. *AI Review*, 27(1), 50–63.

Tan, L., Guo, J., Mohanarajah, S., & Zhou, K. (2021). Can we detect trends in natural disaster management with artificial intelligence? A review of modeling practices. *Natural Hazards*, 107(3), 2389–2417. DOI: 10.1007/s11069-020-04429-3

Teja, N. B., Kannagi, V., Chandrashekhar, A., Senthilnathan, T., Pal, T. K., & Boopathi, S. (2024). Impacts of Nano-Materials and Nano Fluids on the Robot Industry and Environments. In *Advances in Computational Intelligence and Robotics* (pp. 171–194). IGI Global. DOI: 10.4018/979-8-3693-5767-5.ch012

Tetteh, S. G. (2024). Empirical Study of Agile Software Development Methodologies: A Comparative Analysis - Pustakas. *Pcbmb.Org.* https://doi.org/http://archive.pcbmb.org/id/eprint/1883/1/Tetteh1752024AJRCOS113678.pdf

Thakur, D., & Zhang, X. (Eds.). (2020). *Wearable human–machine multi-interface: Human body weight transfer and augmented reality.* Springer.

Thorngate, S., & Hoden, A. (2017). Exploratory Usability Testing of User Interface Options in LibGuides 2. *College & Research Libraries. College & Research Libraries*, 78(6). Advance online publication. DOI: 10.5860/crl.78.6.844

Thota, A. K., & Jung, R. (2024). Accelerating neurotechnology development using an Agile methodology. *Frontiers in Neuroscience*, 18, 1328540. Advance online publication. DOI: 10.3389/fnins.2024.1328540 PMID: 38435056

Timms, P. (2021). *Transformational HR: How human resources can create value and impact business strategy*. Kogan Page Publishers.

Tiriticco, R. (2021). Evaluation and implementation of accessible methods to perform remote moderated usability testing on websites. *Theseus.Fi*. https://doi.org/http://www.theseus.fi/handle/10024/503653

Tomlin, W. C. (2018). *UX Optimization*. SpringerLink. DOI: 10.1007/978-1-4842-3867-7

Tucker, R., Callaham, J. A., Zeidler, C., Paul, A.-L., & Ferl, R. J. (2020). NDVI imaging within space exploration plant growth modules–A case study from EDEN ISS Antarctica. *Life Sciences in Space Research*, 26, 1–9. DOI: 10.1016/j.lssr.2020.03.006 PMID: 32718674

Tullis, T., & Albert, B. (2024). Measuring the User Experience. In *Google Books*. https://books.google.co.in/books?hl=en&lr=&id=bPhLeMBLEkAC&oi=fnd&pg=PP1&dq=User+Personas+%09Usability+Bug+Tracking:++%09Heatmaps+and+Session+Recordings:+&ots=RbKjksUXrM&sig=xqfosMVraUVftu-fABIaHZFPpjY&redir_esc=y#v=onepage&q&f=false

Tullis, T., & Albert, W. (2013). *Measuring the User Experience: Collecting, Analyzing, and Presenting Usability Metrics*. Morgan Kaufmann.

Tulu, C. N., Kaya, M., & Kocamanlar, M. (2021). MaLSTM for Short Answer Grading. *Computers & Education*, 42(4), 255–269.

Tulu, C. N., Ozkaya, O., & Orhan, U. (2021). Automatic short answer grading with SemSpace sense vectors and MaLSTM. *IEEE Access : Practical Innovations, Open Solutions*, 9, 19270–19280. DOI: 10.1109/ACCESS.2021.3054346

Uber. (2020). How Uber leverages machine learning with AI compute. https://eng.uber.com/machine-learning/

Uto, M., & Uchida, Y. (2020). Automated Feature Extraction with IRT and LSTM. *Journal of Educational Technology & Society*, 23(2), 110–122.

Uto, M., & Uchida, Y. (2020). Automated short-answer grading using deep neural networks and item response theory. *Proc. Int. Conf. Artif. Intell. Educ.*, 334–339. DOI: 10.1007/978-3-030-52240-7_61

UX Design Institute. (2024). Adapting products to meet teachers' changing needs. Retrieved from *https://blog.google*

UX Design Institute. (2024). *Leveraging creative hacks: How the Airbnb community inspired a global check-in tool. Retrieved from*https://uxdesigninstitute.com

Vallejos, S., Leonardo, D. R. A., Rodríguez, G., Berdun, L., & Toscani, R. (2020). Preference-Based AI Planning for Web Service Composition. IEEE Latin America Transactions, 18(11).

Van Wynsberghe, A., & Robbins, S. (2019). Ethical by Design: Ethics Best Practices for Natural Language Processing. *AI Ethics Journal*, 2(1), 1–12.

Vangeri, A. K., Bathrinath, S., Anand, M. C. J., Shanmugathai, M., Meenatchi, N., & Boopathi, S. (2024). Green Supply Chain Management in Eco-Friendly Sustainable Manufacturing Industries. In *Environmental Applications of Carbon-Based Materials* (pp. 253–287). IGI Global. DOI: 10.4018/979-8-3693-3625-0.ch010

Vaswani, A.Attention is all you need. *Proc. 31st Conf. Neural Inf. Process. Syst.*, 5998–6008.

Velev, D., & Zlateva, P. (2023). Challenges of artificial intelligence application for disaster risk Management. *The International Archives of the Photogrammetry, Remote Sensing and Spatial Information Sciences*, 48, 387–394. DOI: 10.5194/isprs-archives-XLVIII-M-1-2023-387-2023

Venkateswaran, N., Kunduru, K. R., Ashwin, N., Sundar Ganesh, C. S., Hema, N., & Boopathi, S. (2024). Navigating the Future of Ultra-Smart Computing Cyberspace: Beyond Boundaries. In *Advances in Computational Intelligence and Robotics* (pp. 170–199). IGI Global. DOI: 10.4018/979-8-3693-2399-1.ch007

Verma, R., Christiana, M. B. V., Maheswari, M., Srinivasan, V., Patro, P., Dari, S. S., & Boopathi, S. (2024). Intelligent Physarum Solver for Profit Maximization in Oligopolistic Supply Chain Networks. In *AI and Machine Learning Impacts in Intelligent Supply Chain* (pp. 156–179). IGI Global. DOI: 10.4018/979-8-3693-1347-3.ch011

Vermeeren, A. P. O. S., Roto, V., Väänänen-Vainio-Mattila, K., Law, E. L.-C., Obrist, M., Hoonhout, J., & Kuutti, K. (2010). User Experience Evaluation Methods: Current State and Development Needs. *Proceedings of the 6th Nordic Conference on Human-Computer Interaction: Extending Boundaries (NordiCHI),* 521-530. DOI: 10.1145/1868914.1868973

Wang, J., Wang, L., Li, J., Li, H., Tao, D., Tang, B., & Chen, J. (2021). Autonomous design system driven by artificial intelligence. *International Journal of Computer Integrated Manufacturing*, 34(4), 311–349. DOI: 10.1080/0951192X.2021.1893138

Welin, F. (2024). Integration of User-Centered Design and Continuous Experimentation in Agile processes: A qualitative study. In *Aalto.fi*. https://aaltodoc.aalto.fi/items/d496aebd-17c9-4c7f-837c-221727c355e1

Weng, F., Zhang, L., & Ngo, T. (2019). Cross-platform application design and development: Emerging technologies for future. In *Future Data and Security Engineering* (pp. 435–445). Springer., DOI: 10.1007/978-981-13-8513-3_42

Wilk-Jakubowski, G., Harabin, R., & Ivanov, S. (2022). Robotics in crisis management: A review. *Technology in Society*, 68, 101935. DOI: 10.1016/j.techsoc.2022.101935

Wu, H.-K., Lee, S. W.-Y., Chang, H.-Y., & Liang, J.-C. (2013). Current Status, Opportunities and Challenges of Augmented Reality in Education. *Computers & Education*, 62, 41–49. DOI: 10.1016/j.compedu.2012.10.024

Xu, W. (2024). A "User Experience 3.0 (UX 3.0)" Paradigm Framework: User Experience Design for Human-Centered AI Systems. In *arXiv.org*. https://arxiv.org/abs/2403.01609

Yang, B., Wang, L., Wong, D. F., Chao, L. S., & Tu, Z. (2019). Convolutional self-attention networks. *Proc. Conf. North Amer. Chapter Assoc. Comput. Linguistics. Hum. Lang. Technol.*, 1, 4040–4045.

Yang, H., & Lee, J. (2018). A study on interaction logging and analysis for conversational systems. *Journal of the Association for Information Science and Technology*, 69(2), 181–194.

Yang, H., Zeng, B., Yang, J., Song, Y., & Xu, R. (2020). A multi-task learning model for Chinese-oriented aspect polarity classification and aspect term extraction. *Neurocomputing*, 419, 344–356. DOI: 10.1016/j.neucom.2020.08.001

Yang, Q., & Evans, A. C. (2019). AI and HCI: How AI Will Change the Way We Design and Use Interactive Systems. *Communications of the ACM*, 62(2), 66–73.

Yerram, S. R., Mallipeddi, S. R., Varghese, A., & Sandu, A. K. (2019). Human-Centered Software Development: Integrating User Experience (UX) Design and Agile Methodologies for Enhanced Product Quality. *Asian Journal of Humanity. Art and Literature*, 6(2), 203–218. DOI: 10.18034/ajhal.v6i2.732

Yin, R. K. (2018). *Case Study Research and Applications: Design and Methods*. Sage Publications.

Zaki, T., & Islam, M. N. (2021). Neurological and physiological measures to evaluate the usability and user-experience (UX) of information systems: A systematic literature review. *Computer Science Review*, 40, 100375. DOI: 10.1016/j.cosrev.2021.100375

Zarghami, S. A., & Dumrak, J. (2021). Implications of artificial intelligence for bushfire management. *Australian Journal of Emergency Management*, 36(1), 84–91. DOI: 10.47389/36.1.84

Zhang, M., Lu, Z., & Li, Y. (2017). Deep Learning-Based Recommender System: A Survey and New Perspectives. *ACM Computing Surveys*, 52(1), 1–38.

Zhang, S., Lee, C., Chan, H., Choy, K., & Wu, Z. (2015). Swarm intelligence applied in green logistics: A literature review. *Engineering Applications of Artificial Intelligence*, 37, 154–169. DOI: 10.1016/j.engappai.2014.09.007

Zhang, T., Sodhro, A. H., Luo, Z., Zahid, N., Nawaz, M. W., Pirbhulal, S., & Muzammal, M. (2020). A joint deep learning and internet of medical things driven framework for elderly patients. *IEEE Access : Practical Innovations, Open Solutions*, 8, 75822–75832. DOI: 10.1109/ACCESS.2020.2989143

Zhang, T., Wang, Z., Zeng, Y., Wu, X., Huang, X., & Xiao, F. (2022). Building artificial-intelligence digital fire (AID-Fire) system: A real-scale demonstration. *Journal of Building Engineering*, 62, 105363. DOI: 10.1016/j.jobe.2022.105363

Zhang, W., & Li, H. (2023). Transformer Models in Student Assessment. *AI in Education*, 34(1), 67–79.

Zhang, Y., Lin, C., & Chi, M. (2020). Going deeper: Automatic short-answer grading by combining student and question models. *User Modeling and User-Adapted Interaction*, 30(1), 51–80. DOI: 10.1007/s11257-019-09251-6

Zhao, W., Ye, J., Yang, M., Lei, Z., Zhang, S., & Zhao, Z. (2018). Investigating capsule networks with dynamic routing for text classification. *Proc. Conf. Empirial Methods Natural Lang. Process.*, 43–48.

Zhou, Huang, Hu, & He. (2020). SK-GCN: Modeling syntax and knowledge via graph convolutional network for aspect-level sentiment classification. Knowl.-Based Syst., 205(3).

Zhou, X., Fu, Y., Najm, A., Ma, Q., He, X., Li, H., & Tu, Z. (2020). Improving user-interface interaction with reinforcement learning. In *Proceedings of the 21st International Conference on Web Information Systems Engineering* (pp. 583-594). Springer. DOI: 10.1007/978-3-030-62008-0_41

Zhu, X., Wu, H., & Zhang, L. (2022, June). Automatic Short-Answer Grading via BERT-Based Deep Neural Networks. *IEEE Transactions on Learning Technologies*, 15(3), 364–371. DOI: 10.1109/TLT.2022.3175537

Zichermann, G., & Cunningham, C. (2011). *Gamification by Design: Implementing Game Mechanics in Web and Mobile Apps*. O'Reilly Media.

About the Contributors

Anacleto Correia (M) is an Associate Professor and lecturer of Management and Information Systems subjects at the Portuguese Navy Academy. He holds a Ph.D. in Computer Science, an M.Sc. in Statistics and Information Management, a B.Sc. degree in Management, and also a B.Sc. at the Portuguese Naval Academy. His research interests are focused on requirements engineering, software engineering, process modeling, data mining, machine learning, and business engineering. With over 30 years of experience, he has led numerous industry-leading software development projects. He is the author of many scientific papers published in journals and conference proceedings.

* * *

Vandana B. S. is Associate professor in Nitte (DU), NMAMIT and has 18 years of experience and worked in the area of medical image processing and machine learning. She has published more than 10 papers in indexed journals and conferences.

Saurabh Chandra is an accomplished legal scholar and currently serves as an Associate Professor at the School of Law, Bennett University, India. With a robust academic foundation, he earned his Bachelor of Arts and Bachelor of Laws (B.A. LL.B.) from the prestigious Aligarh Muslim University (AMU). He further specialized in Business Laws, completing his Master of Laws (LL.M.) at the renowned National Law School of India University (NLSIU), Bangalore. Dr. Chandra's academic journey culminated in a Doctorate in Law (Ph.D.) from the esteemed National Law University. In addition to his impressive legal education from some of India's most prestigious institutions, Dr. Saurabh Chandra also holds a master's degree in Management with specialization in Human Resources in Management and another in Journalism and Mass Communication. With 16 years of teaching experience, he has established himself as an expert in Business and

Corporate Laws, with numerous publications to his credit. Dr. Saurabh Chandra is a distinguished expert in Business and Corporate Laws, with a profound understanding of the intricate legal frameworks that govern the business world. His expertise is complemented by a robust portfolio of scholarly publications, which underscores his commitment to advancing knowledge in his field. Throughout his career, Dr. Chandra has consistently produced high-impact research that addresses critical issues in business and corporate law. His publications are widely recognized for their depth of analysis, innovative perspectives, and practical relevance. He has contributed extensively to leading journals, where his work has often set new standards for legal scholarship. His publications not only reflect his scholarly rigor but also his dedication to addressing contemporary challenges faced by businesses and policymakers. By bridging the gap between theoretical insights and real-world applications, Dr. Chandra's work serves as a valuable resource for academics, legal practitioners, and industry professionals alike. Dr. Chandra brings a wealth of experience in Academic Administration, having successfully held various key administrative positions. His diverse qualifications and extensive experience make him a distinguished figure in the academic and legal communities.

Sahil Manoj Chavan is a faculty member in the Department of Electrical Power System at Sandip University, located in Nashik, Maharashtra 422213, India.

Lazarus Jegatha Deborah completed her Ph.D in Computer Science and Engineering in Anna University Chennai in the year 2013 and completed her Master of Engineering in the field of Computer Science and Engineering in Karunya Institute of Technology in the year 2005. She completed her Bachelor of Engineering under Madurai Kamarajar University, Madurai in the year 2002. She is presently working as an Assistant Professor at Anna University Chennai (University College of Engineering, Tindivanam), Chennai, India.

Ushaa Eswaran is an esteemed author, distinguished researcher, and seasoned educator with a remarkable journey spanning over 34 years, dedicated to advancing academia and nurturing the potential of young minds. Currently serving as a Principal and Professor in Andhra Pradesh, India, her vision extends beyond imparting cutting-edge technical expertise to encompass the nurturing of universal human values. With a foundation in Electronics Engineering, Dr. Eswaran delved into the realm of biosensors, carving a pioneering path in nanosensor models, a remarkable achievement that earned her a well-deserved Doctorate. Her insights have been encapsulated in her acclaimed book, "Internet of Things: Future Connected Devices," offering profound insights into the evolving IoT landscape. Her expertise also finds its place in upcoming publications centered around computer vision and

IoT technologies. Dr. Eswaran's commitment to literature is rooted in her unwavering passion to equip the younger generation with the latest knowledge fortified by ethical principles. Her book stands as a beacon of practical wisdom, providing a roadmap through the intricate IoT terrain while shedding light on its future societal impacts. Her forthcoming contributions unveil her interdisciplinary perspective, seamlessly integrating electronics, nanotechnology, and computing. Bolstering her scholarly contributions is her ORCID identifier, 0000-0002-5116-3403, a testament to her prolific research journey that encompasses over a hundred published papers. Dr. Eswaran thrives in merging her profound academic insights with her dedication to nurturing holistic student growth. Her tireless exploration of the dynamic interface between technology and human values continues to shape her works. As the author of "Secure Connections: Safeguarding the Internet of Things (IoT) with Cybersecurity," Dr. Ushaa Eswaran's voice emerges as a beacon of wisdom in the realm of IoT. Her work encapsulates her dedication to enhancing the interconnected world while ensuring its resilience against cyber threats.

Vishal Eswaran is an accomplished Senior Big Data Engineer with an impressive career spanning over 6 years. His fervor for constructing robust data pipelines, unearthing insights from intricate datasets, identifying trends, and predicting future trajectories has fueled his journey. Throughout his tenure, Vishal has lent his expertise to empower numerous prominent US healthcare clients, including CVS Health, Aetna, and Blue Cross and Blue Shield of North Carolina, with informed business decisions drawn from expansive datasets. Vishal's ability to distill intricate data into comprehensive documents and reports stands as a testament to his proficiency in managing multifaceted internal and external data analysis responsibilities. His aptitude for synthesizing complex information ensures that insights are both accessible and impactful for strategic decision-making. Moreover, Vishal's distinction extends to his role as a co-author of the book "Internet of Things - Future Connected Devices." This book not only underscores his prowess in the field but also showcases his visionary leadership in the realm of Internet of Things (IoT). His insights resonate with a forward-looking perspective, emphasizing the convergence of technology and human life. As the author of "Secure Connections: Safeguarding the Internet of Things (IoT) with Cybersecurity," Vishal Eswaran's reputation as a thought leader is further solidified. His work is a manifestation of his commitment to ensuring the security of interconnected devices within the IoT landscape, a vital consideration in our digitally driven world. Vishal's dedication to enhancing the safety and integrity of IoT ecosystems shines through in his work.

Vinay Kumar Gaddam is an Associate Professor of Civil Engineering at Velagapudi Ramakrishna Siddhartha Engineering College.

Ankitha K. is working as Associate Professor in Nitte(DU),NMAMIT, Nitte, Karkala and has 15 years of experience. She published more than 20 papers in indexed journals and conferences.

Suma K. is working as Assistant Professor in Mangalore Institute of Technology and Management, Moodabidri. She has 23 years teaching experience and 15 years of research experience. She has published more than 35 papers in indexed journals and conferences.

Gopal Krishna is an esteemed academic and educator in the Department of Computer Science and Engineering at Supaul College of Engineering, located on Beena Road, Supaul, Bihar. With a strong foundation in computer science, Gopal Krishna has made notable contributions to the academic community through his teaching and research. His work is focused on advancing knowledge in computer science and engineering, mentoring students, and fostering innovation in technology. Gopal Krishna is recognized for his dedication to academic excellence and his commitment to preparing the next generation of engineers in Bihar.

D. Maruthi Kumar is a dedicated academic and researcher in the Department of Electronics and Communication Engineering at Srinivasa Ramanujan Institute of Technology, Ananthapuramu, Andhra Pradesh. His contributions to the field are marked by his focus on cutting-edge technologies in electronics and communication. With a strong background in engineering education, he has mentored numerous students and has been involved in various research projects aimed at advancing knowledge in his domain. His work reflects a commitment to innovation and excellence in both teaching and research, making him a respected figure in his field.

Annie Micheal works for the Department of Computer Science and Engineering at Sathyabama Institute of Science and Technology.

SureshkumarMyilsamy completed his undergraduate in Mechanical Engineering and postgraduate in the field of Engineering Design. He completed his Ph.D. from Anna University, Chennai, Tamil Nādu, India.

Busra Ozdenizci Kose is an Associate Professor of Management Information Systems at Gebze Technical University. She teaches courses in a wide range of topics such as Management Information Systems, Computer Science, Business Analysis, Software Design and Development, Business Process Management, Mobile and Wireless Technologies, Near Field Communication (NFC), Internet of Things (IoT) and Blockchain. She co-authored Near Field Communication: From Theory to Practice, (2012) and Professional NFC Application Development for Android,

(2013). She gives importance of academia & industry relationship, and takes roles such as project manager, researcher, and consultant for national and international companies in this manner.

Sumathi S. Pawar is working as an Associate Professor in NMAMIT, Nitte, Karkala. She has 23 years teaching experience and 15 years of research experience. She has published more than 35 papers in indexed journals and conferences.

S. C.Rajkumar is a highly accomplished individual with a strong background in Computer Science and Engineering. Currently, I hold the position of a Teaching Fellow at Anna University Regional Campus Madurai. My academic journey includes a B.E., M.E., and Ph.D. in Computer Science and Engineering, showcasing my dedication to knowledge acquisition and expertise in the field. With close to 10 years of experience in teaching. My research contributions have been significant, and I take pride in the publication of multiple papers in esteemed international journals such as Elsevier and Wiley. I have also served as a reviewer for esteemed journals and conferences including International Journal of Communication Systems, (wiley), International Journal of Cybersecurity and Applications (Elsevier), International Journal of Multimedia Tools and Applications (Springer), Security and Communication Networks (wiley), IEEE ITS, and PLOS ONE.

K.Hemanth Reddy is working as Associate Professor Vellore Institute of Technology, TamilNadu, Karnataka and has got 16 years of experience. He published more than 50 papers in indexed journals and conferences.

Index

A

AERSCAE 155, 156, 157, 158, 160, 161, 163, 171, 173, 174, 175, 176, 182, 183, 187, 191, 192, 198
Age Estimation 249, 250, 251, 252, 254, 255, 256, 257, 258, 259, 260, 261, 262, 263, 264, 265, 266, 267, 268, 269, 270, 271, 272, 273, 274, 275
Age Learning Algorithms 250, 271
Agile 16, 49, 50, 51, 52, 53, 54, 55, 56, 57, 58, 59, 60, 61, 62, 63, 64, 65, 66, 67, 68, 69, 70, 71, 72, 73, 74, 75, 76, 77, 78, 79, 80, 81, 82, 83, 222, 223, 225, 226, 229, 239, 244, 246, 247
Artificial Intelligence 13, 17, 19, 20, 22, 25, 27, 43, 45, 47, 74, 78, 82, 83, 85, 87, 111, 112, 114, 115, 117, 118, 122, 126, 140, 143, 145, 147, 150, 152, 163, 195, 208, 220, 243, 245, 247, 260, 264, 272, 274, 275, 279, 280, 282, 283, 291, 293, 298, 300, 302, 304, 305, 306, 307, 336, 338, 339
Augmented Reality 1, 2, 16, 17, 18, 19, 20, 39, 45, 47, 74, 83, 101, 110, 115, 117, 118, 119, 120, 123, 125, 127, 136, 137, 140, 145, 147, 152
Autonomous Robots 280, 281, 292, 295

B

Bi-LSTM 155, 156, 157, 158, 164, 165, 168, 169, 173, 174, 176, 177, 183, 188, 191, 192, 198

C

Challenges 1, 2, 3, 5, 6, 13, 14, 16, 17, 19, 20, 23, 24, 31, 32, 33, 34, 40, 42, 43, 51, 52, 56, 61, 62, 63, 64, 65, 70, 71, 72, 73, 78, 86, 87, 89, 92, 93, 110, 112, 117, 118, 119, 120, 123, 124, 125, 127, 130, 131, 133, 135, 145, 152, 155, 157, 161, 165, 168, 186, 228, 241, 244, 246, 249, 251, 253, 254, 257, 274, 282, 287, 293, 294, 295, 297, 298, 306, 307, 312, 334
Continuous Learning 40, 45, 222, 223, 224, 225, 226, 228, 229, 244
Crop Monitoring 310, 321, 323
Cross-Platform Design 19, 20, 21, 29, 31, 32, 33, 35, 37, 39, 40, 41, 42

D

Dynamic Composition 199, 201, 202, 203, 204, 208, 217

E

Early Detection 56, 72, 73, 100, 109, 279, 280
Electronic Waste 86, 87, 91, 92, 93, 97, 98, 102, 103, 106, 107, 112
Emerging Entrepreneurship 221, 223
Energy Efficiency 14, 29, 30, 31, 85, 89, 96, 102, 103, 104, 105, 107, 110, 115
Environmental Impact 14, 85, 86, 90, 92, 93, 102, 105, 106, 107, 110, 297
Evaluation 21, 22, 41, 49, 50, 51, 52, 68, 73, 77, 78, 80, 81, 82, 114, 121, 124, 131, 133, 135, 137, 138, 147, 148, 150, 152, 153, 155, 156, 157, 159, 172, 175, 176, 183, 187, 196, 198, 205, 219, 231, 232, 235, 245, 255, 257, 296, 310

F

Facial Aging 250, 266, 269
Fire Disaster Management 279, 281, 282, 283, 286, 287, 288, 289, 290, 291, 292, 293, 294, 298, 299, 300, 302, 303
Fire Safety 280, 305

H

Healthcare 7, 26, 86, 87, 88, 89, 92, 96, 100, 101, 104, 105, 106, 107, 108, 109, 110, 111, 112, 113, 114, 262,

268, 274, 280, 306, 338
HRD Strategies 222, 224, 225, 233, 234, 235, 236, 237, 239

I

Innovation 1, 4, 6, 15, 16, 39, 42, 44, 45, 46, 87, 89, 90, 91, 96, 99, 100, 101, 104, 105, 110, 118, 119, 120, 124, 130, 134, 145, 219, 222, 223, 224, 225, 227, 228, 229, 230, 233, 235, 236, 237, 239, 240, 242, 243, 244, 280
IoT 1, 2, 4, 5, 6, 7, 10, 11, 13, 15, 17, 18, 19, 20, 77, 112, 141, 272, 275, 285, 297, 336, 338

L

Language Processing 14, 20, 22, 26, 27, 32, 33, 35, 36, 39, 43, 151, 158, 194, 196, 198, 283, 308
Lifecycle Management 85, 86, 90, 92, 94, 106, 107, 110
LMS 201, 203, 204, 207, 208, 210
Low-Power Consumption 96

M

Machine Learning 12, 13, 16, 20, 22, 23, 24, 26, 28, 30, 31, 33, 35, 36, 40, 43, 44, 45, 47, 87, 113, 114, 115, 117, 118, 122, 125, 126, 141, 143, 145, 153, 161, 181, 198, 208, 209, 251, 252, 254, 260, 264, 272, 273, 280, 283, 284, 296, 301, 305, 308, 332, 336
Multi-Modal Interaction 19, 25, 26, 27, 41
Multi-Platform 49, 50, 51, 52, 55, 58, 64, 66, 68, 72, 73, 75, 212, 217

N

NDVI 309, 310, 311, 312, 313, 314, 315, 316, 317, 318, 320, 322, 324, 326, 327, 328, 329, 330, 331, 332, 333, 334, 336, 337, 338, 339, 340, 341

O

Opportunities 1, 2, 16, 22, 31, 40, 42, 63, 86, 89, 96, 98, 105, 110, 112, 117, 118, 119, 120, 124, 129, 130, 145, 152, 200, 223, 224, 225, 228, 229, 235, 236, 241, 242, 244, 302, 339

P

Performance Optimization 19, 29, 30, 31, 35, 41
Personalization 3, 7, 12, 13, 23, 27, 28, 36, 37, 38, 39, 41, 45, 120, 122, 126, 128, 184, 185, 231, 243, 262, 264
Predictive Models 267, 268, 269, 270, 279, 280, 301, 302

R

Renewable Energy 86, 89, 96, 103, 107
Risk Reduction 304
Robotics 16, 26, 245, 247, 279, 280, 281, 282, 286, 289, 290, 291, 292, 293, 294, 295, 296, 297, 298, 299, 300, 301, 302, 303, 304, 305, 306, 307

S

Sensor Networks 285
SOA 199, 201, 206, 219
Startups 222, 223, 224, 225, 226, 227, 228, 229, 230, 231, 232, 233, 235, 236, 237, 238, 239, 240, 241, 242, 243, 244, 246
Student 43, 80, 156, 157, 158, 159, 163, 164, 165, 168, 169, 171, 172, 173, 174, 177, 178, 181, 182, 183, 184, 185, 186, 187, 188, 193, 194, 195, 197, 198, 200, 201, 217
Sustainability 14, 16, 86, 87, 89, 90, 91, 92, 94, 96, 97, 101, 102, 103, 104, 105, 106, 107, 108, 110, 111, 112, 113, 114, 131, 237, 239, 240, 243, 304, 310, 336, 338
Sustainable Digital Growth 221, 222, 225, 229, 233, 237

T

Talent Acquisition 222, 223, 225, 226, 227, 229
Team Empowerment 222, 225
Textual Entailment 194, 198

U

Usability 1, 2, 14, 16, 19, 20, 21, 22, 23, 25, 27, 29, 31, 35, 37, 39, 40, 41, 43, 46, 49, 50, 51, 54, 55, 56, 57, 58, 61, 62, 63, 65, 66, 67, 68, 69, 70, 72, 73, 76, 77, 78, 80, 81, 82, 83, 106, 117, 118, 119, 120, 121, 122, 123, 124, 125, 127, 129, 130, 131, 132, 133, 134, 135, 136, 137, 138, 139, 140, 145, 147, 149, 150, 151, 153, 158, 159, 162, 180, 181, 182, 183, 185, 186, 187, 193, 195, 196, 198, 212, 213, 231, 232, 233, 236, 247, 248
Usability and User Experience 19, 20, 21, 25, 27, 29, 31, 35, 37, 41, 49, 50, 82, 117, 118, 125, 131, 132, 134, 136, 138, 140, 145, 158, 159, 162, 182, 183, 185, 193, 212
User-Centered Design 21, 63, 64, 65, 71, 80, 81, 83, 121, 125, 153, 183, 193, 239, 241
User Experience 1, 4, 5, 11, 12, 16, 17, 18, 19, 20, 21, 23, 24, 25, 27, 29, 30, 31, 35, 36, 37, 38, 39, 41, 43, 44, 45, 46, 49, 50, 51, 53, 54, 55, 56, 57, 58, 59, 65, 68, 70, 71, 72, 73, 74, 75, 76, 77, 79, 80, 81, 82, 83, 87, 101, 106, 117, 118, 119, 120, 121, 124, 125, 126, 127, 128, 129, 130, 131, 132, 134, 136, 138, 139, 140, 145, 147, 148, 149, 151, 152, 153, 158, 159, 162, 181, 182, 183, 184, 185, 186, 193, 198, 208, 212, 217, 222, 223, 225, 230, 233, 237, 238, 239, 240, 241, 242, 244, 245, 246, 247, 248, 251, 259, 261
User Research 19, 20, 22, 23, 24, 41, 49, 50, 51, 52, 53, 57, 59, 60, 61, 62, 63, 64, 65, 66, 67, 68, 69, 70, 71, 72, 73, 74, 76, 151, 183, 212, 235, 236, 240
User Testing 14, 50, 59, 70, 76, 80, 83, 134, 136, 239
UX Design 1, 2, 5, 7, 12, 13, 15, 16, 23, 27, 40, 79, 82, 117, 118, 119, 120, 121, 122, 123, 124, 125, 126, 127, 128, 129, 130, 131, 132, 133, 134, 140, 141, 142, 143, 145, 146, 151, 180, 182, 221, 222, 223, 224, 225, 230, 231, 232, 233, 234, 235, 236, 237, 239, 242, 243, 244, 246, 248

V

Virtual Reality 1, 2, 18, 19, 39, 45, 74, 83, 140, 243, 247
Voice User Interfaces 117, 118, 119, 123, 125, 127, 136, 145

W

Wearables 1, 2, 3, 4, 11, 15, 16, 17, 18, 87, 90, 91, 93, 100, 101, 104, 105, 107, 108
Web Services 31, 199, 200, 201, 202, 203, 204, 205, 206, 207, 209, 210, 213, 217, 218, 219, 220